A.S. Byatt and the
Heliotropic Imagination

A.S. Byatt and the
Heliotropic Imagination

Jane Campbell

Wilfrid Laurier University Press

This book has been published with the help of a grant from the Canadian Federation for the Humanities and Social Sciences, through the Aid to Scholarly Publications Programme, using funds provided by the Social Sciences and Humanities Research Council of Canada. We acknowledge the financial support of the Government of Canada through the Book Publishing Industry Development Program for our publishing activities. We acknowledge the Government of Ontario through the Ontario Media Development Corporation's Ontario Book Initiative.

National Library of Canada Cataloguing in Publication Data

Jane Campbell, 1934–
    A.S. Byatt and the heliotropic imagination / Jane Campbell.

Includes bibliographical references and index.
ISBN 0-88920-439-X

    1. Byatt, A.S. (Antonia Susan), 1936–   —Criticism and interpretation.
2. Imagination in literature. 3. Women in literature. I. Title.

PR6052.Y2Z62 2004   823'.914   C2004-901534-6

© 2004 Wilfrid Laurier University Press
Waterloo, Ontario, Canada N2L 3C5
www.wlupress.wlu.ca

Cover design by Leslie Macredie, using a painting by Vincent van Gogh entitled *Olive Trees* (1889). Reproduced courtesy of The Minneapolis Institute of Arts, The William Hood Dunwoody Fund.

In memory of my parents

Charles Appelbe and Edith Ditchburn Appelbe

Contents

Acknowledgments

THE DEPARTMENT OF ENGLISH AND FILM STUDIES at Wilfrid Laurier University provided the context in which this work was undertaken; I deeply appreciate the contribution of its faculty, staff, and students. Among many others who were helpful in countless ways, I wish to thank especially Paul Tiessen, Michael Moore, and Gary Boire, successive chairs of the Department, for their support and practical help, and Michael Ballin, Viviana Comensoli, Maria DiCenzo, Lynn Shakinovsky, and Eleanor Ty, for their interest and encouragement. Joanne Buchan prepared the manuscript in its many versions with heroic patience, cheerfulness, and expertise, and both she and Susan Mück, her colleague in the Department office, were always helpful and resourceful. The friendship of two former colleagues, the late John Chamberlin and the late Gerald Noonan, is gratefully acknowledged. Each of my research assistants over the years made an indispensable contribution. In chronological order they are Sally Braun-Jackson, Elizabeth Shih, Kristin Mathies, Andrea Penny, and Jennifer Bell. To the graduate students who deepened my understanding of A.S. Byatt's writing, as well as to the undergraduates who shared my interest in reading and thinking about texts, I owe an incalculable debt.

My thinking about *Angels and Insects* was much enriched by Dame Antonia Byatt's generosity in sharing with me her then unpublished essay on the genesis of that work. I benefited greatly from her gracious encouragement and her prompt responses to my queries.

Sandra Woolfrey, former director of WLU Press, first led me to consider shaping my interest in Byatt into a book. I am very grateful to Brian Henderson and his staff at the Press, who have expertly moved the project to publication. Brian's guidance has been invaluable. Special appreciation goes to Carroll Klein, managing editor, for her wise counsel, and to Leslie Macredie, for her artistry in designing the cover. Copy editing was meticulously done by Stephanie Fysh, and the index was provided by Dorothy Hadfield.

Finally, I thank my friends and family, both those who have engaged with me in a long conversation about fiction and others who have helped in a multitude of ways. I especially thank Gwen Brickett, Marilyn Chapman, Leonard Cottrell, Joseph Lee, Margaret Moran, Elizabeth Sauer, Marilyn and Max Sutherland, Clara Thomas, and my sister, Lynda Nanders. My husband, Craig, has patiently followed the book through all its stages, never losing faith in what sometimes seemed to us both to be a project without an end.

Early phases of my research were funded by Wilfrid Laurier Research Grants, and I am pleased to acknowledge this support.

1 Introduction

"ALL MY BOOKS ARE ABOUT THE WOMAN ARTIST—in that sense, they're terribly feminist books—and they're about what language is." In this statement, made in 1990 in an interview with Nicolas Tredell (66), A.S. Byatt described her fiction up to the end of the eighties, supplementing her definition the following year when she said that her novels "think about the problem of female vision, female art and thought" (Introduction, *The Shadow of the Sun* xiv). With one exception, *The Biographer's Tale* (2000), her fiction has continued to explore and expand this subject. Her two early novels, *The Shadow of the Sun*, originally titled *Shadow of a Sun* (1964), and *The Game* (1967), look at the possibilities of and the barriers to female vision, and the first two volumes of her "Powerhouse" quartet, *The Virgin in the Garden* (1978) and *Still Life* (1985), chronicle the intellectual and emotional progress of two sisters as they encounter the world of the 1950s. Byatt's first collection of short stories, *Sugar* (1987), begins with a portrait of a bright, frustrated schoolgirl with a passionate love for Racine's plays and concludes with a mature woman's reflections on the shaping work of the imagination. In the fiction of the nineties and in *A Whistling Woman* (2002), which, with *Babel Tower* (1996), completes her quartet, the focus widens. Although some of Byatt's women, most notably Christabel in *Possession* (1990), are literary artists, Byatt now seems even more concerned with women as thinkers and searchers for wisdom. In the two novellas that make up *Angels and Insects* (1992), Byatt continues the reconstruction of nineteenth-century women's lives that she began in *Possession*; the women in both novellas, "Morpho Eugenia" and the

"Conjugial Angel," work to counter patriarchal structures. The three short story collections of the decade, *The Matisse Stories* (1993), *The Djinn in the Nightingale's Eye* (1994), and *Elementals* (1998), place women in relation to non-literary art forms, to storytelling, and to the challenges of assuming the authorship of their own lives. With *Babel Tower* (1996) and *A Whistling Woman,* the quartet—whose first two volumes appeared to promise a portrait of the artist as a young woman—has become a study of women's experience, physical, mental, and emotional. Byatt's description of her work as "heliotropic" (Introduction, *Shadow* xiv), turning to the sun of creativity, holds true in two senses: she explores and develops her own relation to the sun, and she shows her women characters experiencing adventures of the mind and feelings that bring them into the sun's light. (The image of the heliotrope has an even more personal relevance for Byatt: she suffers from SAD, seasonal affective disorder, and does much of her writing in the summers in the Cévennes in France.) In this book I hope to address both aspects and to show how, in fiction published over a span of thirty-eight years, Byatt has constantly deepened her thinking about her craft and extended her range of knowledge and practice; using a variety of forms, she has worked to encompass more and more of reality. While doing so, she has kept women's lives, past and present, at the centre of her attention.

From her earliest work, however, Byatt's interest in male ways of seeing has been evident, and, as well, the first volumes of her quartet are social and intellectual history as well as family chronicle. Her imagination grapples with the whole world of the given and the contingent. This breadth of view underlies her objection to being classified as a "woman's novelist." In the complex worlds of Byatt's fiction, women's voices are in dialogue with those from the male tradition. Her feminism is thoughtfully described by Richard Todd, who sees Byatt (and Marina Warner) as working in a "total field" that includes a wide range of artistic forms. Within this field, he says, feminism "operates as *an augmentation of a total discourse,* rather than as a simplistic replacement of what has been traditionally privileged by what has been traditionally marginalized" ("Retrieval" 99). In my study I have tried to respect Byatt's own principles, offering close readings of her texts as wholes while giving particular attention to the portrayal of the experience and especially the creativity of women. In arguing for the feminist power and relevance of her fiction, I have made use of feminist scholarship when it seems helpful and appropriate, but I have avoided the imposition of any one theoretical feminist framework on texts that exist as part of a "total discourse."

Among the early contributions to the understanding and appreciation of Byatt's work, three stand out. Juliet Dusinberre's pioneering critique of the first novel of Byatt's quartet, *The Virgin in the Garden* (1978), appeared in 1982 and began the examination of Byatt's relation to the realist tradition. In 1988, Olga Kenyon, in a chapter of her *Women Novelists Today*, included Byatt's first four novels in a wide-ranging account. *The Virgin* and *Still Life* were also discussed by Flora Alexander in her *Contemporary Women Novelists* (1989). All three studies are wise, balanced, and prophetic of Byatt's later achievement. Following the dazzling success of *Possession*, which won the Booker Prize in 1990 and has since been made into a film, critical interest in Byatt was greatly heightened. *Possession* opened up multiple avenues for exploration and called forth a large body of essays on feminism, history, the romance genre, the realist-postmodernist issue, intertextuality, and other topics, many of which relate to other Byatt texts as well.

Byatt was now recognized as a major novelist, and beginning in the mid-nineties, four full-length critical studies of her work were published, as well as a volume of essays. The two general surveys, Kathleen Coyne Kelly's *A.S. Byatt*, in Twayne's English Authors series (1996), and Richard Todd's briefer book of the same title, in the series Writers and Their Work (1997), are extremely useful and illuminating. Kelly's is organized chronologically, Todd's thematically; both include the short stories. Celia Wallhead's *The Old, the New and the Metaphor* (1999) and Christien Franken's *A.S. Byatt: Art, Authorship, Creativity* (2001) are more specialized. Wallhead's study helpfully examines metaphorical patterns in the novels (but not the short stories) up to and including *Babel Tower*, while Franken's feminist study provides a thoughtful and detailed analysis of *The Shadow of Sun*, *The Game*, and *Possession*. In the same year as Franken's book, the first (and to date the only) collection of essays on Byatt appeared. *Essays on the Fiction of A.S. Byatt: Imagining the Real*, edited by Alexa Alfer and Michael J. Noble, brings together twelve essays spanning Byatt's development from *The Shadow of the Sun* to *Babel Tower* (including a contribution by Byatt herself, on the genesis of *Angels and Insects*). With a fine introduction by the editors and a full bibliography, this collection is invaluable for its range of subjects and its diversity of critical opinions and theoretical approaches. Most essays on Byatt are on *Possession*, alone or in comparison with similar texts by Byatt's contemporaries. A few studies, like Franken's book, place *Possession* in relation to Byatt's earlier novels; the most extensive and important of these is Beate Neumeier's discussion of "female visions" from *The Shadow of the Sun* to *Possession*. Several studies of the novellas in *Angels and Insects* have been published; two of these provide feminist readings of "Morpho Eugenia." Now, with additional texts by Byatt in print and the quartet completed, the time seems ripe for a comprehensive study of this multi-faceted, many-voiced writer.

My book builds on and is enriched by the earlier work on Byatt but goes beyond it in including all the fiction published to date. It traces Byatt's development as far as *A Whistling Woman* and shows the place of the short stories in the whole body of Byatt's work. My specific focus is on women's lives and creativity, and my framework includes, as well as the texts highlighted in Neumeier's and Franken's feminist discussions (the four early novels and *Possession*), the four collections of short stories, *Angels and Insects*, and the concluding volume of the quartet. My broader focus is on Byatt's overall growth as a novelist who has been constantly moving into new fictional territory, engaging with new subjects and devising new methods.

My introductory chapter establishes the basis for my approach. It provides an overview of Byatt's thinking about the challenges of writing fiction in the second half of the twentieth century and proceeds to explore her ambivalent response to feminism. Following this, a chapter is given to each of her books in order of publication. Inevitably, *Possession* is analyzed at the greatest length; I hope that this chapter shows the pivotal significance of this multi-generic text for both Byatt's ongoing experiments with form and her construction of stories for women, past and present. My last three chapters break new ground by examining in detail recent texts which have received little critical attention: the six stories that make up *Elementals*, *The Biographer's Tale*, and, together in one chapter, *Babel Tower* and *A Whistling Woman*.

Byatt has distinguished herself as a writer of short fiction, a form admirably suited to her gifts for compression. Some of her most subtle and nuanced observations on women's lives and art are contained in her stories and tales. Apart from Kelly's section on *Sugar*, the briefer discussion by Todd, and my own two essays (combined and revised for inclusion here), criticism of these texts has been sparse and specialized, confined to a few individual stories in *Sugar*, to the title story of the *Djinn* collection, and briefly, in combination with other works by Byatt and those of others, to "Art Work" from *The Matisse Stories*. I hope that by discussing each of the four collections in turn I can illuminate the importance of this form in Byatt's canon. My account of *The Biographer's Tale* in chapter 11 argues that this book, which may initially appear as an anomaly in Byatt's fiction (and which has elicited a divided response from reviewers), is in fact an extension of the author's earliest concerns. Here she addresses again the fundamental questions about language, narrative, and truth-telling with which she began. In form, this tale both exemplifies and examines the problem of "real people" and "images." My final chapter offers an analysis of the quartet as a completed whole from the perspective afforded by A Whistling Woman. We can now trace Byatt's impressive depiction of women's experience within the complex world of thought and discourse in the fifties and sixties. We can also see how her conclusion of her long story represents, in its avoidance of closure and finality, the open-endedness of her search for understanding.

Byatt has said that she needs to be writing a "theoretical book at the same time ... as a novel" (qtd. in Dusinberre, "A.S. Byatt" 193). Her non-fiction writing, in books, essays, and reviews, together with the lectures and interviews she has given, constitutes a sustained reflection on the nature of fiction. As a young writer she was deeply influenced by Iris Murdoch; in 1965 she produced a book-length study of Murdoch's early novels, entitled Degrees of Freedom, and followed this in 1976 with a British Council pamphlet on Murdoch. The two Murdoch studies appeared, respectively, between her first and second novels, The Shadow of the Sun and The Game, and between The Game and The Virgin in the Garden. All of these writings, as well as other early essays and reviews (some of which were published in Passions of the Mind in 1991), deal with a central concern that Byatt shares with Murdoch: the tension in fiction between "real people" and "images," that was the subject of Murdoch's essay "Against Dryness" (1961). In addressing this problem in Virgin and its sequel Still Life, and in the short stories in Sugar and The Matisse Stories, Byatt developed a characteristic blend of traditional and postmodern techniques that she calls "self-conscious realism" (Introduction, Passions 4). In the nineties and afterward, her work moved further from realism, into historiographic metafiction in Possession and Angels and Insects, fairy tale and fantasy in The Djinn in the Nightingale's Eye and Elementals, and the more fragmented, many-faceted, idea-laden narratives of Babel Tower and A Whistling Woman. The Biographer's Tale paradoxically presents Byatt's most explicit critique of postmodernism within a structure that is itself heavily postmodernist. Her work has never lost sight of the need to present the reader with credible characters evoking sympathy and with the related challenges involving story, narration, and morality. Byatt's position with respect to the tradition-versus-postmodernism debate—with tradition represented especially by her undergraduate teacher F.R. Leavis[1]—is, like her relationship to feminism, one of both/and, not either/or.

In Encounter in 1966, Byatt reviewed Patrick White's novel The Solid Mandala. She was then thirty years old and had recently published her first novel, *Shadow of a Sun*, and her first important piece of criticism, *Degrees of Freedom*. Her review, entitled "The Battle between Real People and Images," argues that White's novels produce "a sense of strain, an attempt to conjure with literary images an experience unrealised dramatically"; the characters fail to become truly tragic figures despite the presence of "many images of tragedy" (76). *The Solid Mandala*, like many other modern novels, tries to work simultaneously on two fronts, the symbolic and the realistic, and ends by being less satisfying than an openly allegorical novel such as William Golding's *Pincher Martin*. Quoting from Murdoch's essay, Byatt concludes by pointing to the paradox of novels such as White's, which sacrifice real people to images yet use images "to make precisely the point that people come first" (77).

In her Murdoch studies and her early reviews, one can see this young novelist pondering the problems she was encountering in her own writing. She praises Murdoch's insistence that no formal linguistic structure can contain the reality we experience first hand; as Murdoch wrote in her book on Sartre, "what *does* exist is brute and nameless, it escapes from the scheme of relations in which we imagine it to be rigidly enclosed, it escapes from language and science, it is more and other than our descriptions of it" (qtd. in Byatt, *Iris Murdoch* 14). In an essay entitled "People in Paper Houses," first published in 1979 and included in *Passions of the Mind*, Byatt continues to work on the problem of the "papery" quality of fiction, especially experimental self-reflexive fiction, as it struggles to discover new ways to convey "what does exist." Here, she comments on novels by Murdoch, John Fowles, and Doris Lessing, and points to "the curiously symbiotic relationship between old realism and new experiment" (170) in Angus Wilson's work, a relationship that forms the basis of her own fiction as well.

During these years, Byatt was constructing her own versions of this relationship. Her three earliest novels establish her preoccupation with language and narrative, especially with the changes in the functions of myth and metaphor as a result of the successive pressures of Victorian skepticism, modernism, and postmodernism. All three of these novels use secularized myth; all, especially *The Virgin in the Garden*, are dense with metaphor. Yet all reflect the demythologized world of our time. By contrast, she began her fourth novel, *Still Life,* with the hope of devising a plain, bare language, shorn of analogy and acting out William Carlos Williams's dictum, "no ideas but in things." She discovered that this task was "in fact impossible for someone with the cast of mind I have" ("Still Life/Nature morte" 13). As Michael Levenson puts it, "things and metaphors inevitably commingle" for Byatt ("*Angels and Insects*" 167). Nevertheless, her "project of, in some sense, naming and describing a demythologized world" (Byatt, "Still Life/Nature morte" 14) persists, with all the complexities it involves, in the novels and short stories after *Still Life*. By nature and education inescapably pulled toward richness of allusion and multiplicity of metaphorical structures, Byatt constantly reminds herself and her readers of the duty not to lose sight of "things" and to strive for accurate, exact language; she praises Ford Madox Ford for avoiding the "mythic symbols" of writers like D.H. Lawrence and Virginia Woolf ("Accurate Letters" 108–09). Her characters think about the same problems: in *Still Life*, Alexander Wedderburn tries to write a play in the kind of precise language his creator was hoping to achieve. In *Possession*, Byatt's two main twentieth-century characters, Roland Michell and Maud Bailey, discover that they have been imprisoned by Freudian sexual metaphors; as Roland says, "we can't see *things*" (254). Coming from a different direction, William Adamson, the Victorian entomologist in "Morpho Eugenia," is increasingly fascinated by ant colonies but resists the temptation of taking analogy too far: "men are not ants," he says flatly (100). Byatt's essay "True Stories and the Facts in Fiction" documents the process by which her own research and invention produced *Angels and Insects*, and concludes with the statement, "We need to look at the exterior" (122). Her most recent hero, Phineas Nanson in *The Biographer's Tale*, abandons first poststructuralist theory and then biography in pursuit of "a life full of *things*" (4) and finds what he needs in the world of nature.

In an interview published in 1983, Byatt speaks of "a third element, … neither people nor images, just what is there," and adds, "Painters know naturally that the artist is concerned with that third element, but writers don't always" (Dusinberre, "A.S. Byatt" 182). This statement helps to explain the prominence of painters and paintings in her work. In *Still Life*, Vincent van Gogh is an important presence: Alexander is writing a play, *The Yellow Chair*, about him, and struggles to find words to describe the immediacy of paint. In an essay, "Van Gogh, Death and Summer," Byatt sees the painter as part of a continuum; poised between Robert Browning and Wallace Stevens, all three striving, like the narrator of *Still Life*, to represent accurately a world where objects are losing or have lost their mythic and religious resonance, where art is merely human. Byatt writes, "We know that we live in a flow of light and lights, as we live in a flow of airs and sounds, of which we apprehend a part, and make sense of it as best we can. The pigments on Van Gogh's palette, with their chemistry and their changing tones, are as much part of this perceived flow as the trees and the variable sky. We relate them to each other, and to ourselves, from where we are. It seems to me that at the height of his passion of work Van Gogh was able to hold all these things in a kind of creative or poetic balance" (330). This ability to achieve a balance "of human and inhuman, vision and artifice" is "human sanity" ("Van Gogh" 330). The special importance painting holds for Byatt is reflected in the presence in her fiction of real and imagined painters: not only van Gogh, but Matisse in *The Matisse Stories*, Velázquez, who appears as a character in "Christ in the House of Martha and Mary" (*Elementals*), and the imagined characters Joshua in "Precipice-Encurled" (*Sugar*), Robin and Debbie in "Art Work" (*The Matisse Stories*), Bernard in "Lamia," and Jess in "Jael" (both in *Elementals*). Paintings by van Gogh, Monet, Matisse, and Velázquez function intertextually through ekphrasis; in addition, characters study and teach at art schools, visit galleries, and discuss the visual arts. The attention given to painting amounts to a separate, ongoing discourse within her writing. As Michael Worton points out, what attracts Byatt to painting is its untranslatability, its existence beyond language. The paintings to which she draws attention, he says, "do not so much tell us *what* to read [in her texts] as *how* to read them" ("Of Prisms and Prose" 24).

Byatt's respect for "what is there" creates a tension in the form of her fiction. On the one hand she has a need and love for order. She does not accept Virginia Woolf's statement that "life hits us as a series of random impressions," asserting instead that life "hits us as a series of narratives, though they may be mutually exclusive narratives. We may be hit by random impressions, but if we're intelligent we immediately put them into an order" (qtd. in Tredell 60). This need for order plays against the sense of contingency—a favourite word of Byatt's as of Murdoch's, which Byatt says describes "what is random, accidental, simply factual, about things and people—what is both immediate, and not part of any formal plan or pattern" (*Iris Murdoch* 11). The impressions must be ordered into narrative—we need beginnings, middles, and endings—but room must be left for randomness. This awareness of the role of the accidental was sharpened almost unbearably by the death at age eleven of Byatt's son Charles, killed in 1972 in a road accident; when she was able to work again (dedicating *The Virgin in the Garden* to Charles), she wrote into the second volume of the quartet, *Still Life*, the horrifying death of Stephanie, brilliantly and shockingly placing the random in the midst of the formed.

Byatt's ideal is that of Wallace Stevens: to find, not impose, order. One of her touchstones is Stevens's lines from *Notes Towards a Supreme Fiction*: "To find, not to impose / It is possible, possible, possible. It must be /

Possible" (see "Van Gogh" 322 and "True Stories" 122). From *The Shadow of the Sun* to *A Whistling Woman*, this complicated hope pervades Byatt's thinking. Reflecting on Wittgenstein's image of language as a net—the image that provided the title for Murdoch's first novel, *Under the Net*—Byatt says that although it is true that the net always gets in the way of contact with things in themselves, "if you make the meshes fine enough, the net is so beautiful that all the bumps and humps of things under it are so, yes, so accessible, you can actually sort of see them under the net" (Tredell 66). From such moments of discovery come the shapes of the metaphors that in turn shape her stories. But, again citing Murdoch, Byatt is aware of the dangers of too much shaping; we can be trapped by fantasy into succumbing to the "consolations of form" (*Iris Murdoch* 16). Art must accommodate "mourning and the final acceptance of the incomplete" (Murdoch, qtd. in *Iris Murdoch* 16). The novelist must strive for Murdoch's "hard idea of truth," an ideal to which Byatt constantly returns. In *Notes Towards a Supreme Fiction,* Stevens speaks of the knowledge "that we live in a place / That is not our own and, much more not ourselves, / And hard it is in spite of blazoned days" (qtd. in "Van Gogh" 322). Byatt interprets "hard" in Stevens's poem to mean "solid, in the sense of *terra firma,* and not merely hostile and rejecting" ("Van Gogh, Death and Summer" 323). Elaborating on Murdoch's view of truth as the opposite of "the facile idea of sincerity," Byatt says that "truth is like stone, sincerity is slippery like butter" ("Sugar/Le sucre" 24). She concludes, "We may be, as Browning said, born liars. But that idea itself is only wholly meaningful if we glimpse a possibility of truth and truthfulness for which we must strive, however, inevitably, partial, our success must be" ("Sugar/Le sucre" 24).

Byatt's combination of theoretical sophistication with traditional attitudes to truth and meaning leads her to value characters that are both openly fictive—"papery"—and "real." She quotes Murdoch's argument that both the "crystalline" semi-allegorical novel and its opposite, the sprawling "journalistic" novel, sacrifice reality of character, and she praises Murdoch's success in creating "free and individual characters, whose experience is diverse and not to be summed up" (*Iris Murdoch* 23). For Byatt, a large part of the pleasure of reading fiction is rooted in a very basic, primitive response to characters, a response that can still be made even when postmodernism has taught us to distrust both language and the concept of character. This paradox draws her to Angus Wilson's work, which, she says, "is not realism, but is intimately and uncomfortably related to it. This is because, although Wilson's insistence on the 'second-hand' quality of his people and their world renders them papery and insubstantial, they do nevertheless think and feel, and author requires of reader an imaginative response to thought and feeling which belongs with realism" ("People in Paper Houses" 169). *Imagining Characters* (1995) records a series of dialogues between Byatt and Ignês Sodré, a psychoanalyst. The two highly educated, self-aware readers engage in what Byatt, summing up their conversations, describes as "an almost primitive mode of discourse that literary criticism has eschewed for a long time"—a discourse that treats literary characters as real. "I feel," she continues, "what you and I have had is a sort of conversation which is sophisticated at one level and very deliberately primitive and naive at another" (*Imagining Characters* 253). This response, on two levels simultaneously, is what Byatt hopes to create in her own readers. It is a response that, she believes, is still possible within postmodern experimental fiction. Commenting on the fairy tales she wrote in the nineties, she asserts that "whereas much postmodern self-reflexive narrative seems somehow designed to show that all narrations are two-dimensional and papery, that all motifs are interchangeable coinage, what I believe and hope to have shown, is that the tale is always stronger than the teller.... What I have always believed is that the human imagination, given any scene, any two people, any danger, any love, any fear, will start elaborating, inhabiting, touching, tasting, feeling" ("Fairy Stories"). For Byatt, postmodernism can still provide us with the excitement of "real" characters. Indeed, her own work uses postmodern techniques to free both her characters and her readers.

Byatt's determination to construct characters who live as free individuals means that although she often shows the mythic aspects of their lives—frequently placing her women characters in relation to Tennyson's Lady of Shalott—she, like Adamson, is wary of pushing analogies too far. She refers to Doris Lessing's character Anna Freeman, in *The Golden Notebook*, who insists on separating her identity from the mythic figures of her dreams and resists her analyst's wish to interpret her experience solely in terms of these figures. Anna feels that such interpretations impose closure and impede what Byatt calls the "quest for the impossible accurate record of *now*" ("True Stories" 98). Byatt's own characters, like Byatt herself, are voracious readers of literature; poems, plays, and novels appear intertextually in her books because they are alive in the minds of the characters, many of whom are themselves writers of literary, critical, or scientific texts. Byatt sets out to imagine characters who think, who will interest thinking readers. She says that she wants "to describe varieties of human experience, like thinking very hard in abstract terms, which most novelists don't describe"; she is convinced that abstract thinking is as immediate an experience as the sensuous one of "standing next to a rosebush" (qtd. in Tredell 70). "I can't stop my people thinking serious thoughts" (Kenyon, *Writer's Imagination* 14), she says. Thinking is never separated from feeling, however; in 1989 Nicci Gerrard astutely observed that in "the most successful of her writing" Byatt reaches "the satisfying and painful state in which emotions are intellectual and the intellect profoundly emotional" (102). An area of mental experience that particularly fascinates Byatt is that of breakdown or disintegration; one thinks first of Lucas Simmonds in *Virgin in the Garden*, but such characters reappear throughout her fiction and are especially prominent in short stories such as "Racine and the Tablecloth," "The Changeling," "The Chinese Lobster," and "Baglady," where the process of losing touch with reality is more frightening because of the compression of its representation. She knows that there is a danger in writing, as she often does, about writers: the book may become "in-turned and self-engrossed" (qtd. in Dusinberre, "A.S. Byatt" 192); she values characters who are "nonliterary" like Daniel Orton and Marcus Potter in the quartet (Dusinberre, "A.S. Byatt" 192). She enjoys, as well, imagining the experience of males. Her description of her characters as "hypotheses let loose in the world,... to see how people react in test situations" (Kenyon, "A.S. Byatt" 55–56) does not do complete justice to their many-sidedness or their mysterious qualities, or to the compassion with which they are portrayed. Byatt admires Murdoch for insisting that in writing as well as in living, we must respect the opacity of persons, and she praises Stanley Middleton's ability to show this opacity acting among his characters: "He works on the borders between people where the nature of the self of the other is a mystery and a blank" ("Art of Stanley Middleton" 201).

Discussing narrative viewpoint with Sodré, Byatt expresses her belief that the third-person narrator as used by George Eliot gets "closer" to the characters than the first-person narrator can (*Imagining Characters* 75), and Byatt herself has developed different versions of the third-person voice. She has used it in all her fiction except for two short stories and one novel. In those two stories, "Sugar" and "Jael," the female first-person narration produces opposing effects: in "Sugar" the narrator is quite openly Antonia Byatt; in "Jael" the narrator is malicious, self-serving, and separate from the author. Phineas Nanson, the male narrator of *The Biographer's Tale*, whose project of truth-telling resembles that of the narrator of "Sugar," is more aloof, less confiding, than that narrator. Despite often acting as a spokesperson for Byatt, Phineas seems to prove his creator's point when she says (in a comment about *Villette*) that first-person narration can be "an interesting barrier between the writer and the reader" (*Imagining Characters* 75).

Perhaps Byatt's usual avoidance of first-person narration has something to do with her rebellion against the idea of art as self-expression. For her, art is a way out of the self, "a way of discovering the world" ("Identity" 23). Nevertheless, she does find that some notion of the self is necessary for her as a writer. As early as 1969, in her essay on Tennyson's *Maud*, she was thinking about "what it means to have sufficient identity to be capable of consistent and meaningful action" ("Lyric Structure" 69) in the nineteenth century, when the sense of individual selfhood was already faltering; her essay on *Maud* analyzes the male speaker's "capacity to discover his own identity, *through his senses*" ("Lyric Structure" 72) in his process of individuation. Contributing to a symposium on identity sponsored in 1986 by the Institute for Contemporary Arts, she tried to describe the basis of her own sense of identity, which is associated with "primary experiences" such as that of perceiving art. Having no theory of selfhood, aware of modern theories that deny the existence of the self, and at first powerfully attracted by T.S. Eliot's stress on the impersonality of the artist, she has come to the conclusion that "if you have no self, there are certain things you simply cannot say" ("Identity" 25). If you are unable to imagine the selves of others, you cannot act morally: "You can't respect people, you can't prevent pain, if you don't imagine individual selves. And I don't want an art which doesn't also represent individual selves, and make people imagine them—even though most of one's consciousness is a fiction and a tale, and imperfect, and very threatened at the edges" ("Identity" 26).

An important way out of the postmodern dilemma of selfhood is to think of the self in relation to history. From the post-Romantic metaphor of the self as a "burning glass … which took in things, and composed them," Byatt has moved on to conceive of identity as a knot. "Things go through us," she says, "And if we are an individual, it's because these threads are knotted together in this particular time and this particular place, and they hold" ("Identity" 26). Frederick M. Holmes argues that although Byatt parodies the "excesses" of a type of criticism (such as Leonora Stern's in *Possession*) that stresses the fluidity of identity, she "seems to be in accord with the notion that identity is a malleable construct that must be actively shaped by the individual if he or she is to be more than the product of historical forces"; such "creative self-fashioning," Holmes suggests, is what Roland and Maud find so attractive in their nineteenth-century predecessors, Randolph Henry Ash and Christabel LaMotte (*Historical Imagination* 70). In practice in her fiction, Byatt shows that the maintenance of the knot requires some effort, and she also knows that the knot may give way, breaking the connection: "There are people"—she cites the failure of Helen Waddell's mind in her later years—"who simply become unknotted" ("Identity" 26).

This shift in metaphors, from glass to knot, is related to Byatt's recent preoccupation (in the 1990s) with reading and writing historical fiction, for the knot of identity exists in a historical context. Years earlier, in 1970, she published her study of Wordsworth and Coleridge in relation to their age. Now, she says, figures like Darwin, Freud, Tennyson, and Swedenborg seem to her to be more "central and urgent" ("True Stories" 94) than contemporary events. Aware of a different perspective as she grows older, she now thinks of her life as "a short episode in a long story" ("True Stories" 94). The appeal of historical figures, for the reader as for the writer, is that they are "unknowable, only partly available to the imagination" ("Fathers" 31). Historical novels thus respond both to the contemporary sense of selfhood as problematic and constructed by language and to the contemporary need to place whatever selfhood exists in relation to earlier selves.

As we have seen, Byatt finds it both possible and necessary to speak of truth and meaning. She distinguishes between truth, which fiction, for all its fictiveness, must strive for, and belief, which she is wary of. She describes her "temperament" as "agnostic"; she is "a non-believer and a non-belonger to schools of thought" (Introduction, *Passions* 2). Truth for her is existential and provisional: as a child she resisted Bible stories because she was expected to believe them, and she questions the truth and usefulness of two biblical narratives in "Jael" and "Christ in the House of Martha and Mary." In myths, especially in the story of Ragnarök, she finds "a kind of human truth" ("First Impressions" 21), but to believe in any one system of myths is foreign to her nature. Visiting the Group of Seven collection at the Art Gallery of Ontario during her 1996 trip to Canada, she was drawn to Tom Thomson but not to Lawren Harris, and, her interviewer reported, she was not surprised to learn of Harris's fondness for representing theosophist ideas in his northern landscapes: "I adore myth.... But I don't like people who believe them," Byatt commented in an interview (Ross, "Art, Myth" D1). Although for her there is no one truth to be found, she is "afraid of, and fascinated by," poststructuralist theories of language as a self-relating system "which doesn't touch the world" ("Still Life/Nature morte" 11). "When my writing is going well I do have a sense of the language making itself, constructing shapes and finding forms of thought which are already there to be found"

("Hauntings" 45), she writes. Asked as a young writer to contribute to a collection of essays entitled *The God I Want*, she not surprisingly spoke of having intuited a God through her reading of the Romantic poets, "not an image, but the primary imager…whatever was behind that purely abstract sense of shape one has when one knows one has an idea but has not given it body" (85). This God, envisioned by her as "growing in chaos and shining" (87), is linked with her earlier concept of individual identity as a burning glass. Such a God is not easy to imagine in the face of the cruelty and suffering of lived experience, and Byatt's later image of the knot is an agnostic concept. But her understanding of the Romantics' intuitions of the divine and of the continuing human need to "dream of spirit" (Levenson, "Religion" 43) explains why Michael Levenson can assert that for her "the religious sense must now live on within a radiant materialism." He continues, "[W]e can abandon the net of Christian theology and still retain the sublimity of transfiguration" ("*Angels and Insects*" 171).[2]

Goodness, understood again in relativistic terms, is important to Byatt. She has never forsaken her Leavisite faith in the moral force of fiction. She values Murdoch's statement that virtue, like freedom, has to do with "really apprehending that other people exist" (qtd. in *Iris Murdoch* 8), and her fiction is filled with characters who fail to acknowledge the uniqueness of others. The duty of "attention," which Byatt defines in Simone Weil's terms as "the constantly renewed attempt to see things, objects, people, moral situations, truly as they are, uncoloured by our own personal fantasies or needs for consolation" (*Iris Murdoch* 9), is the task of the novelist, as it is of the character striving for goodness. In *Imagining Characters,* Byatt praises Jane Austen for showing in *Mansfield Park* "people who don't notice other people's feelings, and the extraordinary rarity of people who do…, or who can act on this noticing" (4). Betrayal of others, whether done consciously or not, is a moral failure she explores throughout the whole range of her work, and she shows that it stems from this lack of attentiveness.

The moral responsibility of writers preoccupies Byatt. She has said that she agrees with Elaine Showalter that women writers tend to be more aware than men of the need to respect the feelings and privacy of real-life models. She herself was careful to dispense aspects of her parents' personalities among the members of the Potter family: "I transferred my mother's anger to Bill" (qtd. in Kenyon, *Writer's Imagination* 14; see also Showalter 303). In addition to creating writers who strive for truth, she depicts their opposite—those, like Julia in *The Game* and Josephine in "The Changeling," who distort and prey on the lives of others, irresponsibly parasitizing their subjects and, in these two instances, bringing about their deaths. Byatt knows that art can eat up life.

She believes that criticism and theory, in turn, can eat up art. She acknowledges debts to contemporary theorists like Foucault, Ricoeur, and Derrida; she has expressed admiration for Bakhtin and argued in print with Barthes (see "Identity"), and her work shows the influence of Lacan and (with many reservations) of feminist theory. Nevertheless, her independent spirit and her eclectic way of thinking prevent her from affiliating herself with any critical school. She believes that ideology imposes readings on a text and thus imprisons and distorts it. She is sharply dismissive of critics who with "huge arrogance ... claim that critical activity is as great and important as the first act of making the work of art" (qtd. in Wachtel, "A.S. Byatt" 84). As an undergraduate she was already aware of the problems that arise when a critic takes over an author; she worried "about what Lawrence would have made of Leavis and vice versa" ("Reading, Writing, Studying" 5), and she dramatized this tension in the relationship between Oliver Canning (the Leavis figure) and Henry Severell (the Lawrence figure) in her first novel, *The Shadow of the Sun*. As the years have passed, she has become alarmed by a larger problem—the role of ideology in determining university curricula and thus politicizing the canon: "The fear of being appropriated by an individual critic modulates into the fear of being appropriated by—or supported by— a group" ("Reading, Writing, Studying" 5-6). She passionately wants her texts to be read "as texts," and herself to be seen as "someone who weaves careful structures out of truths, lies, slanted comment, several originals" ("Reading, Writing, Studying" 6). This resistance to the imposition of critical and theoretical frameworks has an additional, personal edge: she is especially unhappy about biographical approaches to her work by readers anxious to explore sibling rivalry or to compare her to her sister, Margaret Drabble. From a broader perspective, the issue is a corollary of Byatt's concern for the preservation of real people in fiction. She describes her own reading, as a student, as "innocent," and she hopes for similar readers for herself, readers who "listen ... to texts until they [have] revealed their whole shape, their articulation, the rhythms of their ideas and feelings" ("Forefathers" 46). She is particularly perturbed by the clash of languages that occurs when current criticism "imposes its own narratives and priorities on the writings it uses as raw material, source, or jumping-off point" ("Forefathers" 45). This awareness of a "gulf" between the vocabularies of various theoretical interpretative approaches and the "feel" of primary texts underlies the ventriloquism of her Victorian poems in *Possession*, where, by resuscitating the voices of the past (as the Victorian poets also did, in their time), Byatt was able to "show one could hear the Victorian dead" ("Forefathers" 47).

In light of these preoccupations and of her personal history, Byatt's ambivalent relationship to feminist theory and criticism can be more easily understood. On the one hand, her attitudes and her writing spring from an intuitive feminism based on experience, observation, and reading. *The Shadow of the Sun*, like Margaret Atwood's *Edible Woman* (1969), anticipates many of the themes and images of the feminist novels of the seventies and eighties. It is worth noting that both Byatt's and Atwood's novels were drafted several years before they were published, Byatt's "between 1954 and 1957" (Introduction, *Shadow* viii) and Atwood's in 1964-65 (Buck 301)—a fact that makes their critiques of traditional views all the more remarkable. Acknowledging the importance of Betty Friedan in calling attention to the need to rethink woman's place—*The Feminine Mystique*, she says, was "written for my generation" (Dusinberre, "A.S. Byatt" 189)—Byatt admits also that she herself suffered from the existence of "a pattern cut out" for women: "Although I've had a good education and I've had chances…, nevertheless, there is this sense of what to be a woman is, that is imposed upon you, that doesn't include being a great artist" (*Imagining Characters* 101). As a writer and critic, she has worked steadily, with growing insight, to explore the creativity of women in the present and in earlier centuries. She understands, as Kelly points out, that "the imagination has a long *gendered* history in Western art and literature" (32). Byatt's heliotropic imagination has required a genderless sun. Her unfinished PhD dissertation would have included the neoplatonic idea that "the Sun is the male Logos, or Nous, or Mind" that engenders life in the inert female Earth. Perceiving the false analogy— "there is nothing intrinsically male about the sun, or female about the earth" (Introduction, *Shadow* xiv)—Byatt went on to explore its ramifications, including the figuring of the female imagination as the moon, reflecting the sun's light. She rejects simple polarizations, such as reason/feeling, which have been used to privilege women but which in fact do them a disservice; she thinks that feminists who follow "earth religions of the Mother" ("True Stories" 111) are misguided. In a similar vein, she is critical of the gnostic belief held by Mondrian, that "the inner, the spiritual, element in man is male, and is enclosed in the solid, the material, which is female"; such ideas, she says, are "silly" ("Fashion for Squares" 17).

On the other hand, Byatt acknowledges male influences—Proust, Balzac, Browning, James, and others—again and again, and her "greedy reading" (Introduction, *Passions* 1) has always eagerly encompassed both sexes. Fearing ghettoization of her works by feminist critics, she is also distressed by the ghettoizing potential of women's studies courses, which separate women's writings from the mainstream women fought so hard to enter—"this seems like choosing a new kind of second-class citizenship" (qtd. in Dusinberre, "A.S. Byatt" 187)—and she worries that the ideology of sisterhood and the focus on women's texts may stand in the way of the pursuit of the universality and objectivity she stubbornly cherishes. Despite her understanding of theoretical arguments that "innocent reading" is impossible, she passionately believes that readers should strive to let texts speak for themselves. Her misgivings about feminist approaches to literature, like her ambivalence about poststructuralism, are a function of her age and education and of what she calls her agnosticism. Having worked for and achieved stature as a writer and the possession of as much knowledge and understanding of the world of ideas as she can encompass, she is not willing to be thought of as simply a "women's novelist." This would be to submit to another set of imposed criteria: "I really don't want, myself, to be ghettoized by modern feminists into writing about women's problems" (qtd. in Tredell 60). She describes herself as "an older and more individualistic feminist" than the feminists of the seventies and eighties ("Reading, Writing, Studying" 5).

Byatt is hard on critics who in her view do not read the *whole* work carefully—as Leavis taught her generation to do—or who wilfully distort texts (by women or by men) by imposing idiosyncratic readings. Mary Jacobus's feminist reading of Wordsworth—her play, for example, with the modern implications of "French letter" in a discussion of his impregnation of Annette Vallon in France—evokes a scathing response ("True Stories" 99-102). Narrow readings of Willa Cather draw Byatt's scorn: "Feminist critics who didn't castigate Cather for not creating positive images of women diligently set about showing that her male narrators were 'unreliable' and their devotion to classical learning 'a faulty literary vision'" ("Justice for Willa Cather" 51). Acknowledging that canons and criteria are constantly undergoing revision as well as that all readings are inevitably partial (in both senses), Byatt stoutly rejects "partisan misdescriptions" of texts: "political frenzy which judges everyone by ahistorical absolutes, without any sense of an obligation to see what an author was trying to do, is at best intolerant, and at worst meaningless" ("Justice" 53). The women novelists she most admires are those who go beyond the exploration of women's issues to look at the human condition: Cather, Murdoch, Doris Lessing, Pat Barker, Toni Morrison, Alice Munro, Penelope Fitzgerald, and, above all, George Eliot. She praises George Eliot for her portrayal of women's experience, which she did "better than most writers" precisely because she was in touch with issues that included but moved beyond the lives of women: "she made a world, in which intellect and passion, day-to-day cares and movements of whole societies cohere and disintegrate" ("George Eliot: A Celebration" 76). The whole realm of the intellect belongs to women; this is the point of her assertion that she would "rather talk about George Eliot's views on German philosophy than her views on women" (qtd. in Dusinberre, "A.S. Byatt" 187). In our own time, Byatt admires Pat Barker for her "true novelist's curiosity about whole people, thinking, feeling, and acting, with complex constraints of background, personal history and language"; Barker, she speculates, "found her great subject partly because she was a woman avoiding the constraints of prescribed feminist subject-matter" ("Fathers" 31). Byatt goes so far as to suggest that the controlling force of feminism may be the reason why there are "no obviously great women novelists" in the present generation, where, as *On Histories and Stories* shows, she has found so many male novelists to admire: her list includes, among British writers, Graham Swift, Peter Ackroyd, Lawrence Norfolk, Ian McEwan, Julian Barnes, and Terry Pratchett. "In my gloomier moments, I think this is not an accident. The women are writing about women's themes for women in what they think are female styles" (qtd. in Miller). Her delight in discovering a young woman novelist whom she can wholeheartedly admire is shown in her generous review of Helen DeWitt's *The Last Samurai*, where Byatt finds the mother-son relationship conveyed in "a genuinely new form" that "both embodies and studies the tug between determinism and chance," and where the patterns are those of "math, grammars, and music"; in DeWitt's novel of ideas, "the love between mother and son is clear, and complicated, and accurately felt" ("Kurasowa Kid" 100, 102). Byatt does not mention George Eliot in this review, but it is clear that she has found a novel that satisfies her in the same way as Eliot's novels do, and a writer who unites the life of the mind and that of the feelings in ways that resemble Byatt's own achievements.

The influence of feminist scholarship can be seen, however, in the gradual modulation of Byatt's position over the years. In her early (1983) interview with Juliet Dusinberre, Byatt stated, "The writer's profession is one of the few where immense sexual-political battles don't have to be fought. There have not been deep prejudices against women writers, except that a woman writer may be set aside and praised like a dog for walking on its hind legs" (186-87). In 1991, in conversation with Eleanor Wachtel, she modified this position, declaring, "Literary scholarship has treated women unfairly for many generations" (Wachtel, "A.S. Byatt" 85).

When her first novel was reissued in 1991, Byatt was able to measure her growing awareness of feminist concerns. Her own original title of the book, which appeared in 1964 as *Shadow of a Sun*, had been *The Shadow of the Sun*. Now, twenty-seven years later, the original title was restored, with an introduction that shows Byatt's understanding of the implications of her title's sun reference. Although Byatt concurs with George Eliot's statement at the end of her essay "Silly Novels by Lady Novelists" that "No educational restriction can shut women out from the materials of fiction" (qtd. in *Passions* 75, 85), she also understands the crucial role of education in opening up language to women: "Men have always presumed to use male and female discourse, and education allows women to do this" (qtd. in Kenyon, *Writer's Imagination* 18). Byatt resists any attempt to define and claim a separate female language, instead, as Olga Kenyon points out, giving to Frederica in *The Virgin* "discourses ... so often in the past only granted to heroes" ("A.S. Byatt" 75). Byatt has personal experience of the educational system's discrimination against women, and refers to it in the introduction to *The Shadow of the Sun*, where she recounts that as a student she automatically lost her grant upon marriage, whereas married men's grants were increased.

Predictably, she also refuses to enter into a discussion of women's separate literary techniques. Her own tendency to write long sentences she attributes to "James and Proust and Eliot" (qtd. in Dusinberre, "A.S. Byatt" 184), not to Woolf's concept of a separate "woman's sentence" as exemplified by Dorothy Richardson. But Byatt's early misgiving about Ellen Moers's identification of a specific female landscape—"I'm sure I've encountered it as much in male writers as in female" (qtd. in Dusinberre, "A.S. Byatt" 186)—becomes, in 1992, a more positive response to Moers and other feminists: "I enjoy their [recent feminist critics'] revaluing of everything that is female. Critics like ... Moers, who thinks there are specifically female metaphors, have made me reflect, though I don't wholly agree with her" (qtd. in Kenyon, *Writer's Imagination* 18). In 1990, in the Tredell interview, she observed that Christabel LaMotte's poetry in *Possession* "contains all sorts of images which modern feminist scholarship has made available for me to see as the powerful guiding images of women's lot" (61). Yet Byatt mocks the imaginary feminist critic Leonora Stern's analysis of Christabel's texts, an analysis exclusively in terms of a female landscape. The point is that Leonora's reading is narrow, imposed, and formulaic. Christabel's images come from lived experience, despite the somewhat ironic fact that Byatt's idea for Christabel's epic *Melusine* originated as a parody of Luce Irigaray (Tredell 61). Like the remarkable sequence in *The Virgin in the Garden* representing Stephanie's discovery of the inner spaces of her body on her wedding night, Byatt's images were discovered, not derived from theory.

As we have seen, Byatt gave no attention to the question of gendered identity in her 1986 lecture "Identity and the Writer." Some feminists are bound to be dismayed by this, and in the fullest feminist discussion of Byatt to date, Christien Franken examines Byatt's ambivalence about both feminist theory and poststructuralism. Franken concludes that Byatt splits herself in two in order to reconcile two conflicting positions on each of the two topics. On feminism, Franken finds that Byatt wishes "to keep 'gender' apart from thinking and writing. 'The woman' and 'the intellectual' are in different categories of identity" (*A.S. Byatt* 28). It seems to me, however, that Byatt takes women's intellectualism as a given (though historically an often unrealized and unrecognized one). I agree with Franken that if Byatt "had emphasized the importance of 'female identity' in her lecture..., she would have had a place from which to criticize both traditional Leavisite notions of the writer as male genius and post-structuralist denials of authorship" (20). My discussion of Byatt's development suggests, however, that the fiction achieves what the non-fiction does not, in its implicit critique of both of the theoretical positions Franken names.

Paradoxically, it may seem, it is Byatt's respect for women's minds that underlies her opposition to some aspects of women's studies, especially those that offer young women only women's texts to read. "It's because I'm a feminist that I can't stand women limiting other women's imaginations," she says bluntly in a 1996 interview (Miller) in which she describes herself as a political not a literary feminist. Byatt follows Lessing in placing women's intellectual life at the centre of her fiction. From Anna Severell in her first novel to Frederica Potter, whose progress is traced throughout the quartet, remaining open at the end of *A Whistling Woman*, Byatt's female characters struggle for knowledge, understanding, and the freedom to *think*. Many, too, share their author's anger at the barriers women encounter—an anger that echoes that of Byatt's mother—and they rebel, with varying degrees of success. The blocking of women's energies by domesticity and social expectations is portrayed again and again—the disappointed wives and mothers, such as Caroline Severell and Winifred Potter, the schoolgirl Emily in "Racine and the Tablecloth," the thwarted scholar Beatrice Nest in *Possession*, and many more. In her conversations with Ignês Sodré, Byatt identifies the stopping off of women's energies as "the theme which for me recurs most powerfully" in all the novels, from *Mansfield Park* to *Beloved*, that the two scholars are discussing (*Imagining Characters* 84). This, for Byatt, is the primary loss women continue to suffer. Linked with it is the biological dilemma embodied for her by the Lady of Shalott. Cassandra Corbett in *The Game* and Christabel LaMotte in *Possession* are both, Byatt says, "the woman closed in the tower who has given her soul for her writing but is also somehow destroyed. They're all the Lady of Shalott" (Tredell 66). Christabel and her descendant Maud utter the same "cry" to the men they love: "you're taking away my autonomy, you're giving me something wonderful that I regard as secondary, my work is what matters" (qtd. In Tredell 60). It is in this sense that Byatt can assert that all her books up to 1990 are about the woman artist, and about "what language is." "If language is as much nature as childbearing, you're all right," she concludes (Tredell 66). She admits to having once found Coleridge's and Woolf's idea of the androgynous mind attractive, and also to having later become "more sceptical and confused" (qtd. in Kenyon, *Writer's Imagination* 14) about the issue. The question of the relation of women to their bodies and to art persists, and for Byatt it can only be represented through the lived experience of characters, not definitively answered.

Byatt's feminism is to be found, then, in her creation of a rich variety of powerfully imagined female characters, not in any ideological position informing her texts. Her sense of female identity is expressed directly, through the bodies, minds, and voices of her characters. She sees characters such as Anna, Stephanie, Frederica, Christabel, Blanche, and Maud as feminist statements in themselves, "as strong ... as any [statement] that I could theoretically make, and as much use" (qtd. in Tredell 61). Stephanie's anger at restrictive hospital rules during labour came from Byatt's own memories, not from "feminist theory" (qtd. in Tredell 61). These women experience the issues immediately, in their lives and in their work (or, in Anna's case, in the work they yearn for). In the nineteenth century, Byatt says, "the powerful images of what it was like to be a woman who couldn't use what she had got" came from George Eliot, not from the statements of the feminists who "accused [Eliot] of not joining in" (Tredell 61). Byatt's first two novels are both incomplete female *Künstlerromane*. The first two volumes of her quartet are more concerned with their heroines' relation to literary, historical, and cultural images than with their potential as artists in the narrower sense, although Frederica and Stephanie are both engaged in finding language in which to tell their own stories. Not until *Possession*, the fifth novel, does Byatt show full-fledged female artistry, in the heliotropic imaginations of Christabel and Blanche. In these two fictive characters, as Beate Neumeier observes, Byatt "finally creates her models of female vision herself" (19), and here at last the creative sun is gendered female in the poems of both Ash and Christabel. True to her understanding of the historical limitations on women's freedom, Byatt imagines Christabel as deprived of both sexual and maternal expression after the birth of her daughter. But there is a crucial difference, for Christabel's story ends with the loss of both sexual and maternal love. In *Angels and Insects*, however, three other Victorian women characters, Matilda Crompton, Emily Tennyson Jesse, and Lilias Papagay, create and interpret narratives and also live in sexual partnerships with men. In *Babel Tower*, Frederica's writing and teaching are parts of a large, complex plot that relates motherhood, violence against women, escape from enclosure, and divorce to broader questions of the use and misuse of language in a world that seems close to breakdown. In *A Whistling Woman,* Frederica moves into television, and her story is joined by that of Jacqueline Winwar, who, as a biologist working in a world controlled by men, has her own struggles to undergo. Through these stories, Byatt charts the gains of women, but she also sets their lives in a broader context of a complex reality that contains elements that do not change.

Byatt explores the relation of women and narrative from many perspectives in the stories in *Sugar*, and in the later short stories of the 1990s —*The Matisse Stories* (1993), *The Djinn in the Nightingale's Eye* (1994), and *Elementals* (1998)—she extends her definition of women's art. Debbie in "Art Work" is a woodcut artist; the Eldest Princess in the story of the same name rebels against the story set down for her and becomes a storyteller; and Eva in "Dragons' Breath" is a weaver (making explicit Byatt's image of her own production of texts). Perhaps most striking in these later volumes are the figures of Gillian Perholt in "The Djinn" and Fiammarosa in "Cold." As a narratologist, Gillian articulates Byatt's concerns with women's enclosure; as a woman, she moves from analyzing narrative to creating it and, in the process, comes to a deeper understanding of her own story, including her sexuality and her death. Fiammarosa's decision to marry the man she loves means that she must leave the environment in which she is able to thrive and produce art. Here Byatt poses again, in the exotic settings of fantasy, the question that remains at the heart of her engagement with the female imagination. She remains wary of the feminist label, however. Her description of "The Story of the Eldest Princess" as "mildly feminist" ("Fairy Stories") may seem odd to readers who see the story as a bold feminist statement, but it must be taken in the context of her stated dislike of the more doctrinaire "resolute feminist rewritings" that have "designs on the reader" ("Old Tales, New Forms" 143).

Whether she is writing at the realistic or the fantastic end of the fictional spectrum, Byatt shows her women characters directly confronting situations that would restrict their growth. Their characteristic response to these situations involves the exercise of intense mental as well as emotional energy. Through this energy, women's plots are changed; plots are never imposed from outside to fit a formula. As Christopher Hope points out in the Contemporary Writers series pamphlet on Byatt, "There is a dogged pride in Byatt's women. Instead of exploiting feminist issues, she puts in place characters who confront existential challenges other writers seem happier merely to discuss" (n.p.). In Sabine Hotho-Jackson's words (she is describing Byatt's historical writing, but her remark is more widely applicable), Byatt is not interested in simply rewriting "from the female perspective" in a way which would "replace one genderspecific reading...by another" (118). The type of feminism to which Byatt objects would require such replacement. Instead, Byatt invents a diversity of plots for her women and gives them many voices and many subject positions.

Like her model George Eliot, Byatt fashions narrators who speak with generosity and humour, as well as with a tragic sense, about a complex reality. Like Eliot, too, Byatt always creates whole worlds; her women's stories are placed in fully realized settings, whether of realism or of fantasy. In these stories—especially in *Possession* and the books that follow it—women help each other, and friendship between women becomes an important subject. Nevertheless, intellectual as well as sexual sharing between females and males is also examined, and male experience is of interest in itself. Male writers, from Henry Severell to Alexander Wedderburn, Randolph Ash, Roland Michell, and Phineas Nanson, are key figures through whom Byatt reflects on her own artistic problems; they often act and speak for her, in a way that shows Byatt's implicit refusal of rigid gender differences and her wariness of all forms of essentialism. Franken points to Byatt's "explicit identification" with Ash (A.S. Byatt 87) and shows its roots in her admiration for Browning, Tennyson, and other Victorian writers. André Brink goes further, finding a merging of male and female stories and value systems in *Possession*; Browning, he says, is "not a Freudian father figure" but "a spiritistic 'medium' *through* which the reader is allowed to reach even further back, into Browning's poetic 'world' where female figures and forces play a significant role" (302). Through Roland and ten years later through Phineas in *The Biographer's Tale*, Byatt continues to contemplate the relationship of words and things with which she began. Roland, as part of his metamorphosis from critic into poet, goes through the same exercise as Byatt set herself after participating in a series of seminars on literary theory: he makes lists of words that "resisted arrangement into the systems of literary criticism or theory" (*Possession* 431; see also Franken, *A.S. Byatt* 136 n. 25). Phineas makes a more drastic move, not only away from theory but away from biography and even from poetry, to the world of creatures. Real and imagined male figures, not only writers and painters but mathematicians, scientists, and a diverse group of others, are important in Byatt's ongoing meditation on the uses humans make of the world.

In fact, a case can be made for viewing Byatt herself as a feminist critic. In both her fiction and her non-fiction, she engages independently in many of the tasks of feminist scholarship and theory over the years. Through a reimagining of history, she has made spaces, "new openings," for women, as she has praised Toni Morrison for doing for her own characters ("True Stories" 101). The same firm sense of history underlies Byatt's awareness of the need to read women novelists such as Austen and Eliot in the context of what was possible for women in their time, rather than applying our expectations to their characters. When she has worked to rescue women like Willa Cather from a specific kind of feminist reading, it has been because she believes that such a reading violates her own first principle of criticism, that texts are to be read as wholes. Through such characters as Frederica and Bill, Christabel, Emily Tennyson Jesse, and Gillian, Byatt scrutinizes male-authored texts, from *The Winter's Tale* to *In Memoriam*, *Sons and Lovers*, *Howards End*, and *Lucky Jim*, not only identifying sexist implications but working out, through her plots, the damage they may do to women readers. Her insistence on reading whole texts, however, means that there is no contradiction for her between her understanding of the way in which Emily's mourning for Hallam is co-opted by her brother's expression of his own grief, in *In Memoriam*, and her admiration for the achievement of that poem as a complex totality. As well, Byatt perceives and analyzes Tennyson's use of myth to present a symbolic statement of women's dilemma in "The Lady of Shalott." Another instance of Byatt's comprehensive reading is Lewis Carroll, whose *Alice* books she draws on especially in *The Game*, *Babel Tower*, and *A Whistling Woman*. Here, we see Byatt's development as a feminist reader. In *The Game*, it is Carroll's use of the looking-glass image that interests her; in the quartet, it is his comic portrayals of an intelligent, brave young girl, Alice, and an irrational, enraged older woman, the Queen of Hearts, in Victorian society. In Byatt's reading, as in her writing, feminist interpretation is part of what Todd calls a "total discourse," and the reading itself changes over time. And while her depiction of patriarchal language and behaviour, in characters from Herbert Baulk and

Mr. Hawke in the nineteenth century to Gideon Farrar, Fergus Wolff, and Nigel Reiver in the twentieth, is chillingly accurate, she is more interested in male figures who are able to share language with women and in the productiveness of those collaborations.

It is Byatt's insistence on openness and inclusiveness, on encompassing more and more of the interest and variety of lived experience, that forms the basis both of her development of the forms and techniques of fiction and of her ambivalent relationship to feminism. As her heliotropic imagination has turned steadily to the sun, she has freed her women characters for creative expression. Her work lays claim to the sun's light on behalf of women. The fact that this process entails the rejection of some aspects of feminist theory and practice is for her a necessary paradox. Nevertheless, her fiction is feminist in that (to use Gayle Greene's definition in *Changing the Story*) it contains an "analysis of gender as socially constructed" and a "sense that what has been constructed can be reconstructed" (2). The multiplicity of women's voices and stories Byatt offers her readers springs from her awareness that the processes of construction and reconstruction are fluid and open ended.

If Byatt were to feel comfortable within any theoretical feminist position, it would perhaps be that which Toril Moi describes: "a feminist vision of a society in which the sexual signifier would be free to move; where the fact of being born male or female would not determine the subject's position in relation to power, and where, therefore, the very nature of power itself would be transformed" (172). This, says Moi, is Julia Kristeva's "third position," which follows the two earlier stages of the feminist struggle: the demand by women for equal access to the symbolic order, and the rejection of the symbolic order in the name of difference. As we have seen, Byatt explores the first path but disassociates herself from the second; by Kristeva's definition, she is a liberal, not a radical feminist. Despite this fact, however, her work asserts the hope that in the future the "third attitude" will prevail and "the very dichotomy man/ woman as an opposition between two rival entities" may be perceived as a mere metaphysical distinction (Kristeva, qtd. in Moi 12). As Kenyon observes, Byatt demonstrates in *Still Life* that the characters' "refusal to be bound by sexual identity releases creative energy" ("A.S. Byatt" 75). Byatt's stories of women's lives are grounded in the real world, however; she is not a utopian writer, not even (perhaps especially not) in her fairy tales. If she is fighting any "theoretical battle," it is, as she told Tredell, "for the work of art not to be propaganda" (61). Her books are open texts that, by eschewing dogmatism, deconstructing binaries of all kinds, and encouraging a plurality of readings, serve women well.

2 *The Shadow of the Sun*

IN BYATT'S FIRST NOVEL, most of her main preoccupations are already apparent. Here she develops character types that, with important variations, recur in her fiction: the ambitious young woman, the disappointed older woman, the visionary genius. Here, too, Byatt introduces specific topics she continues to explore in later work: the tendency of fiction to be parasitic on life and the tendency of criticism, in turn, to feed off and distort creative writing. The human cost of the writer's life, the toll it can take on human relationships, is to be returned to again and again in Byatt's fiction. Above all, in *The Shadow of the Sun* Byatt begins her exploration of the female imagination.

In 1991 Vintage published a reissue of Byatt's first novel, under the title Byatt had originally preferred, *The Shadow of the Sun* (rather than *Shadow of a Sun*, the title suggested by her editor, Cecil Day Lewis, and used for the book's first appearance in 1964), and with an introduction by Byatt. Reflecting retrospectively on her novel's genesis, Byatt identifies the two problems the novel presented: the human and the literary. The primary human problem was the issue of women, work, and men; the second problem was the relationship of the creative writer to the literary critic who interprets his or her work. These two subjects form the two intertwined plots of the novel. The literary problem was that of finding a suitable form. "I had awful problems with the form," says Byatt in the introduction, adding that she lacked appropriate models. The novels of Elizabeth Bowen, Rosamund Lehmann, E.M. Forster, and Virginia Woolf were "too suffused with 'sensibility'"; on the other hand, the "joky social comedy of [Kingsley] Amis and [John] Wain" appealed even less (xi). There were other influences—Françoise Sagan's *Bonjour Tristesse*, another novel of sensibility, and two much more significant and lasting ones, Marcel Proust and Iris Murdoch, whose work Byatt read between the first and second drafts of *Shadow;* "but the underlying shape...is dictated by Elizabeth Bowen and Rosamund Lehmann, and a vague dissatisfaction with this state of affairs" (xii).

Although this inherited underlying shape is discernible in *Shadow*—in its use of the form of the female *Bildungsroman*, its diffuseness (reminiscent especially of Lehmann), and its descriptions, both praised and deplored by the original reviewers, of what one reviewer called "the emotional convolutions behind each utterance" ("Living with a Genius" 21)—Byatt goes further beyond these models than she may have realized.

Through Anna, Byatt examines a problem from her own experience, the contradictions faced by young women in the fifties and sixties who, having fought hard for their places at university, felt forced to choose between work and love: "Men could have both..., but it seemed that women couldn't" (ix). She recalls the attitude of her thesis supervisor, Helen Gardner, "who believed, and frequently said, that a woman had to be dedicated like a nun, to achieve anything as a mind"—an ideal of an "unsexed mind" that Byatt instinctively rejected (ix). These conflicts underlie Byatt's portrait of her heroine, who, with creative ambitions of her own, lives in the shadow of her father, Henry, a visionary and a successful novelist. He, "being male, could have what [Anna] and I felt we perhaps ought not to want, singlemindedness, art, vision" (ix). Anna's problem—of finding her own vision and the means of expressing it—is thus the same as that encountered by her creator. Anna and her search for a female vision are set off against the figure of Henry, the male visionary who is derived in part from D.H. Lawrence, a presence who both attracts and repels Byatt; she finds his writing "powerfully moving" (xiv) but also "violent and savage" and "coercive" (xii). Henry does not share Lawrence's views, nor does he wish to force his vision on others, but his single-minded dedication and, above all, the dangerous alluring brightness of his imaginative world link him with Lawrence, challenging the would-be woman artist. Anna is important in the secondary plot also, for she is the figure over whom her father and his leading critic, Oliver Canning, confront each other, each claiming a natural affinity with her. The "battle" of the novel, Byatt observes, inevitably "fought itself out between sexuality, literary criticism, and writing" (viii). "[In] any male version of this story," says Byatt, Oliver "would have been the hero" (xi). But she makes it Anna's story.

Byatt's version of the underlying shape inherited from Bowen and Lehmann uses a two-part structure. It opens in an atmosphere of waiting—for a break in the summer heat and for some movement in the static Severell family. The plot of part 1 focuses on Anna's attempts to escape from her country home, Darton, where, aware of her mother Caroline's disapproval (Caroline much prefers Jeremy, Anna's young brother, who, unlike the anti-social Anna, is eager to please everyone) and envious of her kind but distant father's access to vision, she is miserably unhappy. Longing for some momentous "event" in the future, which she vaguely associates with being able to write something herself, she has, the previous winter, run away from school to York, simply to experience being "out without leave from somewhere where she should have been shut up" (35). For this she has been dismissed from the school. We first see her leaving the house to hide in a hut in the garden, in order not to be present to greet her parents' house guests, Oliver Canning, a literary critic and obsessively admiring explicator of Henry's work, and Oliver's wife, Margaret. As the narrative progresses, Anna's inability to escape, her sense of being confined yet growing, is contrasted with Henry's freedom to write, inspired by his experiences of heightened, intense vision. Oliver begins to tutor Anna in preparation for university application; at the same time, Henry sets off on one of the periodic tramps around the countryside which help to nourish his imagination. The contrast between the worlds of father and daughter is underlined by the fact that Anna and Oliver are working on Matthew Arnold; they will be studying a critic who, viewing himself as an unsuccessful poet, advocated poetry of human action, while (in contrast with their stasis) Henry is off in quest of experience that will enable him to create what Arnold admired: epic, impersonal works shaped around "whole men, whole actions" (59). Oliver and Anna are thus at two removes from Henry's first-hand creativity. In the next chapter, Anna and Oliver visit the riding stables where Anna had once hoped she might feel at home (and where Michael, a well-off young student with whom she imagines herself to be in love, is working). Their errand is to fetch liquid fertilizer, and this banal task is set off against Henry's adventures at the "edges of experience" (84) and his exhausted, triumphant return home. In this chapter, Byatt depicts Anna as the battleground between two men—Michael, who wants to resume their tentative romantic relationship, and Oliver, who regards Michael as a member of a useless privileged class that wastes university places, avoiding the "real world" which, Oliver insists, Anna must face.

Part 1 ends with a seaside picnic at St. Anne's Crane, an outing carefully and ritualistically organized by Caroline and enjoyed by none of the participants. Henry vents his frustration at Oliver's possessive preoccupation with Henry's work and ideas; Margaret confides to Henry her loneliness in her marriage and appeals to Oliver to be closer to her. That night the weather breaks and Anna, in the bathroom at Darton, watches the storm gather; she sees the moon illuminate the glass to produce a "miracle" of light and feels that she does after all have visionary capacity: "She felt balanced and complete, between all this trapped, plotted light and the approaching storm; she said to herself..., 'I can do something with this, that matters'" (134). Her elation is arrested by Oliver's arrival in search of a drink of water, and by his insistence that she accept his definition of reality, "a combination of one's own limitations and, in some form or other, the eternal kitchen sink" (135). Nevertheless, Anna manages a temporary escape into the rain and lightning outside, taking Oliver with her. Oliver kisses Anna violently, and she tries to dismiss this as a predictable, insignificant act, marking the end of their time together. The next morning the Cannings leave Darton, and Henry gratefully resumes his work.

Part 2 opens with Anna in Cambridge. A fellow undergraduate, Peter Hughes-Winterton, is in love with her; he has given a party in his rooms and she, rather drunk, has gone outside and is waiting for Peter to take her home. Oliver finds her there and takes her to the house in Barton Road that he has been lent by his old tutor; the resemblance between "Barton" and Darton suggests that Anna is exchanging one enclosure for another. Oliver makes love to her, but Anna, experiencing her loss of virginity with emotional detachment, still feels "left free" for her "event" in the future (164). Back at Darton, Henry receives a letter from Margaret, who, obviously very unhappy, pleads with him to come to London to see her. Despite a conversation in which Caroline firmly upholds Henry's right as a gifted male to resist the demands of others, and advocates the feminine resignation to "duty" and practicality that has governed her own life, he decides he must "try and help" (175). Reaching the Cannings' house, he finds that Margaret has enclosed herself in a dark house smelling of stale food; pitifully glad to see him, she expects him to solve all her problems. Over dinner in a restaurant, she begs him to force Oliver to return from Cambridge and respond to her needs in the marriage; she insists that there "isn't anything" she can do except be married. Arriving in Cambridge, Henry first visits Anna, who tells him of her inability to decide what to do with her life and confesses her hope that she will find a way of seeing the brightness in the world that nourishes her father. Delighted to hear this, Henry offers to send her "into the sun," far from his shadow, so that she can discover what she wants to do, but when he talks about Margaret, as an example of a wasted life, a woman consumed by a man, Anna responds so violently that Henry realizes Anna is involved with Oliver. Declaring that she and Oliver are alike, she asks Henry to leave. His interview with Oliver the next day is hostile and resolves nothing: he accuses Oliver of first "grabbing…, pulling down" his books and now taking possession of Anna, while Oliver, in turn, challenges Henry to leave Anna to make her own way as "Anna, Herself" (219). After Henry leaves, Anna goes to see Oliver, from whom she now feels "distant" (229). Waking in the night to the overwhelming thought that she has "not lived one moment of her life, and probably would not" (233), she leaves the house and, on a bridge, has a visual experience of a bottle in the water in the moonlight—a moment that seems to promise real vision and a "sense of valuable loneliness" (237). But the expected event does not come; the vision dissipates into a "secondhand reflection…, in Oliver's manner" (238), and, in despair, she accepts the fact that "there would be no event, no transforming knowledge…. 'I can't do it. I am not going to know. I am going to have to go on just as I am. I shall not change'" (239).

At this point in the narrative, Anna begins to recede: in the next three chapters she is offstage, present only through a letter in chapter 14, and in the following two chapters simply as the subject of confrontations between other characters. Her letter to Henry tells him that she is spending Christmas with the Hughes-Wintersons. Pregnant by Oliver, she wants, with Peter's knowledge, to have an abortion and marry Peter as soon as possible. Caroline, shocked and angry, summons Oliver to Darton. Margaret intercepts the letter and arrives there too, and after an exchange of accusations between Caroline, Henry, and Oliver (Margaret, like Anna, is in the shadow offstage for most of the discussion), Oliver sets off to find Anna. The final chapter begins with Anna at the Hughes-Wintersons, where despite having received an heirloom engagement ring and approval as a future daughter-in-law from Peter's mother, she answers Oliver's telephone call. She runs away for the last time, to meet Oliver in York, and during the journey decides that the baby should be born and "live its own life" (296). The fact that the meeting with Oliver takes place in the Station Hotel in York, the scene of her earlier, unsatisfactory escape, suggests that she has achieved very little: "What I always do, she thought, is run not quite far enough" (296). Although still at this time planning to deal quickly with Oliver, run farther, and try to write, she capitulates when she sees Oliver himself: "Greyness, and remembered brightness, things done and things to do; one had to contain them, and continue somehow. Seeing Oliver, now, Anna saw that it was silly to imagine it could have been done without him. This really was the feared and expected end. At that time, she was surprisingly content" (298).

Within this basic plot of the female *Bildungsroman*, Byatt is innovative in four interconnected ways. First, she finds a way to address not only women's experience but issues that go beyond that subject to explore the function and uses of art. Byatt explores the relationship of the narrative imagination to its living subjects and that of the critic to the work and its author. The moral responsibilities of the writer, which will become central in *The Game* and will continue to be addressed throughout Byatt's career, are examined here for the first time. Henry uses the distressed human beings around him as copy, and thus marginalizes both his own moments of pain and the sufferings of others: "...there was always a point at which misery snapped in him, at which he was impelled to stand aside, and watch" (249). Despite feeling real sympathy for Margaret's despair, he is "interested" in its "female intensity" and thinks he "could use it and might write about it, some day" (184); later, although deeply worried by Anna's pregnancy, he experiences a "secret excitement" over "the way things were working" (249). He has enough self-knowledge to recognize the inhuman aspect of his work—that when he is absorbed in writing he is "abandoned to what ... was not human"— yet he also knows that this is where he is "alive" (288) and, paradoxically, most himself. There is satire in Byatt's portrayal of Henry—he grandiosely sees himself as a Samson figure—but he is not as severely dealt with as are other morally irresponsible authors in Byatt's later work. Henry's attention is usually directed inward, but when he is awakened to an awareness of crises in others' lives, he does make an effort to act constructively.

In her creation of Oliver, the male who struggles with Henry for Anna's allegiance, Byatt is, I think, less sympathetic. She says that his character grew out of the "moral ferocity" of F.R. Leavis, who, at Cambridge, upheld such high standards for art that he nearly convinced the aspiring writers among his students that "anything you wrote yourself would fall so woefully short ... that it was better not to try" (x). Oliver's effect on Anna is to threaten her dream of achieving something herself. When she says, watching the storm, that at such times she feels she has "no limitations," he responds cuttingly, "And that is when you are most limited" (135). If Henry represents the apparent limitlessness of the visionary, Oliver stands for the rigidly defined boundaries of the "real." His ambivalent relationship with Henry is half envious, half scornful; Oliver is, says Byatt, "someone with a chip, who can think..., who makes too much of literature in one way, and doesn't understand its too-bright aspect" (xi). In Oliver and Henry, Byatt shows "the paradox of Leavis preaching Lawrence when if the two had ever met they would have hated each other" (xi). From this perspective it is Oliver who is the parasite, always probing into the details of Henry's life and thought. Henry complains that Oliver "pries, he nibbles, he draws conclusions, he defines, on scraps of information no one with any tact would try to make anything out of" (6-7). The battle between the two men is thus about abstract issues as well as about Anna's fate. Byatt came to see that both men contain aspects of herself; she describes Henry as "my secret self," the creative mind that sees "everything too bright, too fierce, too much" (x), and Oliver as "a kind of public version of what I was about" as critic, "a *user* of literature, not a maker" (xi). The interrelationship of literature and criticism, so fully worked out in *Possession*, is provocatively sketched in Byatt's first novel.

A second way in which Byatt begins to move beyond more conventional women's fiction is in her self-reflexive search for a language for vision, especially for ways of capturing the heightened sense of reality when things are "too much," and of doing so without implying that these shining objects have any significance beyond themselves. Like van Gogh and Wallace Stevens, Byatt and her "secret self," Henry, inhabit a demythologized world. As Henry tramps across the countryside watching the hay fields in the moonlight change "from grey, to straw, to gold, to glass" and the sheaves become "almost bodiless, cages for light," he remembers the biblical sheaves bowing down to Joseph: "How arrogant it was, and how organized…, and how he would hate to be placed in that way, with the sun and the moon and the stars and the clear sheaves flopping down so submissively" (63). Resisting the image of man at the centre of a world of meaningful symbols, Henry prefers "the sheaves as they were, leaning away from him, holding their own shape, their own tension, giving off their own light, nothing to do with him" (64). From these luminous, larger-than-life objects Henry draws primary creative energy, but they do not take their places in a hierarchy; they are not linked to anything transcendental. He ponders the role of language in this demythologized universe, and the triteness of our well-worn superlatives. "One must find a language new and washed clean," he thinks (84). He is fascinated by Platonic thought and by religious symbolism, but becomes angry "when these figures were translated into assurances and the leap was made into faith…, the assurance that there was a creative mind behind the universe" (84-85). Oliver understands, but cannot share, what Henry sees, and, implicitly evoking Wordsworth's "tree, of many, one" from the

"Immortality Ode" (which figures more explicitly in *Still Life*), compares Margaret's tree with Henry's. Margaret, he explains, sees a solid tree that can be touched, whereas Henry's is "an ideal and shining tree, a visible witness to the fact that you are there and you *see* it so, and are alive" (276). Unlike both Margaret and Henry, Oliver and Anna see *no* trees, only "a hole," although they "scan the horizon for trees" (276): they are not content with the world of sense data, but they cannot reach the world of visionary experience. For Henry, it is enough that he can some-times see his tree, but he knows that the vision may at any time go "black," leaving him with "the other thing, the knowledge of nothing, which was always present enough, a warning, just over the edge of the height he constantly walked" (62). Meanwhile, despite Oliver, Anna strug-gles to find her own vision and its appropriate language. The precarious-ness of any kind of visionary experience in a world without faith—and the challenge to the writer who tries to convey the paradox in language—are expanded on again in Byatt's later work.

Third, Byatt innovates within the female *Bildungsroman* by giving her novel the shape the title suggests. Dividing its focus between Henry, as sun, and Anna, as shadow, she secures the reader's sympathy for Anna by showing the power of what Anna lacks. When Henry is at the centre of the narrative, Anna dwindles away; when Anna and her urgent needs are dominant, it is Henry's world that is marginalized. In this way, the tensions within Byatt's subject are dramatized, and the structure recalls equivocal figures such as the silhouette that can be seen as either bride or crone, used by psychologists to demonstrate ambiguity. Byatt's form, which places the image of male power (Oliver, of course, joining Henry here) against that of female passivity, requires the reader to choose, in effect, whether to read a male or a female text, at the same time as it draws the reader into active participation in the drama.[1]

It is in the fourth area, the book's feminism, however, that Byatt most distinguishes herself. In 1983, looking back over her achievement so far, Byatt told an interviewer that she now saw that *Shadow of the Sun* was very much a feminist text, showing the need for women to think care-fully about their choices or be "trapped by decisions of marriage." She wanted, she said, to show that women "do things [they] think are tem-porary and they turn out to be permanent because of women's biology" (Musil 196–97). In her 1991 introduction, she defines women's entrapment in terms closer to those of the novel: her heroine, she says, is "someone who had the weight of a future life, amorphously dragging in front of her, someone whose major decisions were all to come, and who found that they had got made whilst she wasn't looking, by casual acts she thought didn't impair her freedom" (viii). Anna is trapped both by her biology and by her culture's assumptions about women and marriage. She admits that her indecisiveness about her future is "possibly" to do with her gender, and adds, "I can always get married. To Peter, for instance. That might use one up, one could put everything into someone else" (159). The fact that she has achieved some growth by the end of the novel is signalled by her sudden vision of her future if she did marry Peter: living with Mrs. Hughes-Winterton in the country while Peter finished his degree would be a "half life," "something intolerably less than was possible" (293). Even when she was with Peter, she sees, her life would lack "weight" (295). Her culture, however, offers her no way of imagining a life that does not include dependence on a man, and the women around her offer unsatisfactory models.

Anna's mother Caroline, fiercely protective of Henry's need for solitude, organizing the household to revolve around him, and resolutely embracing the conventional wisdom that women must sacrifice, provides Anna with a dangerous example. When Caroline sees that Margaret is desperately appealing to Henry to solve her problems, she delivers a significant speech urging him not to allow himself to be imposed on: "People [women] won't grow up and accept life as it is. They can't cope with the fact that marriage can be boring, that it isn't all love and companionship, it can't be, not if a man is worth anything. They get bored, they say they aren't fulfilled and shout for help. They should learn to sacrifice themselves. Where would you be, for instance, if I was always trying to talk to you, or 'fulfilling myself' instead of coping with the bank and the grocer and the telephone? I don't suppose I find these any more fulfilling than anyone else might. But they have to be dealt with" (173). The inadequacy of this ideology of marriage is hinted at when we learn that Caroline has a pathetic fantasy, a "private life in which she sang Mozart at Glyndebourne"; she sings while she works and imagines the "rapt silence" of her audience (177). Her "deepest security" has pathos also: "the fact that however little effort Henry put into his marriage, at least he had no relationship outside it" (259). In her introduction, Byatt says that only then, in 1991, was she "beginning to dare to try to imagine" her own mother's life; with Caroline she made her first step in this direction, although she avoided confronting her mother's "perpetual rage, depression, and frustration" (ix).

The Shadow of the Sun also shows Byatt's understanding of the effects female self-sacrifice can have on the male. Henry believes "that it was not enough to live a life for someone else" but is aware that "he had accepted ... the sacrifice as it had been offered" (173). As Margaret's frantic letters and his own wife's state of resignation "came to a horrid whole in his mind," he "saw other people suddenly, life after life, occupied with margarine and the milkman, pastry and the telephone, elevating these from nothing into Christian sacrifice or causes for suicide and symbols of the failure of love, and he was ashamed and afraid" (175). Henry is unwillingly cast in the role of patriarchal authority; Anna reflects that she is "kept inactive in the garden" by "his mandate" (91). When he was a Cambridge undergraduate, Henry had "thought it splendid for the women to be allowed" to attend (194), and when his daughter is a student there, he is exasperated by her "submissive feminine gesture" of kneeling to make his tea (197). A few moments later, Anna confides to him her uncertainty about her potential and her longing for the "event" that would make everything "important" so that she, like him, could make things "bright just by looking at them," but adds that perhaps she should "get down to something more obviously possible—my own limitations and the kitchen sink." Henry, delighted by his discovery of kinship with her, rejects Oliver's definition of reality: "Pay no attention to the kitchen sink" (200). Perceiving that to write or to accomplish anything of her own she would need to be far away from him and his reputation, he offers her money to go to "Mexico or somewhere" where she could "move into the sun" (201–02). In the end, however, he fails Anna and loses her to Oliver. Henry's uncomfortable, if intermittent, awareness of the inadequacy of his culture's view of gender roles demonstrates the destructiveness of patriarchy to both marriage and father-daughter relationships. The narrator's repeated descriptions of Henry's face as partly hidden from both Anna and Margaret calls attention not only to the genius that sets him apart, but also to the alienation between the sexes that the culture perpetuates.

Caroline also fails, more drastically, to provide nurturing for Anna. To Caroline, Anna is an annoying presence, especially in contrast to Jeremy, who, perfect in his mother's eyes, already radiates masculine self-assurance. Telling Margaret that she feels "repudiated" by Anna, Caroline cites as proof Anna's "lack of comprehension about ordinary things" such as pressure cookers and Hoovers: "And she'll have to cope with them some day, she's a woman, nobody'll cope for her" (100). Completely unaware of Anna's ambitions, she wants only to "get rid of" her in order to enjoy her own life, and she is grateful to Oliver for "disposing of Anna" both for the summer, by tutoring her, and, she hopes, for the next three years at university (42). Oliver is quick to see that Caroline does not like Anna, and to tell Anna so. When Caroline learns that Anna is pregnant with Oliver's child, she summons Oliver to Darton in order to get him to "betray"

Anna by making her come home—to which Oliver chillingly replies, "She has no home" (267-68). Asked by Oliver what Anna wants to do about the baby, Caroline bursts out, in a final desertion of her daughter, "What she wants is immaterial" (268). Possessing only conventional attitudes to women's work, their role in marriage, and, worst of all, their sexuality— she believes that unwanted pregnancies are "always the woman's fault.... It was a woman's responsibility to keep out of harm, and her intelligence to know what men were and how to manage them" (247) —Caroline can offer Anna neither love, nor support, nor respect.

Byatt recalls that she began to write *The Shadow of the Sun* in the mid-fifties (Introduction viii), two decades before women's issues drew widespread attention. The depiction of Margaret shows Byatt's early understanding of women's problems of self-definition in an environment where their identity seems dependent on the male gaze. When Oliver is in Cambridge pursuing his relationship with Anna, Margaret, at home and aware only that something is badly wrong in her marriage, finds her world dissolving: "The carpet slippers before the fire, her own eyes and nose and mouth and skin, disappeared like the tree in the quad without the male eye on them, and Margaret was lost" (177). She begins drinking in the mornings, keeps the curtains drawn, and obsessively bathes and grooms her body, which is now "the residue, what was left" (179). In the bathtub, she sees her body as fragmented and objectified: "... all these bits are me. It is almost as though one might fall apart without the bath, as though all these lumps and circles might just float away from each other and not belong to me any more" (179). Her shift from "me" to "one" underlines her disorientation. Looking at a magnified image of a woman's face in *Vogue*, she is terrified by what she perceives as her grotesque, empty mirror image and feels that "nothing held, everything was a jumble of bright dead things" (182). When Henry arrives at what he rightly identifies as her "prison," he becomes aware that she is depending on him to "change her life with a word or a gesture" (189). After Henry has escaped on the train to Cambridge, Margaret shifts her attention back to the absent Oliver, carrying on a conversation with him out loud as she walks home. Only in the presence, real or imagined, of a male can Margaret find even the most fragile sense of self. Alone in her house again, she hears both men's voices, telling her "that everything was for the best..., that she was necessary to them and they loved her" (254). Her cherished image of marriage as an enclosure—"Come in with me, and be married," she implores Oliver at a picnic (130)—has turned on itself; she now feels "contained helplessly in a great yellow ball" (254). In her portrait of Margaret, Byatt's satirical gifts are at their sharpest, yet there is sympathy mixed with the satire. For Margaret is aware that she has lost her life. "It's my life they're taking to bits," she cries to Henry in the last scene at Darton. "I don't know what's going on…, but I know it's happening to me. It's terrible" (263). Now that Oliver is lost to her, she again tries to offer love and submissiveness to Henry. Incapable of seeing herself as autonomous, Margaret is an extreme example of the problems of female dependance that Betty Friedan explored in *The Feminine Mystique*, a text that Byatt describes as "written for my generation" (Dusinberre, "A.S. Byatt" 189)—and that was published nine years after Byatt began to write *The Shadow of the Sun*.

Oliver Canning is the most mysterious and most menacing of the males in *Shadow of the Sun*. Byatt says that he is "the Other," a character "whose thoughts are opaque" (xi). By hiding him from the reader, making him known only through his sharp speech, small, wiry body, and precise movements, Byatt effectively conveys the threat he poses to women. Margaret's accusation that he is sadistic is reinforced by his remark to her, when he comes back to their bed at Darton after kissing Anna in the storm, that she (presumably in contrast to himself) has "never wanted to damage any one" (139). Self-contained, curious, dogmatic, intently focused on his work, Oliver comes to represent to Henry "a black destructive hole into which everything gets sucked, and churned out again, dead and masticated and labelled for future reference, my books and Margaret's sexual energy—and love" (203). Yet Byatt gives Oliver enough moments of apparent self-knowledge—of the roots of his competitiveness, his loneliness, and his insecurity—to avoid alienating the reader. In the background from which he came, he tells Henry, girls were "things you had to make," and he had planned a "campaign" to win Margaret, thinking "she'd teach me to rest": "But she wanted a god, and a master… and I couldn't *be* that man, no one could" (275). And, he says, he has been with Henry "like my wife was with me, waiting to be allowed to share, angry at my own inadequacy" hoping that Henry would "see that I was a proper person to be let in" (274). His own sense of exclusion makes him able to identify the repressive effect that living in her parents' house has on Anna, and, although he does care for her, he does nothing to encourage her ambitions. The ambiguities of Byatt's depiction of him were touched on by a *TLS* reviewer in 1964, who asserted that Oliver is not "as forgivable as [Byatt] would have us accept" ("Living with a Genius" 21). Looking back, Byatt says that Oliver "would have been the hero of any male version of this story, l'homme moyen sensuel, suspicious of Henry's wilder edges, guilty about his wife and the girl, but essentially 'decent.'" But, she adds, "this novel doesn't see him quite

that way. It is afraid of him, though I only understand now how much"
(xi). The fear stems from Oliver's power to keep Anna in the shadow. As
Caryn McTighe Musil points out, he makes her think she must choose
between two world views, the "visionary" and the "realistic" (196); Oliver
is thus deeply guilty of manipulation.

In *Shadow of the Sun* Byatt begins her exploration of the female imagination. She comments that her choice of a phrase from Sir Walter
Raleigh's poem "False Love" as her title (and of a stanza from it as her epigraph) points both to women's "illusion" of the need to be "in love" and
to Anna's sense of herself as insubstantial, "a substance like the shadow
of the sun" (xiii). In this book women are put and kept in their places by
men. Margaret, arriving with relief at Darton at the beginning of the
novel, and talking conventional women's talk with Caroline, feels that the
two of them, through their conversation, "knew where they were" (27).
Anna, in her infatuation with Michael, hopes that she has found her
"place" in the world of horses where he works. Beginning daily lessons
with Oliver, she feels "placed" (42); Oliver in turn tells her that because
Henry is "his own" future and does not focus on his children's future like
other parents, Anna is displaced in her family (56). It is Oliver who gives
her the image of herself as "living under" her father's shadow (53)—language she quickly appropriates and later passes on to Peter so that he can
"construct" her story for himself (281)—along with the cliché of the
kitchen sink. Oliver, whose inverted snobbery, derived from his working-
class roots, leads him to eat canned luncheon meat and beans, is, Anna
thinks, using this food "as a way of keeping her in her place as a Severell,
and of emphasizing Oliver's own natural place" (226). At the Hughes-
Wintertons', Anna, now transported to a different social milieu, sees
that she has again been positioned, however kindly, by a male. When the
book ends, she has not yet won a room of her own.

Through the motif of women's reading Byatt shows, self-reflexively, the
scarcity of acceptable women's texts, which hindered her as a beginning writer, as well as the need for women to become what Judith Fetterley calls "resisting readers." Margaret finds no texts that represent
the reality she experiences, and is misled and confused by what she
does read. We first see her reading, secretly, one of the women's magazines that Oliver despises, but to which she is "addicted": "She believed
in love, and the power of love to invigorate and transform and illuminate,
in love as a last resort from dullness, and derived genuine comfort from
the stories, with their endings so final and certain, cast as she was on a
shore where things were strange and dry, and both love and dullness
wore forms so alien and complicated that she could not always distin-

guish one from the other or recognize either for what it was until too late" (22). At a picnic she tells Henry of her attraction to advertisements that show a domestic world "all closed away and cared for," and even adds the cliché, "With a warm glow" (123). After she begins to realize that Oliver is leaving her, when these escapist texts have become, even for her, "intolerable mockery," she turns to another set of false images, *Vogue*, which is "full of things" and provides "a sort of jungle retreat" of close-up photographs, including men with "enormous, remote eyes" (180)— eyes that are grotesque exaggerations of the masculine eye Margaret requires to confirm her existence but that now offers no reassurance.

Anna, much more intelligent and better educated than Margaret, is, unlike Margaret, conscious that she lacks meaningful examples of writing about women. Her knowledge that she does not really fit into the world of the stables is expressed through her alienation from the books that inscribe its rituals: "The whole ethos of the pony books with their emphasis on the tomboy, their bludgeoning mockery of sentiment and sensibility, was against her" (70). Confiding her misery to Henry after his return from his adventures, she cites her frustration with books that, she thinks, simply reproduce her emptiness and confusion while offering no solutions: "I *hate* adolescent novels, they're so boring ... they're not important, and neither am I, they're all about nothing, and so am I. People think muddles are interesting—anything at all, if it can be put on paper— but I don't and I'm not" (93). At Cambridge, she tells Oliver, she dislikes the elevation of literature into a religion, and she singles out Lawrence as her example of her fellow students' compulsion to "see everything in terms of someone else's seeing"; at a party she was asked by a man if she was "a Lawrentian woman" (157). Instinctively rejecting Lawrence's ideal of woman as, in the terms used by Byatt in her introduction, "blind wholesome passivity" (xiv), she asks, "Who am I? I don't want to find out, in those terms" (157). Anna is an early example of the feminist reading advocated in the 1970s by Fetterley, Patricinio Schweickart, and other feminist critics. The male-authored novels, which she knows have no place for her, and the women's magazines, which represent working women's lives through images of "the bed-sitter, the 'cocktail party,' the boy meets girl in London" (91), also offer false images. Near the end, Anna's involvement with Peter seems to be following the plot of the "woman's novel," with the heirloom engagement ring and the suitable marriage—"a happy ending," exclaims Oliver when he hears of the plan (267). Her decision to leave Peter, have the baby, and be with its father suggests a different conclusion, but one still within the framework of traditional women's fiction, with its formulaic "marriage or death" ending.

Byatt hints at a life for Anna beyond this ending through her shift from "this" to "that" in the penultimate paragraph: "This really was the feared and expected end. At that time, she was surprisingly content" (298). This tentatively open ending resembles Byatt's description of Lehmann's endings, with the central figure "looking out on the world not knowing what was going to happen to her" (qtd. in Wachtel, "A.S. Byatt" 87). Here, however, the uncertainty is primarily the reader's, not Anna's. By using the unavailability of alternatives to the current women's plots as a subject, Byatt makes her "vague dissatisfaction" with these narratives active within her novel.

Caught between the constructions of women's lives that her culture offers, Anna remains powerless to find her own language. Struggling to define her experience, she discovers, as an adolescent, ordinary words that have importance for her because she has "only just met them [and] taken possession of them": "light like knives," "we are all alone," and "half a poem, 'Why trees were green once Was of course yourself'" (16). She plans a novel that would, predictably, have a Heathcliff hero and a timid but self-willed heroine. Unlike other girls in her situation, she cannot "indulge herself ... with vague dreams of literary fame in the future" (16) because of her father's presence and the unattainable standard he represents to her. She daydreams about a cottage of her own on the cliff at St. Anne's Crane, where she would write good novels. In these fantasies Henry is always "dead, or removed to the Mediterranean or Mexico" (109); but when Henry proposes that *she* should go "into the sun," her tie with Oliver and her pregnancy cancel the dream. To the end, her view of the world is largely provided by males, and her own texts remain fragmentary, unformed, and hidden.

"There is no female art I can think of that is like what I wanted to be able to do [in *Shadow*]," says Byatt (x). She wanted to construct a female visionary with power and authority, and Anna does have visionary capacity, although she can express it only in Henry's terms. Both of her visionary moments, however, lack the intensity of Henry's visions, and both have a faintly parodic aspect. In Part 1, where Henry tramps freely, alone and unafraid out of doors, Anna sees light reflected through a bathroom window and makes only a brief foray outside with Oliver. Henry becomes so united with the things he sees that he seems to move with them, appearing like a figure in a van Gogh painting, surrounded by "gold figures" that "walked in the sea of corn ... like reapers" (80), and like the farmer in Samuel Palmer's *Cornfield by Moonlight, with the Evening Star* which Byatt associated with *The Shadow of the Sun* and used as the cover for the Vintage edition. Anna, on the other hand, remains a spectator, and her visionary world is moonlit only, rather than offering access to both sun and moon. Her second vision, on the bridge in Cambridge, is more explicitly parodic than the vision in the bathroom. Anna, whom Byatt sees as a "descendant" of Lawrence's Birkin, "a portrait of the artist with the artist left out" (Introduction, xii), watches the moonlit river, with the mundane object of the bottle now replacing the bathroom. She struggles to see "what [her father] would have seen," but the vision recedes, and she realizes that she has "been moved only as far as a secondhand reflection…. She was still small, and self-contained and watching, and the glory was gone" (238).[2] This, I think, is the passage Byatt describes as "a parody of the comical and magical chapter in *Women in Love* where Birkin apostrophizes the full moon" (Introduction, xv). As Beate Neumeier observes, Anna "has no female spiritual tradition to connect her own visions to" (13). At this time, Byatt believes, she herself followed tradition, taking the moon that reflects the light of the male sun as "an image of women's creativity" (xvi); her problem, in her work and in her life, was to find a way of growing her own harvest, which requires the sun. Through Anna, who is "not even a reflected light, [but] a shadow of a light only" (xiii), she made her first steps toward her harvest.

3 The Game

IN A COMMENT PUBLISHED IN 1967, the same year as her second novel, *The Game*, Byatt described the material of her fiction: "habits of mind—the nature of the imagination, the ways in which different people take in the world, the uses they make of what they think or see" (qtd. in Page 214). Her statement defines both the subject of *The Game* and its form. This novel presents and demonstrates contrasting uses of the imagination and shows the impossibility of the imagination's ever fully taking in the world, the difficulty of breaking out of private worlds into communication, and the devastation that can result from the misuse of imagination—especially from attempting to invade the mental space of another person. In many ways *The Game* is Byatt's most Murdochian novel. Like Murdoch's fiction, *The Game* examines complicated relationships among characters and highlights Murdoch's warning against the dangers of private fantasy and the need to respect both the autonomy of persons and the contingency of events. *The Game* is filled with documents and fictions, which, in their relations with each other and with the central narrative, prove Murdoch's point about the incompleteness of experience. In addition, the main characters' relationships to various forms of interpretation become central to the novel's meaning.

The Game goes beyond *The Shadow of the Sun* in its investigation of the female imagination. The main characters are two sisters, Cassandra Corbett, an unmarried Oxford don, and Julia Eskelund, a successful novelist who is married to Thor, a social worker, and has a teenaged daughter, Deborah. Cassandra, whose reclusive, celibate life recalls Helen

Gardner's ideal of the dedicated, nun-like existence of the woman scholar, yearns for pure visionary experience like Henry Severell's in *The Shadow of the Sun* but is also aware of its destructive power. In creating her, Byatt builds on her portrait of Anna and continues her exploration of female vision. In her introduction to *The Shadow of the Sun*, Byatt remembers her impression, as a young woman reading about the mythological Cassandra, that traditionally "female visionaries are poor mad exploited sibyls and pythonesses" (x). Cassandra is exploited, only half-intentionally, by her sister Julia. Julia herself writes women's novels of the kind Byatt dismisses as "self-indulgent creation, the 'waste fertility' with which Comus tempts the Lady" (Dusinberre, "A.S. Byatt" 186). Although she is no visionary, Julia also resembles Henry Severell, for she insensitively appropriates the lives of others as material for her novels. Byatt's division of the qualities of her male writer, Henry, between the two sisters enables her to examine female art more deeply than she had done in *The Shadow of the Sun*. The plot of *The Game* shows the dangers of fiction in a very concrete way, for Julia's new novel, based on her version of Cassandra's obsessive love for the herpetologist Simon Moffitt, causes Cassandra's suicide. Through the third major figure, Simon, Byatt represents a form of perception opposite to that of either sister; his ideal is a neutral, impersonal vision that refuses to impose interpretation on what is seen. He is the most extreme example in Byatt's fiction of the attempt to see nothing beyond "what is there," and he shows that such perceptual innocence is impossible.[1]

The Game of the title is, first of all, the childhood game, with its intricate rules, that the sisters created in Brontë fashion from their imaginations and that continues to exist physically in the form of ledgers, a pack of cards divided into four armies, a set of clay figures representing characters in Arthurian legend, and a map. This game, which continued well into adolescence, was their way of taking in the world by making patterns: first the physical conflicts of warfare, then the intrigues and torments of courtly love. When the sisters, with Julia's Norwegian-born husband, Thor, and their daughter, Deborah, are brought together at the Corbett parents' Northumberland house by the imminent death of Mr. Corbett, they pass their time by taking the Game out from storage in a window seat and playing at it. As they leave after the funeral, Cassandra packs it away, saying that it has "done enough damage." She is echoing Thor's recent rebuke to her: "Don't you think you've done enough damage?" He was referring to Cassandra's obsession with Simon, whom both sisters had, in different ways, loved and lost years earlier, and especially to Cassandra's feeling that Julia stole Simon from her (121). "Why don't you let go?" Thor urged, "Julia is afraid of you. Let him go, let Julia go" (107). Cassandra's repetition of Thor's words shows that she understands the relationship of the Game to her estrangement from her sister. Before they met Simon, there had been an earlier instance of appropriation, directly involving the Game and bringing its shared storytelling to an end. Julia had taken a story of Cassandra's concerning "paths taken and escapes made" by Sir Lancelot, revised it, adding control and irony, and published it as her own. This, as Cassandra recognized at the time, was not simple theft, since "the story was, or had been, common property" (84), but she had deeply resented it.

The overlapping of the sisters' inner lives has continued, with unusual intensity, although they have seldom met as adults. Cassandra has found that Simon's appearances on television have made him "accessible to the imagination, to dispute, to thought, to dreams," but she still feels herself "an object of Julia's speculation, Julia's tale-telling" (108). For her part, Julia has felt shut out and judged inadequate by her older sister. While Cassandra puts away the Game, the two sisters achieve a moment of adult understanding, each confessing to a sense of loss arising from what Cassandra calls "a gulf between the life we created and the life we lived." She says that she "had hoped to be able to bridge it, in time," but does not say whether she hoped to use her scholarly work on Malory's *Morte d'Arthur*, her devotion to Anglo-Catholicism, or her fantasy life with Simon for this purpose. She then, in an attempt to act on Thor's plea, tells Julia that "one should make a real moral effort to forgo one's need for a sense of glory," and that she and Julia should try to see each other "more on the surface" (123). Yet Julia, despite her hope that she and Cassandra can attain ordinary friendship, and despite pity for her sister, whom she sees as betrayed by the Game into a life of solitary imaginings, feels "a little flicker of irrational envy; Cassandra had appropriated their world, taken it over" (123). Julia herself, by contrast, has turned away from the particular imaginative demands of the Game to achieve popularity by writing novels about her own daily life, exploring the imprisonment of women by love and domesticity. The Game thus becomes a symbol of the sisters' continuing relationship as well as of their childhood interdependence, and it represents both their invasion of each other's mental territory and their shared awareness of the "gulf."

The Game also provides language for Byatt's novel, as well as its basic structure. Julia's publication of her version of Cassandra, in a novel called *A Sense of Glory* that marks a new departure for her as a writer, is described as "one of those destructive moves we are only enabled to make by rigidly refusing to consider their nature, until too late" (260). In fact, it causes Cassandra's death. The evidence at the inquest into Cassandra's suicide includes a psychiatrist's statement that it was, "in these cases, just possible to assume that there was an obsessive attempt to 'play fair'"; the thoroughness with which she had sealed herself into her room, before taking pills and turning on the gas, suggested a concern "to prove she was no gambler" (279). Later Julia tells Simon that she has felt controlled by Cassandra: "She always made the rules.... She made me what I am" (280). The language of games is used also in the activity of the imagination. Simon tells Cassandra of his attempt to see with the eyes of his dead friend Antony Miller—"a silly game...that got to be not a game" (241). Earlier, Cassandra, after watching one of Simon's television presentations, writes in her journal about her need to pursue metaphors "to the death": "Is this a game, or an action? Is that a real question?" (170).

The structure of the novel is patterned on that of a game with two players, alternating between Cassandra's and Julia's perceptions and between retrospective and present narrative. The question of who has won this larger game becomes crucial. When Julia publishes her novel, using Cassandra's phrase, "a sense of glory," as its title and Cassandra's relationship with Simon as its subject, Cassandra, who has painfully achieved, at last, a real relationship with Simon, feels that the book's existence destroys their new-found freedom. She tells Simon that they can never say anything to each other "that won't be seen in terms of Julia's fiction" because "Our course is plotted for us in it"; the theme of *A Sense of Glory*, she says, is "what Dr. Johnson called 'the hunger of the imagination that preys incessantly on life'" (271). Shortly after this conversation, she kills herself. Nevertheless, we are left at the end of the novel with the question of who has been the winner. "Who had stolen whose action?" Julia asked herself when she heard that Simon, as she had "made" him do in her book, had gone to Oxford. She saw that "she could not, now, if Cassandra had possibly seen Simon, ask Cassandra to forgive her for the book in which she had imagined such a meeting" (252). And as, with Simon's help, she clears Cassandra's papers from her Oxford rooms, she fears that her sister's death may have "simply loosed" the imaginary Cassandra who will "gnaw intolerably at her imagination in the future" (285). Malcolm Bradbury observed in his review of *The Game* that "in one sense the triumph of Julia is the triumph of this world" (74)—but, as he saw, Julia's triumph is open to question. Both sisters are trapped by the Game. Julia sees that in trying to come to terms with Cassandra she has imprisoned herself: "We think...that we are releasing ourselves by plotting what traps us, by laying it all out to look at—but in fact all we do is show the trap up for real" (251). Cassandra, meanwhile, is, as Byatt observes, "very much in danger of being overwhelmed" by her obsessive fantasies (*Imagining Characters* 252).

Clearly, then, *The Game* is more than a study of sibling rivalry or of obsessive love, although it takes both these topics seriously. Its central topic is the activity of perception. Admittedly, the subject has a personal edge for Byatt, who says that the novel is shaped around "various metaphors of the writer…as one who eats up reality," adding, "I have known, personally, human beings whose lives have been wrecked or mutilated by being made the object of other people's fictive attentions" ("Sugar/Le sucre" 22). But despite the temptation to read *The Game* as an angry response to Margaret Drabble's novel *A Summer Bird-Cage*, published four years earlier and also containing two sisters, Byatt's text is much more responsive to the kind of "gender-sensitive" reading proposed by Christien Franken (*A.S. Byatt* 73) than to a biographical approach.[2] There seems to be no reason, from within the text, to question Byatt's assertion that she "felt very alienated from each of them [the sisters] in turn" (Dusinberre, "A.S. Byatt" 190). Through both sisters, Byatt is continuing her exploration of the possibilities of the female imagination, and through both she shows its dangers. Furthermore, and most importantly, Byatt continues to make the human imagination and its products her primary subject. In what Franken calls a "pre-emptive strike," Byatt "anticipates" the sisterly paradigm used by some critics of *The Game* and "successfully disarms" such readings (*A.S. Byatt* 64).

Each time Julia raids Cassandra's imaginative life, the resulting product is a distortion. Julia's reworking of Cassandra's earlier story (already extensively revised by Cassandra for her own public version) had a more elegant, less "lumpy" form. Similarly, *A Sense of Glory* gives shape to Julia's version of Cassandra's imagined relationship with Simon and, inevitably, distorts it. Annexing for her purposes Father Rowell, Cassandra's priest and friend—and, in the process, neglecting his suggestion that she try to enlarge the possibilities of Cassandra's daily life—Julia makes the imagined lover a priest rather than a naturalist. She succeeds, according to one fictive reviewer, in telling the story of "hopeless love, felt in intelligent if cranky middle age" (264) with genuine sympathy for the central character, whom, with an obvious allusion to Emily Brontë, she calls Emily Burnett. Her book has an open ending. After Emily's meeting with the flesh-and-blood man whom she has nourished in her imagination for so long, the reader is left, says the reviewer, "with the question of whether the cold breath of reality on the glittering imaginative structure will prove absolutely destructive, or be the beginning of a more restricted, but more mature existence" (265).

As Julia tells her lover, Ivan, she tried to give her character some freedom; she wanted to convey both limitations and possibilities and to go beyond the semi-autobiographical subject of her earlier books. "And I meant to try and write a *real* book—a complicated book—not about myself," she says (160–61). But her imagination was not equal to the task she set herself; she has failed to recognize and respect individual freedom, the opacity of persons. Since she has used real-life models whose emotional states are precarious, the results are disastrous. Deborah, who had herself resented being material for her mother's novels, points out that Julia's use of Cassandra is more damaging than her use of her husband and daughter because earlier books "weren't really about *me*, they were about you, what you felt about me. But this was *about her*" (273). In a sense this is true, yet, as Ivan shrewdly observes, it is also about Julia: he sees—and Julia admits—that Emily is to some extent a composite portrait of Julia and Cassandra. The "sense of glory" and the failure of reality to measure up is something both women understand. Ivan also observes that Julia's story provides a "one-sided equation" because Julia has "left out the persecuting female novelist" (175–76). Further, the irony implicit in the art-life relationship is greatly deepened by Julia's failure to imagine the possibility that Cassandra might be able to reach out to Simon despite the "*forests* of imagination between them." In her version, she tells Ivan, when Emily meets her priest in Oxford, "she lets him go, she won't put out a hand" (176). In fact—as we learn later—Cassandra, after the first shock, is able, with great effort, to reach out to Simon. After Simon, in Cassandra's college rooms, tells her the story he has to tell—of his friend Antony being eaten alive by piranhas before Simon's eyes—Cassandra is able to respond to his emotional and physical needs and to discover that "it was also surprisingly painful to be in a position to consider what was good for him" (236). When Simon, after making an incoherent sexual proposition and falling into a drunken sleep, awakes and asks her out to dinner, Cassandra reaches an important realization:

The romantic moment of recognition would not happen—although she had come closer to that than she could possibly have considered likely, and she had refused it. But what she had now, though not absolute, was more than that grey recognition of defeat, of pure limiting impossibility, that was the romantic recognition reversed. Simon, chatty, gossipy, nervous, kindly—which?, having made of her pictures—what? and of herself, too—what? was asking her out to dinner. And she had preached to him that the complete, the absolute feeling was not desirable. She did not know what he thought, and would not know. But she would take what was offered. Painfully, deliberately, still terrified, Cassandra, for the first time in her life, rose to an occasion. (247)

She can now put into words what went wrong between them years earlier—"you didn't like things to mean too much. I loved you too much" (247)—to smile at him, and, until Julia's book ends their relationship, to enjoy a release into an ordinary friendship. Cassandra has lived beyond Julia's ending, but Julia's failure to conceive of Cassandra's freedom and potential for growth proves fatal. When *A Sense of Glory* is published, Cassandra feels trapped in the book and rejects Simon's pleas that she try to continue to live in the world with Julia. Knowing that we all create each other in normal life, she insists that Julia has gone beyond what is allowable: "she does a little more than simply see me, and that little is intolerable" (276).

Failing to do justice to the autonomy of Cassandra, Julia has also failed to imagine Simon. In her book, she tells Ivan, the priest "sort of remembers" Emily, "and the pathetic thing is he likes her, he really likes her" (176). Simon, in fact, has dreamed of Cassandra in the years between their meetings, has made professional use of quotations she gave him, and has unconsciously saved up things to tell her. He has needed Cassandra, and Julia has been incapable of imagining either his need or her sister's response. She has, however, been dimly aware of other possibilities lying beyond her creative scope. Her own love for Simon, she reflects after the completion of *A Sense of Glory*, has remained (as she had imagined Cassandra's remaining) that of a child for "an imaginary hero, or a television idol." Yet she thinks that "another kind of love, from another person might... call out in him another reality; but that was only idle speculation. She had imagined him" (261). She also admits to Ivan that she may not have tried hard enough to "tug" the story away from Cassandra, and that perhaps she ought simply to have written the book for her private satisfaction, not published it. She has been guilty of self-deception and, in Bradbury's words, of "moral clumsiness" (74) rather than of deliberate cruelty. Her book is an example of what Murdoch would label fantasy rather than imagination, and she has failed to achieve the freedom that, for Murdoch and for Byatt, comes from really apprehending the separate existence of others.

If Julia uses her fiction to give shape and finality to the persons and events of her life at the risk of distortion, Cassandra, living in another kind of fantasy, leaves behind only unfinished pieces of writing: her journal (once intended to grow into some larger work), her edition of Malory, her poems about Morgan le Fay. It was in her journal that she tried to contain her imaginative life after Julia's first theft, which ended their shared storytelling. The function of the Game as a recorder of romantic imagining has also been continued in Cassandra's professional life by her work on Malory (where, Julia thinks, her sister's inner life has been sterilized by footnotes) and by the poems. The journal has helped Cassandra to escape from her sense that her life is "weightless and meaningless"; by recording details she has distinguished "between what was real and what was imagined" (26-27). In her journal, too, she carries on a sporadic one-sided conversation with Simon, commenting on his television presentations and continuing arguments they had had in the past.

Shortly before Simon's arrival in Oxford, she turned to painting as a way of coping with reality, creating a version of Simon's world and of Simon himself. These paintings, she tells Simon, were a way of making the world "manageable": "It's a matter of weight. If one doesn't occupy one's space in the world, the world does have to be warded off—immobilized, reduced, kept down. Trimmed to size" (254). From this experience of what an earlier journal entry called the "tyranny of objects" (166), Simon releases her. In turn, she, by listening, has released him from his nightmares of Antony's death. As she and Simon find themselves able to talk like old friends, Cassandra experiences a new world, transfigured by its ordinariness: "Buses, pillar-boxes, telephones, staircases were there to be used. Food was there to be bought and eaten. She was balanced on her feet, she had weight, and was related to things. Distances were measurable and each distance was the proper distance. The air shone" (254). She no longer needs either the paintings or her journal.

Julia's book drives Cassandra back to the journal to make one last entry, which repudiates the "limp doll" that Julia has made of her: "My shoes, my nightdress, my pens, my papers, little dirty details of me lifted. Pinned out—oh yes, even my underwear—like a limp doll to be filled with puffs of her breath. What was missing filled in by her with dotted lines, pieces of new string to jerk the joints, or wood to replace limbs, as they do in museums, and never a footnote to say, this material is conjectural. This is an eclectic and conflated text" (276). Like A Sense of Glory, Cassandra's papers have power: the last journal entry is read out at the inquest, and the papers taken from her room became the final image of The Game. The novel's last sentence describes Simon and Julia driving away from Oxford while behind them, in the trunk of the car, "closed into crates, unread, unopened, Cassandra's private papers bumped and slid" (286). The papers' continuing existence, like that of the Game in the window seat, undercuts the apparent optimism of what immediately precedes—Julia's determination to be a new woman, free of Cassandra and Simon and of the judgments of the past. Cassandra's papers, with their capacity to hurt Julia but also—perhaps—to educate her, refute Julia's naive hope and suggest that genuine growth is more difficult and less tidy than her idea of it.

Simon, at the other extreme from Julia, does his best to avoid interpretation. He insists that he chose his work because it was something neutral, "where curiosity was simply curiosity" (196). "You watch a snake eating. You watch *it eating*," he tells Ivan's television panel. "You might just be curious about how it does it" (195). He is angry when the other members of the panel want to interpret his snakes, and his interest in them, in psychological or religious terms, and is bewildered when they talk of him as an artist. If there was an artist in the television series, he says, it was Antony, his collaborator. After Ivan's program, Simon complains to Julia that he felt "savaged," made "food for thought" by the discussion and that he finds "all this tying up of loose ends" dishonest (200). When *A Sense of Glory* is published, he tries to make Cassandra resist its impact, arguing vehemently that their relationship is real whereas the book is "a lie, at worst, and—and a piece of imagination at best. You can't destroy a reality with fiction" (270).

A reminder of the distortion inherent in all interpretation is provided by the reviews of *A Sense of Glory*. Even the fullest and most thoughtful review exemplifies the reductiveness of all reviewing (as well as of all fictional representation) as it notes that Julia "can sum up a whole woman by describing... the distressing juxtaposition of a dangling crucifix and tinned college spaghetti" (264). A second review provides facts we had not known. We learn that Julia betrays not only Cassandra and Simon but Julia's accomplice, Professor Storrin, who had planted the seed of the book in her mind and who is portrayed as a "suave don" with a "false charm." We also observe how Julia has coarsened Cassandra's intellectual interests by replacing Malory with the earl of Rochester. The third review, a brief snippet, airily summarizes: "Miss Gee had nothing on Julia Corbett's Emily Burnett" (265). Together, the reviews cannot sum up the original, which remains inaccessible within *The Game*.

When the characters in Byatt's novel try to imagine each other—and this is the central action of the book—the result must, then, be failure. Julia has tried all her life to "come to grips with" both the Game and Cassandra (148). At Oxford, as she renews her scrutiny of her sister, she

feels that they have "at last reached a point where the inevitable knowledge of long acquaintance could become an intelligent love" (135). But
Cassandra's reality escapes Julia. Cassandra is more successful in her
imagining of Simon. In the course of her long study of him, she has
begun to find that, despite the unreality of television, some of her
thoughts of him are "not fantasy, but knowledge. What he says, what he
shows, I am occasionally, by careful attention, able to know and pre-
dict.... I know to a certain extent what he is afraid of.... And what he
thinks. Love is attention, though that is only a part of the truth" (168–69).
When Simon, in her presence, compulsively relives his experience of
Antony's death, "she thought she saw what he saw; this was what, over
the years, she had been training herself to do" (233). She has not yet, however, grasped Antony's relation to Simon. Antony, according to Simon,
made the films and therefore stood, unknown to her, between herself and
Simon; it was often his voice that she took as Simon's. The shock of this
information forces Cassandra to make a further effort of imagination, and
this effort in turn leads to new uncertainties but also to new understanding. Remembering the looking-glass world of Lewis Carroll, which
she has earlier used as an analogy for Simon's world on the screen, she
sees Antony as the Red King, who (according to Tweedledum and Twee-
dledee) dreamed the whole story. "We create each other," Cassandra
thinks. "Through hard glass, one comes across the Red King, snoring
and dreaming. Wake him, look him in the eyes, break his dream and
you vanish. Apparently this dead man was the Red King; Simon and the
programmes were his. And thus myself? And Julia? Again, I pursue
metaphors. Nothing is as we see it, as we imagine it. But we must go on
seeing and imagining" (244).

After this recognition, she is able to meet Simon on the level of friendship. Her tragedy is that although she intuitively understands more than
Julia does about the relationship of love and imagination, she finally
refuses to try to live beyond her role in Julia's book. Now that Julia has
replaced Antony as the creator of Simon (and of Cassandra herself),
Cassandra can think only of escape through death. In killing herself,
she fails to do justice to Simon's reality and to her own—and thus, in the
book's final irony, mirrors Julia's failure of creativity and love.

Byatt's use of symbols, myths, and allusions is extremely subtle and
intricate, as we would expect from a writer who is so much concerned
with the play of the mind with its materials. She has taken to heart Iris
Murdoch's warning against too heavy a reliance on a controlling myth:
much more difficult than finding a structural myth for a novel, Murdoch
says in "Against Dryness," is preventing myth from becoming rigid and

interfering with the contingency of the characters. In her use of symbols and their controlling myths, Byatt sacrifices completeness and consistency in order to let the structure grow in a more natural way.

In *The Game*, the dominant myth is the story of the Lady of Shalott, but it does not function alone, and it does not become a straightforward parallel to the action. Like the Lady, Cassandra has woven a web of reflected images that has become her world. In a note in her journal that is at once a self-revealing description of her own activities and a gentle parody on Byatt's part of academic language, Cassandra says that Tennyson's poem, with its images of "the mirror, the knight with the sun on him, reflected in the mirror and woven into the web," is "a great deal more intelligent than we commonly give it credit for. Tennyson has here both indulged, and provided a commentary on, his mediaevalist romanticism. Cf. *The Palace of Art*. Solitude concerned with reflections" (171). This entry follows Cassandra's realization that through her sympathy with Simon's presentation of his snake, she has reached a point where "the Church seems to me (to its discredit) to diminish him and his serpents"—a point that recalls the crisis of the Lady's story: "The threads of thought I had believed securely fastened to seem suddenly loose, floating wild and unattached" (170). Later, watching her Sir Lancelot, the sleeping Simon, and recognizing that "nothing will be the same" now, she again remembers Tennyson's poem: "When the lady looked out of the tower—seeing, simply, a lump of flesh and blood and a patch of sunshine—the mirror cracked and the web flew out" (244). When Julia enters Cassandra's room after the inquest, she too recalls Tennyson's lines—

Out flew the web, and floated wide
The mirror crack'd from side to side,
The curse is come upon me.... (283)—

and experiences a recurrence of the old terror that Cassandra's storytelling had caused in her as a child. Like the Lady, Cassandra has seen the real world, left her weaving and her mirror, and died. Byatt gives the story a revealing twist, however. What killed Tennyson's Lady was entering so belatedly into the real world, leaving behind her shadow-world of art; what kills Cassandra, who has safely completed that task, is her sister's world of art. The problem of perception is basic to both Tennyson's work and Byatt's. As Simon tries to show Cassandra, she is trapped by Julia's book only if she lets herself be—only if she creates her own version of its power, weaving it into her web. "You spin ideas, Cassandra, so you can't see for them. After all, here I am. Here I am," says

Simon (271). But Cassandra is now convinced that she can never escape the "shadow" (277) created jointly by herself and Julia, and, like the Lady, she is sick of shadows. The fact that her death comes after her brief taste of a life free of shadows deepens its poignancy.

If the myth of the Lady charts the course of Cassandra's entrapment by Julia, it also represents Julia's imprisonment by Cassandra. When they were children, Cassandra controlled the Game, and her refusal to allow happy endings caused nightmares for both the child and the adult Julia. In their adolescent narrative, Julia wrote about Malory's Elaine—the original of Tennyson's Lady—and came to see both herself and Cassandra as Elaine figures. When Simon appeared on the scene, he naturally became Lancelot, the object of Elaine's hopeless passion. Cassandra's possessive intellectual relationship with Simon prompted Julia to pursue—and briefly achieve—a sexual one, and the result of so much intensity was Simon's withdrawal from both sisters. Both sisters have continued to imagine him, however. When Simon returns, Julia, who has already completed her fictional version of him, knows that although he is no longer Sir Lancelot, he is still not available to be loved by her in any ordinary way. Her writing of A Sense of Glory, intended to free herself from the Game's "veiled subtleties" (147) and thus from Cassandra, does not do so completely. Julia knows that Cassandra has always been "the mirror where she [Julia] studied the effects of her actions" (283) and fears that after her death Cassandra will continue to take this role. By using the myth in this twofold way, Byatt has made it suggest, in a more complex usage than Tennyson's short poem could do, the limiting patterns formed by the imagination.

Byatt also extends the myth's main symbols, web and mirror, and in doing so demonstrates the incompleteness of all structures. The web appears as the "beautiful network of designed movement" that first Simon, then Cassandra, believed to be the structure of the universe. When Simon was a Christian, suffering and sin were "rents in this network" (90). Cassandra, after finding Christianity inadequate, continues to use the same image, replacing suffering and sin, which in Simon's earlier faith were capable of being mended, with the less reassuring concept of "accident" (256). Here, as in Julia's hope that her visit to Cassandra in Oxford will knit up "a rent that ran across the whole web of her life" (124), the web holds possibilities of order, whether created by God or man made. The image also has associations with webs that can trap us. Julia, on arriving in Oxford, briefly thinks of Cassandra as sitting in the college "like a spider, in a web, waiting" (134), and the narrator briefly extends the spider image by telling of the college's Havisham room, which has, because of its name, connotations of "dedicated and cobwebbed emotion" (136). Most obviously, the web links the story to those other weavers of webs, the Brontë sisters. One of *The Game*'s two epigraphs is from Charlotte Brontë's poem "Retrospection"—"We wove a web in childhood / A web of sunny air"—and Cassandra's suicide provides proof that the web, in the words of the poem, had "spread its folds" into adult life. This menacing aspect of the imagination's weaving work is reinforced by the use of the Brontës' biography and fiction as further examples (along with *Great Expectations*) of unfulfilled longing. Julia thinks she knows that Cassandra has felt like both sisters: "like Charlotte Brontë, cut off from Branwell and Zamorna, like Emily, silently pining for another world" (122). Despite Emily Burnett's name (and despite the fact that Cassandra has "always despised Jane Eyre's prudery" [243]), it is with Charlotte and M. Héger that the first reviewer of *A Sense of Glory* associates Emily and the priest. The web shows both the human longing for pattern and the absence of any pattern that is finally adequate.

The symbols of mirror and glass are even less open to a tidy interpretation. Like the web, this group of symbols has to do with the question of how we create what we see, and it also relates to our ability to visualize what we have never seen, as when Julia compares Cassandra's room to "the room you have seen just a corner of in a mirror" (132). Like the web, glass offers dual possibilities, of imprisonment and of creative freedom. Four lines from George Herbert's poem "The Elixir" sum up the possibilities for Cassandra:

> A man that looks on glass
> On it may stay his eye
> Or if he pleases through it pass
> And then the heaven espy. (166)

Cassandra has occasionally passed through the barrier, at moments when the television screen, usually simply a "mirror of our desires," has yielded her "an image, not only of myself, but of a real man" (167–68). But such accesses to visionary love are rare. Perception and our preoccupation with it can trap us, and the effort to share in another's world can bring us to the point of madness, as both Cassandra and Simon know. "I live in two worlds," Cassandra concludes. "One is hard, inimical, brutal, threatening, the tyranny of objects where all things are objects and thus tyrannical. The other is infinite: heaven, through the pane of glass, the Looking Glass world. One dreams of a release into that world of pure vision and knows that what would be gained would be madness; a single world, and intolerable" (170-71). The tyranny is felt when the mind does not take in the objects of perception: they remain, in Coleridge's words, which Cassandra recalls, "fixed and dead" (167). The opposite experience is also described by Coleridge in his "Dejection" ode, in lines which Cassandra has shared with Simon; in the same poem he writes of our ability to give life to nature. Yet too much effort of vision can be dangerous. As Father Rowell warns Julia just before Simon's unexpected return, Cassandra is in danger of losing touch with reality and knows it. The characters discover that the possibilities of perception are less clear-cut and less easily controlled than Herbert's lines would suggest. Julia, usually less vulnerable than Cassandra, experiences panic when her dead sister's possessions refuse to remain neutral, but become "heavy with Cassandra" (282).

Mirrors, as reflections of one's own features, are threats to both sisters. Cassandra dislikes their superficiality: "They do not reflect the hollow in the skull"; they are "partial truths, like certain putative works of art. Like almost all works of art" (167). Julia, usually gratified by her own reflection, breaks down before Cassandra's mirror when she senses the presence of Cassandra's dead face as well as her own.

Glass also represents the worlds we create for ourselves. Even before she knows of Julia's book, Cassandra has a premonition of her glass-house retreat, which she and Simon share, being "bombarded with stones" (257). Her last words are "I want no more reflections" (277). Julia, who has felt sympathy for the anaconda in the zoo, lit up and exposed in its glass box, tries to believe that she can live the rest of her life free from others' judgments, but acknowledges that her growth will be hard. Even in solitary thought, there is no permanent escape from the glass as barrier or as reflector. The division of the self into the experiencing and the watching creature, Cassandra tells Simon, forces each of us to become "*both* the suffering creature under the glass and the watching eye over the microscope" (241).

The last major symbol, the snake, also proves the impossibility of final interpretations. Its obvious reference is to the Genesis story; Julia, who has always hated snakes, thinks that "we are *meant* to be repelled by them" (13). Simon studies the snake as the thing-in-itself, which demands respect by its simple existence. He admits to loving snakes—although he does so less as he knows more about them. Curiosity, he tells Julia, is the beginning of love, and "most of us would do best to stop there since we aren't capable of anything better" (211). Cassandra has made a much greater effort than Julia to see as Simon does; Julia's gift to her sister of a glass snake shows, perhaps, her recognition of this difference between them. Nevertheless, Cassandra's need for metaphor draws her to mythical interpretation. The story of how Psyche's curiosity led her to discover Eros embodied as a serpent, Cassandra "tells" Simon in her journal, is interpreted as showing the transformation of spiritual love into lust. The snake is thus "a symbol for our horror at finding ourselves necessarily embodied" (27). She quotes Coleridge's poem "Psyche," which depicts the snake as deforming and killing what it feeds on, and which presents this activity as the usual human lot: the reptile is a more apt image for humans than the butterfly. This allusion links the snake with the activities of predation and ingestion and thus with the novel's main subject, the devouring power of the imagination. "There is no love," writes Cassandra grimly, "that does not deform and kill" (28). In her last conversation with Simon, she returns to Coleridge's lines. She sees that she, in the hunger of her imagination, has fed on Simon, sees that Julia has depicted this process, and also sees that Julia has engaged in the same predatory activity. (The most extreme instance of predation is, of course, the devouring of Antony—a story that Ivan, whose imagination lacks subtlety, finds funny.)

The snake has other traditional associations, however. It is also an emblem of life, creativity, and eternity, and Coleridge uses it in this way as well. In a passage that Byatt takes as her second epigraph, Coleridge makes the serpent, "by which the ancients typified wisdom and the universe," an emblem of the imagination. Simon, on television, speaks of the worship of the snake "in association with running water and with lightning" (22) and of its connection with the idea of rebirth. Byatt herself, in her interview with Juliet Dusinberre, describes the snake as "both sex and destruction, and imagination and preservation" ("A.S. Byatt" 193).

The snake, like the web, glass, and mirror, carries both hopeful and depressing possibilities, and like them it contains opposing meanings that are, in Byatt's words, "curiously and intimately combined" (Dusinberre, "A.S. Byatt" 193). These images come together in Cassandra's journal entry, although their implications are not exhausted there: "We wove a web in childhood, a web of sunny air…. But there is no innocent vision, we are not indistinguishable. We create each other, separate. It is not done with love. Or not with pure love. Nor with detachment. We are simply specimens, under the bright light, in the glass case, in the zoo, in the museum. We are food for thought. The web is sticky. I trail dirty shreds of it" (276).

Byatt has made her own combination of myths, symbols, and allusions, but her method of doing so constitutes her own admission that no order of language can hold the chaos of experience. As she does so often,

Cassandra appears to speak for the author when she tells Simon that "fictions are lies, yes, but we don't ever know the truth. We see the truth through the fictions—our own, other people's" (271), and adds that no metaphors—not even, as she had once believed, those of religion—are true. In life as in art, we cannot avoid interpretation; Thor's uninflected English, the speech of a foreigner, frustrates Julia since she is often uncertain of his meaning. Yet all interpretations must ultimately fail.

A large part of the effectiveness of *The Game* comes from Byatt's skill in using the novel-within-the-novel. This device is one that attracted her in Murdoch's work. Byatt has shown how, by having novelists as characters in both *Under the Net* and *The Black Prince*, Murdoch has communicated "the tension between the attempt to tell, or see, the truth, and the inevitability of fantasy, the need for concepts and form and the recognition that all speech is in a sense distortion, that novelists are fantasy-mongers" (*Iris Murdoch* 35–36). The contrast between Julia's novel, as we hear of it from her and from the reviewers, and *The Game* itself embodies Byatt's struggle to respect the contingency of events and the autonomy of persons. Simon's visit to Cassandra in Oxford is the best instance of contingency in *The Game*: it arises from a need Julia could not have imagined and produces results she could not have foreseen. It also precipitates two "firsts" in the lives of the sisters. Cassandra, confronted by Simon, rises to an occasion for the first time, and Julia, facing the probability that Simon's visit will have disastrous consequences, for the first time loses her novelist's curiosity: she does not want to know what he is doing there. Byatt recognizes the limits of freedom, but her respect for individuality enables her to create, as she has praised George Eliot for doing, "characters who were both determined and free" (Byatt, Introduction, *The Mill on the Floss* 29). By including the novelist in her novel—as Julia did not in hers—Byatt takes account of the moral problems of art and shows herself to be a better novelist than Julia. Yet Julia has her own claim to sympathy, and it is one of the strengths of *The Game* that she receives her due. She has felt oppressed by Cassandra and the lingering influence of the Game; she has felt patronized by Thor's self-containment and exploited by Ivan; she is unable to reach sexual satisfaction. As an artist, she is capable of humility: she knows that the use of external details to sum up a character somehow misses the "essence" (131). Despite her wistful self-justification, Ivan's facile reassurance, and Thor's refusal to judge her, she knows that she cannot escape guilt for Cassandra's death. When Deborah tells her that she should not have published *A Sense of Glory*, Julia thinks, "Here was judgment" (273). Although we sense at the end that Julia's determination to live differently will be frustrated, there is reason to forecast a better relationship with Deborah, resulting from the outburst of creative anger between mother and daughter as well as from Julia's realization that her daughter is the only one who has made real allowances for her. The ending is left open. The reader's question—"Can Julia learn?"—parallels the question about Emily's future that, according to one fictitious reviewer, was implied at the end of Julia's novel, and Julia's opacity is preserved.

The Game is another step in Byatt's project of writing beyond the woman's novel of the mid-century, finding new forms that will communicate the experiences of women but not limit the author to domestic or familial issues, and that will show sympathy for men as well as women. Simon sees himself as the victim of too much female imagining, and both Thor and Father Rowell suffer as the result of the sisters' intense preoccupations. At a time when many women on both sides of the Atlantic were writing fiction that focused on the restrictions of women's lives within domesticity,[3] Byatt critiques that subject. Her novel contains probing analyses of the relationship of sisters, of the mother-daughter tie, and of sexual obsession, but it does so within the framework of Byatt's other subject, "what language is." Through the descriptions of Julia's earlier novels, Byatt shows the limitations of the form of the "woman's novel," and in *The Game* itself she points to larger possibilities for women's fiction.

4 *The Virgin in the Garden* and *Still Life*

IN THE QUARTET OF NOVELS that began to appear in 1978, Byatt embarked on an ambitious project: the fashioning of a shape to accommodate the complexity of her vision of women and language. Conceived as a historical sequence, this "Powerhouse" quartet[1] covers the period from 1953, the year of Elizabeth II's coronation, to 1970. However, the prologue to *Still Life*, dated 1980, marks the chronological end of the sequence, which concludes without closure. In these novels Byatt finds a form capacious and flexible enough to hold her development of the female *Bildungsroman* in combination with her ongoing exploration of language. The four texts are very different in language and styles: the first, *The Virgin in the Garden* (1978), is dense with myth and metaphor; the second, *Still Life* (1985), represents the attempt at—and inevitable failure to achieve—a plain demythologized style, bare of metaphor; and the third and fourth, *Babel Tower* (1996) and *A Whistling Woman* (2002), even more ambitious in scope, reflect the jangling fragmentation of the sixties and make more use of visual art. The four volumes place women—not only the central figures, Stephanie and Frederica Potter in the first two, Frederica alone in the third and fourth, but a shifting cast of others—in relation to history and culture. They constitute an extended reflection on women's power, actual and mythologized, in the context of the intellectual developments of two decades. The fully realized social worlds that are represented enable Byatt to avoid the vague, inconclusive, individual-oriented endings that she dislikes in "women's novels" like Rosamund Lehmann's, for now the whole world, not just the characters' individual lives, is open and problematic at the end. The structure also subverts the "marriage or death" endings of the traditional novel about women. At the end of *Still Life*, Stephanie's life is cut short (*within* her marriage to Daniel Orton) as she falls into the stillness evoked by the book's title, but life continues, and her life is a force in the lives of others throughout the rest of the story. Frederica, married to Nigel Reiver and mother of Leo when the third volume begins in 1964, is divorced at the novel's conclusion and is involved in an affair with John Ottokar. A *Whistling Woman* ends with Frederica pregnant by Luk Lysgaard-Peacock, her future undetermined. The scope of Byatt's undertaking allows her to show female identity in process, growing and changing over time.

The first two volumes, the story of the two sisters, form a unit and will be discussed together. The story begins with the Potter family in North Yorkshire, where the father, Bill, is head of English at Blesford Ride School. Bill is a follower of F.R. Leavis, an agnostic, and an ardent believer in the humanizing moral value of literature. "[I]nspired, dogged and ferocious" (*Virgin* 22), he dominates his wife, Winifred, who, with their children, suffers through his unpredictable rages and his certainty of being always rational and right. The three children are, first, gentle, reflective Stephanie, who despite achieving academic distinction at Cambridge has returned home to teach at the Girls' Grammar School; next, Frederica, still a schoolgirl, filled with curiosity and fierce ambition; and Marcus, the youngest, who is believed to be a mathematical genius and who is subject to visionary experiences that both delight and disturb him. The Potters' friend Alexander Wedderburn teaches English at the boys' school but aspires to be a playwright; he has written a play, *Astrea*, which is to be the focal point of the coronation year celebrations organized by the local millionaire and art connoisseur Matthew Crowe. During the course of the novel, Stephanie is surprised by falling passionately in love with Daniel, a curate for whom Christianity means service to others rather than dogma. Their marriage coincides with the production of *Astrea*, in which Frederica plays the young Elizabeth. Meanwhile, Marcus undergoes mental and emotional anguish leading to breakdown. In *Still Life*, Frederica follows her sister to Newnham College. Marcus makes some friends, Jacqueline and Ruth, and finds a precarious mental balance. Stephanie gives birth to a son, Will, and a daughter, Mary. In a bizarre, shocking accident, she is electrocuted by an unearthed refrigerator and dies, watched by Marcus who, paralyzed by horror, can do nothing to help his sister. Frederica is consoled by a passionate relationship with Nigel Reiver, whose wealthy, powerful milieu she welcomes as the opposite of her family's world. Daniel, driven wild by his loss, puts his children in Bill and Winifred's care and sets out on a long trek that finally takes him to Alexander's flat in London.

The Virgin in the Garden extends the blend of realism with a more experimental metaphorical structure that Byatt had used in her two earlier works. A much more complex patterning is required for this more ambitious project of placing women's stories against a background of culture, art, and history. The metaphors, Byatt says, are "blood and stone, flesh and grass, music and silence, the heard and the unheard melody, the red and the white rose" (Dusinberre, "A.S. Byatt" 191); these are also the images of Alexander's play (which we never read, although its language and staging are described). Botticelli's *Primavera* is the central image, and the colours are "red, white and green" (Byatt, qtd. in Tredell 65). Through these images, Byatt sets out to construct a female mythology: "The male mythology is the Dying God and Resurrection. The female one is birth and Renaissance, and that is what the Elizabethans recognized, and what Alexander wanted to show in his play," she told Juliet Dusinberre in 1983 (193). Later, in 1990, Byatt described the pattern that, she said, she "always" has, "a kind of linear narrative, and then an enclosed space which is a metaphor, or an object, or … a poem, which you interrogate differently, but which is part of the narrative movement" (Tredell 65). She was describing *Possession*, but the pattern is easily seen in *Virgin*, where *Astrea* and the figure of Elizabeth occupy the enclosed space. As Olga Kenyon observes, in *Virgin* Byatt anticipates feminist criticism in "analysing the potent images of virgin mother that circumscribe, describe, distort and mythologise both ordinary and extraordinary women" ("A.S. Byatt" 72). The complexities of the image are represented in the women in Byatt's novel and, within the novel, in Alexander's play, where the necessity of using two players to represent Elizabeth at two stages in her life symbolizes both the elusiveness and the division of the female. The characters in the main narrative both encounter and represent the possibilities of the conflicting images, and as they do so the novel enters a mythic dimension beyond realism. The existence of *Astrea* within the linear narrative, and the resulting interplay between the two texts, demonstrates the impossibility of the nostalgic enterprise of recovery of past glory—if that glory ever existed in the first place. Both the play and the televised coronation—another enclosed space[2]—comment self-reflexively not only on the loss of the irretrievable past but on the gap between subject and representation.

The prologue, dated 1968, has already drawn attention to this gap. As Kenyon observes, it provides a Proustian way of viewing time: the characters look "backwards and forwards…, from a present they are partially in and partially outside" ("A.S. Byatt" 69). The first sentence of the prologue, when we read that Frederica "had invited Alexander...to come and hear Flora Robson do Queen Elizabeth at the National Portrait Gallery" (9), highlights the idea of performance. Alexander, waiting for Frederica and Daniel to join him, ponders the words *national* and *portrait* and their denotation of identity, "the identity of a culture (place, language, and history), the identity of an individual human being as an object for mimetic representation" (9). When Frederica arrives—followed by a figure whom we will later recognize in *Babel Tower* as her current lover, John Ottokar—Alexander's thoughts, and the conversation, turn to parody, a form of performance that Alexander has never understood in its modern manifestations. In the clothes of the women around him he sees forms of parody; Frederica appears to him as Britomart from *The Faerie Queene*, Lady Antonia Fraser as Belphoebe. (The "dumpy woman in a raincoat" [12], whom we guess to be Byatt herself, is not dressed in an obvious parodic fashion, however; she is the representer, not the represented.) Looking at the Darnley Portrait of Elizabeth I, Alexander is unhappy about his own attempt to represent Elizabeth, and feels "terrible sadness.... He wished, he thought, that he had never written that play" (15). All representation is doomed to fail.

The gardens in Alexander's play resonate with other gardens of innocence and naming, especially Eden, and also with the real and imagined gardens of the characters' worlds. We are shown Crowe's garden at his estate, Long Royston, where *Astrea* is produced, the Masters' garden at the school, the Easter garden at Daniel's church, Marcus's secret mental garden of pure geometric forms, the school's "Bilge" (Biology) Pond, and gardens and worlds in Shakespeare, Marvell, and Milton, which haunt the text. Byatt has commented on the frequent representation, in earlier narratives, of "the temptation of a virginal figure through the senses in a garden" (qtd. in Kenyon, "A.S. Byatt" 66).

Byatt relates her fascination with the virginal figure of Elizabeth I to the problem of marriage and the loss of "separate identity" for women; by refusing to marry, Elizabeth became "the archetypal virgin, with power," a "paradoxical female figure [who] 'hath both kinds in one'" (qtd. in Kenyon, *Writer's Imagination* 13). This figure became associated in the Renaissance with England itself, with Astarte, Cynthia, and Cybele, and with Virgo-Astrea, the last of the immortals, who was goddess of justice and, conflated with the Virgo of the zodiac, of harvest.[3] The iconography of the play—which already has parodic elements—takes on aspects of irony and farce in relation to the real-life participants.[4] Frederica is informed about the significance of female figures of power by Crowe while he tries to combine sexual with intellectual instruction. In her role as the young Elizabeth, Frederica runs from her stepmother's husband, Thomas Seymour, wearing paper skirts that are being slashed to ribbons as she runs, signifying threats to her virginity. In fact, however, Frederica views her own virginity as burden rather than power; it is always knowledge that is power for Frederica. Later, she pretends to be no longer a virgin in order to entrap Alexander. As the young Elizabeth, she declaims fiercely, "I will not bleed"; when Wilkie matter-of-factly relieves her of her burden, she in fact bleeds profusely. Anthea Warburton, who plays Astrea, is already pregnant on opening night, and the power of her role contrasts with the queasiness of her own body.

In the real world, the gardens are degraded and parodic. The mock Tudor garden that Crowe (a mock Prospero) has contrived is a place of furtive sexual intrigue and, during performances, of the schoolboys' parodic bottle chorus. The walled Masters' garden, where Stephanie and Daniel's wedding reception takes place (with Bill both present and, by his own declaration, not present), is compared to "the ultimate garden in *Alice*" (269), where things also are not what they seem. Stephanie, required by custom to be a virginal bride, is not one, and the walls and locked gate lose their power. She and Daniel talk in the garden of St. Bartholomew's, after the service at Easter, a festival that she finds particularly "alien"; she prefers Christmas because birth is "a real miracle ... believed" and "needed" (155). The garden that Felicity Wells has lovingly constructed, of spring flowers with "stems encased in cotton wool in meat paste pots beneath the stones" (156), shows the falsity of the male myth of resurrection. Marcus, a virgin in his lack of knowledge, led by his teacher Lucas Simmonds into attempting experiments with the paranormal, "remembered his secret garden of forms and felt pure rage that Lucas should have connected gods and electricity to cairns or cones of stone" (342). This relationship and his confused, frightened awareness of Lucas's sexual needs threaten the "cleanness" (342) of Marcus's mental world, and when Lucas attempts to castrate himself and is found naked, garlanded with flowers, in a mad parody of King Lear, Marcus slips into breakdown.[5] The Bilge Pond, where Lucas, another virgin, mutilates himself, is another degraded garden. Once used by the students for biological studies, it is now neglected and defunct. Lucas, who hopes for revelation of ultimate truth through experiments with light, is taken forcibly from this fallen garden to a mental hospital. "I want the reader to stop and read the meaning of these gardens," Byatt has said (qtd. in Kenyon, "A.S. Byatt" 62).

Byatt says that *The Virgin in the Garden* represents "nostalgia for a *paradis perdu* in which thought and language and things were naturally and indissolubly linked" ("Still Life/Nature morte" 9). This statement relates to what is arguably the primary paradox that the text considers, the stillness of art's representation of flux. Stephanie, in many respects the novel's wisest character, teaches Keats's "Ode on a Grecian Urn" and reflects that this, her favourite poem, says "ambivalently that you could not do, and need not attempt, what it required you to do, see the unseen, realise the unreal, speak what was not, and that yet it did it so that unheard melodies seemed infinitely preferable to any one might ever hope to hear" (78). It is Stephanie, too, who can view the piecing together of costumes for the play in a "double" way: "She saw what things meant to be, and missed no detail of how they, in fact, presented themselves" (110). Through its metaphors, Byatt's novel moves constantly between the ideal and the real, and asks us to think about our own mind's construction of lost paradises, "infinite unchanging vistas ... from the height of one year old, out of suburban gardens or municipal parks in summer, endless grassy horizons and alleys which we always hope to revisit, rediscover, inhabit in real life, whatever that is" (317). Recognizing that this novel is a hybrid of two forms, functioning both "as naturalistic fiction in the George Eliot mode and as the Proustian self-reflecting text," Dusinberre sees the reader as "harried between opposing perceptions of the power of the imagination and its impotence" ("Forms of Reality" 55, 58). The characters are similarly harried.

The novel's narrative asserts that although there is no true renaissance, there is the possibility of new beginnings. Frederica's splendid examination results will take her to Cambridge. Alexander escapes from the garden to pursue a career in writing; he leaves behind both the Masters' garden at the school and the Potters' garden, scene of his botched tryst with Frederica. To the sisters he still represents, as he had at the beginning, "male mobility," in opposition to the "female provincial rootedness" (47) that Stephanie has chosen but that Frederica hopes to avoid. Stephanie and Daniel, who have experienced a rebirth through passion in their encounter with another Venus, Anadyomene, by the sea at Filey,[6] wait now for the birth of their child at Easter time. Marcus has seen that he can do nothing to help Lucas and has escaped from his father's anger. Although the last scene takes place in an almost paralytic stillness, the seeds of growth and change, both intellectual and biological, are present.

The prologue to *Still Life* demonstrates, even more clearly than the prologue to its precursor, how far Byatt has moved beyond social realism and straightforward narration. Its date, 1980, signals discontinuity as well as continuity: Alexander, Frederica, and Daniel are meeting seventeen years after the end of *The Virgin in the Garden* and thirteen years after Stephanie's death, which concludes *Still Life*. Stephanie is absent from this prologue, as she already was from the earlier prologue, dated 1968, and the reader has yet to find out why.

In the *Still Life* prologue, incompleteness and the reaching beyond boundaries are further suggested in the canvas of van Gogh's *Poet's Garden*, which Alexander, the first to arrive at the Post-Impressionist exhibit, examines. The painting shows "a great pine, still widening where the frame interrupted its soaring" (1). The breaking of patterns is suggested by references to Frederica (which precede her appearance in the text) in Alexander's reflections on their relationship as one of continuity through change: she is "no longer" likely to be late because "her life [has] schooled her"; she does not fit into the "pattern … in the events and relationships of his life"; "She had been a nuisance, a threat, a torment and was now a friend" (1). Frederica has constructed a pattern of repetition within difference: they have met to look at van Gogh, as, Frederica now reminds him, they met earlier at the National Portrait Gallery, and she recalls "the eclectic Sixties parodies" of that time (5). Linearity is disrupted; any concept of beginnings and endings is called into question.

With Frederica's arrival, the text becomes more playfully self-reflexive. Mixing real people with her invented characters (as she did also in *Virgin*), Byatt includes herself, for she is surely the "smallish woman in a pine-green tent-like coat" (3) to whom the art historian John House (one of those whom Byatt thanks in her acknowledgments) attempts to introduce Frederica. House is not certain what name Frederica is now using— "women these days are so protean" (3); she subsequently signs the Visitors' Book "Frederica Potter." Meanwhile, she is not interested in her creator, believing her not to be "of real concern"; the smallish woman, however, examines her character "with an apparently absent-minded scanning attention" (3).[7] Naming, the shifting identities of women, and the problematic relationship of author to text are all invoked as topics here.

The postmodernist consideration of language leads to further questions about representation, when Frederica overhears an old woman telling her friend, as they view Monet's *Au Cap d'Antibes,* that Winston Churchill painted the same scene. Alexander's reflections on his own failure in his play about van Gogh to "write a plain, exact verse with no figurative language, in which a yellow chair was the thing itself, a yellow chair" (2) is compared with Daniel's distrust, for "completely different reasons," of figurative language: "He never now made a sermon from a metaphor" (10). Alexander and Frederica discuss the relation of signifier and signified: "Olives ... could not *not* recall the Mount of Olives, the Garden of Gethsemane, in the day of Van Gogh the pastor's son, the lay preacher. As the cypresses must always, differently, mean death" (7). A passage from a letter of van Gogh's shows his own thoughts about the relationship of colours to signification: "one can try to give an impression of anguish without aiming straight at the historic Garden of Gethsemene" (8). We note that Byatt, still concerned with how minds take in the world, is now shifting her attention from dramatic to visual representation, two modes linked by similar problems.

Continuity and change, the persistence and the rupture of connections, are represented also in the last part of the prologue, through Daniel and Will. Daniel is a figure of stability in the midst of change. In contrast to Frederica, who, like Alexander, has followed fashion, Daniel has worn "the same black clothes" (5) through two decades. Yet he has "become a specialist in wild blows of chance" (9) through his work with victims of violence and is estranged from his son, Will; Will, now on his way to the famine in Uganda, communicates with his father only indirectly through Frederica. Although Frederica and Daniel disagree briefly over how to name Will—"'Hippie,' said Daniel. 'Helping out,' said Frederica" (10)—father and son are engaged in the same kind of work. They last met in a hospital where Daniel had come to comfort a mother, Will to wheel a trolley bearing her dead daughter. But Will, like van Gogh, is "in flight from his family" (7). Sameness and difference, as well as dispersal, continue to the end. Daniel, refusing Frederica and Alexander's invitation to have coffee with them in Fortnum and Mason's (it was tea, in the same restaurant, that he declined at the end of the prologue to *The Virgin in the Garden*), separates himself from the other two.

The prologue, then, does much more than simply spur narrative curiosity. It introduces a postmodern project containing gaps, broken lines, fragmented experience, and open endings, at the same time as it gestures toward linearity. The story doubles back on itself in a series of loops, reaching back to the two texts set in the fifties; to the prologue to *The Virgin in the Garden*, dated 1968; and also to *Babel Tower*, which ends just before the first prologue, and to *A Whistling Woman*, in which the action of the first prologue is reconfigured. The 1980 prologue is the chronological end of the quartet; *Babel Tower* and *A Whistling Woman* (both without prologues) bring the story only to 1970. The quartet, says Byatt, "avoids endings" (Wachtel, interview).

The enclosed space within the linear narrative of *Still Life* is, once again, a play by Alexander, but this time, instead of Elizabeth I and her power, the character and narrator interrogate van Gogh. His paintings are the primary intertext; they embody one of the meanings of Byatt's title. In the prologue, Alexander recalls the fact that language, with its inescapable tug toward metaphor, worked "against" his goal of plain language: "Metaphor lay coiled in the name sunflower" (2). He and the narrator share this problem. In a central chapter, Alexander looks at the bowl of fruit on the Pooles' breakfast table and ponders the relationship between words and things: "How would one find the exact word for the colour of the plum-skins?" The narrator joins him: "You may use the word 'bloom'…. But you cannot exclude from the busy automatically-connecting mind possible metaphors, human flesh for fruit flesh, flower-bloom, skin bloom, bloom of ripe youth for this powdery haze, human clefts, declivities, cleavages for that plain noun" (165). And as if to show where metaphors can lead us, a few pages later Alexander makes love to his landlady, Elinor Poole.

Meanwhile, Alexander is troubled by his knowledge that his subject, van Gogh, could, with paint, "get nearer to the life of the plums than he ever could" (163). Toward the end of the book the narrator confesses, "I had the idea, when I began this novel, that it would be a novel of naming and accuracy" (301). Such a novel, with many nouns and adjectives, could describe the world of Marcus and his grasses (after the disaster with Lucas, Marcus has no more visionary experiences). But in Frederica's world, as she prepared for her finals, "to make comparative images was to have great power, to be a small god making wholes" (302). Despite her own distrust of analogies when they lead us away from "things," Byatt is in Frederica's world. In her essay on *Still Life* in *Passions of the Mind*, she tells us that the project, which, using a plain, bare style, would "emphasize contiguity rather than analogy," "was in fact impossible for someone with the cast of mind I have" ("Still Life / Nature morte" 13). She gives as an example the cyclamen, offered by Stephanie as a welcoming gift to her mother-in-law, who rejects it: "The cyclamen *would not stay* at the level of exact description." It turned out to be "bristling with threads of connection" to the flowers in *The Virgin in the Garden* and to "language-flowers in general" ("Still Life/Nature morte" 13), as well as to Mrs. Orton. The plant, "almost maroon in its dark red-purple" (25–26), becomes linked to Mrs. Orton's swollen legs, the "purplish cast" of her hair, and the "crimson apple-round" of her cheek; "in Stephanie's mind" the flower "resembled bruised flesh" (26). Byatt says that the colours of *Still Life* are "purple and blue" (Tredell 65), and the cyclamen's purple shades into the pale violet irises that Daniel brings to Stephanie after Will's birth, into Alexander's purple-black plums, and into the backdrops for the staging of his play, which displayed van Gogh's "purple and gold

Sower" and the painting of violet and Prussian blue irises that the painter feared as a "terrible" painting (310). Finally, the last colour image in the book is the "blue enamelled Polish [coffee] pot" from which Alexander hopes to put "life" (358) into the exhausted, grief-stricken Daniel. This small cluster of colour images encapsulates the novel's preoccupation with life and death as humans experience them and as they struggle to represent them through art.

When she was still engaged in the writing of *Still Life*, Byatt told Juliet Dusinberre that she had been reading some theoretical books "which have started to persuade me that metaphorical writing is not necessarily the antithesis of literal writing, but that metaphor itself can be literal" ("A.S. Byatt" 194). This discovery informs the whole text: it is openly present in the narrator's statement that "the germ of this novel was a fact which was also a metaphor": a young woman, a child, a pack of nasturtium seeds, and a tray of young plants that have "died in the struggle for survival" (237). We have already seen Stephanie planting nasturtiums, which flourish only after she has learned to thin out the seedlings. Immediately preceding the reference to the germ (itself a metaphor), the narrator showed how chance produced Mary's conception: the image cluster of plant seeds, human sperm, and ova is both a celebration of Stephanie's fruitfulness and a warning of what will happen to her. Nature demands that not all life survives. In keeping with Byatt's wish to write a demythologized novel, *Still Life* contains more literal (and fewer literary) metaphors. It fulfills Byatt's hope that she could "write about birth, about death, plainly and exactly," and that this novel would "move from an undissociated paradise to our modern dissociated world" ("Still Life/ Nature morte" 11). The chapter about Stephanie's giving birth to Will has become justly famous,[8] and the narrative of her death is stark, swift, and appalling. Byatt loves and searches for order, writing of moments when we have what we take to be "a privileged insight into the order of things, in which all things are to be experienced as parts of a whole" (175). She shows us many examples of order, from Will learning to speak, naming and drawing flowers, to Marcus finding peace through learning the classification of grasses. Yet she also knows about contingency and, lurking behind it, chaos, and courageously writes from within Stephanie's own consciousness of the moment when "the refrigerator struck" (334), pain invades her body, and her life is cut off.[9]

In a narrative intervention after Stephanie's death, Byatt speaks of "the decorum of the novel," which "requires that time not be given to grief," and of the "temptation to hurry over the next part of their lives" (343). Modern novels, she reflects, no longer end with marriage but "lumber on inconclusively"; death, "more of an end than marriage," concludes tragedies. Shakespeare knew about the "waking eyes of grief" hurt by "the unacceptable" (she cites Cordelia's death) that "makes that play too uncomfortable for the Aristotelian relief" (344). In giving space in her novel not only to Daniel's grief but to the different, individual grief of Bill, Winifred, Marcus, and Frederica, Byatt breaks the conventions, leaves her ending open, and provides for the survivors.

Soon after his meditation on plum skins and metaphor, Alexander is present at a dispute between the novelist Juliana Belper and the grammarian and mathematician Gerard Wijnnobel. The novelist proclaims postmodern chaos and randomness and the resulting need for art forms to reflect "the fragmented and subjective nature of our perception of the world"; Wijnnobel dismisses her viewpoint as "silly" and "simplistic" (177): "We cannot have the idea of random happenings or chaotic conditions without ... having had a concept of order" (178). Byatt is on Wijnnobel's side, but her novel shows sympathy as well for Belper's view and for the woman herself, reduced to tears by Wijnnobel's rude condescension.

The form of *Still Life* has been the focus of critical debate. The reviews were more mixed than those of *The Virgin in the Garden*, with Patrick Parrinder, for example, responding to the book's "gravely humanistic vision of tragedy" (17), and John Naughton praising both *Still Life* and its predecessor for being "rooted in metaphors that make sense" (31). Others, however, found the author's display of learning pretentious and her characters difficult to care about because they are not "whole and satisfying models of humanity" (Conant 18). The most significant critical objection was to the self-reflexive authorial comments. Roger Lewis, seeing the Proustian inheritance, found that these passages work as Byatt intended them to: "Byatt, at last, shows that a novel can think about itself without resorting to nervous Borgesian paper-puzzles, tricks, tics" (29). Lorna Sage also thought that the blend of tradition and Murdochian experiment succeeded; Byatt's "sense of fictional possibilities is deliberately distanced from naturalism.... The acquired characteristics [are] nicely at odds with the inherited ones" (22). But Peter Lewis found that the "avant-garde methods" (42) did not suit the form of historical fiction, and Adam Mars-Jones, in the review that gave the most extended consideration of Byatt's methods, agreed that the instances of "self-subversion" were the least successful; he singled out as the book's "only seriously misconceived passage" (720) an aside by the narrator that describes the happiness that Frederica would have found with Ralph Tempest, whom, "by chance" (*Still Life* 297) she missed meeting.

In an essay published in 1989, "The Hard Idea of Truth," Michael West-lake addresses what he sees as the central problem in *Still Life*: an "oscillation" between an empiricist epistemology that separates knower and known and that implies the "transparency of language transmitting knowledge" and a "post-structuralist alternative which remains cloistered behind the novel's formal structures…. Shoring up the dubieties of the novel's questioning metaphysical discourse are the pillars of organic, humanistic belief" (37). To this critique, Alexa Alfer responds by suggesting that the apparent "flaw" in Byatt's "fictional argument" can be seen as a sign of the symbiotic relationship "not only between literary realism and experiment, but also between the creative and the critical imagination" ("Realism" 48). Byatt, she argues, has always seen the problems implicit in realism; her novels are valuable because they internalize the challenges of poststructuralist theory. Drawing on Ricoeur's theory of metaphor, Alfer proceeds to a probing exploration of the ways in which Byatt's fiction questions and reshapes mimesis. Byatt's image of lamination, I would suggest, is helpful too. In the Tredell interview, Byatt speculates that Frederica's idea of lamination as a way to keep things separate, first introduced in *The Virgin in the Garden* and becoming more prominent in *Babel Tower*, is relevant not only to women's experience but more widely to the activity of perception in general. Frederica thinks that a sexually passionate, intellectual woman might survive by laminating "facts and things" so that they can "lie alongside each other" (*Virgin* 209). In the interview, Byatt suggests that lamination can apply also to our "reading" of landscape: you know that "the Wordsworthian vision is no longer accessible. You *know* that, even while you're looking at the moors in an almost Wordsworthian way. But if you laminate it, you can have the Wordsworthian feeling and you can have the consciousness that you ought not to be having it" (Tredell 69).

This divided perceptual experience of theoretically sophisticated late-twentieth-century people is something Byatt is consciously and deliberately working to capture. The fiction that follows *Still Life* clarifies this part of Byatt's project. *Possession* presents what Westlake calls the "larger cultural crisis" (33) in a direct comparison between nineteenth- and late-twentieth-century thought, showing that the twentieth-century scholars who fall passionately into romantic love are having an experience they are conscious they ought not be having in the poststructuralist era (at the same time showing that the Victorian world was already questioning its own assumptions). My point is that Byatt is conscious in *Still Life* of what Westlake describes as the novel's "hesitations, contradictions and formal equivocations, its failure to secure the stability it seeks" (33). Put very simply, her aim is to convey in language how it feels to be living with these contradictions, knowing that both self and language are unstable. She thus succeeds, as Flora Alexander argues, in "negotiating for herself a position that accommodates both the realist tradition and her theoretical understanding that the written text is both less and more than a representation of the real world" ("A.S. Byatt" 6).

Byatt has said that the books that preceded *Possession* were written "more painfully because I was trying to tell the truth about real things"; they "engaged the whole of me including the rather tortured me" (qtd. in Stout 24). In *The Virgin in the Garden* and *Still Life*, she excels in her portrayal of real people living with pain and joy in a real world. Unlike her character Raphael Faber, Byatt does not believe that the time is past when art worked at "inventing people and giving them names and social backgrounds and amassing descriptions of clothes and houses and money and parties" (*Still Life* 215). George Eliot, whose texts are rooted in such descriptions, is the guiding spirit in these two novels. Byatt's characters, like those she admired so much in Eliot's fiction, "*think*: they worry an idea, they are, within their limits, responsive to politics and art and philosophy and history" ("George Eliot: A Celebration" 73). Also like Eliot's characters, they feel deeply. Frederica's greed for knowledge and experience; Stephanie and Daniel's blind, instinctual falling into passion; Winifred's sense of exclusion and suppressed rage within her marriage; Bill's stubborn idealism, his bullying, and his angry tirades; Marcus's terrified visionary moments and his growing fear of his half-mad mentor, Lucas Simmonds; Stephanie's joyful recognition of the newborn Will; and Daniel's wild plunge into grief and despair at Stephanie's death—all make direct impact on us. In her short study of Byatt in *Contemporary Women Novelists*, Flora Alexander praises Byatt's ability to give "artistic form to things that verge on the unbearable" (38). Like Eliot, Byatt gives life to her minor characters as well, and many of these are shown undergoing suffering. The frustrated young mother Jennifer Parry, the miserably unhappy and sexually tormented chemistry teacher Lucas, the vicar's wife, Clemency Farrar, disgusted by her sexually predatory, manipulative husband, and the headmaster's wife, Mrs. Thone, who has lost her young son, are made real along with the others of Byatt's large cast. Mrs. Thone, one of the most briefly glimpsed, becomes an emblem of grief as Byatt transfers to this character the grief she herself felt at her son's death: Mrs. Thone "had understood exactly that between a good breakfast and an end of break bell a boy could run, fall, smash, twitch, stop moving forever and begin to decay" (243). In her apprentice novels, *The Shadow of the Sun* and *The Game*, Byatt had learned how to represent characters in a few sentences of description or conversation without being merely dismissive, like her imagined novelist Julia.

There are memorable comic scenes in these two novels, too, as Byatt gives free rein to her satiric gifts and her sense of the ludicrous. The best comic scenes are all tinged with sadness and loss. In *The Virgin in the Garden*, there are, among many other moments, Bill's disruption of Stephanie and Daniel's wedding despite his self-proclaimed non-particcipation; Crowe's unwelcome fondling of Frederica while she is fiercely asserting her wish to become cultured by learning to appreciate his collection of erotic paintings; Frederica's achievement of her loss of virginity with Wilkie after failed attempts with Alexander whom she is convinced she loves. In *Still Life*, Frederica, now at Cambridge, tries to impress men with her quick mind while her body, a scarce commodity in this male-dominated world, is more in demand. No longer a virgin, she performs the Lady in *Comus* (repeating the irony of Anthea Warburton's playing the Virgin Queen while pregnant with Thomas Poole's baby) before an audience containing some of her previous lovers. Because the Tempter figure has a hangover, Frederica is forced to speak both parts, hers loudly, his in a prompting hiss; the scene encapsulates both her sexual and her linguistic immaturity and confusion in a world in which she is moving between roles and discourses. Stephanie, pregnant and exhausted, painstakingly prepares a traditional family Christmas dinner that no one really enjoys. She had intended this, the first Christmas in her own home, to be "different," but in fact her family, who do not know how to celebrate, get through the day as they always have: "they watched each other and waited for Christmas to be over" (35). Stephanie's only consolation is that the members of the ill-assorted group (Marcus has moved into her cramped house in order to recover from his breakdown; Daniel's egocentric, censorious mother also lives with them) have "behaved well" (47). The festivity is manufactured, and both she and Daniel experience a sense of loss, as Daniel reflects that what he had wanted in marriage was just Stephanie, not a "Home" (47), and feels that his gift to his wife, a nightdress, pales beside Frederica's books. The whole Christmas celebration is sadly comic.

Byatt says that in the sixties she thought that she had lived long enough to be able to write "a historical novel"; in *The Virgin in the Garden* she "wanted to say something about English society." Although she later thought this to be an "absurd" hope, and said self-deprecatingly that she wished she "had more feeling for social patterns" (qtd. in Kenyon, "A.S. Byatt" 75), she did achieve considerable success in depicting both the wartime years of scarcity and austerity, which the Potter sisters remember, and the fifties, when England, buoyed by the coronation celebrations, began to experience renewed prosperity and hope. Through the activity surrounding the production of *Astrea*, Byatt provides a range of attitudes to English history and culture. As Kuno Schuhmann observes, Byatt chooses not to reduce all views to her own, but to "present a number of views, qualifying each as a limited one" ("Concept of Culture" 118). In *The Virgin in the Garden*, Bill, Alexander, Crowe, and the television coverage of the coronation offer diverging views. Bill, with his insistence on the tie between literature and community and his Leavisite proclamation that "life" is to be found in texts like *King Lear*, not in what he takes to be Daniel's Christianity, is impatient also with Crowe's elitist connoisseurship. With subversive intentions, he agrees to help in the festival Crowe is sponsoring: "He would see that information was purveyed about the Tudor police state and judicial barbarities" (67). To Bill, Crowe's hopes of giving the people a glimpse of a Golden Age are empty, frivolous nostalgia. For his part, Crowe uses his wealth to foster local Yorkshire culture while surrounding himself with paintings and sculptures reflecting the European artistic heritage. Alexander is somewhere between the two: he hoped that in his play he could participate in "the renovation of the language," following T.S. Eliot and Christopher Fry, but, inhibited by the presence of Shakespeare, he finds that his goal of "vigorous realism" conflicts with "a natural warp in the work itself towards pastiche and parody" (17). He has tried, nevertheless, "to write, to discourse, in verse, about history and truth" (241). In 1973, on television himself, he critiques the televised coronation proceedings of twenty years earlier, as a "huge misguided nostalgic effort of archaism … a true shadow of blood and state, a real fantasy and trick of fame" (241).

Amidst these male attempts to represent what is valuable in tradition, Frederica and Stephanie strive for their own understanding. Frederica, viewing the coronation, senses that at her age, "What a farce!" is "the right response"; she sees "that the Coronation was not only not the inauguration of a new era, it was not even a contemporary event" (241-42). Later, in 1973, she thinks that Alexander's later view is "oversimplified"; she recognizes both the real "innocence" and the "hope" of a new Renaissance in 1953 and the absence of any "objective correlative" (241). With more maturity, she perceives England as a series of disconnected historical images, only partly represented for her by T.S. Eliot's idealistic *Four Quartets*. The coronation "had tried and failed to be now and England. There had been other worse failures. In the sense in which all attempts are by definition not failures, since now is now, and the Queen was, whatever the People made of it, crowned, it *was* now, and England. Then" (242).

Stephanie, too preoccupied with domestic worries to pay much attention to the media's representation of the young queen, is surprised later by Alexander's success in representing the earlier hope of renaissance through the "density and energy" of his play. Like him, she connects the first Elizabeth with myth—Virgo-Astrea, Gloriana—and with the images of rebirth in Shakespeare's *Winter's Tale,* and responds to the "weight of language" (362). Meanwhile, however, she is already experiencing the loss of connection to language and the life of the mind that had been prefigured to her in her dream before her wedding. In the dream, images from Keats's "Ode on a Grecian Urn," Milton's "When I consider how my light is spent," and Book Five of Wordsworth's *Prelude* combined to warn of the threats to art and thought and the duty to preserve what Milton says "is death to hide." Waking in terror, like Wordsworth's dreamer, she reflects on the paradoxical relationship of the dream images to her own life. At first "she thought she thought... that she should not marry, she had lost, or buried, a world in agreeing to marry," then that marriage to Daniel would require her to be wholly present, "body and imagination at once," so that "there would be no place for urn or landscape in their own terms. But if it was death to hide them, it was, it surely was, death to immure oneself with them" (252). Powerfully drawn in both directions, she commits herself to the world of growth and change rather than to the stillness of art. When she listens to Alexander's language about renaissance, she is already pregnant, about to experience birth through her body.

In *Still Life,* other definitions of history and culture confront both sisters. In the summer she spends in France as a mother's helper, Frederica encounters another landscape, culture, and history. Like another northerner, van Gogh (the subject of Alexander's new play), Frederica is startled by the southern landscape and must try to reconcile it with her "tradition of looking at landscape, [which] was deeply Wordsworthian" (59). She learns about Nîmes through its architecture and its traditional bullfights (which repel her), and, reunited with Alexander and Wilkie at Crowe's beach party, she is taken by Alexander to see ancient images of St. Mary Jacobus and St. Mary Salome in a church where the historical saints and their black servant, Sarah, according to legend, journeyed after the death of Christ. Frederica sees the two Marys as identical sweet-faced, doll-like figures that contrast with the image of Sarah, which shows "austerity and arrogance or contempt" (82); they are two opposing cultural and racial representations of the female. More important to Frederica, however, is the fact that she is once again with Alexander (whose play involved her in other, English performances of femininity) and is discussing art and ideas with him. Drawn together by "reciprocal need"—Frederica, as always, needs to learn more, and Alexander needs encouragement about his new project—the two draw closer to "an understanding that they two were friends." They do not fully know this yet; Frederica is aware that sex inhibits conversation, but she thinks, too, that "to be talked to by Alexander was a pleasure not readily to be forgone" (83). The terrible news of Stephanie's death brings them together again, and the prologues to both *The Virgin in the Garden* and *Still Life* confirm the narrator's observation, after their conversation in France, that they will "know each other for a long part of a life-time" (83). Her experience in France, like that of the coronation, will be revised in Frederica's memory; "In later years, say 1964, 1974, 1984, the first vision of Nozières took on its perfection and primacy," says the narrator (53). D.J. Taylor points out that the first two volumes of the quartet are "built upon a steady forward dynamic, the comparisons always those of an unseen future, the judgments those of a wiser retrospect" (*After the War* 94).

When she returns to England and enters Cambridge, Frederica's cultural and sexual horizons continue to expand. One of her new friends is Tony Watson, whom she privately labels a "fake" because he has carefully surrounded himself with possessions that are meant to signify humble working-class origins but that both conceal his privileged background and parody his father's educated leftist views: "Tony could not refute his father's beliefs, only reproach him by adopting the style, the attitudes, of the workers he admired, studied and did not resemble" (125). Frederica is beginning to see some of the subtle contradictions of class in England. She is not taken in by Kingsley Amis's *Lucky Jim*, whose hero is lauded by her male friends as "some kind of moral hero...the decent man, the common man, the scrupulous man" (123); instead, she identifies him as a perpetual child and objects to his categorization of women by their clothes. "Jim is so *sure* he knows what a nice and nasty skirt for a girl is, and what's more that nice girls are in nice skirts and nasty ones in nasty ones" (124), she rages at Tony. Tony's friend Alan Melville she labels a "chameleon"; Alan is in fact working class but can "respond with skill to the behaviour of those round him" (125). She has more sympathy with the chameleon because, she thinks, women are "naturally driven to that state" (126). She has become a chameleon herself, sleeping with some of her new friends while not believing their declarations of love yet enjoying the company of "those who had interests other than herself" (183), who are absorbed in painting or theatre, and ironing sheets and darning socks in return for inclusion in discussions of poetry. Reflecting on the contradictory cultural messages that women receive—a fellow student is sent down for being secretly married, yet society presents marriage as "the end of every good story" (127), and part of Frederica believes this— she thinks, in panic, "surely it was possible … to make something of one's life *and* be a woman" (184). When she falls unrequitedly in love with Raphael Faber, this German-Jewish refugee, the only male of his family to escape Belsen, both forces her to define her own "roots" as "Northern lower-middle-class. Nonconformist" (213) and threatens her sense of having a place. Recognizing the "gulf between Bill Potter and what had happened in Belsen…, seeing that he [Raphael] could not even define 'lower-middle-class,'" she struggles to clarify. "I have roots like D.H. Lawrence: my people better themselves a little, like Lawrence's ambitious women." But Raphael is repelled by her example; she sees that he hates Lawrence. Meanwhile she, who "had never had occasion to say 'my people' before, like that" (215), is floundering, her assumptions shattered. At the end of *Still Life*, after the horror of Stephanie's death, Frederica is still without a place, in the throes of a passionate relationship with Nigel Reiver, whose alien, enclosed country-house world is to entrap her.

Stephanie, meanwhile, is experiencing other aspects of culture and society. Her life, giving help and comfort to needy people as the wife of a curate in the working-class parish of St. Bartholomew's, is geographically much narrower than her sister's. "Sunk in biology" (13), she gives birth first to Will and then to Mary and becomes "obsessed with growing things" (227), attached to life. She—whom Byatt describes in an interview as the more "intelligent" sister (Tredell 71)—is so busy with her family and with helping Daniel (despite her lack of religious belief) that she has almost no time to think. Snatching some time for herself in a library, she first thinks of knowledge in terms of remembered pleasure—"grasping an argument, seizing an illustration, seeing a link, a connection, between this ancient Greek idea here and this seventeenth-century English one, in other words" (153). This pleasure seems lost, but now, in the present, she makes new connections: "She thought of … various lights, Plato's sun, Daniel's body, that first moment of Will's separate life, herself in sunlight" (153). She has an understanding of connectedness, of mind and body; five years older than Frederica, she has internalized her knowledge. Pulling herself away from this "wool-gathering," which has now led her to think about the "desired shape" of her own life, she turns to her morning's project, thinking about Wordsworth's "Immortality Ode." She discovers that she was already thinking about it; "the poem was about all these things, the splendour in the grass, the need for thought, the shape of a life, the light" (153).

Despite these moments of insight, and despite her joy in watching Will—named for Wordsworth and also, unintentionally, for Bill—become a namer of his own world, Stephanie is acutely conscious of what she has given up. Near the end of her life, she speaks to Daniel about her loss of language. The fact that she can do so shows the strength of their bond, but afterward, instead of continuing to talk together—which would have been best for Stephanie's "solitary self"—they do what at that point she sees as "second-best" (307) and make love. In the last scene in which she and Frederica are together, the two sisters listen without comment to Wijnnobel's inaugural speech as vice-chancellor of the new coeducational university, to his extolling of "the education of the complete man" (275), and his illustration of his discussion of perception with a series of objectifications of "a girl" (276). They move on to contemplate a pair of Henry Moore sculptures at the New University, which is being built on Crowe's estate. The figures are female and male, and the sisters are drawn together by a "compulsion to belittle the female figure" (277). The statue's wide hips remind Stephanie of her own, broadened by child-bearing; its small head is pronounced by Frederica to be "hardly an inspiration to a generation of female undergraduates" (277). Meanwhile, two generations of males provide standard responses to this cultural artifact. Two-year-old Will recognizes the stability of the earth mother, and Wilkie sees her as "content," whereas the male, erect with head raised, "has aspirations." Stephanie says that the pair is "powerful"; Frederica, speaking for both herself and Stephanie, reports that they find the female "threatening" (278). In Stephanie's last moment, the word *altruism* comes into her mind, both summing up her life and restoring to her a fragment of lost language. Depicting women's experience within a range of sharply observed social settings, these two novels show the difficulties of being intelligent, young, and female in England in the fifties.

5 *Sugar and Other Stories*

BYATT'S FIRST COLLECTION OF SHORT STORIES, *Sugar and Other Stories* (1987), extends her exploration of the relationship of art and reality. Byatt says that she turned to this form, relatively late in her career, because of her awareness of the shortness of the time for writing: "I suddenly realised that there were more and more and more things in the world that I noticed, and that I haven't got enough life to write already the novels I have thought of.... And so I started seeing things in this very condensed clear way, as images, not necessarily to be strung together in a long narrative, but to be thought out from" (Chevalier, "Entretien" 26). What the characters and the narrator—who are usually intimately related—make of the images is what the stories are about. The difficult process of "extracting meaning from experience" (Spufford 23), central in the four novels that preceded *Sugar*, is brought into sharper focus by the compression of the new form. With two exceptions, "The July Ghost" and "Precipice-Encurled," the stories are narrated from the perspective of their female central characters. Even in the two exceptions, women characters—in each story, women who experience premature loss—are poignant presences. Several of the stories make feminist statements—concerning, for example, the discouragement of girls from academic achievement, the domination of women's lives by the needs of aging parents, and the social and cultural oppression of postmenopausal women—but Byatt's most significant feminist contribution is quieter and more pervasive. It lies in the steady, compassionate gaze she directs on the minutiae of women's lives, in the depiction of the female imagination, and in the qualities of endurance, courage, and hopefulness that her characters display in painful, often desperate situations.

In its progressive melding together of thematic and narrative strands and its steadily increasing focus on the shaping work of the imagination, the ordering of the eleven stories represents the process of confection that is Byatt's metaphor for storytelling. The first four, "Racine and the Tablecloth," "Rose-Coloured Teacups," "The July Ghost," and "The Next Room," are linked by the motif of parent-child relationships. Next comes a pair, "The Dried Witch" and "Loss of Face," both set in Korea. (The nation is not named, however; the reader is left to deduce the setting from the narrator's clues.) "The Dried Witch" provides an implicit comment on "Loss of Face." Only with the seventh story does the figure of the writer become central. "On the Day that E.M. Forster Died" and "The Changeling" present two vignettes about women writers: the first is a sympathetic portrait, the second sharply critical. "In the Air" repeats from "The Dried Witch" the figure of the solitary, threatened woman, but transports her from a Korean peasant village to a British urban setting. The last two stories, "Precipice-Encurled" and "Sugar," openly reflect on the relationship of the imagined and the real. The first features two Victorian males, a poet and a painter; the second a contemporary woman writer and her family history. With "Sugar" the collection comes full circle: the adult narrator shares with her dying father the same respect for justice and truth that the girl Emily in the first story projects onto her imaginary Reader. Both the child Emily in the first story and the adult in the last story contain aspects of the author. Byatt, who suffered at the Mount School from the lack of value placed on individual achievement, has also said that when she began to write, she too constructed an ideal Reader (Dusinberre, "A.S. Byatt" 188; Chevalier, "Entretien" 25). The narrator of "Sugar," the only first-person narrator in the collection, is Byatt herself, "the daughter of my father, trying desperately to be accurate" (qtd. in Wachtel, "A.S. Byatt" 89). Emily's understanding, like her power, is limited; the mature woman writer who speaks in "Sugar" exemplifies the richness and variety of women's creativity. Taken in sequence, the stories move from the more realistic to the more metafictional end of the scale. The confecting process, the imagination's shaping activity, itself emerges gradually as the subject; simultaneously, the reader, warily addressed in "Racine," is invoked more confidingly in "Sugar." The collection fits into the category that Patricia Waugh places at the centre of the spectrum of metafiction: "those texts that manifest the symptoms of formal and ontological insecurity but allow their deconstructions to be finally recontextualized or 'naturalized' and given a total interpretation" (*Metafiction* 19).

"Racine and the Tablecloth" is about a power struggle in a girl's school; it is also about the making of moral and literary judgments and the destructive power of language. The protagonist, Emily Bray, confronts her antagonist, the headmistress, Martha Crichton-Walker. A third figure is Emily's imaginary Reader, for whom she writes her essays: "He was dry and clear, he was all-knowing but not messily infinite. He kept his proportion and his place. He had no face and no imaginary arms to enfold or heart to beat: his nature was not love, but understanding.... It is not too much to say that in these seemingly endless years in that place Emily was enabled to continue because she was able to go on believing in the Reader" (6). In opposition to the silent impartiality of the Reader, Emily perceives the "essential denial" (1) of Miss Crichton-Walker, who uses language to condemn: she labels Emily's laboured handwriting "aggressive" and her essays "nastily presented": "the judgment dropped in heavily and fast, like a stone into a pond, to rest unshifted on the bottom" (5). When Emily, in an act of mild rebellion, disobeys the school's rules by walking back from church by a private shortcut, Miss Crichton-Walker finds her looking at a willow tree and calls her act of walking back alone "depraved" (or did Emily invent the word? In any case, "the word must have been in the air ... for her to pick up" [9]).

Socially awkward, unathletic, and scholarly, Emily is a misfit among the other girls; she clings miserably to her belief that "at the end of the tunnel there was, there must be, light and a rational world full of aspiring Readers" (20). In the face of the headmistress's insistence that the academic achievement of girls must not be valued too highly—"there [is] as much lasting value, as much pleasure for others, in a well-made tablecloth as in a well-written book" (21)—Emily is determined to excel in her finals and especially to do justice to her passion, the works of Racine. She relates the tablecloth example to her great-aunt Florence, who, prevented by the needs of others from fulfilling her dream of travelling, spent her days doing embroidery until arthritis stopped that too. After this vision of her own possible fate, Emily becomes "double"; she breaks into a "feeling part" that has "given up" and a "thinking part" that "chattered away toughly" (25) as she prepares for her examinations. Crying uncontrollably except when she is actually writing the papers, she manages to achieve the highest marks in the school's records.

Near the end of this story of the oppression of women—in this case most directly by other women—the narrator asks who has won. She shows Emily as an adult, having "made up" her "account" (5) and passed judgment on Miss Crichton-Walker, appearing to win (going to university, specializing in French, marrying happily, having clever daughters, and working part-time as a translator) yet also feeling, though "in a fluctuating and intermittent way," that she has "somehow lost" (30). The story ends by moving on to the next generation, where the pattern of thwarted female ambition threatens to repeat itself. Emily confronts authority at her daughter Sarah's school and insists that Sarah, who is good at both French and mathematics, be allowed to do both; the authority, now ironically represented in the male figure of the headmaster, accuses Emily of projecting her own "unfulfilled ambitions" on her daughter. In an updated but still sexist version of Miss Crichton-Walker's rhetoric, he says that his school cares about "the whole human being": it exists to educate Sarah "for forming personal relations, running a home, finding her place in society, understanding her responsibilities" (31). Emily, hearing the echo of Miss Crichton-Walker's "old mild voice" (31), leaves in defeat. Sarah, however, is glimpsed briefly: she has created her own (now ungendered) Reader and lays out her solution to a problem in geometry "for the absent scanning of an unfalteringly accurate mind, to whose presence she required access" (31–32). The open ending puts the reader in the position of judge, replacing the two actual authority figures and the two imagined readers, and charged with creating a future in which Sarah's heliotropic imagination can turn toward its own sun. "You can believe, I hope, you can afford to believe, that [Sarah] made her way into its light" (32), says the narrator.

"Racine and the Tablecloth" grimly demonstrates the horror of manipulation and coercion. It also shows self-reflexively that too much control will lead to a breakdown of order. By interspersing interludes of disorder and misrule with the episodes of imprisonment, Byatt demonstrates the imagination's need for openness and freedom. The girls and their counterparts at a boys' school conspire to reverse the girls' and boys' seating at church; the girls (unconsciously countering Miss Crichton-Walker's neatly allegorical, moralizing stories) concoct stories of their headmistress swinging naked in the garden. But Emily cannot participate in these carnivalesque trespasses, nor can she confront the headmistress directly through speech. As Laurent Lepaludier has shown, she must find her own form of opposition: her essays, especially her analysis of Racine's texts, provide her with "artistic discourse in its perfection" (42).[1] Emily is fascinated by Racine's control of passionate excess, holding it within "the flexible, shining, inescapable steel mesh of that regular, regulated singing verse" (17). However, in contrast to Racine's beautiful but rigid form, Byatt's form allows for indeterminacy. Despite the depressing similarity of the mother's and daughter's situations (with, in the background, two earlier generations of self-sacrificing, caregiving women, Great-Aunt Florence and Emily's mother), there is some hopefulness in this story: in the strength of the four generations of women, in Sarah's ability to excel at both a "female" and a "male" subject, and in the handing over of the ending to a non-mythical, small r reader whom the narrator, after a rather skittish earlier relationship, now appears willing to trust.

The second story, "Rose-Coloured Teacups," is much briefer, encompassing only a few moments in the consciousness of Veronica, the main character. It again explores women's history and its repetition through four generations. Veronica, middle-aged mother of two daughters, tries repeatedly to visualize her own mother as a student, waiting with friends in a college room to entertain a group of male students—one of whom is to be Veronica's father—at a tea party. Her imagination creates the scene only to the point of the young men's arrival and the mother's smile of "pure pleasure, pure hope, almost content. She could never see any further: from there, it always began again, chairs, tablecloth, sunny window, rosy teacups, a safe place" (38). The teacups represent the irretrievable past, the fragility of loved objects, and the barriers between the generations. They had been passed on to Veronica by her mother's friend "to take back a new generation to the college" (36), but Veronica, disliking their old-fashioned prettiness, had allowed most of them to break, although she now finds the surviving pieces "exquisitely pretty" (38). Her reverie about this tea party is her only form of mourning for her mother, who had become embittered at being trapped by marriage and children. Her mother had tried to hold on to her happy past by seeing Veronica at the same college but had then felt "excluded ... from her own memories of the place. The past had been made into the past, discontinuous from the present" (37). Now Veronica experiences the same discontinuity with her daughter Jane as Jane impatiently breaks the sewing machine on which Veronica's grandmother had made clothes for Veronica's mother. Veronica, hearing "in her mind's ear" her mother's "howling plaint" about the smashed teacups—"how *could* you"—restrains herself from reproducing that fury against the new generation, and again, as in the first story, there is the possibility of a happier future. Veronica and her sisters all "partly evaded" (37) their mother's frustrations. Veronica has not vented her mother's anger on her daughter, and the physical features of the older generations persist in benign recombination: Jane has her father's eyes and the "wide and shapely smile" (38) that Veronica has imagined as belonging to the young man at the tea party, Jane's grandfather.

"The July Ghost" and "The Next Room" are ironically contrasting ghost stories. In the first, a mother who (like Byatt herself) has lost her eleven-year-old son acquires a lodger who sees the boy's ghost; the mother, who longs to see the boy, cannot do so. In the second, a daughter who has faithfully nursed her widowed mother and believes herself to be free, at fifty-nine, to live her own life, finds herself pursued by the quarrelling, complaining voices of her parents. In both stories, time defeats hope and creativity, keeping pain alive. These stories also introduce another narrative thread in the collection; like "The Dried Witch," they contain the weird or strange, "what haunts"—elements that, Byatt says, she wanted to use the short story form to "accommodate" (Chevalier, "Entretien" 13).

"The July Ghost" is told through the consciousness of an unnamed male character who, in the first sentence, confides to an American woman at a party, "I think I must move out of where I'm living" (39). This, it turns out, is the second time he says these words. The first time, also at a party, he says them to Imogen, who, hearing that his lover Anne has left him, suggests that he become her lodger. Near the end of the story, after the man has narrated some of his experience to his American friend, he packs his bags, intending to move to the house where she is staying. The ending itself, however, leaves his departure in question. Within this framework of repetition is the ghost story (if that is an appropriate label—it has some of the conflicting possibilities of Henry James's *Turn of the Screw*). The man repeatedly sees a boy in Imogen's garden and then (in her presence) in the house, and learns from her that her son, who was the same age and wore the same clothes, had been killed in a traffic accident two years earlier and that her prolonged, isolating grief has driven her husband away. The man tells Imogen what he has seen, and she confesses that after the boy's death she had hoped to "go mad enough" to see him again and had once half seen a "ghost of his face." But she had resolved to do no outward mourning; she had willed herself not even to dream of him: "Only my body wouldn't stop waiting and all it wants is to—to see that boy" (47). The man becomes convinced that the boy wants him to make love to Imogen in order to re-engender the boy in another child. He does not ask the boy for confirmation: "Possibly this was out of delicacy.... Possibly there were other reasons. Possibly he was mistaken: the situation was making him hysterical" (52). He tries to comfort Imogen with sex, but she, passive but receptive at first, becomes immobilized and begins to scream. When he sees the boy again, he uses the same expression as her husband, Noel, had used to Imogen before he left her, that he cannot "get through" (42, 55), and asks the boy to release him. Meanwhile, he has made the experience into a story, giving the American woman a "bowdlerized version" (49), which presents the boy as only the dead boy's look-alike, just as he had, earlier, given Imogen a softened, abbreviated version of his loss of Anne.

Not only Imogen and the man but also the American woman, who has come to England to get away from a love affair with her married professor and who, it seems, is about to begin an affair with her new friend, are trapped in eerie repetition. When the man, having told his version of the story, confesses that he now feels that he and Imogen are no longer helping each other and that he must leave, she says that he has to live his life. He repeats, "Yes…, I've tried to get through, I have my life to live" (54)—repeating Noel's words as well as the woman's. Imogen and the lodger ponder the grammar of loss. When Imogen heard her son was dead, she thought, "is dead … it's a continuous present tense" (47). The man, in his turn, feels that "Anne was worse lost because voluntarily absent" (48); as he prepares to make love to Imogen, he thinks of Anne and, in another linguistic formulation of loss, "what was never to be again" (53). As the man packs to leave Imogen's house, he feels that the boy may want him to stay: "as he stood helplessly there, the boy turned on him again the brilliant, open, confiding, beautiful desired smile" (56). The end, like the interpretation, is left open. Have his own experience of loss and his intuition of Imogen's needs created what he saw? Has he, as Imogen suggests, tried to do her psychic work for her? "I am too rational to go mad," she says, "so I seem to be putting it on you" (50). The story shows, in Imogen, the tension of repressed feeling and, in the man, the human need to shape experience by narratives that accommodate it; at the same time, it explores the possibility of surviving presences. The meaning of time and the function of memory (including the question of whether memories can be communicated by one person to another) are hauntingly mysterious in this story. What is indisputable is the power of loss.[2]

"The Next Room" begins with Molly Hope's cremation and her daughter Joanna's sense of relief. "She had dutifully given her mother a large part of her life"; now that her mother is "free carbon molecules and potash" (58), she hopes to be able to travel again on the foreign tours that her work had offered her before her mother's illness. Certain, like Imogen, that death ends everything and, like her, self-controlled and rational, she dismisses a toothache as psychosomatic until its persistence forces her to allow her colleague and former lover Mike to make a dental appointment for her. At this point her certainty about the finality of death begins to be countered by other versions: a television program in which a North American Indian speaks of his ancestors still living "in the grass and trees and stones we know and love" (65); a conversation with her co-worker Bridget (who has replaced her as Mike's assistant), who in Japan "had breakfast every day with the family's grandfather, who was dead" (67); most insistently of all, the "well-polished narration" (69) of the near-death experience of Bonnie Roote, a fellow patient at the dentist's. Bonnie had seen her mother's idea of heaven, a bungalow and peonies, and her dead relatives waiting, with her mother, for her. Joanna rejects Bonnie's story and her footnote, that their meeting was brought about by higher powers because of Joanna's need to hear it. She recalls her mother's complaints of hearing the quarrelling voices of Joanna's grandparents, waiting for her in the room next to her bedroom. Joanna herself now begins to repeat this experience, hearing her own parents' voices arguing. The voices persist even in a Durham hotel room, where Mike, after shattering her vision of travelling again to the desert—"the African moon faded and the horizon contracted like a brace" (76)—has sent her on an assignment. Here, one of her interviews provides a darker instance of Bonnie's comfortable belief in planned coincidences; she talks to an unemployed steelworker, now, like her, "written off" (82) by a changing society. Depressed by the evidence, Joanna is forced to revise her own version. Why should the dead be different from the living, she asks—"Why should not the worst and most tenacious aspects of our characters persist longest?" For the voices are attached not to her parents' house, but to "her own blood and presence" (83). Like the Christmas cactus "Joanna Hope," bred by her father and perpetuating the ironic family name, the individual life is determined, "bearing its eternal genes which dictate its form and future forever and forever" (83) and ensuring that she, confined, disappointed and angry as her parents and grandparents had been, will "in her turn pass, none too quietly, into that next room" (84). Having determined as a young woman to live differently from her mother, she, like her, has been trapped. The presence of the dead among the living is for Joanna a terrifying reality.

In the next two stories, the clash of cultures hinted at in "The Next Room" is foregrounded. Set in Korea, these stories present conflicting views of the same culture, for the first, "The Dried Witch," shows a woman ritually killed by the same decadent society that in the second, "Loss of Face," has become enshrined in a museum. If it were not for the harsh perspective given by the first, the second would invite us to romanticize the primitive aspect of the society. Moreover, the central figure in "Loss of Face," a British woman scholar at a literary conference, aspires to a global perspective that precludes the privileging of any culture, any language, and that, inevitably, fails at a crucial moment, defeated by the limitations of her own culture.

In "The Dried Witch" an old woman, A-Oa, has reached the "dry" time of her life. She has lost her children, her husband has been taken by the army, and her brother-in-law, Da-Shin, with whom she had lived, sharing the only bed and forbidden to touch by the taboos (which prescribed death for the woman, presumed to be the temptress, and expulsion, rarely enforced, for the man), has mysteriously vanished. A-Oa recognizes her opposite number in Kun, an aging, effeminate old man, alone and childless like her. Both "singletons on the edge of the circle, not woven in by kin or obligation" (88), they are marginalized, but Kun, as a male, has power. Because he spies on them, the other villagers fear him; his wife has been executed for (allegedly) trying to bewitch him, and it was after Da-Shin had been followed by Kun that he disappeared. Now A-Oa sets out to make herself feared in the only way available to her: by becoming a jinx. Following the instructions of the female shaman, she sets up an altar in her kitchen, where she is safe from Kun's observation because of the taboo forbidding men to enter the woman's part of the house, and she lays out objects to dry or, if already dry, to be plumped out. She becomes accepted as a jinx and when a young man, Cha-Hun, comes to her for a charm to win (in a repetition of Da-Shin's relationship to A-Oa herself) the forbidden love of his sister-in-law An-At, she provides it, although she is "privately sure" it is "unnecessary" (104). She knows that Kun has learned of her complicity. When the young woman becomes pregnant and when Cha-Hun's young brother, A-Oa's first "cure," is found dead, the "witch" is resigned to her fate: "Let us look into this, Kun said, as she had always known he would say" (105). The lovers accuse her of putting them under a spell, and Cha-Hun, frantic to save himself, repeats, at Kun's prompting, the traditional remedy: "We sun the jinx. We put the jinx to dry in the sun" (107). A victim of Kun's manipulation of the debased collective imagination of the villagers, who take up the cry, A-Oa experiences the ultimate dryness. Tied to a stump in the burning sun, her body dies horribly. Some of her last thoughts are of An-At; she wonders if she—another victim of patriarchy—will be beheaded. Yet in the end, seeing a tree nearby burst into flames, she experiences power and creativity. Remembering the superstition that a jinx can set trees on fire, her imagination dances to the sound of the flames, and the last image, as her mind and body separate, is of freedom: "The eddies of heat…took her with them, away from the strapped and cracking thing, away" (111).[3]

In "Loss of Face," a reconstructed version of A-Oa's village is visited by

Celia Quest, a British literary scholar whose name echoes E.M. Forster's Adela Quested in *A Passage to India*. Like Adela, who wants to see the real India, Celia tries to approach the foreign culture with openness. Their hosts at the conference show the Western visitors their folk village, which preserves their vanishing past. All occupations are represented— there is even a female shaman (Celia knows from her guidebook, one of the many texts that compete for authority within the story, that the country is "Confucian, Buddhist, Catholic, residually shamanistic" [114]). Their guide, Professor Moon, explains the segregation of the women's quarters, and Celia, thinking, in terms of her own scholarship, of lares and penates, asks if there is an altar. Professor Moon avoids answering, making her aware that she has "trespassed" (121), and instead points out the contrast between the ugly Western clothes of the modern Koreans and the beautiful traditional dress of the folk dancers, and demonstrates his own skill at Korean kite flying. Celia realizes that she can never escape the language and images of her origins: she cannot help substituting Chinese kites for those he describes, and, like the Korean people themselves, is torn between two visions. When she next sees Professor Moon, she reflects that although she has been in his company for three days, she knows nothing about him; he has become for her "what she was aware of not knowing, a form of absence" (122). Meanwhile, the reader who has moved from "The Dried Witch" can fill in some of the blanks: the uses of a household altar, the consequences of the rigid separation of the sexes.

Celia's experience of linguistic and cultural difference in Korea is summed up in the image of the Tower of Babel, which—again pointing to the impossibility of separating ourselves from familiar landscapes— she associates with Breughel's painting. Representing fractured speech and the resulting cultural differences, the Tower of Babel duplicates itself in the two plate-glass towers where the conference takes place: the lecture tower which, following Asian superstition, has no fourth floor, and the hotel tower, which, in deference to Western fears, has no thirteenth. Further exploration of linguistic barriers occurs when Celia wonders how her Asian audience hears Milton's linguistic transitions and what they see when they read of George Eliot's sense of place. Yet these scholars can meet Celia on her intellectual ground: Professor Sun corrects her view of the English Civil War, and (unlike Celia's students) he can suspend his disbelief in Milton's "patriarchally predestined cosmology" (113). Celia is aware of the ironies involved, for both sides, in these acts of cultural appropriation. She realizes that if art is, as she believes and as T.S. Eliot implies, "a work of rescue," the decision to privilege some fragments in this way entails the failure to "canonize" others (120). She knows that there can never be a complete and universally accessible text. Yet she makes a disastrous faux pas at the concluding banquet. Seated beside what she takes to be a "younger, gentler, more shy" (123) version of Professor Sun, she assumes that he is a young lecturer and asks his name. He retrieves his name tag from his pocket and she sees in horror that "He was not like Professor Sun, he *was* Professor Sun. Not to have known him was to annihilate everything that had been said or acted, to break the frail connections that had been made" (126). She, who prided herself on enjoying difference, has failed to distinguish his face from other Korean faces. By losing his face she has herself lost face. After discussing Harold Bloom's *Map of Misreading* with her fellow scholars, she herself has misread. The title, "Loss of Face," is a triple pun, for history has deprived the Koreans of their collective identity, their national face. Colonial rule has taken their language and art, and even the names they use are "versions of their names.... So there were many Suns and many Moons also" (115). Celia discovers that she knows neither Sun nor Moon. The real Korea, like the real India that eludes Adela Quested, remains inaccessible to her.

Flying home, thinking of the Tower of Babel, Celia finds the idea of England "irrelevant": "It was required that one think in terms of the whole world, and it was not possible" (127). Professor Sun had confided to her his belief that his people should be studying not British but Third-World literature; for Celia, the Third World is "not one, it was many" voices, like the literature of "women, or blacks, or homosexuals, voices contradicting or modifying a voice, now unheard, that had once claimed to be the best that was thought and said in the world" (125). As a woman, she does not like to be marginalized, but "Loss of Face" shows that both she and Professor Sun, in different ways, are being pushed to the margins of a shifting text. In the airplane, she thinks about the clash between "the human speech of particular men" and the "universals ... the plate-glass tower, the machine gun, the deconstructive hubris of grammatologists and the binary reasoning of machines" (127). Despite the gentle humour with which Byatt describes Celia's predicament, the story is deeply pessimistic about both the survival of individual differences and the possibility of global communication.

With the next two stories, "On the Day that E.M. Forster Died" and "The Changeling," the collection moves toward more explicitly metafictional concerns. Both are cautionary tales about women writers whose imaginative freedom is challenged by the intractable external world. However, Mrs. Smith, in the first story, is presented with a distanced sympathy, while Josephine Piper, in the second, is an alienating and alienated figure.

"On the Day" begins, "This is a story about writing" (129). Mrs. Smith is a middle-aged writer who, in 1970, believes that the "time for writing about writing was past" (129). She would not have liked the narrator's story, because Mrs. Smith "never wrote about writers. Indeed, she wrote witty and indignant reviews of novels which took writing for a paradigm of life. She wrote about the metaphysical claustrophobia of the Shredded Wheat Box on the Shredded Wheat Box getting smaller ad infinitum" (130). For her, art is an addiction, not a cure; she prefers to separate life and art and likes "things to happen" in fiction. The narrator, although "much in sympathy" with Mrs. Smith's views, nevertheless thinks her own story about writing is "worth telling"; indeed, it is "overloaded with plot, a paradigmatic plot which … takes it beyond the narcissistic consideration of the formation of the writer, or the aesthetic closure of the mirrored mirror" (130). This plot of the narrator's shows the failure of human plotting; in it, time and fate are triumphant.

On the day in question, Mrs. Smith has an idea for a long novel that will combine several plots. Her time has come, she thinks, to write a book that will contain the historical and biological time she has lived through. Her planning of it, as she sits in the London Library, becomes "a growth, a form of life, her life, its own life" (133). Exhilarated, she experiences for the first time the paradox of "limitation" (for her project, huge as it is, will necessarily be limited by her own "history, sex, language, class, education, body and energy") as "release and power" (132). In the midst of her elation, however, the narrator tells the reader, "the plotting and over-plotting I wrote of … is … stalking Mrs. Smith" (135). Confident of her power to control her own plot and, with it, time, she is moving to meet the plot beyond her control. She meets an old acquaintance, Conrad, who (as his name suggests) has been involved with many plots. After a very active professional and sexual life—a psychologist, he has worked for the prison service and the army, and he has had children by several women—he was found to have tuberculosis. His active plotting abruptly suspended, he had a vision of life's finitude and decided to study music as "the most important thing." When Mrs. Smith last saw him, he was absorbed—with a concentration that parallels her own recent experience of planning her novel—in this "story of the music … a plot almost needing no character" (139). Now, apparently mad, he has moved into a new plot. He now knows, he tells her over lunch, that time is an illusion and that humans can live forever. Meanwhile, he must have her help, he says, in protecting the world from nuclear war by guarding a duplicate set of plans for a machine that uses music to drive its listeners mad; he is delivering the original plans to the Israeli embassy for use against the Arabs. Mrs. Smith refuses to be part of his espionage plot, escapes with the package from his frenzied attempt to force her to stay in the restaurant (their scuffle is misread by a spectator as a rape plot), and weeps for the music that Conrad has so madly misused. As the story ends, her idea for her novel is interrupted (as Conrad's earlier plots had been) by illness—a lump (ironically recalling the "growth" of her imagined text) that the surgeon says must be removed at once. She spends the three weeks before the operation trying to think of "short tales, of compressed, rapid forms of writing, in case there was not much time" (146). As the narrator promised, this plot goes beyond the "mirrored mirror" (130); it is the paradigmatic plot of the triumph of time, and it reflects not writing but life. Mrs. Smith is defeated by the biological clock that Conrad's grandiose delusion dismisses as unreal. The narrator's ominous use of tense (the present story "would not have" pleased Mrs. Smith [130]) suggests that the interruption, unlike Conrad's illness, is a final one. The irony is underscored by the reference in the title: seeing the headline announcing Forster's death after a long life, Mrs. Smith feels free to proceed as a writer: he was simultaneously "removed ... as a measure" and made "more accessible to learn from" (136). Mrs. Smith knows that Forster believed in "recognizing the complicated energies of the world in which art didn't matter" (135)—the world that now claims her.

"The Changeling" continues Byatt's examination of the writing process. At its centre is a successful fiction writer, Josephine Piper, whose subject is fear. She specializes in the excruciating suffering of young boys. Her prototypical hero, Simon Vowle, finds a temporary haven from the horrors of boarding school life in the school's boiler room. Josephine is using her own experience here—she wrote her first stories in such a retreat—and Byatt herself did the same thing (Musil 195). The "Shredded Wheat Box" structure is shattered, however, by the entrance of Henry Smee, a recent graduate of the school, which Josephine's son Peter had also attended. He is introduced to Josephine by her friend Max McKinley, the headmaster. Max is in the habit of sending difficult and lonely boys to stay with her, and he now asks her to keep Henry—who, he says, "is Simon Vowle" (147)—until he goes to Cambridge in the autumn. Josephine sees the resemblance: "You could have used ... the same little groups of words indifferently to describe either" (149-50). However, although the language fits Henry, the image does not encompass him; his troubling presence in her house becomes increasingly disturbing to her, and their strained relationship reaches a crisis when Henry, directed by Max, reads Josephine's story about Simon, "The Boiler Room." Reaching out for help to Josephine, who, he now knows, understands his torment (and, we are chillingly told, would have enjoyed writing about it), he is given a dismissive response, but persists: "the world is more terrible than most people ever let themselves imagine. Isn't it?" (155). After this, Josephine finds that Henry's "reading of Simon Vowle" has destroyed her freedom, for "Simon Vowle was herself, was Josephine Piper: there was no room for another" (156). Henry has given solid form to both her subject and her reader, and her writing becomes blocked. Finding Henry in her room looking in her mirror, she screams at this further invasion and orders him to leave. He does so, and kills himself. Josephine, freed from his demand that she imagine his "inside," resumes her endless task of exorcising her fear: "Her imagination tidied Henry Smee into a mnemonic" (159); "The next day she was able to start again with nothing and no one between her and the present Simon Vowle,... making a separate world, with no inconvenient reader or importunate character in the house" (160). All that is left of Henry is the ghost of his hands, which she appropriates for the new Simon.

"The Changeling" is a frightening study of the artistic process. Reminiscent of both *The Shadow of the Sun* and *The Game*, it explores the moral failure of the artist through irresponsible opportunism and refusal of empathy. Like Julia, the novelist in *The Game*, Josephine is the artist as consumer, attacking her human subjects with what Byatt (speaking of *The Game*) has described as "the sharp teeth and gaping jaws" of her imagination ("Sugar/Le sucre" 22). With rigid compartmentalization and iron control, Josephine pushes away the challenge of "real people" in the interests of self-preservation. In her struggle to avoid the nameless terrors of her agoraphobic mother, she entraps herself; in her frantic flight from her own fear, she avoids confronting her mother's fear, nor can she face Henry's. Henry, like Josephine's divorced husband and like her son Peter, sees through the facade of the cosy domestic household that Josephine has "made up" and forces her to acknowledge its falseness. "Perhaps she had not done wrong. She simply was wrong" (158), she reflects, while trying to understand Peter's decision to drop out of college and help the homeless. Both Henry and Peter also see through Max, who, with his urge to plot others' lives and his provision of Josephine with copy, is her accomplice and procurer. Despite his apparent sensitivity to the sufferings of adolescent boys, Max does not respond to their needs, and the narrator's statement that he reports Henry's suicide "with circumspection and tact" (159) suggests a detachment that parallels Josephine's own.

Strategically placed in relation to Byatt's developing theory of fiction, the next story, "In the Air," moves away from the artistic concerns of the preceding two. Reasserting Byatt's need to imagine the lives of non-literary characters, it explores the subject of fear—a pervasive subject in *Sugar*—more sympathetically than Byatt allows Josephine to do. At the same time, like "The Changeling," it deals with the materialization of an obsession. Mrs. Sugden, the widowed, aging central character, has found a way to "organize" (165) her fear. Living alone with her dog, Wolfgang, she is provided by the media with ample evidence that an attacker lurks in every neighbourhood, and she imagines her own future attacker in protean terms: "He was black, he was white, he was brown, he was dirty grey.… He had all the time in the world" (163). She knows that it is "civilized" to discuss violence more openly than in the past but her fear is increased by this openness. Fear, for her, is "in the air" (168), and it is in the open air that she expects to meet her attacker. On one of the daily walks that, steeling herself, she takes with the dog, she sees a young man who moves in an oddly exaggerated way, carries a knife, and is following a blind woman and her guide dog. Mrs. Sugden forces herself to go to the blind woman's rescue. The woman, Miss Tillotson, invites her new acquaintance home to tea, and the young man invites himself. Miss Tillotson has found her own courageous way of dealing with the ubiquitous terror; seeing the blind woman's much more vulnerable situation crystallizes Mrs. Sugden's fear. "In my position," says Miss Tillotson, "you could be afraid of everything.… I'd rather come out in the air" (177). As the guests leave, the young man, who has identified himself as Barry and has admitted that he "might be any kind of maniac" (182), promises that he will cross Mrs. Sugden's path again; he too likes to be out in the air. "I'm around a lot. I'll look for you, specially," he says, "tossing the blade" of his knife "in the air" (184). The atmosphere of male threat is intensified by the "jeering filth" (169) shouted by some of the small boys Mrs. Sugden passes on her walks, as well as by her knowledge that Wolfgang bites people "for his own pleasure, not for her protection" (171). Like "The July Ghost" and "The Changeling," this story poses questions about the mind's construction of reality. Is Barry a thief, a rapist, a murderer waiting his chance, or only a sadistic bully? Has Mrs. Sugden, in her lonely, desperate, contracted life, needed her fear to materialize before it became unbearable—since "Every day she feared him a little more" (163)—and is Barry its projection?

The penultimate story, "Precipice-Encurled," moves back to the world of art. Combining actual events near the end of Robert Browning's life with an invented story of a young painter, Joshua Riddell, it brings the principles of the whole collection into sharp focus. Byatt's narrative practice, blending fact and fabrication, demonstrates the duplicitous relationship of the imagination to its materials. In her essay "People in Paper Houses," Byatt observes that Julian Mitchell's novel *The New Satyricon* provides a criticism of "the relation of the novel, the writer and his world." She continues, "It plays games with truth, lies and the reader, teasing him with the knowledge that he cannot tell where veracity ends and games begin. It is the game all novelists play anyway, raised to a structural principle" (180). She is predicting her own practice in "Precipice-Encurled," an art that was to be expanded to a large scale in *Possession*, *Angels and Insects*, and *The Biographer's Tale*.

The title of the story comes from Robert Browning's poem "De Gustibis—," in which the poet declares, "What I love best in all the world / Is a castle, precipice-encurled, / In a gash of the wind-grieved Apennine" (14-16). Ostensibly, the story tells of an occasion in 1882, in the last decade of Browning's life, when the poet and his sister, Sarianna (his companion after his wife's death), fail to carry out their plan of visiting friends at a villa in the Apennines. What prevents them is the death of their friends' house guest, a young English painter named Joshua Riddell. Intent on capturing the appearance of an approaching storm, Joshua is swept from his perch on a cliff and dashed to pieces. The young painter and the old poet, the reader is made to feel, would have understood each other: they share a passion for accuracy about the most minute and insignificant details of the human and natural worlds. The plot thus embodies one of Browning's favourite themes, opportunity missed. This narrative itself is enclosed in, and encloses, two more stories on the same theme—stories of unfulfilled love. Joshua's death cuts short a tender relationship with his host's daughter Juliana, and (according to the hypothesis of another of Byatt's characters, a twentieth-century scholar) Browning is falling in love with Mrs. Bronson, his hostess during his visits to Venice, who returns his affection but remains unaware of his passion. The Brownings plan to visit Mrs. Bronson later that year but are prevented, by flooded roads and illness, from reaching Venice, although they do so in 1883. Both love stories are left without conclusions; the image of Mrs. Bronson, waiting for Browning, begins the story, and Joshua's unfinished portrait of Juliana ends it.

The plot thus represents the intrusion of destructive chance happenings into the life of imagination and emotion. The title, "Precipice-Encurled," refers to the precariously occupied spaces of love and art, and the narrative method demonstrates the hazards of creativity. Through Browning's and Joshua's work and in its own movement, the story shows the creative mind's encircling, assimilating work—and the inevitable escape of "the real thing" from the mind's grasp. In the words Juliet Dusinberre has used of *The Virgin in the Garden*, this short story "seems to declare that the real is beyond form" ("Forms of Reality" 61).

It is the epigraph, however, rather than the title, that provides the most telling clue to the story's special qualities:

> What's this then, which proves good yet seems untrue?
> Is fiction, which makes fact alive, fact too?
> The somehow may be thishow. (185)

The lines, with some interesting omissions and a significant change in punctuation, are from Browning's *The Ring and the Book*:

> Well, now; there's nothing in nor out o' the world
> Good except truth: yet this, the something else,
> What's this then, which proves good yet seems untrue?
> This that I mixed with truth, motions of mine
> That quickened, made the inertness malleolable
> O' the gold was not mine,—what's your name for this?
> Are means to the end, themselves in part the end?
> Is fiction which makes fact alive, fact too?
> The somehow may be thishow. (I.698–707)

Byatt uses Browning's words to hint slyly at her own way of using biography. At the centre of her story, surrounded by documented details of Browning's life and quotations, by his work, and by an unnamed work of twentieth-century scholarship, Byatt has placed an example of "fiction which makes fact alive." By adding the comma where Browning did not use one, she suggests that fiction making is inevitable whenever the imagination is at work on facts. The story of Joshua and Juliana (which even the dust jacket of *Sugar* encourages us to read as fact, "an almost unremembered incident on Browning's Italian travels") is invented. The facts are that the Brownings had been invited by the Cholmondeleys (not the Fishwicks) to visit them on the island of Ischia (not in the Apennines); their visit was cancelled because the Cholmondeleys' guest,

Miss Wade, accidentally fell from a ledge while sketching the sunset and died of her injuries.

On the other hand, the scholar and the hostess, who both may appear to be invented, are real. Although, unlike Mrs. Bronson, he is never named by Byatt, the scholar is Michael Meredith. His 1985 book *More Than Friend* contains, after a long introductory essay, the Browning-Bronson letters, edited with meticulous attention to fact—including the proposed visit to Ischia and the death of Miss Wade (15 n. 3).[4] The craftsmanship with which Byatt mixes fact and fiction is so skilful that a reviewer of *Possession* praises "Precipice-Encurled" for its achievement as historical fiction; in comparing the story with the novel, the reviewer says that for the story the details of Browning's life were "all there, the art was in the gathering and sorting" (Karlin 18). It is, however, the "something else" that was *not* "there" that gives life to the story. By calling into question the existence of the boundary line between fact and fiction, Byatt daringly shows both the impossibility of originality and, conversely, the inevitability, in all writing, of invention and "confection." Embedded in her story are additional texts. Meredith's book, which provides Byatt's starting point, contains other texts as appendices: Mrs. Bronson's two published reminiscences of Browning and a memoir by an American acquaintance, Daniel Sargent Curtis. Several other works are intertextually present in Byatt's text, including Browning's poems, Henry James's *Aspern Papers* and "The Private Life," Christopher Smart's *Song to David*, Andrew Marvell's "Mower's Song," Shakespeare's *As You Like It*, and John Ruskin's *Modern Painters*. Byatt's imagination combines these texts and adds a new love story.

The story's four-part structure represents the encircling work of the imagination as it appropriates its material. The first two parts are very short. The story opens with the "lady," Mrs. Bronson (she is not named until the fourth part), sitting in her house in Venice, waiting for Browning. This part appears reliably factual: there are descriptions of the lady as she appears in portraits and photographs, and details of her life—the number of her servants, the names of her dogs, and her love of delicate objects, together with the information that James gave her a small role in *The Aspern Papers* and planned to make her the central character in a novel. Yet even here fiction creeps in, as the narrator speculates on the party to which the lady's daughter may have gone in the afternoon when her mother "sits, or might be supposed to sit" in the window, and on the umbrella the daughter may have taken with her. The narrator also interprets the lady's expression as shown in "portraits, more than one, tallying" (Meredith reproduces three portraits and two photographs) as "an indefinable air of disappointment" (185).

In the second section, set in the twentieth century, the scholar is introduced, working with letters and other documents to construct his story. He "combs" the facts—including Browning's poem "Inapprehensiveness," which the scholar interprets as a confession of Browning's love—in the direction of the hypothesis of the old poet's "dormant passion" for the lady. The scholar's work borders on fiction as he gives a shape, "subtle, not too dramatic" (188), to the facts, as his imagination curls around the woman whom "he likes ... because he now knows her, has pieced her together" (187). After recording Browning's missed visit to Mrs. Bronson in 1882, Meredith writes, "He was in danger of allowing the friendship to cool," and the narrator adds possible interpretations: "perhaps anxious on her behalf, perhaps on the poet's, perhaps on his own" (188). As Mrs. Bronson and Browning have been enclosed by the scholar's biography, so the scholar is now enclosed by Byatt's narrative—and both the scholar and the narrator are "piecing together" their subjects.

Browning, who has been at the periphery of the first and second sections, is at the centre of the third. In his hotel room in the mountains, he reflects upon his two selves—his expansive public self, which pursues facts in the other world, and his creative private self, which uses these facts and which he imagines as "a brilliant baroque chapel at the centre of a decorous and unremarkable house" (189). The stream of his associations leads him to the idea that Descartes would be a suitable subject for a poem, and he thinks of how he could "inhabit" the philosopher, making the "paraphernalia" of Descartes's world spin around "the naked cogito." "The best part of my life," he thinks, "has been the fitting, the infiltrating, the inventing the self of another man or woman, explored and sleekly filled out, as fingers swell a glove." Yet he himself, who gives "coherence and vitality" to these other selves, is "just such another concatenation" (191). He reviews his favourite characters—the Duchess, Karshish the Arab physician, the risen Lazarus, David, Christopher Smart—noting that they have all shared his own "lively, indifferent interest in everything" (193). These thoughts take him to Sludge the Medium, through whom, following his principle of giving "true opinions to great liars," he has expressed his own vision of the creative intelligence "at the back" of the universe: "something simple, undifferentiated, indifferently intelligent, alive" (193–94). His reverie is interrupted by Sarianna, who tells him of a fellow guest, Mrs. Miller, who wears "an aviary on her head" (194); the next day, Browning's public self autographs Mrs. Miller's birthday book and tells her of the proposed visit to the Fishwicks, and she recites the lines about the precipice-encurled castle. In this section, Browning is both enclosed by Byatt's narrator and encloses other creative selves, and his imaginative piecing together of fact and fiction mirrors Byatt's.

The fourth section, much the longest, presents the—literally—precipice-encurled heart of the story. As she and her family prepare for Browning's visit, Juliana wonders what the poet will "make" of them. The process of creativity is the subject of this section, but this process is either, like Joshua's, broken off in the middle or, like Browning's as imagined by Juliana, never begun. Joshua begins to sketch Juliana's "extremely pleasant" (197) but unremarkable face, and feels their souls meet, and they kiss. The next morning, after spending the night wrestling alone with the conflict between his new love and his responsibility to the "empty greenness" of his "primitive innocence, before," Joshua goes up the cliff to paint; he wants to look at "the land beyond habitation" (204). Remembering Ruskin's words about mountains and a painting by Monet, he perches in an "eyrie" on the precipice and begins to work. He is alternately "miserable" at his "failures of vision" and "supremely happy" as he experiences self-oblivious absorption, "unaware of himself and wholly aware of rock formations, sunlight and visible empty air" (209). As the sky suddenly darkens, he resolves to try to follow Monet's example, painting light itself and "the act of seeing" (210). Losing his footing as the ice pellets strike him, "still thinking of Ruskin and Monet" (211), he falls to his death. The narrator then records the impact of the death on Browning, who reflects briefly on the unknown young man: "his imagination reached after him, and imagined him, in his turn … reaching after the unattainable" (212). When Mrs. Miller asks if he will compose a poem about the death, he replies that he is left "mute" by such events; he does, however, write a poem about Mrs. Miller, "clothed with murder" in her hat of birds' wings (213). In the twentieth century, the scholar is at first hopeful that Browning will now visit Mrs. Bronson, then disappointed as he reads more letters. The last image is of the unfinished sketch that "Aunt Juliana" keeps pressed in the family Bible, of "a young girl, who looked out of one live eye and one blank, unseeing one, oval like those of … [angels on] monumental sculpture" (214).

With this image, the encircling process is concluded, but all the narratives—and all the creative experiences they examine—are left incomplete, and all hold within them potential subjects that are not mined by any artist. Mrs. Bronson's story is described by the scholar, Meredith, as "the novel Henry James missed" (xxv). Descartes never becomes the subject of a poem by Browning, nor does Browning ever "make" anything of the Fishwicks or of Joshua; Joshua never completes either of his sketches.

In its use of fact and fiction the story produces an effect of *trompe l'oeil*. The scholar, who to the uninitiated reader appears imaginary (as Mrs. Bronson herself may), is real. Joshua (the Riddell/riddle), who seems real to the same reader, is imaginary. The impression of the reader who does not have a prior knowledge of the facts is that the scholar, in his eagerness to reclaim Mrs. Bronson—to do what James had merely planned to do—and to construct a love story for Browning's old age, has missed the poignant story of youthful ambition and young love that Browning also missed. In fact, there was no story to miss. Byatt, marginalizing both the scholar and his subject, and altering the facts of Browning's itinerary in 1882, creates a story for the fourth section of "Precipice-Encurled" that has more apparent authenticity than any other part. "A good scholar may permissibly invent, he may have a hypothesis, but fiction is barred," observes the narrator (187–88). Byatt's own procedures explore and threaten the line between scholarly invention and fiction. She moves from dependence on Meredith to innovative use of James to bolder manipulation, finally departing from fact—and other texts—altogether.

Byatt also shows that both Meredith and—much more daringly—Browning combine fact and fiction. Browning imagined Smart noticing not only the whale and the polyanthus, which Smart did include in his *Song to David*, but also the blossoms of Virgin's Bower, which he did not (Browning, "Parleyings" 195–98; Smart, *Song to David* 310, 456–57). Starting with the account of the raising of Lazarus in John 11:1-44, he imagines the life of Lazarus afterward, about which John is silent—and encloses this story in that told by Karshish, whom Browning has also imagined. The narrator's work in this third section of "Precipice-Encurled" parallels Browning's. When Sarianna opens the door of her brother's room, the windows are described in the words used by James's narrator in "The Private Life" when, coming upon the poet Claire Vawdrey (modelled on Browning) writing in the dark, he sees "a couple of vague, starlighted apertures" (194; "Private Life" 227) and concludes that there are two Vawdreys, the public and the private. Mrs. Miller is an invention of Byatt's, but the French words uttered by Browning when he hears about her are a version of those that he is recorded as having said on a different occasion.[5] When, in Byatt's story, Browning writes in Mrs. Miller's birthday book, there is more unacknowledged borrowing from James. In "The Private Life," however, it is the narrator who cannot remember his own birthday; in "Precipice-Encurled," it is Browning. Immediately after this there is explicit reference to James's dislike of Browning's lack of discrimination, and an image from James is used literally when Mrs. Miller nods "under the wings of the dove" (195). The language of the fourth section is the most original and independent, movingly creating the feelings of Joshua and Juliana and the moments just before Joshua's death. The narrator then parries Meredith's "hypothesis" about the personal reference of "Inapprehensiveness" with a "fiction" of her own, making Mrs. Miller's hat the stimulus behind "The Lady and the Painter."[6] The point is clear: while Meredith's hypothesis may have more basis in fact, the truth about the subjects of both poems—like the truth about Lazarus, Smart, Mrs. Bronson, and Browning himself—remains beyond reach.

Browning wrote that Smart "pierced the screen / 'Twixt thing and word" ("Parleyings" 113-14). These are brave words, but Browning knew, and Byatt demonstrates, that the screen is impenetrable. "Precipice-Encurled"displays the predatory activity of the imagination as it raids other texts in its fruitless attempt to get to the "thing." More optimistically, Byatt also shows the fertility of language. In her novel *Still Life,* her narrator confesses, "I had the idea that this novel could be written innocently, without recourse to reference to other people's thoughts, without, as far as possible, recourse to simile or metaphor. This turned out to be impossible" (108). In "Precipice-Encurled," Byatt shows why the experiment must always fail. The scholar, dutifully retracing Browning's steps to Asolo, hears the sounds of the place through Browning's words as he listens to the "contumacious grasshopper" (*Sordello* VI.787). Even Joshua, the painter, sees through others' words, recognizing the accuracy of Milton's description of the fallen leaves in Vallombrosa (199; *Paradise Lost* I.300-04), experiencing first love through Marvell's Mower: "She / What I do to the grass, did to my thoughts and me" (203; Marvell wrote "did," not "does"), and applying to himself Shakespeare's description of lovers who "no sooner looked but they loved" (202; *As You Like It* V.II.32). Even when painting and sketching, he sees through Ruskin's language. When he tries to reach beyond language, remembering simply Monet's canvas and sketching the unmediated subject, he dies. On one level, his death is paradigmatic.

In "Precipice-Encurled," the language of incompleteness and shattering, like the structure, testifies to the failure of enclosure. On the precipice, Joshua sketches a broken snail shell, "the arch of its entrance intact, the dome of the cavern behind shattered to reveal the pearly interior involution" (209). In a few moments, he himself has vanished in a "shattering of bone and brain" (211). Despite the many invocations of enclosure, epitomized by Browning's fantasy that the "pothooks and spider-traces" of his handwriting contain the world (189), the broken shell more accurately images the story Byatt tells. Yet if fiction stops short of holding reality, it also extends it. It is like Monet's *Vétheuil in the Fog,* which so startled Joshua: "You could see, miraculously, that if you could see the town, which you could not, it would be reflected in the expanse of river at the foot of the canvas, which you could also not see" (210). Like Browning's resuscitation of his source, the "Yellow Book," in *The Ring and the Book,* Byatt's fiction has made fact alive. "The somehow may be thishow."

In "Sugar," the author speaks for the first time as Byatt and explores, through fictionalized autobiography, her own imaginative history. Its rambling form is also its subject. Setting out to write about her paternal grandfather, the narrator finds she must describe her father's death, her mother, her other grandparents, and family history as it has been received by her, and she traces her imagination's involvement with myth from the family myth to her favourite childhood reading, the Norse myth of origin and destruction. The narrator begins by contrasting her parents as makers of fictions, and by preferring her father. A judge, he had a respect for "evidence" and a "wish to be exact, a kind of abstract need which is somehow the essence of virtue" (217). As he lay dying in an Amsterdam hospital, he tried "to construct a ... satisfactory narrative of his life" (231). On the other hand, her mother "had a respect for truth, but she was not a truthful woman" (215). Some of her lies were told "to make a story better;" others were complaints, "fabricated evidence of non-existent wickedness" (215-16). She told of her husband's parents, who neglected their healthy children in order to care for their crippled eldest son and who forced their son Freddie, the narrator's father, to work in the family candy factory until faced with his determination to go to Cambridge. Her version of her husband's neglected childhood focuses on the horse trough where his siblings left him as a baby and forgot him while they played. The father's own memories are more benign—of a life of freedom: "we had each other and the fields and the stables ... we ran wild" (231). The narrator recognizes that she herself has interpreted these stories and others, of the escapes of aunts and uncles to more exciting worlds, with the help of written texts, just as her mother borrowed from the story of the Prodigal Son for her depiction of her father-in-law's response to her husband's declaration that he would go to Cambridge with the wages he had saved: he had delightedly "fallen upon your father's neck" (224), she always said. The imagination's need for shape is examined here, and the narrator begins to see her own resemblance to her mother.

Paintings, too, have contributed to the family story. There are the van Gogh prints that the narrator always associated with her mother, whose own family myth traced the family's descent to Dutch Huguenots. The prints were, in fact, her father's choice; she talks about van Gogh with him as he is dying; she is writing a novel that includes van Gogh, and she hints at a parallel between the artist and her father, both men who struggled toward accuracy of representation: "he [van Gogh] remained steadily ... intelligent and analytic, mixing his colours, *thinking* about the nature of light, of one man's energy, of one man's death" (236). Later she "recognized with shock" (234) boats on a French beach, having seen them first in one of these prints, and she "saw that tortured and aspiring cypresses were exact truths, of their kind" (236). (Here "exact" and "of their kind" bring together the father's and the mother's versions of truth.) A paradigm of all representation, the cypresses combine factual accuracy with imaginative shaping.

The narrative progressively becomes its own subject. The narrator sees that she is herself partly her mother's invention—"I saw that much of my past might be her confection" (240)—and that she is truly her mother's as well as her father's daughter. Just as she has seen her grandfather's face in her father's, so she feels her mother's face "setting like a mask in or on my own." She is a storyteller too—"I select and confect" (241)—and, inevitably, she tells lies. In this story, she has left things out—the tear gas and police in Amsterdam—which she now returns to retrieve: "To omit them is a minor sin, and easy to correct. But what of all the others? What is the truth?" (241). Reflecting later on this story, Byatt concludes that "in some curious way" the mother became "the heroine of that story ... the ground of the fiction" (qtd. in Wachtel, "A.S. Byatt" 89).

"Sugar" concludes with two incidents. The first modifies the narrator's mother's construction of the paternal grandfather as a stern patriarch, and shows him as a kindly man, proudly showing his grandchildren how the light streaks in humbug candy were made: "It's the air that does it....Nothing but whipping in air" (244). The twisting together of the dark and light ropes of sugar to make humbugs is the dominant image of Byatt's collection, with the candy's name recalling the mother's lies, which were "sugar-coated pills, grit and bitterness polished into roundness by comedy and by ... worked-upon understanding of ... real meaning" (229). The candy factory is, appropriately, the subject of the first piece of writing that the narrator remembers "clearly as mine." In it—borrowing Frances Hodgson-Burnett's "spun glass" and Coleridge's "as green as emerald" (245) and thus demonstrating that we can never be free of others' language—she wrote of the texture and colours of the discarded bits of candy. The second concluding event epitomizes the whole collection by asking the central question about the dividing line between lived events and mythmaking. The narrator tries to recall her father's return from the war, "a storied event, already lived over and over, in imagination and hope" (248). She remembers the figure in the doorway of her room, herself leaping out of bed and over her sleeping sister, and the experience—"this is surely memory, and no accretion"—of "a terror of happiness." But "the real thing, the true moment, is as inaccessible as any point along that frantic leap." As she writes, other images return to her—"the gold-winged buttons on his jacket"—but neither "words" nor "things" can recall her father's reality. His return takes its place with the other "markers" of the narrative. The last sentence is a list of objects, some "storied," some experienced *and* storied (for "After things have happened…, we begin to know what they are and were, we begin to tell them to ourselves"), ending with the "melded and twisting hanks of brown and white sugar" (248). In this story especially, Byatt has put into action the lesson she attributes to Proust, who narrated "his own life, *beside* his life," and who showed how autobiography could contain "its own precise study of the nature of language, of perception, of memory, of what limits and constitutes our vision of things" ("Sugar/Le Sucre" 23).

In *Sugar and Other Stories*, Byatt successfully blends the self-reflexive and the mimetic. She shows how the imagination constructs its mosaic, and she acknowledges its limits, the dark corners where it cannot go or which it chooses not to include, "the long black shadows of the things left unsaid" (241). Situations and events recur; versions of the past are both terrifyingly powerful and frustratingly inconclusive. Repetition is sometimes oppressive and imprisoning, sometimes enriching and illuminating.

Byatt has noted that "language relates things as well as controlling them" (Dusinberre, "A.S. Byatt" 183). Her own metaphors, like the "branching and flowering" (133) pattern envisioned by Mrs. Smith, suggest endless relationships rather than containment. Her least sympathetic characters are those who, like Miss Crichton-Walker, Kun, Conrad, and Josephine, attempt too tight a control of their own and others' narratives. Her more admirable are those who, like Celia and Mrs. Smith, have the wisdom to see that no text can encompass the whole world and that no imagination can transcend its own limitations.

The stories in *Sugar* are deeply concerned with narrative—not only with its methods but with its uses and abuses, as exorcism, manipulation, self-projection, self-forgetfulness, rescue, paradigm. Some of the finest moments show characters experiencing creative exhilaration, as

Mrs. Smith does in the library, planning her novel, and as Joshua does while sketching on his precipice. Such moments are timeless and wordless, however, and they are often doomed to premature shattering. Loss is a central fact in most of the stories, and it is often suffered by figures who are isolated—by age, gender, grief, culture, or simply difference. Opportunities are missed, or were never really there. These stories celebrate bravery, tenacity, empathy, and honesty; they show characters who, despite their obvious fictiveness, think and feel. Through their author's scrupulous attention to "what is there," they demonstrate her allegiance to the writer's goal as defined by Wallace Stevens, "accuracy with respect to the structure of reality" (qtd. in Byatt, "The Omnipotence of Thought" 121).

6 *Possession: A Romance*

WITH POSSESSION, BYATT MOVED into a new mode. Always fascinated by the impingement of the past on the present—as well as by the impossibility of reconstructing the past—she set out, she says, "to find a narrative shape which would explore the continuities and discontinuities between the forms of nineteenth- and twentieth-century art and thought" (Introduction, *Passions* 6). The shape she found enabled her to combine in a new way the issues and preoccupations of her earlier work, and at the same time to move further away from the use of autobiographical material. Byatt's enduring concern with moral goodness is implicit in her analysis of "possession": the novel looks at right and wrong ways to possess, in personal relationships and in learning. Understanding that romance is both a method of defamiliarization and, in Rachel Blau Du Plessis's words, "a trope for the sex-gender system" (ix), Byatt uses the form to explore continuity and discontinuity in women's lives over the two centuries. Her creation of a series of literary works purportedly by her two main nineteenth-century characters enables her to show, as well, both the process of demythologization and the power and attraction of myth (including, especially, myths about women). Metafictionally, her romance reflects upon its own methods and those of all fiction, particularly that which charts women's lives. It returns to the subject of "Precipice-Encurled": the imagination's manipulation of its historical material, of the "something else" that "proves good yet seems untrue," the invention that "makes fact alive." Within the romance framework, Byatt encloses a mix of other genres, among them mystery, detective story, academic satire, Victorian novel of ideas, contemporary feminist novel, epistolary fiction, diary, and fairy tale. The result is a book that constantly shifts its shape and that, despite being tightly plotted, remains open ended in structure. Byatt both uses and subverts romance; she uses the genre to suggest ways of transcending the assumptions of patriarchy. As Linda Anderson asserts, "Juxtaposing stories with other stories or opening up the potentiality for multiple stories … frees the woman writer from the coercive fictions of her culture that pass as truth" (vii). In *Possession*, Byatt uses both these techniques, freeing both herself and each of the women writers in her text and completing the work begun in *The Shadow of the Sun*.

In *Possession* there are two sets of characters, one in the Victorian period and one in the late twentieth century. Byatt's Victorian figures, both poets, are Randolph Henry Ash, well known in the twentieth century and believed to have enjoyed an exemplary, monogamous married life with his wife, Ellen, and Christabel LaMotte, a more obscure figure assumed to have lived in a lesbian relationship with the painter Blanche Glover. In the late twentieth century, there are two British scholars, Roland Michell, an Ash scholar, and Maud Bailey, a LaMotte scholar. Their predictable love story begins with texts, as Roland discovers drafts of a letter from Randolph to Christabel and Maud finds, hidden in a doll's bed at Seal Court where Christabel spent the last part of her life, what they—mistakenly—take to be the entire correspondence. Reinterpreting the now defamiliarized biographies, they uncover a Victorian love story that produced a daughter, Maia. An American Ash scholar, Mortimer Cropper, hears about the letters and embarks, with Ash's heir, on a scheme to rob Ash and Ellen's grave where, it is suspected, crucial documents are buried. Roland, Maud, and a group of friends and fellow scholars interrupt him, and the final letter from Christabel to Ash is found. The letter proves that Christabel is Maud's great-great-great-grandmother, not her great-great-great-great aunt as she had believed; Maia was brought up at Seal Court by Christabel's sister, Sophia Bailey, and her husband, and became Maud's great-great-grandmother. The story ends happily: Roland and Maud declare their love for each other, and Val, with whom Roland had been living in an increasingly unsatisfying partnership, is paired with a young lawyer, Euan, who, we hope, will also help Maud establish ownership of the papers and keep them in England.

The book has two epigraphs. The first is Nathaniel Hawthorne's distinction, in his preface to *The House of the Seven Gables*, between novel and romance. Insisting that romance is not lawless, that it must be faithful to "the truth of the human heart," Hawthorne asserts the prerogative of the writer of romance to "present that truth under circumstances, to a great extent, of the writer's own choosing or creation." The second is a passage from Robert Browning's monologue "Mr. Sludge, the Medium" in which Sludge defends the mendacity of poets, writers of "plain prose," and mediums like himself. What can any of them do, he asks, "without their helpful lies?" In *Possession*, both Byatt and her characters are engaged with the question of fictive truth as it relates to literature, criticism, biography, history, and moral experience.

In creating her two main Victorian characters, Byatt makes her own blend of fact and invention. Her male poet, Ash, is a version both of the historical Robert Browning and of Byatt's own earlier version of him, in "Precipice-Encurled." She gives Ash qualities that also marked the historical figure: intellectual curiosity, an appetite for actual and vicarious experience, and the human warmth and empathy that enabled him to speak ventriloquistically through the voices of many characters. Like Browning, Ash is interested in everything. Like Browning, Ash grapples with the central question of the work of the imagination: how invention can be true to reality in a way in which fact can never be—and, indeed, whether fact as such even exists. In *The Ring and the Book*, Browning showed his fascination with the biblical story of Elijah's resuscitation of a corpse (Byatt, "Robert Browning" 47); Ash, too, wonders whether his projection of life into his characters is comparable to Elijah's act (168). Other characters in *Possession* perceive Ash in ways that resemble Byatt's understanding of Browning. Beatrice Nest, the twentieth-century scholar who originally hoped to work on Ash but has been set to work instead on Ash's wife's journals, values Ash for his love poems. As a student, she was caught by their dramatization of "true conversation between men and women" (113). Similarly, Byatt, praising Browning's love poems, says that "he sees women as complex human beings, with their own minds and desires, and hopes for dialogue" ("Robert Browning" 29–30). When James Blackadder, the Scottish scholar who is head of the "Ash Factory," is forced by a television interview to condense his lifelong study of the poet into a short statement, he uses language close to that in Byatt's essay on Browning: "He understood the nineteenth-century loss of religious faith. He wrote about history—he understood history—he saw what the new ideas about development had done to the human idea of time" (400).

Ash is not Browning, however. Byatt gives Ash the same year (but not the same day) of death as Browning, and her footnote (445) crediting Swinburne with providing information about Ash's funeral, if checked, leads to a letter in which Swinburne declines the offer of tickets to Browning's funeral. Both poets write about Lazarus (as did Tennyson), but the ordinary objects that Ash's risen Lazarus notices with new intensity are, in Christabel's words, "the Goat's yellow barred Eye—the bread on the Platter with the scaly Fishes waiting for the oven" (166), not the parallel but different objects that Browning's Lazarus sees. Browning himself is referred to in *Possession*, although not by name, when Ellen Ash, struggling with her own religious doubts, quotes "the Poet" who made a character (Renan in the epilogue to *Dramatis Personae*) ask, "where may hide what came and loved our clay?" (223; qtd. in Byatt, "Robert Browning" 68). Ash writes a monologue for the Dutch scientist Jan Swammerdam; Byatt, in *Passions of the Mind*, compares Swammerdam's discovery of the microscope to Sludge's sense of the dreadful immensity of the very small (65), but Browning did not write about Swammerdam. Furthermore, Ash's interest in Norse myth is more reminiscent of William Morris than of Browning. Most crucially, in *Possession* Byatt counters the story of the Browning's married happiness with a tragic one. Married after a long courtship, Ellen is incapable of responding sexually, and the Ashes' long, celibate marriage is based, in Ellen's view, on his forbearance, her gratitude, and their deep mutual affection.

Christabel LaMotte, the poet with whom Ash has a brief, passionate love affair, is "an English version" of Emily Dickinson, "the greatest woman poet of all" in Byatt's opinion, but with a Breton background that gives her an un-English "sexual frankness" (qtd. in Wachtel, "A.S. Byatt" 80). The rest of Byatt's Victorian cast mix fact and invention in a different way. Crabb Robinson, in whose diary Roland finds the first clue that Ash knew Christabel, did, in February 1858, write an entry mentioning Coleridge, Wordsworth, and Lamb, and Byatt quotes it (24); the diary entries for June 1856, referring to Ash, and for June 1858, recording Ash's meeting with Christabel at one of Robinson's breakfast parties, are, of course, "helpful lies" invented by Byatt. The pallbearers at Ash's funeral include Lord Leighton and Hallam Tennyson, both historical figures, and an invented character, Sir Rowland Michaels; this last character's name, a playfully invented near homophone for Roland Michell, seems to foreshadow Roland's claim to a special relationship with Ash. The other Victorian characters, Ellen Ash, Blanche Glover, and Sabine de Kercoz, are pure fabrications, a fact that itself poignantly indicates the unseen lives and lost unknown potential of multitudes of women in history. In them Byatt again shows how fiction makes fact alive.

In the writings of her two Victorian poets, Byatt creates poetry and prose that are richly evocative of nineteenth-century writers but too distinctive to be dismissed as mere pastiche or parody, although they contain elements of both. Byatt has said that both these techniques are "ways of pointing to the fictiveness of fiction" ("People in Paper Houses" 176), and the poems written in Ash's and LaMotte's voices do this pointing in a special way. The forthright, urgent immediacy of speech in Ash's poems catches some of the qualities of Browning's monologues, although Byatt states that Tennyson also influenced the rhythms (Rothstein C22). In Christabel's poems, the interrupted and incomplete syntax, the dashes that indicate fragmented reality, refusing closure, and the persistent image of enclosed spaces recall Dickinson (who, like Christabel, saw enclosure as both imprisonment and opportunity for women). The last feature, also, suggests Christina Rossetti, identified by several reviewers as the most likely original for Christabel, although Byatt denies this link (Wachtel, "A.S. Byatt" 80). But both Byatt's poets have different interests from their models and use different forms and metaphors. They become creators in their own right, originals. When the Victorian models' voices are heard alongside theirs, the effect is what Byatt notes in George Eliot's reworking of German texts: "not parody, not pastiche, not plagiarism— but a good and greedy reading" ("People in Paper Houses" 167).

   Possession is metafiction, but it is also about "real people." In 1992, in one of the earliest attempts to categorize this novel, David Lodge placed it within his definition of "crossover" fiction, which uses "foregrounded intertextuality, the overt citation or simulation of older texts in a modern text" to combine metafiction and realism (208). Two years later, Frederick M. Holmes ("Historical Imagination") suggested that *Possession* is an example of postmodern historiographic metafiction as defined by Linda Hutcheon. In her *Poetics of Postmodernism,* Hutcheon places in this category "novels which are both intensely self-reflexive and yet paradoxically also lay claim to historical events and personages" (5). Responding to Brian McHale's statement that modernism is epistemological in its focus while postmodernism is ontological—as well as to definitions that would reverse the adjectives—Hutcheon argues for "both/and": "Historiographic metafiction asks both epistemological and ontological questions. How do we know the past (or the present)? What is the ontological status of that past? Of its documents? Of our narratives?" (50). In creating what McHale calls a "tension between ... two versions" of the past, the "official" and the "apocryphal," *Possession* "induces a form of ontological flicker between the two worlds" (McHale 90); the status of both versions is questioned by their juxtaposition. At the same time, Byatt blurs the lines between past and present, both by moving constantly between them, thus decentring both, and by making her twentieth-century characters repeat the experience of their predecessors. In acts of what Holmes calls "faith in the freedom of her own historical imagination" ("Historical Imagination" 332), Byatt also offers passages of conventional omniscient narration—Christabel and Ash in Yorkshire, Ellen and Ash in London, Ash and Maia in Lincolnshire—that provide the reader with information withheld from the twentieth-century sleuths. Combining realist and experimental techniques in these ways, *Possession* opens itself to many interpretive possibilities, as the critical commentaries of the nineties testify. (See Appendix 1.)

Byatt has observed that her twentieth-century characters are so "possessed" by contemporary theory, so constantly "asking themselves so many questions about whether their actions are real and whether what they say can be thought to be true, given that language always tells lies, that they become rather papery and are miserably aware of this." Part of the joke of *Possession*, she says, is that "the dead are actually much more alive and vital than the living" (Wachtel, "A.S. Byatt" 82–83). However, the very fact that Roland and Maud *are* painfully aware that language can be an imprisoning force makes them accessible to the reader, who shares their self-conscious preoccupation with "paperiness." The reader follows with sympathy as their entrepreneurial zeal for literary detection turns into personal involvement with their subjects, and as their scholarly collaboration becomes romantic attachment. Beatrice Nest, with her bemused sense of a mystery hidden in Ellen Ash's journals, and James Blackadder, with his dogged dedication to Ash's texts, are also appealingly believable. Even the two twentieth-century American scholars, Leonora Stern and Mortimer Cropper, whose depiction borders most closely on caricature, are capable of surprising us, although their critical texts are predictable and self-parodic. Inspired by French feminist theory, Leonora's analysis of Christabel's supposedly lesbian writings sees their landscapes as "a multitude of hidden holes and openings through which life-giving waters bubble and enter reciprocally" (244), while Cropper's somewhat prurient, apparently authoritative view of Ash's marriage proves to be far from reliable.

Byatt uses plot, in both the Victorian and the twentieth-century narratives, to question traditional women's plots. She does so in three closely interrelated ways: by showing, in both centuries, the destructive effects of the culture's construction of the female and, at the same time, the richness and variety of women's creative potential; by exploring the possibilities for women of working together in solidarity; and by imagining love relationships between men and women that begin and remain rooted in intellectual sharing, "passions of the mind."

In the nineteenth-century plot, Byatt uses four women—Christabel, Blanche, Sabine, and Ellen—to explore the restrictions of women's lives and their limited opportunities for self-expression. It is, of course, in Christabel that one most fully confronts the paradox of the idea of the woman of genius. As Rachel Blau DuPlessis observes, this idea "sets in motion [for bourgeois women] not only conventional notions of womanhood but also conventional romantic notions of the genius, the person apart, who, because unique and gifted, could be released from social ties and expectations" (84–85). Christabel's struggle with these contradictions is central to *Possession*. A sign of her conflicted position is her hiddenness in the text. Although for most readers she is the dominant character, we never enter her consciousness. Yet her voice is heard powerfully, in her letters to Ash, in her conversations with him in Yorkshire (where we are privy to his thoughts but not to hers), in her discussions with Sabine, and, most emphatically of all, in her writings.

The first reference to Christabel in the text is in Ash's first draft of a letter to her, and it refers to his recollection of her speech—"our extraordinary conversation," toned down to "our pleasant and unexpected conversation" (5), and finally becoming conventionally polite, as he refers to the "great pleasure" of talking to her (86). What attracted Ash so strongly on that first meeting, we learn later, was her speaking of "the power of verse and the Life of the Language" (172). In Christabel's own texts Byatt represents women's linguistic creativity in direct, unmediated form. In her interview with Eleanor Wachtel, Byatt says that it is in their poems that the reader encounters the two Victorians "most nakedly" ("A.S. Byatt" 81), and it is fitting that the first evidence of their physical love relationship appears in their texts. Roland and Maud, pursuing the mystery surrounding their subject, find identical passages, which they and other readers have until now interpreted differently, in Ash's *Ask to Embla* and Christabel's *Melusine*. Both poems contain the question "shall those founts / Which freely flowed to meet our thirsts, be sealed?" (237). Rereading these, Roland and Maud begin to realize that the anguished regret expressed by the speakers was experienced personally by both poets. Notwithstanding the passionate poignancy of Ash and Christabel's conversations in Yorkshire (which only the reader, of course, hears), the most moving moments of their relationship are contained in their texts.

In her letters to Ash, Christabel begins by denigrating her genius in the conventional terms of her culture and progresses, as she comes to trust him, to self-affirmation. In an early letter, she is the "dead Moon" reflecting Ash's brilliance. But also, already in this letter, she presents herself as an "honest craftswoman" like Arachne, the spinner (87). As their correspondence becomes more intimate, she discusses with him her intention to embark on the traditionally male form of the epic, although she again draws back in double-edged self-mockery: "how can a poor breathless woman with no *staying-power* and only a Lunar Learning confess such an ambition to the author of the *Ragnarök*?" (161). Soon after this, she tells Ash that she sent some of her poems to "a great Poet," asking him "Are these Poems? Have I—a Voice?" She recalls his lukewarm patriarchal response: the poems "would do well enough to give me an interest in life until I had—I quote him exactly—'sweeter and weightier responsibilities'" (180).[1] This recollection is immediately preceded by a passage that shows her perception of Ash's interest in her work as very different from "the usual response" of "oh, it is excellently done—*for a woman*. And then there are Subjects we may not treat—things we may not know." She proceeds to share with him her vacillation on the topic of women's abilities—"I do not say but that there must be—and *is*—some essential difference between the Scope and Power of men and our own limited consciousness and possibly weaker apprehension"—but follows the important word "possibly" with a forthright declaration that "the delimitations are at present, all *wrongly drawn*—We are not mere candleholders to virtuous thoughts ... we think and feel, aye and *read*—which seems not to shock *you* in us, in me" (180).

In her tales and poems, Christabel explores both the possibilities for women and the received opinions about them. One of her *Tales for Innocents*, read by Roland on his first meeting with Maud, begins as a new paradigm for the female quest. It tells of a queen who desired above all things a silent bird that "lived in the snowy mountains, nested only once, raised its gold and silver chick, sang once only, and then faded like snow in the lowlands." The second paragraph introduces the heroine, a shoemaker's daughter, a dreamer who, inefficient at ordinary tasks, and not beautiful like her two older sisters, has a desire of her own, to "go even a little way into the wild wood," where women's traditional work would not be required but where there "might well be a need of such things as she knew she had it in herself to perform" (51-52). This story, left unfinished by Byatt, suggests a plot in which a woman finds for another woman a desired object, and thus counters the familiar stories in which males perform difficult quests in return for women's favours. It is significant that all three—the shoemaker's daughter, the queen, and the bird—are mysterious, rare, and female; the story marginalizes males.

Another story of Christabel's, "The Glass Coffin," also resists the predictable ending of its original, one of the Grimms's tales. It begins as a familiar story about the rescue of a lady by a male, a little tailor. The lady, silenced and imprisoned by a magician because she refused to marry him, wishes instead to live with her twin brother and hunt with him in the woods. The tailor finds the sleeping woman and, with a glass key, releases her from her glass coffin. In a parodic moment, she recognizes him: "You must be the Prince" (63). But the tailor rejects the name of Prince and questions the prescribed ending. He offers instead a generous, common-sense revision of the old story: "Of course I will have you,... for you are my promised marvel.... Though why you should have me, simply because I opened the glass case, is less clear to me altogether, and when, and if, you are restored to your rightful place,... I trust you will feel free to reconsider the matter, and remain, if you will, alone and unwed" (66). Christabel adds mystification and complexity by asking the reader to consider "whether he spoke there with more gentleness or cunning, since the lady set such store on giving herself of her own free will," and instead of moving swiftly to the expected conclusion, she imagines the two "disputing, politely, the moral niceties of their interesting situation" (66). Their discussion is interrupted by the reappearance of the evil magician; vanquishing him, the tailor also releases the lady's beloved twin brother from the spell that had transformed him into a dog. The tale ends ambiguously: the tailor, the lady, and the brother live together, the twins occupy themselves with hunting in the "wild woods," and the "one thing... missing" from the happiness of the household is not, as one might expect, a child. Rather, it is work for the tailor, who now orders cloth and threads so that he can make for pleasure what he once made "for harsh necessity" (67), thus fulfilling the genre's expectation of a "happily ever after" ending but with a difference. Unlike her prototype, Snow White, who, as Sandra Gilbert and Susan Gubar point out, is freed from her first coffin only to be trapped by the male voice speaking from "her second glass coffin, the imprisoning mirror" (*Madwoman* 42), the princess in this story is liberated from the controlling voice of patriarchy. She is free to pursue her own choices, including that of chastity, which is suggested by her parallel with the huntress Diana. Despite its revisions of the source story, "The Glass Coffin" remains tied to its nineteenth-century context; Christabel imagines liberation for the woman but takes it for granted that male power is needed to bring this ending about. Although she acknowledges the story's "obvious Freudian imagery," which would interest Leonora Stern in the twentieth century, Byatt says that her own interest, like Christabel's, is in ways of breaking the "narrative structure" of the Grimms's tales (Todd, "Retrieval" 108). Nevertheless, Byatt makes Christabel slyly innovative in her ending. Although readers may assume with Ann Ashworth that "the ending is a happy wedding" ("Fairy Tales" 96), and although Byatt herself speaks of marriage as the outcome ("Ice, Snow, Glass" 157), the tale itself does not make this ending explicit, and in a commentary on the story, Byatt says that "the nineteenth-century and twentieth-century feminist note" in the story is "the sense that the expected marriage, the rescuing of heroine and house from captivity in glass, is a lesser thing than the freedom to walk in the Forest and to work" ("Fairy Stories").

Christabel uses a more self-conscious narrator in "The Threshold," which tells of three female figures offering three gifts to the questing male Childe. They appear as images of the sun, the world of growth; the moon, who, the knight thinks, knows his secret soul and who offers "The secret place / Where lovers meet"; and the shadow world of "Rest" (154). The Herb of Rest, or death, is what the Childe's suffering father had sent him to find: "And you know, and I know…, that he must always choose this last, and the leaden casket, for wisdom in all tales tells us this…. But let us have a moment's true sorrow for the silver blisses the Childe would have preferred, and the sunlit flowery earth which is my own secret preference, and then let us decorously follow as we must." By pausing before the inevitable conclusion to insert regret for the two lost choices, and by declaring that "one day we will write it otherwise," even allowing the Childe to refuse all three gifts and "live free of fate," the narrator opens up not only other plots for men and women—including ones not tied to female-male interaction—but also other parameters for narrative, ways of avoiding "the power of necessity in tales" (155).

Christabel's lyrics explore a wide range of female experience. One, expressing delight in domesticity, states, "I like things clean about me" (37). Another, enclosed in a letter to Ash, retells the story of Psyche, in love with Cupid and forced by the jealous Venus to sort a heap of grains and seeds; she is helped in her task by "Spinster Ants." Ignoring the love plot of the story, Christabel rewrites it as an allegory of females helping females, one that recalls the life of equality and shared labour she had with Blanche:

> The Ants toil for no Master
> Sufficient to their Need
> The daily commerce of the Nest
> The storage of their Seed
> They meet—and exchange Messages—

But none to none—bows down
They—like God's thoughts—speak each to each
Without—external—crown (162)

Women's ability to enjoy small spaces is suggested in a poem that begins
"All day snow fell" and that celebrates the prospect of "Delight" presented by an apparently female "Creature" inside the house (128). But
enclosure is also potentially dangerous: "hearts may tap like loaded
bombs /…And walls break outwards—with a rush—" (210). Like Dickinson, whom many of these lyrics recall (and like Sabine), Christabel presents women suffering from inactivity:

Men may be martyred
Any where
In desert, cathedral
Or Public Square.
In no Rush of Action
This is *our* doom
To Drag a Long Life out
In a Dark Room. (112)

On the other hand, "My subject is Spilt milk," written in Brittany, speaks
of the irreparable damage that action can do and encodes a reference to
Christabel's divided self, torn between Blanche and Ash:

This cannot be restored
This flow cannot redeem
This white's not wiped away
Though blanched we seem. (382)

Byatt has said that she needed Christabel to provide "a misleading clue"
about the fate of the child, and describes the lyric as "a feminist poem
at its deepest level" (Tredell 63). In it and its untitled counterpart, which
begins "Our Lady—bearing—Pain," Christabel is "actually inventing a
whole feminist religion" from her sense of exclusion from male-cen-
tred Christianity and her experience of woman's pain, which is "not part
of a redeeming icon" (qtd. in Tredell 64).

In this and other poems, the threats posed by desire are inscribed. In
The City of Is, Dahud's lover hears the "Ocean at the door" and foresees
death, despite his lover's reassurances (330-31). A version of the Rapunzel story, a poem beginning "The Thicket is Thorny," focuses on the

witch's malicious deception of Rapunzel by pretending to be the male lover while the lover himself watches helplessly. Another poem, the one that first attracted Maud to Christabel's work, sums up complexities of "freedom" for women. In this poem, the Cumaean Sibyl speaks about her bitter knowledge and her weariness of immortality:

> Desire is a dowsed fire
> True love a lie
> To a dusty shelf we aspire
> I crave to die. (54)

For the Sibyl, enclosure in the jar provides the safety that Christabel, writing to Ash, praises. For women, she tells him, the "Donjon" that confines them offers a kind of freedom that men "do not need to imagine" (137). But there is a price to be paid for this enclosed freedom. As Maud tersely summarizes, "The Sybil was safe in her jar, no one could touch her, she wanted to die" (54). Taken together, Christabel's lyrics grapple with the issues of innocence and experience, solitude and relationship, virginity and sexuality.

Christabel's most extensive meditation on the nature of the female is *The Fairy Melusine*. The figure of Melusine, Christabel tells Ash, contains "two aspects—an Unnatural Monster—and a most proud and loving and *handy* woman," who, the legend says, built castles and made fields grow (174). The long section provided from the poem begins, "And what was she, the Fairy Melusine?" (289)—a version of the question Christabel poses to Sabine: "Who knows what Melusine was in her freedom with no eyes on her?" (373). Here, the cousins are discussing the male construction of women as "double beings, enchantresses and demons or innocent angels." Christabel has just declared her intention to write a "Fairy Epic" that, as romance, would be free of the restraints of history and fact; romance, says Christabel, is "a proper form for women" because it provides a place "where women can be free to express their true natures ... women's two natures can be reconciled" (373). In *Melusine*, Byatt has Christabel address both the issue of male construction of femaleness and the question of woman-in-herself. The proem to the epic picks up where this conversation ends, following the questions about women's nature with reports about Melusine by various speakers: "Men say ... The old nurse says ..." (289). The narrator then, after evoking the "Mystery" that surrounds "our small safe place" (290), recalls John of Arras, the monk who wrote the original story, and finally, speaking openly as a woman telling a woman's story, associates Melusine with other figures—Medusa, Scylla, Hydra, the Sphinx—who suffer for being powerful and female: "…let the Power take a female form / And 'tis the Power is punished" (292). Returning to the original question—"what was she?"—the speaker asks for help from another empowered female, Mnemosyne, in order to tell the story once more. Book One then introduces the knight, Raimondin, on his mysterious, despairing journey. He hears Melusine singing and, seeing her, finds his whole being concentrated in that instant, "so that he was one thing" "Under the steady and essential gaze / Of this pale Creature in this quiet space" (297). Other fragments of the poem are presented earlier in the text, so that at the moment of meeting, the outcome—the suffering of both Raimondin and Melusine that results from his breaking her prohibition and spying on her while she is bathing—is already known. We have already read the description of Melusine as a sea creature below the waist "of argent scale and slate-blue coiling fin" (121) and, at the point where Christabel's text merges with Ash's, have already heard Raimondin's desperate question on confessing his betrayal: "Is there no remedy?…shall those founts…be sealed?" (237). The identification of author and heroine is foreshadowed in another passage that describes Melusine's domain. Its language, Roland and Maud recognize, derives from Christabel's Yorkshire idyll with Ash; there is even a punning reference to "ash-saplings" (266). In her last letter to Ash (which he never reads), Christabel completes the story. She writes that she has become her heroine, who in the legend is transformed into a dragon flying about the battlements of the castle she has built. Christabel, in her brother-in-law's house, has, she says, "so to speak flown about and about… crying on the wind of my need to see and feed and comfort my child" (501). *The Fairy Melusine*, Maud tells Roland, was rewritten at least eight times, a fact that suggests that Christabel was never satisfied with her answer to her own question about the "true" nature of women. For her, as the versions of female experience in the tales and lyrics also indicate, female subjectivity is hidden, diverse, in process, constantly reconstituting itself, and always vulnerable to the male gaze that attempts to fix it. Most important is the creativity—in singing, in building, in making a private space—that Christabel's rewriting of Melusine's story stresses. In *Melusine* (as in *The Threshold*), Christabel makes the sun female, rejecting the old association of nature and woman as passive recipients of warmth and light from a male source. In *Melusine* the sun is "mother" (293), and Raimondin reflects Melusine's light:

... his face took the brightness of her glance
As dusty heather takes the tumbling rays
Of the sun's countenance and shines them back. (298)

What Christabel could not yet claim for herself she later boldly achieves for her heroine.[2] "Christabel's feminism in the nineteenth century, which was partly instinctive, is a wonderful thing," says Byatt (Tredell 60).

The figures and images through which Christabel constructs her personal identity represent the Victorian and modern dilemmas of the woman artist. To Ash, Christabel presents herself as Arachne, the spider who *"must spin out"* her "huge Burden of Silk"; "the silk is her life, her home, her safety—her food and drink too" (180), and as the egg in her riddle, a crystal casket enclosing a gold cushion, "a perfect O, a living Stone, doorless and windowless" (137). Both of these images underline her need for solitude to produce her art, and for something else—security from the penetrating male gaze. As she and Ash come closer to their decision to go away together, she writes to him about the "injustice" of the fact that "I require my freedom—from *you*—who respect it so fully," inserting at this point an account of her pact with Blanche to renounce "the outside World—and the usual female Hopes" in order "to *make good things*." She concludes by relating herself to the Lady of Shalott, who chose "to watch diligently the bright colours of her Web—to ply an industrious shuttle ... to close the Shutters, and the Peepholes too" (186–87). After she and Ash have met in Richmond Park, her images change to those of cataclysmic flood and fire, and to a juxtaposition of the paradoxical connotations of protection and destruction that Ash's name contains: "Ash the sheltering World-Tree, Ash the deadly Rain / So Dust to Dust and Ash to Ash again" (194). "I cannot let you burn me up" (194), she exclaims. Yet what follows immediately is an unconscious slip, a shift from "I should" to "I shall," which acknowledges female desire and makes the consummation a *fait accompli*: "I shall go up—like Straw on a Dry Day" (195). Near the end of her life, in her last letter to Ash, the problem of the creative woman is still there for Christabel. She regrets her loss of solitude: "I would rather have lived alone.... But since that might not be—and is granted to almost none—I thank God for you—if there *must* be a Dragon—that He was You" (503). From this perspective the story ends, like its earlier segment about Blanche, as a failed experiment. But this is not the whole story; Christabel says also, at the end of her life, that without Ash she would neither have had the experience of motherhood nor have written *Melusine*: "I owe you Melusine and Maia both" (501). Thus, years later, she reaches her own answer to Ash's question, "Could the Lady of Shalott have written *Melusine* in her barred and moated Tower?" (188). And her image of Ash is not simple either: he is the dragon in *Samson Agonistes*, "assailant" on the "tame villatic fowl." But she also imagines herself and Ash together becoming Milton's Phoenix, "that self-begotten bird ... that no second knows nor third" (502). In her portrait of Christabel, Byatt poignantly explores the ambiguities of freedom for creative women, and does so in a way that speaks to twentieth-century women who, recognizing Christabel as a victim of Victorian repression and stereotyping, also see her, with Blanche and Sabine, as affirming qualities of strength, insight, and versatility that persist throughout the generations.

Blanche Glover, Christabel's companion, shows women's longing to live an autonomous, self-sufficient life without dependence on men. Like the other women artists, Christabel's cousin Sabine de Kercoz and Christabel herself, Blanche "encodes," in Du Plessis's words, "the conflict between any empowered woman and the barriers to her achievement" (84). She and Christabel tried to live an experiment, in a harmonious, non-hierarchical partnership where each would pursue her own creative impulse and each would do her share of the household's work. Twentieth-century LaMotte scholars label their relationship lesbian, but Byatt's text is not explicit about this. In 1860, after Christabel, pregnant with Ash's child, has left their house, Bethany (named for that of the biblical family of Mary, Martha, and their brother Lazarus), to take refuge in Brittany, Blanche drowns herself. Her suicide note tersely lists her reasons: "First, poverty.... Second, and maybe more reprehensibly, pride. I cannot again demean myself to enter anyone's house as a *governess*.... I would rather not live than be a slave." The third, "failure of ideals," comes to the heart of the issue: "I have tried, initially with MISS LAMOTTE, and also alone—to live according to certain beliefs about the possibility, for independent single women, of living useful and fully human lives, in each other's company, and without recourse to help from the outside world, or men" (307). They failed, she thinks, both because society "fiercely" opposed their radical attempt and because they themselves lacked the necessary strength. The collapse of Blanche's life after Christabel's flight is symbolized by the disappearance of her large canvasses. She painted Christabel as her namesake in Coleridge's poem, "before Sir Leoline" (308) (presumably in supplication, imploring her father to send away the temptress Geraldine), and Merlin and Vivien, portraying, in Christabel's words, "the moment of triumph" when Vivien receives Merlin's power (354). Both paintings thus depicted a female-male power struggle. Blanche gave both of them to Christabel, and her note stipulated that she not dispose of them but provide for them after her own death "as I myself would have." She also left her other works in Christabel's hands in the hope that in time "a taste may be created and a spirit may prevail where their true worth may be assessed" (308). Twentieth-century scholars have been unable to find the paintings—although Maud and Leonora speculate that they may be still "mouldering" at Seal Court—and they become one of the unsolved mysteries in *Possession*. They are more than this; their history is an allegory of the fate of women's art. When Maud and Leonora try to imagine them they can do so only in terms of paintings by males, Albrecht Dürer and Henri Fantin-Latour, although Leonora, as a good feminist, insists that they would not be "derivative" (312). Some smaller, more conventionally feminine flower paintings by Blanche were to be used, according to her instructions, to pay for her funeral. All that is known to survive of her art is the series of woodcuts that illustrate Christabel's tales. When Maud and Roland look at these, they see the artist's sensitivity to situations of terror and threat. They particularly notice Blanche's engraving of a hedgehog child, which shows, not surprisingly, her sympathy for the hybrid-misfit. (Providing a contrast to the obscurity of Blanche's art, the dust jacket of the hardcover edition of *Possession*, displaying the well-known version of the Merlin and Vivien story by Edward Burne-Jones, is a silent reminder that male art survives.) Unlike Christabel's poems, which find their proper reader in Maud, Blanche's canvasses remain hidden in the twentieth century.

Very different from Blanche, but sharing her commitment to artistic expression, is Christabel's young Breton cousin, Sabine. Motherless from infancy, living in isolation with her scholarly father, Raoul, and, although without real power, nominal mistress of his household since her girlhood, she is the creative female controlled by patriarchy. In young adulthood, she writes in her journal, "whenever I think too rebelliously, or ride too fast," she feels the pressure of her father's anger and love as "gentle tugs" on the bond that, like the linen rope that attached her to his desk as a toddler, still holds her to him (341). As an adult, her sense of their bond is so strong that it leads her to fantasies of incest; at the same time she knows that her father "has no knowledge of what I fear. Or desire" (341). Sabine understands that women's tragedy is "*inaction*" (340); as a child she had "played at being Sir Lancelot, before I learned I was only a woman and must content myself with being Elaine aux Mains Blanches, who did nothing but suffer and complain and die" (339). Preoccupied with the idea of female power, she writes about the Princess Dahud, the "good sorceress," who represents for her "our desire for freedom, for autonomy, for our own proper passion" (349). Dahud is thus, for Sabine, an alternative to the figures of powerless, suffering women who predominate in

Breton culture. Dahud's story contrasts with the fate of the girl who, stumbling in the May Day dance, is physically attacked by the other dancers. (Christabel, hearing about this custom, identifies the girl as the Fallen Woman.)

Sabine also relates "Gode's Story," told every year by the family's female servant as part of the November storytelling. In this traditional Breton tale, the miller's daughter is, it seems—for the tale is filled with indirection and innuendo—made pregnant by a sailor, and her dead (murdered?) child appears as a "little thing dancing" (359) that leads the mother over the edge of the cliff to her death. The sailor, frustrated by the girl's mysterious behaviour and ignorant of her pregnancy, marries another woman. Now, compelled by the power of the mother's language to hear the dancing feet, he sees the child and in time wastes away and dies. The story reasserts the tie between sexuality and death while exploring the form of fairy tales that cross the threshold between natural and supernatural. It also, as Byatt points out ("Fairy Stories"), reiterates an old motif in nineteenth-century literature. Told in the presence of the pregnant Christabel, "Gode's Story" inscribes the entrapment of women throughout history. In real life, Sabine recognizes a counterpart of these women, the girl who, pregnant out of wedlock, was mistreated by nuns at her convent refuge, lost her child, and died young. As Christabel's body swells with her pregnancy, Sabine identifies her as potentially another such figure.

When Christabel arrives in Brittany, Sabine, knowing that her cousin is "both an acknowledged ... writer ... and a woman," sees her as "a sign of hope, a leader, for all of us" (336). She shows her work to Christabel, who reads it as a "*good* reader," with respect and understanding (350). Christabel's own poem about Dahud, *The City of Is*, is also about the complexity of women's power, and Christabel's interpretation of the tale of Merlin and Vivien, told by Sabine's father every November, parallels Sabine's view of Dahud, so that both become feminist readings of male stories. When Raoul says that Vivien represents "fear of Woman ... the sleep of reason under the rule of ... desire, intuition, imagination" (354), Christabel offers a "different" interpretation (he calls it "perverse"): that Vivien's is "a tale of female emulation of male power—she wanted not him but his magic—until she found that magic served only to enslave *him*" (354). Similarly, Sabine, resisting the version of the story of Dahud given by the editor of one of her father's books, who wrote that it is "the terror of the passion of the senses, let loose in women," challenges this phallocentric reading that relegates women to the position of the feared Other. "Why should desire and the senses be so terrifying in women?"

asks Sabine. "Who is this author, to say that these are the fears of man, by which he means the whole human race? He makes us witches, outcasts, *sorcières*, monsters ..." (349). Despite Sabine's partial comprehension of Christabel's dilemma—she perceives that her cousin deals with her pregnancy by splitting herself into a physical self and a "conscience" and "public self" (372), in contradiction of Christabel's earlier insistence to Sabine that body and soul cannot be separated—she is unable to help her. Christabel gives birth in secret, returning to England soon afterward. Sabine's journal breaks off at this point, and when Ariane Le Minier, her twentieth-century editor, summarizes the rest of her story, it is the familiar one of marriage "after a prolonged battle with her father" (380), who wished to keep her with him, and (repeating her mother's story) an early death in childbirth. In her work, however, Sabine achieved her goal of writing "the history of the feelings of a woman" (348): she produced several novels and depicted in one, *La deuxième Dahud*, a heroine whom Ariane describes as powerful, mesmeric, and independent.

The fourth Victorian woman in *Possession*, Ellen Ash, displays the hidden, thwarted energies of women in a different form. Her journal, with its "carefully edited, ... carefully *strained*" version (461) of her life with Ash, is the basis of divergent twentieth-century views of her life and personality.[3] To Blackadder she is simply "*dull*"; to feminist scholars in the next generation she is, like Dorothy Wordsworth, a repressed genius, one of "the female companions of the great," in Blackadder's words, "raging with rebellion and pain and untapped talent" (31). Feminists like Leonora Stern are intrigued by Ellen's journal's silence on the subject of sex. Beatrice Nest, having begun by seeing Ellen as a dutiful wife, has become aware of a mystery that the journals protect, and now thinks that Ellen wrote "to baffle"; there are, she suggests to Maud, "things flittering and flickering behind all that solid ... *panelling*" (220). Through the journals, Ellen gradually reveals herself. We read of her wish, as a young girl, to be "a Poet and a Poem"—to play both the conventional male and female roles—and of her finding, at the age of sixty, "a kind of creeping insidious vigour" (122) that she has no way of using productively. Her perceptiveness as a critical reader is shown in her comments on *Melusine*, which respond to the mobility of the poem's world and to the terrible tragic power of its heroine, as well as to the parallels between Melusine and Coleridge's Geraldine, with her blue-veined feet and white skin (121, 296). Ellen praises Christabel's avoidance of "softly gloved lady-like *patting* of the reader's sensibility" (120). Later, with Ellen's perception of the beauty of Christabel's alter ego already established, we discover that when she read the poem, she had known for years of the affair between Ash and Christabel. As a Victorian woman, Ellen's potential as a "Poet" remains unknown—that is precisely Byatt's point—but her ability as a reader does more than hint at its existence.

In her sense of self-division, Ellen stands for many women in both centuries. On the one hand, she has been made into a "Poem," or, in an early love letter from Ash, objectified as a "picture," a girl in a white dress (460). This image, after she is told by Blanche of her husband's affair, turns on itself to become a terrifying combination of Christabel's imprisoned lady and her Sibyl enclosed in the jar. Ellen sees herself as a Snow White "suspended ... in the glass casket" waiting, not for the prince's kiss, but for sleep (232). Her journal contains flashes of resentment of male freedom: she sees the contrast (even before Blanche's revelation) between the "delightful free forces" that surround Ash in Yorkshire and the heaviness of London (227). Her need for activity and self-assertion is grotesquely played out in her chess games with the clergyman Herbert Baulk, about which she acidly comments, "He was pleased to tell me that I played very well for a lady—I was content to accept this, since I won handsomely" (227). Her dreams, however, show her sense of the real state of things; there, Baulk unfairly controls her queen's moves, and on waking she formulates the paradox that "in chess the female may make the large runs and cross freely in all ways—in life it is much otherwise" (228).

Although, as she admits, she has in some ways lived a lie in her unconsummated marriage, Ellen has a devotion to truth, which she images in terms of the geologist Charles Lyell's description of crystals below the earth's surface. "I keep faith with the fire and the crystals," she thinks: "I do not pretend that the habitable surface is *all* and so I am not a destroyer nor cast into outer darkness" (458). Like Christabel, she uses her intelligence to ponder questions of religion. She accepts that Noah's flood may convey symbolic not literal truth, but, like Christabel, she finds the idea that the New Testament narrative may be only an "invention" a "threatening" one. She resents Baulk's patronizing reassurance that she "should not trouble my intellect with questions which my intuition (which he qualifies as womanly, virtuous, pure and so on and so on) can distinguish to be vain" (223). Although she feels compelled to ask Baulk's advice in dealing with her pregnant unmarried servant, Bertha, she also sees that in agreeing to send Bertha to a workhouse for "fallen women" she has "done wrong" to a fellow woman (231). To avoid the workhouse, Bertha runs away, after voicing her helplessness by repeating, "What can I do?... It all continues on whatever I will" (226), and disappears from the text as so many of her counterparts disappeared from history.

Ellen's journals, in Beatrice's keeping, are available for Byatt's twentieth-century characters to read, but only the reader of *Possession* is privy to facts that come closer to the truth of Ellen's life. We share her understanding that silence (both about her husband's love affair and about her sexless marriage) is at the heart of her marriage. We are given at least a partial explanation (besides the cultural one) for her terror of sex (made vividly explicit in a stream-of-consciousness passage), through the narrator's comment that "A young girl of twenty-four should not be made to wait for marriage until she is thirty-four and her flowering long over" (460). We know that although she does read and destroy Ash's never-posted letter to Christabel, which reveals that he knew that Christabel bore him a child, she preserves Christabel's last letter to Ash, unopened, and buries it with her husband, together with the plait of hair he had kept in his watch, the hair bracelet she had woven of her own hair and Ash's, and the love letters exchanged between Ash and herself. She does this so that these things will have "a *sort of duration*," and, if they are dug up and read, so that "justice will ... (perhaps) be done to *her* when I am not here to see it" (462). By these actions Ellen keeps her pact with the crystals, and, by ensuring the survival of Christabel's letter about Maia's birth and adoption, she gives Maud her heritage. She thus achieves both authority in her own story and authorship in the stories of others.

The twentieth-century women in *Possession* enjoy more mobility and freedom of vocation than their nineteenth-century counterparts, but Byatt shows them still bound by both inherited and modern constraints. Beatrice, who stands between Ellen's world and Maud's, is a woman academic who has been directed to work on Ellen by her forceful male professor, Bengtsson. Bengtsson took for granted that, as a woman, Beatrice would find editing Ellen's journals "a suitable undertaking" (114). Taught in the 1940s to look for "Influences and Irony" (115) in literature, she finds none in Ellen's writing, and her work, documenting Ellen's domestic life, is outdated before it is completed. Confiding in Maud, she describes her capitulation, as a "dependent and excluded" person in a male preserve—"*They* said it would be better to—to do this task which presented itself so to speak and seemed appropriate to my—my sex"—and she glimpses the lost possibility of female self-assertion: "A good feminist in *those* days ... would have insisted on being allowed to work on the Ask and Embla poems." Maud's challenging "Being allowed?" leads Beatrice to revise her words to "On *working* on" (220)—and to an angry outburst in which she contrasts Maud's apparent equality with males with her own generation's experience of isolation, of being turned into witches (in eerie repetition of Christabel's self-description) and made the subject of "*witch hunts*" (221). Nevertheless, Beatrice attains real understanding of her subject. With surprising decisiveness, she acts "on behalf of" (438) Ellen when she suspects Cropper of planning to rob the grave, and thus assists Ellen in putting the documents into Maud's possession.

Val, in the next generation, suffers in another way from male control of the academy. Her graduating essay on Ash is "discounted" because the examiners assume that because she lives with Roland, it is "largely" by him (13)—an ironic assessment, for Val's reading of the love poems conflicts with Roland's (and with Beatrice's); she views them as being about narcissism, "the poet addressing his Anima" (13). Her story is a familiar one. She (often grudgingly) encourages and facilitates Roland's work, and splits herself in two—a smartly dressed breadwinner working at jobs she dislikes, and a shabby, depressed, increasingly silent partner at home in their basement flat. Roland, tired of their life together but feeling affection and concern for her—in Byatt's words, a "nice man" (Wachtel, "A.S. Byatt" 87), not an intentional exploiter—is unable to help her, and she is rescued and transported to a happier life by the sunny, wealthy lawyer Euan McIntyre.

More fortunate, in her professional and, ultimately, in her personal life, is Maud. Nevertheless, she faces a twentieth-century version of Christabel's dilemma. Like the poet she discovers to be her ancestor, Maud lives in tension between her need for solitude to do her work and a half-admitted longing for relationship. An unquestioned academic success as director of the Women's Resource Centre at Lincoln University, and possessing a remote, apparently self-contained beauty, she appears to men to be "icily regular, splendidly null," like her namesake in Tennyson's poem. She works, appropriately, in a glass tower that bears Tennyson's name and, as a self-protective gesture, keeps her strangely beautiful golden hair hidden. As a self-conscious post-Freudian postmodernist, she ruefully acknowledges to Beatrice that contemporary scholars "question everything except the centrality of sexuality" (222), and finds both pleasant and unpleasant the Lacanian theory that selfhood is but "a matrix for a susurration of texts and codes" (251). She is drawn nostalgically to the Victorians because, as she tells Roland, "they valued themselves. Once, they knew God valued them. Then they began to think there was no God, only blind forces. So they valued themselves, they loved themselves and attended to their natures—" (254). Becoming increasingly aware of the complexity of the Victorian poets, she sees the reductiveness of Cropper's biography of Ash. It is, she thinks, "a peculiarly vicious version of reverse hagiography; the desire to cut his subject down to size" (250). Equipped with this insight, she is ready, with Roland (who has arrived, simultaneously, at a similar dissatisfaction with Leonora's work on Christabel) to confront the relationship they uncover. And her friendship with Roland, which involves collaboration in the study of their Victorian predecessors, offers her the opportunity to move into a loving relationship that, since it acknowledges its existence within the postmodern context, can encompass other dimensions.

Byatt shows the reductive, cramping construction of women in two periods of history, but she also shows women's potential for creative self-assertion and empowerment, available especially when women work together. In both centuries, communal action among women characters is a valued resource. Reviewers, as well as Byatt herself, have remarked on the vividness and vitality of the Victorians as compared with the twentieth-century characters, and it is, moreover, disturbing to some readers that none of the contemporary women engage in creative activity. In their attempts at solidarity and mutual encouragement, however, it is the twentieth-century women who have the greatest success. Although Blanche and Christabel's experiment was made possible by a foremother, Christabel's aunt, they cannot maintain the pattern of women helping women. Blanche's possessiveness and jealousy and what appears to be lack of trust on both their parts destroy what they have made. Ellen cannot help Bertha, although she believes that she has at least been kinder than women from the previous generation; she remembers her own mother beating their servant. Sabine and Christabel, who empathize and encourage each other as women and as writers, cannot do more than this, and their relationship ends with Christabel's return to England. In contrast, the twentieth-century characters are more successful in nurturing each other and therefore illustrate a more optimistic paradigm for the future of women. Joan Bailey, with her appreciation for her husband's concern with "the history of things" (78), persuades him to give Maud and Ash access to the letters they find. In return, Maud hopes to be able to buy her disabled benefactress (whose immobility is a physical image of the inactivity and dependence endured by women) an electric wheelchair. Ariane Le Minier, the French feminist scholar, shares Sabine's journal with Maud and Leonora, following the "feminist principle, co-operation" (334). Together, the women work to uncover the loves and work of their foremothers. Leonora, whose bisexual private life is as comically complex as her approach to women's texts is disconcertingly simple, has a generous spirit, which shows itself in the hilarious scene in which she and Blackadder are interviewed (in a three-minute segment of *Events in Depth*) by the bewildered television presenter Shushila Patel. Leonora surprises Shushila by agreeing with Blackadder that the newly discovered Ash–LaMotte correspondence should remain in England: "The days of cultural imperialism are over, I'm glad to say" (404). Maud's intellectual, if wary, sharing with Leonora survives Maud's rejection of Leonora's sexual advance. Beatrice turns to Maud for help in thwarting Cropper's scheme, and Maud has reached a better understanding of Beatrice's subject, Ellen: she has seen that Ellen's journals do not "make a whole picture" (232) and why Beatrice called them baffling. Maud is the "discerning reader" for whom, Christabel said in her last letter, *Melusine* was waiting (501). Meanwhile, in France, Ariane will edit and make available Sabine's novels. Together, the women arrive at a sense of kinship with their predecessors, and at a recognition that they are all, as Leonora says, sisters. In this respect, *Possession* incorporates some aspects of the subgenre of fiction proposed by Sandra Zagarell as particularly appropriate for women's stories, the "narrative of community" (499), which resists the teleological, goal-oriented plot and the notion of separate selves. In *Feminine Fictions*, Patricia Waugh, too, praises novels by women that stress collectivity rather than reinforcing the idea of separateness, and declare that "freedom, harmony, human dignity, and love lie not in the realization of any 'essence' of the human individual but in the relationships with others which construct our *social* identity" (209). It is not part of Byatt's intention to go as far in breaking down individual subjectivity as the authors cited by Waugh: Joanna Russ, Angela Carter, and Brigid Brophy. Part of Byatt's project is to explore the area where some form of autonomous selfhood may still be posited. However, the shadowy presence of the framework suggested by Zagarell and Waugh further compounds the multiplicity of the plots of *Possession*, at the same time as it demonstrates the novel's openness to many critical paradigms.

The heterosexual love plots of *Possession* transform the plot of traditional romance in two ways. First, the two main relationships are rooted in shared intellectual concerns, and the two males must, in order to be deserving lovers, cross over into female territory to meet the women on equal terms. Second, the twentieth-century partners enter into a type of new romance within a shared postmodern consciousness that views love itself as a "suspect ideological construct" (267) and the self as "a discontinuous machinery and electrical message-network of various desires, ideological beliefs and responses, language-forms and hormones and pheromones" (424), developments that have their roots in nineteenth-century skepticism. Ash already confronts the mechanistic explanation: love may be, he suggests, no more than the "kick galvanic"; "Are we automata / Or Angel-kin?" (273). Both pairs of lovers live in a world that demystifies romance.

For Ash and Christabel, language is both the object and the origin of love. In the final version of his first letter to Christabel, Ash speaks of his wish to discuss with her "Dante and Shakespeare and Wordsworth and Coleridge and Goethe and Schiller and Webster and Ford and Sir Thomas Browne" (86). As their friendship progresses through their correspondence, he goes further: he feels himself to be speaking to her as he "might speak" to "all those who most possess my thoughts," and again lists male writers, Shakespeare, Browne, Donne, and Keats (177). At this point, still before a second meeting has taken place between them, he is scrupulously aware that, in imagining such conversations, he has been "unpardonably lending you, who are alive, my voice" and that he, a writer of monologues, must now try to "construct a Dialogue" (107). Christabel is his best reader, and he in turn reads her with understanding; he is ready to revise his list of writers to include women. While Christabel is contemplating her "Fairy Project," he encourages her. He takes for granted that women can aspire to the epic form as well as to the lyric, which the culture grudgingly allows them. Christabel, he sees, is able to embrace the contradictory aspects, the demonic and the earthly, of her heroine. For the first time, he says, he writes a poem —Swammerdam—with a specific reader, Christabel, in mind. And after they have become each other's text in another sense, he shows his awareness that Christabel is Melusine: in their first sexual embrace he thinks of "holding Proteus" (283), and in Ask to Embla, his hero, the first man, Ask (the ash tree), praises Embla, the first woman, for being "ever-constant in ... changefulness" like the current in a river: "You ... are the force / That moves and holds the form" (262). As the hero of new romance, Ash must face the issue Ellen also recognized as her own: can a woman both inspire art and be an artist? Christabel is becoming "a sort of Muse" to him, he writes, and he anticipates her reply: "Well, you will say, you are too busy writing the poetry itself, to require employment as a Muse. I had not thought the two were incompatible—indeed they might even be thought to be complementary" (188). Years before meeting Christabel, he had already prefigured her vision of female creativity by portraying the sun as female, creating light, and presenting Ask and Embla's first sight of each other as mutual, not one-sided, reflection:

> ... he saw that she
> Was like himself, yet other; then she saw
> His smiling face, and by it, knew her own— (242)

As Byatt observes, her two Victorian poets destroyed "the old Nous-Hyle creation myths without even shouting about it" (Introduction, *Shadow* xv).

After their affair, Ash's *Garden of Proserpina* inscribes equality between lovers. Even his "Mummy Possest," described by Maud as "that nasty anti-feminist poem" (42), shows, besides the obvious personal anger at the mediums' trickery, some sympathy for the women who, powerless in the "cold" Victorian world of "objects Reason rules," turn to the "reversed world" of spiritualism:

> Here we have Power, here the Irrational,
> The Intuition of the Unseen Powers
> Speaks to our women's nerves. (410)

At the same time, the poem shows the poet's own complicity with the mediums' ventriloquism. Early in their correspondence, Ash proves himself as a worthy lover of Christabel by tearing up a first version of a letter that offered, in response to her expression of religious doubts, a conventional response like that which Baulk gave to Ellen. In this rejected text, Ash says, he "wrote, what may not be nonsense, that women's minds, more intuitive and purer and less beset with torsions and stresses than those of mere males—may hold on to truths securely that we men may lose by much questioning" (163). Despite his willingness to admit that the conventional view may have some validity, he knows that it will not satisfy Christabel: "you would not be best pleased to be exempted from argument by an appeal to your superior Intuition ..." (164). Instead, he addresses her as an equal, answering her urgent question about the truth of the Gospels—"Tell me—He Lives—for you" (167)—with his speculations about the truth of fact and of myth and about the poetic imagination. Again, she is an exception, unique in his experience. How unusual their conversation is for him is signalled by his automatic use of the masculine pronoun: "I have never before been tempted to discuss the intricacies of my own writing—or his own—with any other poet ... but with you I felt from the first that it must be the true things or nothing—there was no middle way" (177). His feeling of kinship with Christabel, that when they write to each other they are "in touch, that is, blessed" (196), is deepened by their sexual relationship. Yet in his last, unposted letter, which implores her to tell him the fate of their child, it is their intimacy of mind that he mourns: "remember that we heard each other's thoughts, so quick, so quick...." In this letter, too, he recognizes "the injustice of the different fates of men and women" (456).

Despite his respect for Christabel's equality and for her need, as an artist and as a woman, to be free, Ash cannot both love her and leave her with her liberty. He is aware during their correspondence that they are contained within a plot that imposes its own conventions, but he persuades Christabel that they can find "a small space, for a limited time—in which to marvel that we have found each other" (193); he sees the exercise of freedom as "cannily and wisely and with grace—to move inside what space confines" (200). The force of necessity, which preoccupies both of them at the time of their affair, prevails, and Christabel becomes, as Blackadder and Leonora agree, a stereotype, "a Fallen Woman and Unmarried Mother" (426). Christabel's reading of their situation, that safety and freedom are mutually exclusive, is the true one. When Ash assures her, "You are safe with me," she replies, "I am not at all safe, with you. But I have no desire to be elsewhere" (284).

Through Ash, Byatt explores the possibility of being a male sympathetic to feminism in the nineteenth century. He tells Christabel that before they met he had seen "the painfulness, the *waste*, of the common restrictions" that women endure (185). In his marriage he has shared his intellectual interests with Ellen, but he has not been able to free her for physical love. Still, as he lies dying, husband and wife agree that they have been happy, "saying little, looking at the same things, together" (448). In his love for Christabel he has failed, in a different way, to facilitate her freedom. But in the attempt he becomes a new kind of romantic hero.

In making Roland another respectful crosser of boundaries, Byatt invites the reader to compare him with his male contemporaries, just as we compare Ash, in his century, with the unnamed male poet who patronized Christabel, with Raoul de Kercoz, and with Herbert Baulk. Roland's contemporaries include Cropper, who has an unspecified sexual perversion, who confuses scholarship with physical possession, and whose slippers, embroidered with a head of Mnemosyne, are emblematic of his method of appropriating what is not rightfully his. Much more admirable is Blackadder, who, by contrast, is capable not only of disinterested scholarship but of the personal growth needed to begin an improbable friendship—perhaps even a love affair—with Leonora. Roland's rival for Maud's favours is Fergus Wolff. Like Fenris Wolf, the devourer of Odin in Norse mythology, Fergus is predatory. He is described in vulpine terms, as "rapid," with a "voracious smile" and a "long mouth terribly full of strong white teeth" (32). Maud's memory of her sexual encounter with Fergus is of "a huge, unmade, stained and rumpled bed," with sheets "like the surface of whipped egg-white" (56)—an image very different from Christabel's unbroken egg and from the chaste white bed that Roland and Maud find is for both of them an image of longed-for privacy and solitude. Fergus is Roland's opposite: he is an academic and sexual opportunist, becoming a follower of Lacan and Foucault at the right moment, and later giving an ostensibly feminist paper (whose title, "The Potent Castrato: the phallogocentric structuration of Balzac's hermaphrodite hero/ines" [57], nicely parodies late-twentieth-century academic discourse) at a conference on Gender and the Autonomous Text. An aggressive crosser of gender lines, he is, unlike Roland, an appropriator of, not a sympathizer with, feminism. Roland's closest counterpart is Euan, who, speaking to Val, revises his own masculine reassurance about their prospects for happiness from "That depends on me" to "On me too, that is" (417). Like Roland, he hopes for an equal relationship; however, what he and Val can achieve is only glimpsed by the reader.

As Roland and Maud move through their romance and, simultaneously, uncover more of the love story of their subjects, they are aware, often uncomfortably, of the parallels between their relationship and that of the two Victorians. The reader identifies more, as we see Roland as the modern representative of the tailor who freed the lady from her glass coffin. Like Ash and Christabel, Roland and Maud begin with a shared intellectual passion that grows from initial wariness to mutual confidence. Both Ash and Roland already have the responsibility of caring for another woman when the new love stories begin. Retracing their counterparts' steps, Roland and Maud discover, as had Ash and Christabel, that they walk well together. Even when they try to "get out of their story" (268) by taking a holiday from their research to visit Boggle Hole, which does not appear in Ash's biography, the Victorian lovers have, we find, gone there before them and for the same reason—they liked the name. When Christabel's last letter is retrieved and read, Maud is overwhelmed by the recognition that the photograph Christabel had enclosed, in order to show Ash his daughter, is that of her great-great-grandmother. (I read "She" in Maud's response to the photograph, "She was my great-great-great-grandmother" [503], as referring to Christabel, not to Maia: faced with this new revelation, Maud moves back a generation to make the obvious but startling deduction.) "There's something unnaturally *determined* about it all. Daemonic. I feel they have taken me over," she confides to Roland (505). When, after a long, deliberate delay, Roland and Maud consummate their love, their language echoes Ash and Christabel's.

Roland, finishing a sentence of Maud's, suggests that she feels "safe" with him, to which Maud responds, "Oh no. Oh no. I love you" (506).

Byatt leaves them, and the reader, with the problem the Victorian lovers could not solve: of preserving the autonomy of the woman while committing themselves to each other. Relating herself to Christabel's metaphor of the egg, which stood for "her self-possession, her autonomy," Maud insists, "I must go on *doing my work*," and Roland reassures her that he has his "own solitude" (506). It is possible to feel more hope for this contemporary pair, I think—partly because Roland and Maud both cherish the same image of solitude, "a clean empty bed in a clean empty room, where nothing is asked or to be asked" (267). At any rate, Maud is able to believe that Roland would not "blur the edges [of her separate self] messily" (506). On the other hand, Roland's empathy with her need to be released from the restrictions she has placed on herself is shown when, at his request, she looses her tightly bound hair, becoming a Rapunzel who is not at risk. As Roland watches, he feels "not exactly... desire, but... an obscure emotion that was partly pity, for the rigorous constriction all that mass had undergone, to be so structured into repeating patterns" (272). When the hair is completely freed, he feels that something in himself has been released. Another factor in the lovers' favour is, ironically, the contemporary phenomenon of the peripatetic scholar. Roland has been offered jobs in Hong Kong, Barcelona, and Amsterdam; he hopes that they can "think of a ... modern way" (507) to make a long-distance partnership. Some readers may find ominous the description of their final union as Roland's taking "possession," but the narrator confesses that the phrase is "outdated" and places against it language of newness and rebirth. The world in the morning had a "green smell.... It was the smell of death and destruction and it smelled fresh and lively and hopeful" (507). Also important is the reference to the odour of "bitter apples," for Roland's flash of illumination, which frees him to write his own poems, results from his rereading of a familiar Ash poem about the golden apples of Proserpina, the Tree in the Garden, and the naming and renaming of the things of the world: "We see it [the garden] and we make it, oh my dear," he reads (465). Biting the apple, which is both Proserpina's and Eve's (and the apples on which the lovers feed in a poem by Robert Graves that Val teaches Euan), Roland and Maud experience the death and destruction of the innocence of their old world; they must construct a new morality and a new language. Their future is still to be imagined.

As a reader of Ash, Roland is able, though reluctantly, to revise his interpretation in light of new evidence. His problems with Val help him to see that Ash's writing of loving letters to Ellen while with Christabel might not be hypocrisy: "Perhaps he did love his wife, too," he says to Maud (264). The same intuitive sympathy with Ash prompts his reading of "In-Pace" in a sense opposed to Maud's. Maud sees the poet as punishing the sorceress for her beauty and wickedness; Roland argues that "He's writing about the people, including herself, who thought she *ought* to be punished.... She colluded with their judgment. He doesn't" (55). It is Roland's patient, honest work on Ash's text that leads to his seeing the familiar words as "living creatures" and to the reward of being able to write poems of his own. He understands "that Christabel was the Muse and Proserpina and that she was not" (472), and sees that his quest for the sources of Ash's "Garden of Proserpina" has ended where it began, with Christabel. Christabel is both a figure from myth and an active woman in the real world; she is both the inspirer of poems and a poet who created a Proserpina of her own, for Melusine, as Christabel tells Ash, is a version of the Proserpina figure (174). This discovery leads Roland to intuit that language can still be used to say something. He begins by writing "lists of words that resisted arrangement into the sentences of literary criticism" (431), thus proving himself a worthy hero for Byatt. After he has fed his absent landlady's cats (described by the narrator in language that demonstrates Roland's insight into the metaphor-creating activity of the imagination), he finds a new voice; poems "came like rain and were real" (475). A hero of modern romance, he has earned both the poems and Maud, for he has become free to recognize all living things—and language too—as unique, with possibilities of newness and surprise.

In proposing a new kind of heterosexual partnership, Byatt creates a couple who must unlearn the orthodoxies they have been taught. For them, language begins by posing a problem, constituting a force of division rather than, as for Ash and Christabel, one of mutual delight. Knowing that after Freud and deconstruction everything is both sexual and textual, and agreeing that "metaphors *eat up* our world," they become troubled by this "horrible over-simplification" (253–54). "They were children of a time and culture which mistrusted love, 'in love,' romantic love, romance *in toto*, and which nevertheless in revenge proliferated sexual language," observes the narrator, who proceeds, playfully, to provide proof of the point: they knew about "phallocracy and penisneid, punctuation, puncturing and penetration, about polymorphous and polysemous perversity..." (423). As Maud points out to Roland, "all the looking-into has some very odd effects on ... desire" (267). When they realize that they nevertheless are becoming part of a love plot, that "a Romance

[is] one of the systems that controlled [them]" (425), they take refuge in silence. Anticipating going to bed with Christabel, Ash was struck by the "absence of language" for his hopes (281); now, the postmodern pair, lying chastely together, know that "Speech, the kind of speech they knew," would destroy the peacefulness they feel. Even here, as they fall asleep, they cannot escape textuality; Roland is jokingly characterized as "a dark comma against [Maud's] pale elegant phrase" (424). They struggle for self-direction and authenticity; both are aware that, "finding themselves in a [romance] plot, they might suppose it appropriate to behave as though it was that sort of plot" (422). When they finally must speak, Roland ruefully acknowledges that he is experiencing "all the things we—we grew up not believing in" (506). It is his and Maud's ability to accept contradictions—to live as self-conscious postmodern subjects and yet also to say "I love"—that gives them credibility and integrity as characters.[4]

The form of *Possession* stunningly balances openness and closure, in a way that feminist critics argue is representative of successful feminist fiction. Gayle Greene's description of Margaret Atwood's *Lady Oracle* is helpful here: Atwood's novel "looks back, but ... uses the 'rearview mirror' to negotiate a new present. [It] 'contains,' as all narrative must, but its metafiction includes commentary on narrative as containment" (189). *Possession* fulfills these criteria. Its ending satisfies our narrative curiosity—a characteristic of the reader's experience that Ash labels "hunger" (476)—but it also answers the postmodern requirement of "narrative uncertainty," of which Maud, early in their quest, reminds Roland (129). Yet the openness of this ending is very different from the inconclusive endings of the women's novels that Byatt found unsatisfactory as models early in her career. In her 1993 interview with Wachtel, Byatt, while granting that coherence and closure are present in *Possession* and that such endings give—and should give—pleasure, also warns against unobservant reading: "I haven't used the plot naïvely ... I am actually going back to writing novels with plots as a technical experiment" (88). (In the 1990 interview with Tredell, Byatt identifies closure as "the really revolutionary narrative mode at the moment" [59].) Although at least one reviewer has accused Byatt of failing to leave room for contingency (Karlin 18), it is precisely an acknowledgment of contingent reality that is achieved in her ending and especially in the postscript, which sends the reader back to the text with questions which prove the impossibility of final interpretations. For Byatt's women characters in particular, this openness is crucial, since it leaves room for reconstruction and revision.

The ending of *Possession* combines the resolution of Shakespearean comedy with postmodern openness. In the Wachtel interview, Byatt says that she decided to "take a purely Shakespearean-comedy way out" ("A.S. Byatt" 87) by providing Euan as a mate for Val. It is fitting then that Euan himself, in the gathering of the characters just before the denouement, suggests that they are experiencing both the ending of a romantic comedy and that of a detective story. The postscript provides a third ending, that of renewal through the daughter whom Ash meets; "In Shakespeare's last plays the daughter is the restoration of something," Byatt adds (Dusinberre, "A.S. Byatt" 193). Each of the endings offers coherence, makes sense of what has preceded, and satisfies our idea of what is fitting, but each is also in some ways open. The lovers must find a way to respect each others' uniqueness, but the way of constructing this new plot is left to each reader's imagination and judgment. In any case, as Roland has anticipated, the romance plot must give way to one of "social realism" (425).[5]

In the detective plot, the villainy of Cropper has been exposed, and Cropper himself has been taken into the circle of scholars, at least temporarily. (Significantly, only Fergus is excluded from this scene.) But the cache of papers answers only some of the questions of the scholar detectives, and the future of the papers themselves remains unknown. The scholars must now rewrite their work in the light of their new knowledge. Blackadder knows that "we shall need to reassess *everything*" in Ash's "post-1859 poems"; Leonora sees that her categorization of Christabel as a lesbian-feminist poet is too rigid; and Maud points out that *Melusine* will be read differently if its landscapes are related to the real ones of Yorkshire—and also that "No use of the word 'Ash' may be presumed to be innocent" (485). Cropper's *Great Ventriloquist*, which makes confident assumptions about Ash's marriage, and Leonora's *Motif and Matrix*, which reads Christabel's work in terms of the female body, with its "sloping declivities,... hidden holes," and "female secretions" (244, 245) are both now in need of rewriting. The work of reading and interpretation is thus shown to be endless, as Roland has already found, and these twentieth-century readers of Ash and Christabel must accept the fact that they will never know "all about" their subjects. Neither we nor the twentieth-century scholars know the circumstances of Maia's conception, which must have been in July or August 1859. The Yorkshire trip ended in June, and in late April 1860 Christabel left her cousins' house to give birth. This gap in the text—which readers enthralled with their glimpse of the Yorkshire idyll may not even notice—is Byatt's most telling assertion of the inaccessibility of the past. In the autumn, Ash tells Ellen that the affair is over, that the woman he loved has "vanished" and that in any case they "agreed that this one summer must see the end—of—the end" (454). For Maud, the Victorian and the contemporary plots are joined by the revelation that she is a direct descendant of Christabel; in studying Christabel with professional detachment, she has been unwittingly, in Blackadder's words, "exploring all along the myth—no the truth" of her "own origins" (503). She now must reimagine herself, both sexually and in terms of genealogy.

Finally, the "Postscript 1868," in which Ash meets his eight-year-old daughter, delights the reader, who has read, as the scholars never do, Ash's anguished (and uncharacteristically sexist) question about the child—"Did he live?" (456)—recorded in his unposted letter. At some time after writing that letter, we realize, Ash guessed that Christabel was at Seal Court; did he know that he would find their child there too? Christabel had written to Ash in her last letter, sent after her anger had dissipated, that there is "a space in [Maia's] life forever, which is yours" (500); Byatt, at the end of her book, lets us glimpse this space. Entering into what Richard Todd calls "readerly complicity with the nineteenth-century narrative" ("Retrieval" 109), we also learn that, like Ellen and the twentieth-century scholars, we have misinterpreted a clue, for the coiled hair Ellen buried with Ash is not Christabel's but Maia's. In exchange for the floral crown Ash makes for her, Maia allows him to cut a lock of her hair. But Maud, who is most crucially concerned with this meeting, is never to know of it. Along with our pleasure in the one-way recognition scene (for Ash is careful to preserve Maia's illusion that Sophia and George Bailey are her parents) there is regret for what might have been. Byatt's ending makes us reread Ash's rambling words on his deathbed: "Summer fields—just in a—twinkling of an eyelid—I saw her. I should have—looked after her. How could I? I could only—hurt her" (452).

Byatt's conclusion is both formally satisfying and true to the contingent reality of the practical world. Her three endings—two for the characters' knowledge, one for the reader's—avoid the "paperiness" she finds in John Fowles's alternative endings for *The French Lieutenant's Woman*. Fowles's endings, she says, "do not suggest a plurality of possible stories. They are a programmatic denial of the reality of any" ("People in Paper Houses" 174). As postmodernist fiction, *Possession* also illuminates a point of Linda Hutcheon's. Commenting on the "paranoia" about patterns and closed systems that is often found in postmodern fiction, Hutcheon notes a paradox: often "the terror of totalizing plotting is inscribed within texts characterized by nothing if not by over-plotting and overdetermined intertextual self-reference. The text itself becomes the potentially closed, self-referring system" (133). By showing that her characters (with good reason) fear overly structured repetitive patterns, and by leaving space for indeterminacy and movement, Byatt conveys a sense of hope. Her postscript is aptly described by Jean-Louis Chevalier as being "outside the narrative, yet at the very heart of the story" ("Conclusion" 131). A final ending, like the message for Christabel that Ash entrusts to Maia, is "never delivered" (511). (In fact, Byatt has provided a fourth ending, which extends the story beyond the covers of the book: see Appendix II).

By crossing genre lines—between epistolary novel, romance, fairy tale, detective story, academic satire, and, as I have suggested, narrative of community—Byatt's plot subverts the concept of unitary narrative. The idea of the centrality of sexuality, which, Maud admits, is taken for granted by post-Freudians, is questioned even as it is apparently reinforced: the passion for language turns out to be even more enduring and rewarding than is the desire for the beloved. Mysteries are solved and secrets revealed, but only to open up more questions. Byatt's characters, too, are like those Byatt values in the novels of Iris Murdoch, "free and individual characters, whose experience is diverse and not to be summed up" (*Iris Murdoch* 23), and the most admirable are those who, correspondingly, are able to respect the uniqueness and irreducibility of others, "paying attention" in Simone Weil's sense of the term. Some of the most memorable passages in *Possession* celebrate pure, wordless moments of intuitive recognition: when Ash knows that Christabel is "to do with him" (472); when Roland experiences a similar conviction about Maud; perhaps most striking of all, when Roland comes into possession of his own poetic language. These moments, like the small space for wonder that Ash and Christabel find, defy linearity by bringing the narrative to a standstill. Similarly, Roland's poems inhabit an imaginary space of their own; only their titles are recorded. The ever-changing versions of plot and character show us that all narrative, like the story of "falling in love," "combs the appearances of the world…out of a random tangle and into a coherent plot" (422). By leaving gaps in the plot, by refusing to follow every line to a conclusion, Byatt implicitly cautions against too vigorous combing.

Byatt leaves room for indeterminacy both in her main narrative and in the intertextual stories it encloses. As their quest nears its end, Roland and Maud list four questions that remain unanswered:

What became of the child?
How or why, in what state of ignorance or knowledge, had Blanche

been abandoned?
How had Ash and LaMotte parted?
Did Ash know of the possible child? (422)

Christabel's exhumed letter answers the first question. The third and fourth are answered at least partially by an excerpt from Mrs. Hella Lees's memoir, *The Shadowy Portal*, and by Christabel's letter referring to the seance held at Mrs. Lees's after Christabel's return from Brittany. Ash had pursued her to Brittany and learned of the child's birth. Back in England, knowing that Christabel would be at the seance, he disrupted the proceedings by angrily demanding to know what had happened to the child. In Christabel's last letter, she tells him that she came to live at Seal Court "not long after you and I met for the last time—as it turns out," and explains that when she had cried out at the seance, "You have made a murderess of me," she had been thinking of Blanche's suicide but had decided to let Ash believe, "if he knows me so little," that she had killed their child (500). Neither Roland, Maud, nor the reader ever knows the answer to the second question, however: Christabel and Blanche's final parting, like the precise nature of their relationship, remains an untold story of its own, and a further reminder of the hidden, mysterious lives of women throughout history.

The stories told by the embedded texts of *Possession* are also incomplete. Not only is it true, as Roland reflects, that "Letters ... are a form of narrative that envisages no outcome, no closure," so that "Letters tell no story" (130–31), but (despite the reassuring title of chapter 10, "The Correspondence"), the letters between Ash and Christabel are never neatly gathered together for the reader. In chapter 6, just after the letters are found, Joan Bailey reads aloud the final version of Ash's first letter and a letter from Christabel that must precede the first one from Ash to Christabel in chapter 10. In the second letter, Christabel's insistence that her stated wish to live in seclusion is not a way of teasing him—"how should I demean you or myself so—or you demean Yourself to think it" (87)—suggests that there are at least two more letters that are lost. Similarly, the last letters of this doll's-bed cache, in which Christabel asks for the return of her correspondence and Ash reluctantly complies, are not, as we know, the last; and as Roland and Maud point out, they are undated. Furthermore, Ash tells Christabel in his covering letter that he has burned two of her letters. Chapter 8 contains fragments of two more letters, which, from their content, belong in chapter 10. The letter to Christabel from "a friend" (379), which Ash's (and Browning's) friend Michelet encloses in his own letter to Sabine's father, is, we assume, from Ash; Sabine does not know whether Christabel ever read it. Like Blanche's paintings, and like Ellen's and Sabine's journals, the letters of the Victorian lovers are incomplete texts. Their fragmented state, together with the circumstances of their discovery as a result of a clue from Christabel and a hunch of Maud's, stresses contingency, the extent to which records are always (to use an often-repeated phrase of Byatt's characters) "in the hands" of others and of fate. The incompleteness of the correspondence also preserves the autonomy of their authors. As Roland thinks, "Letters ... exclude not only the reader as co-writer, or predictor, or guesser, but they exclude the reader as reader ..." (131).[6]

The texts of Ash's and Christabel's major poems, too, are present only in fragments, and, in the case of *The Garden of Proserpina*, in different versions (see Brink 298). *Melusine* was rewritten eight times. And Cropper's autobiography can never be completed, not only because he does not know his own inner self but also because he feels prohibited from writing about his powerful mother, whom he feels he will ultimately fail and who becomes one more woman whose power remains hidden from us. This brief reference opens up possibilities in our understanding of Cropper, but our curiosity is never satisfied. Cropper's versions of his own story always break off at the point where he inserts Ash's letter to Cropper's great-grandmother warning against spiritualism, a "high point" (105) for Cropper that marks how completely Ash has taken over the life of his biographer. Although we come to know much about Byatt's characters and their texts, opacity is preserved and the mysteries run deep.

In a letter to Ellen written in Yorkshire, Ash defines his main subject as "the persistent shape-shifting life of things long-dead but not vanished" (256). His immediate context is geology, but he is also describing both Byatt's subject and the form of her narrative. For Christabel, too, "metamorphosis" is "one of the problems of our time—and all Times, rightly known" (161). In her letters she explores metamorphosis in religious thought, and in her poems she examines, among other forms of change, shifting images of women, the chief of whom, Melusine, is herself a figure of metamorphosis. For the twentieth-century scholars, the problem of changing interpretations is never-ending. They must continue to interpret, but their discoveries—together with what remains undiscoverable—affirm the impossibility of a final reading. Maud works on "liminality. Thresholds. Bastions. Fortresses" (506), and the instability of boundaries is proven both in her scholarship and in her life.

Brittany, where Christabel experiences her private, painful metamorphosis into motherhood, is a metaphor for the novel itself. Raoul de Kercoz describes Brittany as a place where "the borderline between myth, legend and fact is not decisive" (339). As Victorians, Ash and Christabel struggle with the issue of unstable boundaries in religion. Christabel accuses Ash of making "Holy Scripture no more than another Wonder Tale" (160), and Ash responds by admitting that once one begins to think in terms of one myth prefiguring another—of the Norse creation story prefiguring the Christian, for example—one is in the presence of "a two-handed engine," for "figuration" is "a slicing weapon that cuts both ways ... to say that the Truth of the Tale is in the meaning, that the Tale but symbolises an eternal verity, is one step on the road to the parity of all tales" (163). In her essay on Browning, Byatt sees the Victorian poet occupying a crucial position in the process of demythologization that was central to the nineteenth century. In *Possession* she makes Ash, Browning's counterpart, face squarely the question of whether his ventriloquistic imagination is true or false prophecy. Is his writing about the raising of Lazarus "lending life to truth ... —or verisimilitude to a colossal Lie ...?" (168). In this letter he rests his case with Keats's faith in the truth of the imagination, adding, however, that "without the Maker's imagination nothing *can live* for us"—to which Christabel, unsatisfied, replies with her stubborn insistence on the unique truthfulness of the New Testament. Christ's self-description as "the Truth and the Life" is not merely "an approximate statement," she insists. It "rings—through eternity—I AM" (169). For Ash, the "road to the parity of all tales" leads to *The Garden of Proserpina*. In his poem, the garden, the place of primary naming "to which all Poets come," is simultaneously Proserpina's garden, the Garden of Eden, the grove where the Hesperides kept the golden apples, and the Norse goddess Freya's walled garden where "the World Ash rose from out the dark" (463-64). His narrator asks the key question, "And are these places shadows of one Place? Those trees of one Tree?" and follows it with a history of mythmaking that answers his question by showing that metaphor and truth are inseparable:

> The first men named this place and named the world.
> They made the words for it: garden and tree
> Dragon or snake and woman, grass and gold
> And apples. They made names and poetry.
> The things *were* what they named and made them. Next
> They mixed the names and made a metaphor
> Or truth, or visible truth, apples of gold.
> The golden apples brought a rush of words.... (464)

Finally, Ash asserts that all humans—and, on the personal level, he and
Christabel—are poets naming our world:

> We see it and we make it, oh my dear.
> .....
> I see the Tree all rugged-thick with bulk
> Of corky bark about its knotted base.
> You see it like a silver pillar, straight
> With breathing skin for bark, and graceful arms. (465)

And he returns to the paradox of the truthful lie: "All these are true and
none. The place is there / Is what we name it, and is not. It is" (465). It is
Roland's rereading of this poem that enables him to take possession of
his own garden (his landlady's, which had hitherto been forbidden
ground and which, centuries earlier, had also been Marvell's garden)
and to name his own world. Like Brittany, the garden exists in instability: it is "at the centre of a maze," and is seen

> through a glare
> Of mirage upon mirage, vanishing
> Like melting ice…, or foam
> Breaking at tide's edge, on the sifting beach. (465)

In her own naming, Byatt plays with the same idea of resemblance and
difference, for her characters' names are both laden with history and
symbolism and yet uniquely their own. Christabel is both Coleridge's
heroine, whose destiny remains hidden in the unfinished poem, and a
distinct individual. Her family name, as a reviewer has noted, recalls
the French writer LaMotte Fouqué whose fairy tale *Undine* has links with
Melusine (Karlin 17); it is also a double pun, on *moat* and on the French
word *mot* (word). Christabel herself combines the first pun with one on
her brother-in-law's name when she writes of her "motte-and-bailey
defences" (502); a bailey is the wall around a castle. The second pun
underlines the female's right to language and her relation to the male
tradition. Ash's name, as he and Christabel are both aware, has connotations of both fruitfulness and destruction. The ash tree, which gave rise
to the first man, is described in Byatt's source, a book on Norse myth, as
a holy tree that makes "wondrous music which told, not of death, but of
eternal change" (MacDowall 253). As Ash tells his goddaughter, the ash
tree also holds up the world and joins the underworld to heaven. Roland's

name recalls Childe Roland, one of Browning's heroes who came to the dark tower on his mysterious quest; Ash's description of the journey to the garden tells, as Browning's poem does, of travelling through a wasteland setting. Maia is both a child of May, and thus a force of renewal, and, like the may tree or hawthorn, a "*threshold-presence*" (181). Christabel reminds Ash of the superstitious belief that the may tree "must never be brought into the house" (178), and Maia lives on the boundary of her mother's world, shut out, for her own good, from knowledge of her true parents. In Greek myth, Maia is a daughter of Atlas, who holds up the world as, in Norse myth, his counterpart the ash tree also does—and so the names of Ash and his daughter are linked through the parity of tales. Ash himself reminds his daughter that Maia is the mother of Hermes, and associates her with both Proserpina and Keats's "Belle Dame Sans Merci"; wearing the crown he gives her, she is "Full beautiful, a fairy's child" (509, 510). Maud, besides bearing the Bailey name, which signifies her strategy of self-defence, is, through her given name, a descendant of Tennyson's beautiful, unattainable woman. Byatt gives Tennyson's silent figure a voice of her own, and a vocation beyond that of the muse who inspires male action. Similarly, Christabel, who in Coleridge's poem is placed under a spell that limits her power of speech, finds a voice in Byatt's text. Maia, though caring "nothing for books," plays like the spontaneously joyful child in "Christabel" (501–02); her son, Walter, however, loves language as Christabel had hoped his mother would, responding "most feelingly" (503) to Coleridge's "Ancient Mariner," which his grandmother teaches him. Walter is Maud's great-grandfather. Ash and Christabel's descendants are thus connected to literary history, yet they are also free and unique. Even minor characters in *Possession* have evocative names. Ariane Le Minier's given name associates her with Ariadne, whose thread led Theseus out of the labyrinth and who, Nancy Miller argues, "remains tied to her gift as a kind of package deal": Ariadne is the enabler of males who allows them to "penetrate the space of the great artist" (285). For Ariane, however, there is a crucial difference, for she provides the thread for the use of *female* explorers. Moreover, as her family name suggests, she is a miner; as a scholar, she excavates in her own right, and in fact, as André Brink points out, her surname indicates a *male* miner (Brink 356 n.13). All these suggestive, resonating names are attached to characters whose difference from those for whom they are named is as important as their resemblance to them.

Byatt's treatment of history and myth establishes that it is each individual person's acquisition of the past, at a deeply personal level, that matters in the end. Ash writes to Mrs. Cropper that the "fragment" of the past that is ours, that we have "read and understood and contemplated and intellectually *grasped*," is what "we must thoroughly *possess* and hand on" (104). Ash, Christabel, Roland, and Maud must all do this in their own ways; each must rename the world. This is the point, I think, of the address to the reader that immediately precedes Roland's flash of insight about Ash's poem. Byatt's narrator speaks of the "primary pleasures" that a writer can "make, or remake at least, for a reader," and, after demonstrating some of them, goes on to discuss a less often treated subject for a writer, "the intense pleasure of reading" (470). "Think of this," she says, "that the writer wrote alone, and the reader read alone, and they were alone with each other"; and, after describing different ways of reading the same text, evokes Roland's reading of "The Golden Apples," asking us to share his experience. His "sense that the text has appeared to be wholly new, never before seen, is followed, almost immediately, by the sense that it was *always there*, that we the readers, knew it was always there, and have *always known* it was as it was, though we have now for the first time recognised, become fully cognisant of, our knowledge" (471–72). In his review, Richard Jenkyns objected to this passage as "would-be post-modern self-reflexiveness" that indicates that Byatt "misunderstands the virtue of her own book, which lies in its solidity" (213). On the contrary, it seems to me that Byatt has opened a space for the reader to enter the book in a new way, as an acknowledged possessor of that solidity. Commenting on her story "Sugar," Byatt says both that it is "overtly fictive and about fictiveness" and that it "does try to be truthful" ("Sugar/Le sucre" 25). In *Possession* she provides plenty of commentary on the fictiveness of fiction, but she also tells the truth, about our relationship to the past, about the complexity and richness of human experience, especially that of women, and—perhaps most important of all—about reading, writing, and creativity.

Byatt fulfills her aim of showing the continuity between past and present, and she does more: by imagining her Victorian women artists and placing them within a recognizable historical context, she insists on the need to rewrite women's history. Ash, a male artist, has real-life counterparts, but Byatt's female artists, Blanche, Christabel, and Sabine, have no obvious parallels in nineteenth-century England or France; they and their work occupy imaginary space, testifying to the lost and hidden potential of countless women. Christabel's "Sibyl" poem, if it "existed," would alter our view of T.S. Eliot's originality in using the same story as the epigraph to *The Wasteland*. Byatt interposes Christabel's text between Eliot and his classical (male) source, Petronius, and thus makes room for a woman to participate in the literary tradition and to enrich it. If *The Fairy*

Melusine "existed," it would correct patriarchal notions of woman as witch, assert the creative power of women, and point to a female artistic genealogy. Through her women artists Byatt transforms old notions of literary history. In the words of Sandra Gilbert and Susan Gubar, Byatt explores two crucial questions about women and possession: "First, given Victorian sexual ideologies, could a creative woman be a lover and a mother without losing her self-possession, her autonomy? And given patriarchal historiography, could a literary matrilineage survive, and if so, who would possess it?" (*No Man's Land* 3: 387).

7 *Angels and Insects*

IN *ANGELS AND INSECTS*, PUBLISHED IN 1992, Byatt continues the probing of
the Victorian mind and its preoccupations that she began in *Possession*.
The book consists of two novellas, "Morpho Eugenia," set in the early
1860s, and "The Conjugial Angel,"whose events take place in the mid-
1870s. The two stories are linked by the presence of one character, Captain Arturo Papagay, who appears at the conclusion of the first and re-
enters at the end of the second, and, more importantly, by two large
subjects: the struggle for meaning in a world shaken by the perceived
conflict between science and religion, and the relationship of women to
this world and to language. *Angels and Insects* is about the ways in which
a society attempts to inscribe its beliefs; in both novellas there is a clash
of texts, a war of discourses, and this conflict reveals the failure of language ever to convey the "hard idea of truth." Both stories also show
Byatt's understanding of the problems of Victorian women in relation to
language—problems that persist into our time—and both depict women
who are able to enter and alter male discourse.

Unlike *Possession*, *Angels and Insects* is restricted to nineteenth-century
events, both recorded and imagined, and thus situates the reader differently. Without late-twentieth-century characters to mediate and confirm
our perspective, we are confronted directly with the issues faced by
Byatt's Victorian characters, and experience for ourselves what Michael
Levenson calls "the old shudder of Darwinism" ("*Angels and Insects*" 172).
Byatt herself, in an essay published in 1995 ("A New Body of Writing"),
drew attention to the prominence of Darwinism as a topic in late-twen-

tieth-century British fiction. Far from seeing this as an anachronistic or nostalgic phenomenon, she clearly thinks it relevant to our time. Levenson goes further: "What animates the historical turn in *Angels and Insects* is not a longing for a past epoch, but a conviction that history is now" (164). In her own discussion of Darwin in recent fiction, Byatt writes in similar terms: "Now, I think, novelists are thinking about what it is to be a naked animal, evolved over unimaginable centuries, with a history constructed by beliefs which have lost their power" ("A New Body of Writing" 443). In "Morpho Eugenia," Sir Harald Alabaster is agonizingly aware of the ebbing of faith caused by, among other pressures, evolutionary theories. Fifteen years later, in "The Conjugial Angel," a group of characters inspired by Emanuel Swedenborg attend seances in the hope of gaining direct evidence of the existence of the spirit world. Thus, Byatt represents two stages in nineteenth-century cultural history. Sally Shuttleworth sees the novellas as "nostalgic texts, but defiantly so, offering a celebration of nineteenth-century sensibility" ("Writing Natural History" 158).

For both novellas, Byatt invents characters who are lively and engaging. The historical figures who appear in "The Conjugial Angel"—Emily Jesse, who had been engaged to Arthur Hallam; her brother Alfred Tennyson, whose mourning for Hallam informs the period's most famous poem; and Hallam himself, whose ghost appears briefly—are convincingly and painfully present to our imaginations. Like *Possession*, these pieces of historiographic metafiction (which Marilyn Butler, in her review of *Angels and Insects*, dubbed "ficticism" [22]), mix realism and romance (including scientific text, ghost story, Gothic horror story, and fable) and use plots that, through patterns of restoration and renewal, both subvert and uphold the romance genre.

The two stories are very different in content but share basic motifs. Both deal with taboos that, while horrifying Victorians, were at the same time invited by the period's social structures. In "Morpho Eugenia," the entomologist and explorer William Adamson returns to England from Brazil after a shipwreck that destroyed most of the specimens he had collected. He joins the titled Alabaster household as a cataloguer of the father's scientific collection, becomes enthralled by the beautiful eldest daughter, Eugenia, and, despite the class barrier, marries her, only to discover later that she has had a long-standing sexual liaison with her half-brother Edgar and that the brood of children, white-complexioned as their mother's family name suggests, are probably doubly Alabasters. Freed now from what he had, even before the discovery, found to be a stifling existence, he begins a sexual relationship with Matty Crompton, his helper and co-author, and together they sail for Brazil. In "The Conjugial Angel," the principal taboo is homosexual love, and we eavesdrop as Tennyson, now an old man, struggles to reassure himself that his love for Hallam was "pure." Emily Jesse has herself been nearly imprisoned by a taboo, against the marriage of a woman whose fiancé has died; her marriage with Richard Jesse, a sea captain, has been affected by the lingering sense of having been "unfaithful" to Hallam. Like William, Emily finally liberates herself, recognizing the strength of her bond with her husband. But the two plots show the problems arising from the Victorians' assumptions about codification and control, which resulted in their idealization of the family unit on the one hand and in their segregation of the sexes through the education system on the other.

Classification, and the final impossibility of rigid categories, are central in both novellas. Attempts to place human existence in the cosmos link William's dialogues with his father-in-law about religion and faith in the first text with the experiences of the seance participants in the second. William's labours of sorting specimens at the Alabasters' well-named estate, Bredely Hall, lead to another, more crucial kind of sorting, as he must separate reality from illusion in his marriage and his partnership with Matty; it is Matty herself, who has presumably known of the brother-sister affair all along, who says meaningfully that she hopes William's "*sorting* may be completed to everyone's satisfaction" (44). William's work for Sir Harald is supplemented by helping Matty to organize the younger children's study of insect communities, and when this in turn leads to his undertaking the writing of a book on natural history, with Matty's help, William's list of possible chapter headings shows the issues of classification that preoccupy him:

Instinct or Intelligence
Design or Hasard
The Individual and the Commonwealth
What is an Individual? (109)

Yet despite his observation and his reading, which reinforce the thought that individuals exist only to serve the group and which call into question the very notion of individuality—in the vegetable world, at least, the individual may be simply the "*variety*" (114)—he is forced to acknowledge the distinctive, fiercely individual qualities of Matty, including, at the most basic level, the smell of her body and clothes. With Matty's help, too, he finally refuses to serve the communal purposes of the Alabasters, in which he knows he is classifiable as a drone. In "The Conjugial Angel,"

Lilias Papagay, the Captain's putative widow, reflects on the definition of what happens in the seances she engineers. At one level, she knows that "it was all a parlour game,... a kind of communal storytelling," yet she also knows that her friend Sophy Sheekhy, the medium, who unlike Lilias is able to move easily between the seen and the unseen worlds, is "not acting" (285) when she describes her visions. In both novellas, persons, events, and objects resist classification; in both, systems that seem to deny individuality and uniqueness break down at crucial moments. The principle of analogy, invoked in both novellas to explain the human relationship to the lower animals, or, alternatively, to link the human and the supernatural, takes us only so far. In "True Stories and the Facts in Fiction," an essay on the genesis of *Angels and Insects*, Byatt comments on the tendency to anthropomorphize insects, and cautions, "I think we should be careful before we turn other creatures into images of ourselves" (115).

As it was in *Possession*, metamorphosis is a key concept in *Angels and Insects*. The biological process that transforms larvae into moths or butterflies, which William and Eugenia witness in the display he has arranged for her, is a metaphor for the changes that are undergone within their marriage and in William's and Matty's relationship, and that are hinted at in the title of Matty's fable, "Things Are Not What They Seem." Matter is as mysterious as spirit and its changes as incomprehensible: William remarks to the tormented Harald that "Mystery may be another name for God. It has been well argued that mystery is another name for matter....The laws of the transformation of Matter do not explain it away" (60). Tennyson, whose questionings of the meaning of matter and of its relation—if any—to spirit are frequently cited by Harald, is shown, in "The Conjugial Angel," to be fond of stating that "Matter is a greater mystery than Mind" (264). His *In Memoriam*, of course, holds out the fragile hope of human metamorphosis into a higher existence at death, just as it unflinchingly imagines the details of the dissolution of the body. Looking back at the process of writing *Angels and Insects*, Byatt reflects, "I found ... that I was feeling out, or understanding, the Victorian fear that we *are* our bodies, and that, after death, all that occurs is natural mouldering" ("True Stories" 108). The title of her two-part work captures this dilemma.

The two stories are also concerned with sexual classification and the special vulnerability of women to rigid labelling. Both novellas show how the Victorian ambivalence about a woman's marrying after the death of her fiancé (let alone of her husband) could be crippling for the woman. Eugenia, whose fiancé died (by suicide, we learn later), is described by her sister as "like … a widow without being married" (6). Emily is perceived by her brother, her fiancé's family, and their circle of friends as having been unfaithful to Hallam's memory: in fact, Hallam's cousin declared that Emily's marriage to Richard Jesse was "just the same thing as marrying again" (Kolb 798), and Elizabeth Barrett, before her own marriage, pronounced Emily "a disgrace to womanhood" (Kelley and Hudson, *Brownings' Correspondence* 7:226-27; see also "The Conjugial Angel" 174), particularly because she continued after marriage to accept an annuity from old Mr. Hallam—an act that, Byatt more sympathetically speculates, Emily "confusedly" links to her "independence" (232). The passionate nature of Alfred's love for Arthur complicates Emily's situation still further, even before Hallam's death. Richard Todd suggests that by becoming engaged to Arthur, Emily may be seen as committing "a form of unconsummated incest" (*A.S. Byatt* 36), and Kathleen Coyne Kelly draws on Eve Kosofsky Sedgwick's theories to consider whether Emily may be seen as "the mediating body through which Hallam and Tennyson pursue their love for each other without public censure" (112). The situation of Mrs. Papagay, who has sorrowfully accepted that her husband has perished at sea, is relatively simple but ambiguous nevertheless, for in the absence of proof of Arturo's death, she is not marriageable because not officially widowed. Both women must identify their place— Lilias by joyfully returning to it, Emily by defining it for herself.

Characters in both books confront the Victorian social hierarchy and participate in its gradual dissolution. William, well aware that by society's ranking he, as a butcher's son, is inferior to Edgar, responds to Edgar's taunts that he is "underbred" (62) by invoking his father's honesty and his own history of courage. His future brother-in-law Robin Swinnerton praises William's refusal to engage in a fist fight with Edgar: William is a "civilized man," whereas Edgar is an "anachronism" (63). But when William discovers that Edgar has impregnated Amy, one of the insect-like horde of servants who maintain the luxury of Bredely Hall, he must bitterly accept Edgar's statement that it is not William's "place" to try to help the girl, now banished to the workhouse: "My mother will send some sort of present. It is her place" (146). Rank, William knows, can be used to justify the cruellest, most callous kinds of exploitation. But despite the persistence of this anachronism, society is changing, and those characters who, like William, are able to separate themselves from class are signs of hope. Matty is thus a suitable mate for William. Before assuming her role of dependant of the Alabasters, she was educated, through the kindness of the bishop's wife, with the bishop's children whom her father tutored; "I was educated with my betters," she tells William (118). Both she and William can be seen, from the perspective of hierarchy advocated by Edgar, as "hanger[s]-on" (108). Whereas William had been disappointed not to discover an "intimate new speech" (69) with Eugenia, Matty's lively, informed mind meets his in a conversation that moves beyond Victorian ideas of male-female relationships. In "The Conjugial Angel" the main trespassers of class lines are Lilias Papagay, whose profession as medium has allowed her to move upward into the world of the Jesses and their friends, thanks to "the democracy of the Spirit World" (171), and her husband, Arturo, whose profession makes him a traveller between hemispheres.

A racial outsider with a "rich mixed smile" (160) and a survivor against the odds, Papagay is much more than a plot device as he crosses textual boundaries to link the two narratives. As a "Hermes figure" (Todd, *A.S. Byatt* 33) conducting William and Matilda from the stagnant world of Bredely to their unknown future, he speaks for the colour and variety that his name represents (Todd, *A.S. Byatt* 33), for curiosity and interest in life, and—implicitly—for acceptance of mortality. Our last sight of the two adventurers records Matilda's response to an exhausted monarch butterfly that has been blown far off course to Papagay's ship. Matilda expresses fear, hope, and wonder at its fragile, battered body: "And yet it is still alive, and bright, and so surprising, rightly seen" (160). Papagay speaks the last words of the novella, universalizing Matilda's statement: "As long as you are alive, everything is surprising, rightly seen" (160). And the three travellers "look out with renewed interest at the points of light in the dark around them" (160). In "The Conjugial Angel" Papagay, presumed lost at sea several years after this voyage to the Amazon, returns home safely after being, as he tells Lilias, "Twice wrecked ... [o]nce cast away" (289). His return provides a satisfying symmetry: as Judith Fletcher points out, "*Angels and Insects* comes full circle, beginning and ending with a shipwrecked man" (231). At the same time, however, Papagay's return reopens the ending of "Morpho Eugenia": did William and Matilda reach the Amazon? Were they, too, wrecked or cast away, and if so, did they survive? Through the doubling back that his reappearance gives rise to, Papagay is once again an agent of curiosity and mystery.

In "Morpho Eugenia," whose events take place two years after the publication of *The Origin of Species*, the scientific and biblical versions of the world vie for dominance and, while the accounts given by Darwin and his fellow scientists are in the ascendency, neither side "wins." Soon after his arrival at Bredely, William becomes aware that he is engaged in a conflict of discourses with Sir Harald. Against Harald's urgent need to prove that there is a design and to name the designer "God," William realizes that his speculations are leading him toward biological determinism, an idea to which, "like almost all his contemporaries, he was half afraid to give full expression" (116). Harald's progress on his book, which he describes as "the kind of impossible book everyone now is trying to write" (33), is circular. He continues, wistfully, to raise consoling arguments that he has already demolished, and ends in a state of intellectual paralysis. William's writing, on the other hand, is progressive; his book on insect life evolved out of his boyhood journals. After he became an observer of nature, he had for a time the same wish as Harald, to discover in nature signs of divine love. Beginning with journal entries in which his terror of God's punishment drove him to minute self-examination, he moved, when he discovered the natural world, to entries in which he searched nature for signs of a divine hand at work, and then, after his interest became focused on insects, to passages cataloguing the details of the natural world. His writing shows a more complex mind than Harald's, one that encompasses both visionary moments and long hours of meticulous analysis, and his text is able to contain many discourses, from the blunt comparison of himself, struggling to survive in the teeming jungle, to "a dancing midge in a collecting bottle" (12) to the passionate appropriation of Ben Jonson's "O so white! O so soft! O so sweet is she" (12) for his newly discovered Eugenia. His narrative for children, depicting the ant colony that he, Matty, and the Alabaster children study, combines imaginative play with scientific description and theoretical discussion. As a writer, William is at home in many genres, and in both the "male" (rational) and the "female" (imaginative) spheres of discourse. As a scientist concerned, as his surname suggests, with naming, he is able also to respond to the imaginative, mythological appeal of scientific names and to appreciate the fact that Linnaeus, who named so many species, was a creative artist. The variety of his style is summarized by the publisher's letter of acceptance: "facts in abundance, useful reflections, drama, humour, and fun" (144). Both his text and Harald's typify Victorian responses to evolutionary theory. Harald, clinging to the image of a loving God—and finding comfort in Tennyson's image of the child in the dark who, "crying, knows his father near"—falls back on "*truth of feeling*" (88) and on the cherishing of family love, while William, having long ago rejected, with relief, the vengeful God of his Methodist childhood, sees that the social instinct in animals may just as easily lead to social organizations that are rigid, intolerant, and authoritarian. It is ironic that Harald, who preaches to his household vague sermons praising the love of family members for each other, is totally unaware of how literally his son and daughter have been practising his injunction, and equally ironic that William, as a husband, has been blind to the relationship between his wife and his brother-in-law. As Todd says, William can give "secular explanations for patterns of communal life and reproductive behaviour" but is shocked by "the implications of those patterns" when he is confronted by them (*A.S. Byatt* 32). In the end, analogies fail to account for lived experience. By the time William's horrifying discovery is made, his writing is completed, although he has not reached any final conclusions. He and Matty have sent off their book and a publisher has accepted it. Harald's text, however, remains entangled in its own maze of argument, and it is obvious that it will never be published; it has reached a dead end.

Although *Angels and Insects* is dominated by male-written texts, women's discourse in a broader sense is highlighted in both novellas. In "Morpho Eugenia," Byatt gives her imagined character Matty empowerment through language, and in "The Conjugial Angel," through a seamless blending of fact and invention, she shows the historical figure Emily Tennyson Jesse moving into assured and decisive speech. Both women free themselves from the scripts written for them by their culture.

The first words in "Morpho Eugenia" are spoken by a woman who has, in the remainder of the text, virtually nothing more to say. "You must dance, Mr. Adamson" (3), says Lady Alabaster, simultaneously conforming to her role as Victorian matron and introducing one of the book's dominant tropes, that of the mating dance. In a verbal gesture that is repeated later, she then prepares to call a woman of inferior rank to act on her behalf: "I shall ask Matty to find you a pretty partner…" (3). Alienated from language, she relies on another of the family's dependants, Miss Fescue, to help her form the words when the family plays anagrams. In her household, although Harald is "master," he is, William sees, a "*deus absconditus*" (76); his wife is the silent, indolent "source of power" (27). This is a community falling into social and sexual decadence; Lady Alabaster's power consists in being able to regulate the work of her inferiors, most of them women and all of them, even the pregnant Amy, more energetic than their mistress. When Philip and Belinda Haas's screenplay for the film version added the death of Lady Alabaster to Byatt's text, it suggested, as Todd points out, that in this hive, as in those of insects, "the queen's death leads to the dissolution of the colony" (*A.S. Byatt* 37). Like her mother, Eugenia exercises her power for the most part in silence. Her most forceful speeches are in praise of her unchanging life at Bredely, where "the same flowers come out every spring in the meadows, and the same stream [is] always running." This declaration of delight in her "*bounded*" existence" (29) relates ironically to her second, longer speech, a defence of her incest with Edgar, in which she insists that this relationship, based on sameness and enclosed by the family tie, seemed "perfectly *natural*" (159). When she knows that her sexual power over William has ended, she assumes that her financial power is still needed and offers to write him a cheque for the expenses of his expedition. He is, of course, able to reject this. Eugenia's power, like her mother's, has played itself out, and, like her mother, she lapses into silence.

Matty, whose power is in the ascendency as Eugenia's peters out, is in every way Eugenia's opposite. Alert, inquisitive, and artistically and verbally skilled, she is interested in differences, not sameness, and in expanded horizons, not boundedness. For Eugenia, the enclosed life of Victorian women is a luxury; for Matty, it is, first, an opportunity for focused observation of the natural world and, later, an obstacle she is able to defy. "My sphere is naturally more limited," she says, contrasting herself with William. "I look naturally closer to hand" (77). The two "pictures" (158) that end the book define Eugenia and Matty as, respectively, conventional and unconventional woman. For her last interview with William, Eugenia has dressed carefully in flattering colours; she appears as an arrangement in a frame, ready, in an ironic flashback to their earlier relationship, to receive the male gaze. Matty's picture includes William—he is in the frame with her—and both the sea and the sky around them are filled with life and motion; theirs is a moving picture. The wind stirs Matty's skirts, and she and William, looking not at each other but out at the precarious world, "breathe salt air, and hope, and their blood swims with the excitement of the future" (160). Unlike the Alabasters, they have exposed themselves to the dangers of open spaces. We do not know what happens to them, but we leave them, as the narrator says, "on the crest of a wave" (160). Eugenia's picture is a traditional representation of woman as static sensuous object; in William and Matty's (which recalls Ford Madox Brown's Victorian painting *The Last of England*), the woman is very much subject.

Matty's role as co-adventurer with William, which begins when they together direct the children's collecting expeditions, leads to textual collaboration, as she first instigates and then co-authors the book that, together with her own book of fairy tales, becomes their passport to the Amazon. Although she initially restricts her self-description to "*assistant*" (93), contributing sketches to illustrate the book, and, like many women of her time, making a fair copy of a male-authored text, William recognizes that her contribution extends much further; he devises "a narrative voice that was a kind of royal, or scientific We, to include both of them, or either of them, at given points in time" (108). Defying Victorian stereotypes of the feminine in her interest in scientific facts, Matty advises William not to disguise his views out of prudence: "I think a man must be truthful, as far as possible, or the whole truth will never be found" (117-18). The idea that William has heard from a friend of Darwin, that women are not "prepared to question the truths of religion" (116), does not apply to Matty, to whom (in a neat reversal of Marlow's protection of Kurtz's Intended in *Heart of Darkness*) he entrusts opinions that he considerately withholds from Harald. Matty can contemplate the possibility of "future generations who will be *happy* to believe that they are finite beings with no afterlife" (117). She thus contradicts the Victorian idealization of the woman as the binary opposite of the man, intuitive and emotional where he is rational and intellectual, and needing to be shielded from the harsher truths. In creating Matty, Byatt says, "I saw that I needed another woman [besides Eugenia], not confined to her biological identity" ("True Stories" 117).

It is as an author in her own right, however, that Matty most fully reveals the quality of her mind. Her text, "Things Are Not What They Seem," combines fable, allegory, and natural history, while putting her knowledge of Milton and Homer to imaginative use; it is described by Byatt as a "metaphor about metaphor-making" ("True Stories" 20). A story about enchantment, imprisonment, and metamorphosis, it comments on William's capture by the deceitful Eugenia and predicts his escape. On this level, as Kelly points out, Seth, the shipwrecked sailor who is turned into a swineherd by the evil fairy into whose garden he strays, represents William. Mistress Mouffet, the "Recorder" or "Spy" (131) of the garden who brings about his rescue, is Matty herself (Kelly 103-04). As narrator, Matty's learning and inventiveness are shown by her play with names. The Circe-like fairy identifies herself as Mrs. Cottitoe Pan Demos; her name, she says, "means, 'for all the people,'... and that is what I am. I am for all the people. I keep open house for everyone who comes" (122). In classical myth, however, Aphrodite Pandemos is the goddess of sensual lust and Cotys or Cotyllo is a Thracian goddess whose worship involved orgiastic rites.[1] Dame Cottitoe is a much more sinister figure than her own bland translation of her name suggests. Her name also echoes Pandemonium, Milton's place for the devils; her devils are the men whom she has changed to swine and other beasts. She thus figures the sensual enthralment of William by Eugenia and the confusion that has resulted from it. Matty's love of language and stories and her preoccupation with naming underlie the plot by which Seth is rescued. He becomes enslaved by Dame Cottitoe when she forces him to eat pomegranate seeds—the same meal that, in myth, ensures the captivity of Proserpina—and the fern seeds provided by the helpful ant (who comes from the story of Cupid and Psyche, which the governess, Miss Mead, told to the Alabaster children) generate the second metamorphosis that leads to his release. Mistress Mouffet, who identifies herself as a relative of an early namer of insects (Thomas Mouffet), is the alter ego of Matty Crompton, whose name in turn, Kelly suggests (104), is derived from John Crompton, the pseudonym used by another authority on ants. Under Mistress Mouffet's tutelage, Seth (whose name, like William's, identifies him as a son of Adam and therefore as concerned with naming) learns about the names of creatures, especially those of the moths. He shares her delight in the work of names in "weaving the world together, by relating the creatures to other creatures," effecting "a kind of *metamorphosis*, you might say, out of a *metaphor* which is a figure of speech for carrying one idea into another" (132). After this instruction, during which the narrator comments, with muted self-mockery, that Mistress Mouffet "obviously...took great pleasure in instructing others" (133), Seth is ready to use language, intuitively, to save himself. He is transported on the back of the moth named Sphinx Acherontia Atropos into the presence of a mysteriously powerful, veiled figure, who, his instructor has told him, is "the source of riddles, but also of answers" (136) and who may change him by restoring him. Commanded to name her, he can only say, "I do believe you are kind" (139)—and thus stumbles on the name that saves him. The figure is Nature, Dame Kind, and through her power Seth is able to break the spell of her false counterpart and return his companions to their natural shapes. On its more general allegorical level, then, "Things Are Not What They Seem" tells of the liberating, perplexing power of nature and, at the same time, asks us to accept her laws without fear. We must internalize both of the voices heard by Seth on his journey, one saying "Fear no more" and the other repeating Tennyson's appalled report in *In Memoriam* of a voice that says, "I care for nothing, all must go" (138). But as the author of the tale, Matty resists any reductive interpretation. To William's tentative identification of Dame Cottitoe Pan Demos with the church, she protests, "I had no such grand aims, I assure you. My message was linked to my title" (141).

Between this text of Matty's, with its encoded message to William, and the second text, their collaborative word game (of which she is again the instigator), lies William's discovery of the facts of his marriage, which exemplifies Matty's title in brutally specific terms. Their participation in a game of anagrams is Matty and William's final textual collaboration; working together with the letters they have received, they compose a terse four-word narrative that sums up their shared knowledge and hints at a future for them. William first makes "insect," to which Matty replies with "incest," shocking him with her knowledge; William's next word is left for the reader to discover, and Matty's final word is "phoenix." I deduce that William's word is "sphinx," for he has just been presented with "incest," already possesses the letters p, h, and x and, we are told, sees a way to "answer her message" (153) with a word of his own. The pause in which the reader engages in the game provides a space, like that in *Possession*, where we are invited to reflect on the act of reading; it enlists the reader as textual collaborator. By offering Matty "sphinx," William not only alludes to the riddle of his marriage and to Matty's fable, which encoded his predicament, but also renames Matty in honour of the Sphinx moth who helped his alter ego Seth to solve his own riddle of naming. "Hold tight to the Sphinx" (136), Miss Mouffet had told Seth, and William's response shows that he has understood.[2] The final word, "phoenix," asserts Matty's hope for transformation, already encoded in her fable and soon to be represented in the novella's final image, the butterfly. Immediately after this, she names herself Matilda, tells William that she intends to accompany him to the Amazon using the proceeds from her fairy tales, and, overruling his protests that the jungle is "no *place* for a woman" (156), orders him to "*Look at me*" (157). William, who has dimly recognized her individuality from the beginning, now does see both "the unyielding Matty Crompton" and "the new hungry Matilda" (158), and in the private space of her room they make love.

Byatt has said that she wants to create characters "who have thought processes which change them, which matter to them. Not beliefs, but thought processes" ("Identity" 25). Both William and Matilda have been changed by the thought processes they have shared, which have enabled them—despite the contrary evidence provided by their study of insects— to experience a moment of freedom and choice. Earlier, William had resisted the chain of analogy, declaring, "Men are not ants" (100); now he is able to assert will and independence and, as well, to use his new power over Edgar to force him to provide for Amy, thus fractionally enlarging her restricted female space. William and Matilda have not, of course, found answers to the intellectual problems of their age—they have not arrived at "beliefs"—but they have engaged in the search with honesty and courage. Each of them, too, has had glimpses of something operating in human lives that is beyond mere chance. Matilda's fable ends with transformation occurring "as if by magic, that is to say, *by magic*" (140), and William, at the climax of the game of anagrams, thinks that the "luck of the letters was uncanny. It gave him the feeling" that "in fact there is Design" (153). The design the two come to perceive in their own affairs is the product, however, of their own hard work. Byatt's ending points to the possibilities of change that were already present in Victorian gender relations. Matilda has entered the sphere of male discourse while remaining creative in the female sphere. She has also rejected her culture's story about women (a story that separates her both from men and, as a white woman, from the women of colour whose world she is to enter).[3]

If Matty Crompton is empowered by participating in the scientific discourse of her time and by creating her own text as a means of communicating with and freeing the man she loves, Emily Jesse, thirty-seven years older, has a different task. The text of her life has been literally written for her: imprisoned in her brother's *In Memoriam*, she has been defined as the grieving fiancée and assigned a life of "perpetual maidenhood" (vi). Long before the events in "The Conjugial Angel" she attempted (after nine years of mourning) to break out of that story by marrying Richard Jesse, but she still feels the burden of society's expectations of spiritual faithfulness to the dead man. In both novellas, the climactic moment is a revelation of the woman's selfhood, but Matty is at the beginning of her adventure, whereas Emily, in her sixties, is nearing the end of hers. Emily's speech of self-realization, when she asserts her choice of the living husband over the dead fiancé, completes the process by which she extricates herself from the role constructed for her by her brother years earlier, as well as from a version of female behaviour enjoined by Mr. Hawke, expounder of Swedenborg's text and of St. Paul.

Emily's moment of truth is a speech passed on in the Jesse family, recorded by the Jesses' granddaughter Fryn Tennyson Jesse, and reproduced verbatim by Byatt. Faced with Sophy's report that Hallam's spirit asserts that he and Emily will be "joined and made one Angel" (283), in the hereafter, Emily responded decisively: "'Well, Richard,' she said. 'We may not always have got on together as well as we should, and our marriage may not have been a success, but I consider that an extremely unfair arrangement, and shall have nothing to do with it. We have been through bad times in this world, and I consider it only decent to share our good times, presuming we have them, in the next'" (283; see also Kolb 802). Using this family record, Fryn Jesse's impressions of her grandparents' marriage, Hallam's letters, and *In Memoriam*, Byatt brilliantly imagines Emily Tennyson Jesse. In doing so, she once again makes fact alive through fiction, creating a compelling figure who, like Matty—and like Christabel, Blanche, Sabine, and Ellen in *Possession*—speaks for silenced Victorian women. In "The Conjugial Angel," as in the other narratives, the woman must define herself in relation to male texts and male versions of the feminine. Writing in 1940, Fryn Jesse herself imagined the grandparents whom she never knew. She speculated that her grandmother "grew tired of being a thing enskied and sainted as the dead Arthur Hallam's fiancée ... and decided to have a life of her own" (Kolb 802). She also commented, in crisp prose her grandmother might have enjoyed, "I believe my great-uncle Alfred [Tennyson] was extremely annoyed at the marriage, which is understandable considering he had written 'to her perpetual maidenhood and unto me no second friend.' One must admit it made him look rather silly" (Kolb 801). Fryn Jesse speculated that Hallam's letters to Emily indicate that he was "a pretty frigid lover" (Kolb 800).[4] A feminist reading of *In Memoriam* detects a disturbing absence of concern for the flesh-and-blood Emily, whose marriage in 1842, eight years before her brother published his poem, is entirely omitted from his text. A reader of Hallam's love letters may also, like Fryn Jesse, be dismayed by the lover's tendency to patronize and preach to his beloved. Quoting copiously from Alfred's poems and Arthur's letters, Byatt produces a collaborative male-authored version of a woman's story. Placing this against Emily's own view of her experience, she also invents the two women mediums who (both consciously and unconsciously) help Emily in completing her long process of self-liberation from the patriarchal story.

In her 1989 review of Alex Owen's *The Darkened Room*, a study of women and spiritualism in the late nineteenth century, Byatt pointed to the ambivalent nature of their "power"; because women were thought to be "receptive," "intuitive," and "passive," they were suited to be the conduits of communications from the spirit world ("Chosen Vessels" 605). Byatt saw that her interest in Owen's subject was "turning into a metaphor for fiction, a seance is a fiction" (qtd. in Chevalier, "Entretien" 17), a recognition that led to the writing of "The Conjugial Angel." She saw that she needed two mediums and that these were "the voices of the writer in me ... there was one woman who was a novelist manquée, who went to seances out of human interest..., and the other one, a woman who would have been a poet, if she hadn't been a medium, who saw a very intense, precise image of the nature of things" (qtd. in Chevalier, "Entretien" 17). Together, these two co-operate as fiction writers. Lilias is the curious, sympathetic natural storyteller who tried to write narratives "from bobbins of gossip or observation..., life-lines..., chains of cause and effect" but with "stilted" and "saccharine" (168) results. Her attempts were hampered by the conventions of women's fiction—conventions she is able to defy in her contributions to the seances. Sophy is the pure visionary, who experiences dream images, images from everyday perception, and images from literature as part of one continuous reality. Describing the genesis of "The Conjugial Angel," Byatt elaborates on her creation of Lilias and Sophy: "I wanted space for the kind of female consciousness I needed, to which perhaps Emily Tennyson did not quite fit." Lilias and Sophy are "named for the female angels often described as having been in Paradise before Adam, Lilith and Sophia or the Shekhinah, who according to some theologies created matter" ("True Stories" 105–06). Thus, like Matty, the two mediums answered their author's need for representatives of female energy and creativity.

In her review, Byatt notes that Owen sees Victorian women mediums as a group "whose sense of themselves was structured by a social perception of their identity, which they tried both to subvert and to reinforce" ("Chosen Vessels" 605). The first seance in "The Conjugial Angel" shows Sophy and Lilias helping a grieving woman, Mrs. Hearnshaw, who has lost five little daughters, all named Amy, and who, Lilias correctly intuits, is again pregnant. Building on Sophy's skilful evocation of the scent of roses in the room, Lilias uses her gift for automatic writing to construct a narrative of consolation in which the five dead children convey their happiness in the rose garden where they live and their knowledge that a new "earthly seed" is "growing in the dark"; she must not, they say, be given "Our Name" but should be called "Rosamund, Rose of this Earth" (198). With tactful kindness, the ventriloquized voices provide for both possibilities for the new sister (the child's gender is taken for granted): if she survives she will bring her mother happiness, but if she joins the dead children "she will be happier and you will bear the pain in that certainty" (198). Somewhat comforted, Mrs. Hearnshaw confirms that she is pregnant and admits that she has tried to avoid conception because of her terror of another loss; silently, Lilias allows her "irrepressible imagination" (199) to create the scene that led to the conception—a scene that, with comic savageness, shows Mr. Hearnshaw forcing intercourse on his wife. Lilias, who is "of imagination all compact" (163) is doing what Byatt does in her construction of Emily. She takes fragments of fact—she knows of Mr. Hearnshaw's egotistical, sexist blaming of the children's deaths on his own "shortcomings of faith" (167)—and makes it the germ of her mini-narrative. Her public contribution to the seance affirms woman's duty to trust in God and bear children, patiently enduring loss, but her private fantasy reveals her understanding of male aggression.

On a much larger scale, Byatt gives a voice and personality to Emily Jesse. Using two reported speeches, the one recorded by Fryn Jesse and another in which Emily commented on the process of grief—"I have felt everything; I know everything. I don't want any new emotion. I know what it is to feel like a stoän" (172; Tennyson and Dyson, 165)—she imagines a discourse and a narrative consistent with these fragments and with the facts of Emily's life. Byatt has said that in this story, whose "original impulse … was … revisionist and feminist," she told "the untold story of Emily…. One of my *données* was Emily Tennyson's *exclusion*" from "the often-told story of Arthur and Alfred" ("True Stories" 104). Before the Hearnshaw seance begins, Byatt depicts Emily beginning her war of words with the dogmatic Swedenborgian Mr. Hawke, who is anxious, on biblical authority, to identify Aaron, Emily's pet raven, with "gross and impenetrable falsities" because of his blackness. Emily counters this with the insistence that "Owls and ravens are God's creatures" (183) and uses as *her* authority her own experience and Wordsworth's passage about the owl-calling boy. Her sparring with Hawke—in which both her husband and Aaron assist her—runs through the narrative as a story of its own; she is well read in a variety of texts besides her brother's and the Bible, and she refuses to accept Hawke's often anti-feminist interpretations of scripture, which, following Swedenborg, viewed Christ's mortal part as deriving from his mother and cast off at the Crucifixion, leaving only the divine part derived from the Father. This sequence of exchanges, which is sometimes accompanied by an aggressive dance by Aaron the raven, who sallies out to do battle with Hawke, culminates in what Lilias recognizes as a spiritual battle "fuelled by texts" (281) in which the Jesses unite against Hawke to challenge his warning against the dangers of female beauty. Byatt endows Emily with a quick acerbic wit and an alert intelligence, and her direct, assured discourse defeats Hawke's repetitious, inflated preachiness.

The second narrative of the seances concerns Emily and her longing—again, like her attraction to Swedenborgianism, a matter of recorded fact—to communicate with Hallam's spirit; she wishes, Byatt asserts, to know that she is forgiven for having married Richard Jesse. In the first of these seances, Sophy relays a message from Hallam that Emily identifies as being for her. It contains lines from *In Memoriam*, cites a theological work by Hallam, *Theodicaea Novissima*, uses some of his pet names for Emily, and—most tellingly, for her—refers cryptically to "Revelation 2, 4" that reads "Nevertheless I have somewhat against thee, because thou hast left thy first love" (205). This, together with a text Emily knows is from Hallam's own translation of Dante's *Vita Nuova*, "You have a bounden duty and you ought / Never forget our Lady who is dead" (204), makes her feel that she is being reproached; perhaps Arthur, like his family, has not forgiven her for ending her mourning.

In the solitary reverie that follows this seance, Emily reconstructs, through memory, the story of Arthur's courtship, death, and memorialization by her brother Alfred, and her eventual courtship by Richard Jesse. She remembers feeling intense romantic love for Arthur, but also that he "treated her like a mixture of a goddess, a house-angel, a small child and a pet lamb" (218). He encouraged her to help him in his translation of Dante, then teased her for the imperfection of her work, and he shared her brother's typically Victorian view that women should not "trouble themselves much with theology" (218). Two memories of their brief time together dominate her meditation, and together prepare for her release. She recalls how Arthur, caught up in—and helping to create—the magic of the Tennysons' home, Somersby, came upon her in a glade filled with flowers, called her "a wandering fairy or dryad," and declared his love for her; she reconstructs their enclosure together in a "leafy, flowery thicket" (224). Arthur, comparing this thicket to groves in Malory, Spenser, classical texts, and Tennyson's *Recollections of the Arabian Nights*, further enclosed her in a network of texts. This image of enchanted containment is contrasted, however, with one of exclusion, as Emily remembers approaching her brother and her fiancé sitting together on the Somersby lawn, their hands outstretched toward each other, discussing the Neoplatonic idea that the female Matter is animated by the male Mind, Nous. This analogy, Byatt says, is one "which … all feminists ought to deconstruct" ("True Stories" 111). When Emily tries to begin the process of deconstruction by asking, "Why is inert Matter female and the animating Nous male, please?" she is patronized, lovingly immobilized as a "picture," and given dismissive answers based on the receptive, emotional nature of women and the intellectual curiosity of men. When she refuses to be satisfied with these trite responses, she is told by her beloved that "Women shouldn't busy their pretty heads with all this theorising" (228). Emily's rejection of conventional flattering language about women—"That isn't the answer....That isn't the answer" (228), she persists—anticipates Julia Kristeva's description of feminist practice that must say "that's not it" and "that's still not it" (137). And the variety of versions of women's lives contained in the basket of books Emily is carrying—Keats, Shakespeare, *Undine*, and *Emma*—reflects her resistance to simple essentialist definition.

The primary text in Emily's stream of memories is, of course, *In Memoriam*. Despite her admiration for her brother's ability to capture "*exactly the nature of her own shock and sorrow, the very structure and slow process of pain, and the transformations and transmutations of grief*" (232), she has also felt that the poem "strove to annihilate her" (233).

Alfred has appropriated her grief, even figuring himself, not her, as Arthur's widow: "Alfred had taken Arthur and bound him to himself…, leaving no room for her" (234). Nor is there room in the elegy for her wedding, "inconvenient" to the poem, or for her first-born child, named for the dead fiancé. Alfred, she muses, "could hardly have celebrated her own wedding-day.… But he had somehow managed to undo it completely, as though it had not been" (235). Her thoughts then move to her courtship by Richard Jesse, who was attracted by her "lively… interesting" (237) face, not by its static beauty, and who respectfully counters her version of her history of love, loss, and finality with "If you loved him so well, it only proves you can love well and be faithful.… We will not forget him, Miss Tennyson, if you marry me—the love can persist" (241). He convinced her that they could be "comfortable" together, but she still felt occasionally accused by the Hallams, the Tennysons, society at large, and the ghost of her young self, "also accusing, also unappeased" (242). This ghost, as well as Hallam's, needs to be confronted.

At the same time that Emily is retrieving her personal narrative, Lilias and Sophy are having adventures of their own, as all three women prepare, unconsciously, for their final seance. Mr. Hawke's clumsy physical assault on Lilias contrasts comically with his abstract verbal pomposity, and Sophy, alone in her room, goes into a trance that brings her in contact with Hallam—not with his spiritual presence, but with his decaying body. During the same moments that Emily is remembering the downward pull of the mourning process on her younger self, Sophy recognizes that being so much mourned has dragged Hallam "down, or back, or under" (250). Cradling his stinking body in her arms to comfort him, she sees a vision of Tennyson as he is now, an old man. This sequence confirms what Emily sees—that the two men have a closeness that shuts out Emily (and Tennyson's wife, another Emily, as well). Whatever he may say later in his spirit form, the reanimated Hallam longs only to see Tennyson, and Tennyson, whose mind we now enter, thinks only of Arthur and the poems written for him.[5] His memory of the day on the Somersby lawn has entirely erased his sister, and in his misgivings about *In Memoriam*—which reflect Byatt's own lifelong concern about the misuse of art—it is Arthur, not Emily, whom Tennyson fears he may have wronged, by allowing the poem to feed off Arthur's death as "a kind of vigorous parasite.… Perhaps he was in some wrong way *using* his beloved to subserve his own gain…" (268). Byatt movingly and delicately imagines his attempts to define his love for Hallam in terms that, while admitting that "there was more excitement in the space between his finger and Arthur's" (260) than in his sexual relations with his wife, steer clear of openly admitting to homosexual love. Sophy is not able to help Arthur to see his friend, but because, Byatt says, "The Conjugial Angel" is "literature and not spiritualism" (Chevalier, "Entretien" 17), it is Sophy, with her poet's power, who sees Hallam.

In the final seance, the two mediums help Emily to complete the narrative of mourning. Lilias's first writings oppose the here and now to the apocalyptic; their centrepiece is a passage from Tennyson's "The Palace of Art" warning against shutting out love. The last jotting, declaring that "The Bridegroom Cometh" (282), ushers in Sophy's terrified vision of Hallam as part winged bird, part formless clay. As she hears his message, which would bind Emily to him forever, she perceives that this figure is "hungry for the life of the living creatures in the room" (283). This message is the catalyst for Emily's declaration of love for her husband (whom she has just heard tenderly reminiscing about the beauty of her hair, in defiance of Mr. Hawke's Pauline insistence on women's heads being covered in church). In a flash of insight, seeing Richard's amazement at his wife's words, Lilias abandons her image of Emily as the tragic heroine of a story of bereavement and composes a new narrative: "it was only when the Angel threatened her with the loss of the husband she had taken for granted that she really saw him, saw him in terms of his loss, his vanishing, that was implied, and was driven to imagine existence without him" (284). The sympathy she had felt for Emily is now transferred to "a kind of bubbling delight at the spectacle of the looks, shrewd and wondering together, that passed between these two elderly people, who might be supposed to have no possible secrets from each other, and yet had this great one" (284). As she had used her automatic writing to comfort Mrs. Hearnshaw, so she now ends the seance with a wickedly comic parody of *In Memoriam*. Combining images from Blake, Swedenborg, and Tennyson, it proclaims the physicality of the body and its decay in terms Mr. Hawke is quick to pronounce obscene (Fryn Jesse records that the seances participated in by her grandmother had to be ended because the writings became "obscene and filthy" [Kolb 802]). Byatt notes in her review that Owen sees the seances of the period as "a way of subverting normative conceptions of a woman's place and decorous behaviour" ("Chosen Vessels" 605). Here, Lilias's poem, with its images of carnality (no doubt influenced by Arturo's crude, exuberant love-talk) countering the "stone" Conjugial Angel, defeats Mr. Hawke and helps Emily to make the decision to end her quest for contact with Hallam. The narrative produced by the seances, which began as a reinforcement of conventional Victorian attitudes to women's place, has ended as a rejection of some of those assumptions. The co-operative women's narrative, like Matty's tale, has corrected the public version of women's lives. As the story ends, the three women, who had been made to feel "too abundantly fleshly" (278) by Mr. Hawke's strictures, take the bodily comfort of tea and biscuits with their ally Richard Jesse. The fleeting present, with its temporary pleasures, has triumphed over longing for the past, and this peaceful scene prepares for the tumult and joy of Arturo's return as Lilias feels "life ... pumped into her heart and lungs" (289). Byatt aptly describes "The Conjugial Angel" as "a ghost story and a love story. As a ghost story it is concerned with live and dead bodies; as a love story it is concerned, among other things, with male and female bodies" ("True Stories" 110).

In "The Conjugial Angel," as in "The July Ghost" and "The Next Room," Byatt provides space for the irrational and the uncanny. Like Alex Owen, whom Byatt praises for being "respectful and careful about the beliefs and mental and spiritual experiences of others" ("Chosen Vessels" 605), Byatt does not reduce seances to mere fraud. Lilias's writings can be explained by her reading, her remarkable memory, and her creative genius. But Sophy's visions remain inexplicable by rational means: she has no access to Hallam's letters, for example. In her interview with Chevalier, Byatt admits that her upbringing led her to view spiritualism as "completely irrational and odd" but says that she now sees it as, "in fact, a much more usual aspect of human nature than 20th century rationalism." Literature, she continues, can be "a way of taming" and giving form to the "violent persons or beings" (qtd. in Chevalier, "Entretien" 16) that are felt as immediate presences in non-rational experiences. As Byatt's recognition of Sophy's being part of herself shows, the line between a medium's activities and those of a novelist is not easy to draw. Pointing to the fact that "both novellas insist on scenes of imaginative transformation," Michael Levenson suggests that "what finally matters is not that [Sophy's visions] were *images of the real*, but that they were *real images*" ("Angels and Insects" 166). Furthermore, he argues that "the activity of speech and writing is itself bound up with belief, spirit, transformation" and that "the very act of writing historical fiction is a raising of the dead" (172).

In both novellas, the happy ending is earned; it comes as a second chance for the characters after their sufferings and disillusionments and after their hard-won expansion of understanding. Although predictable, these endings are not simplistic. The characters have acknowledged the doubleness of perception and therefore the impossibility of arriving at a final system to explain the world. For William, the English landscape is superimposed on the Brazilian jungle and the two visions of the world are constantly present. For Emily, Somersby remains a magical place, partly constructed by her imagination, but it is also a place "made by men, made for men" (225) that shuts her out—and after Hallam's death it is a place of stark, numbing loss. The dangers inherent in the imagination's constructions of false paradises are clear in both texts, but so are the glories of real insight—and, above all, the intricacy and power of language. The central text linking the novellas, *In Memoriam*, is given many readings, not one: Emily's feminist interpretation is paralleled with the fragmented reading produced in the seances, with Harald Alabaster's desperate grasping at the poem's consoling passages, and with Tennyson's own reading, which especially, and fittingly, focuses on the "threads of living language" (269). This plurality of readings affirms both the poem's complexity as a Victorian artifact and its ability to withstand parody. Byatt's assertion, made outside the text, that *In Memoriam* displays, above all, Tennyson's "intelligence" ("A Hundred Years After" 8) is amply demonstrated. With its multiplicity of perspectives, its juxtaposition of texts and interpretations, and the intelligence, compassion, and generosity of its central vision, *Angels and Insects* proves, once again, that in Byatt's world "everything is surprising, rightly seen" (160).

Both the novellas in *Angels and Insects* celebrate openness and plurality of vision. The dividing of narrative perspectives between male and female characters is one way in which this takes place. In "Morpho Eugenia," we are privy only to William's thought processes, but we are also aware of Matty's perspective through her speech and writing. In "The Conjugial Angel," the viewpoint is predominantly female: we enter the consciousnesses of Lilias, Sophy, and Emily, but, with Sophy's help, we also overhear Alfred's ruminations. Both narratives assert the freedom of the human imagination and both provide a space within which humans can act authentically.[6] In both stories, life, energy, and individuality in the real world are valued. William remembers Matty's distinctive smell and Lilias keeps alive Arturo's "live smell…, unlike any other hair and skin in the whole world" (289), and both of the central love relationships privilege the interesting and the unexpected. "I have become interested in knowing things that concern you" (155), Matty tells William, and Richard surprises Emily in the midst of her mourning: "You aren't cut out to be a maiden aunt, I know, I've watched you ever so sharply. I know you think you *ought*, but you haven't thought of me, have you? You didn't expect *me*, did you?" (241).

At the end of "Morpho Eugenia," Matilda is struck by the life and brightness of the battered butterfly. In a parallel scene near the conclusion of "The Conjugial Angel," Sophy reflects on the "miracle" of sharing tea and biscuits with the Jesses and Lilias: "Any of them might so easily not have been there to drink the tea, or eat the sweetmeats … but here they were and their eyes were bright and their tongues tasted goodness." "This too was a miracle" (287), Sophy thinks, still recovering from the shock of her encounter with the Angel, as she imagines the history of the tea, the biscuits, and the china. And Sophy has the last words in the book, as she understands that the true "life in death" (290) is the safe return of the living Arturo, rather than—as her friend had thought—the perpetuation of the other, lost Arthur through the naming of the Jesses' son. Byatt says that both novellas are "studies of the danger of thinking with images that think with images themselves" ("True Stories" 122). Both texts show that analogies—whether they involve insects or angels— cannot (in Levenson's terms) "stabilize the world" ("*Angels and Insects*" 170), and both texts end by celebrating mystery, surprise, and contingency.

8 The *Matisse* Stories

In conversation with Ignês Sodré in *Imagining Characters* (1995), Byatt reflects that as she grows older, she requires "different problems, as a reader" than "for instance, choice of partners" (241-42). As a writer, she has moved steadily away from the mating or marriage plot, and her short stories in particular have explored other issues, although most keep women at their centre. All of the stories in the three collections published in the 1990s — *The Matisse Stories* (1993), *The Djinn in the Nightingale's Eye* (1994), and *Elementals* (1998) — explore the lives of women, offering implicit comments on the changes and challenges of women's experience in the late twentieth century. They thus extend the preoccupations of *Sugar and Other Stories* but offer a wider definition of women's creativity. In some of the shorter pieces, such as "Medusa's Ankles" from *The Matisse Stories*, "Dragons' Breath" from the *Djinn* volume, and "Baglady" from *Elementals*, Byatt comes close to the effect she fantasized about after the large-scale achievement of *Possession*. Speaking with Val Ross in an interview in 1991, she agreed that she would probably never become a minimalist writer, but predicted, "I'll trust more that I'll be able to write with a single gesture, like a good lyric." In the same interview she observed that "writing would get simpler" with experience: "you do things simply after you can do them complicatedly" (C5). These stories are often complicated in subject, but the writing is dextrous and deft, the images are used with economy and subtlety, and the language is glowingly sensuous, whether it is describing the brilliance of coloured objects, the jangle of background music in a restaurant, the delicate blend of flavours in a Chinese meal, the paradoxical burning sensation of ice on the skin, or the visual impact of a painting.

The three *Matisse Stories* are based on small English domestic or academic events. They are more realistic in mode than the stories in the two later collections, and thus closer to the *Sugar* stories, although like those earlier stories they contain elements of the weird. Both volumes examine the processes of perception—what we choose to look at, what stories we invent or repeat to ourselves. In *Sugar*, discoveries are made through literature and writing; in the *Matisse* volume, the visual replaces the literary. In each of these three stories, paintings by Matisse are evoked as icons of achieved calm, joy, and power; in each, they are associated with a release of energy that at least temporarily frees the characters from being trapped in repetition. There is a personal dimension here, too. Speaking with Mira Stout in 1991, Byatt confided that her work had recently become lighter as she began to see the world again after the blackness of her grief at the death of her son. Matisse's paintings were important in this process: "If one day you regain the sense that these colors and this tension are extraordinarily beautiful, it feels like an incredible gift. The human condition is horrible; all this beauty is extra" (15).

Susannah, the middle-aged woman in "Medusa's Ankles," finds that professional success has come "too late," for she is to appear on television but her aging body has "lost the desire to be seen or looked at" (19-20). In an attempt to redeem at least her hair from decay, she has entrusted it to Lucian, a hairdresser who, with unconscious irony, promises her a "natural" look. What lured her into his shop was a print of Matisse's *Rosy Nude*, which Lucian had chosen to suit his rose and blue colour scheme, thus creating a soft illusionary world in which, Susannah felt, she could "trust" him with the "disintegration" that her intelligence tells her is "indeed natural, the death of the cells" (7). As he works, Lucian confides that he is having an affair with a young girl; weary of his wife, he "must have beauty" (10). The cruel, inevitable contrast between youth and age is sharpened by his subsequent redecoration of his shop. Contemporary colours of grey and maroon replace the *Rosy Nude*, and Susannah now thinks, "Dried blood and instruments of slaughter" (15). When Lucian tells her that he intends to leave his wife, whose fat ankles disgust him, Susannah, whose own ankles are swollen, feels empathy for the wife. Compelled to remember her younger self, now replaced, like the painting, by the harsh colours of age, she sees her grey face in the mirror and feels rage "like a red flood ... it must flare like a flag in her face, but how to tell in this daft cruel grey light?" (23). Meanwhile, she, like the wife, has been abandoned: Lucian goes to work on another client, and his assistant makes an artificial coil of "Sausages and snail-shells, grape-clusters and twining coils" (23) on Susannah's head. The mirror terrify-ingly asserts that Susannah is now repeating the futility of her mother's visits to the hairdresser: "The Japanese say demons of another world approach us through mirrors as fish rise through water, and, bubble-eyed and trailing fins, a fat demon swam towards her, turret-crowned, snake-crowned, her mother fresh from the dryer in all her embarrassing irreality" (23). Susannah is at once her mother, Medusa, and the old queen in "Snow White," a hybrid with grotesque head and swelling ankles. Furious, she blurts out the truth, "*I look like a middle-aged woman with a hair-do....* Not natural" (24) and, in a wonderfully satisfying unleashing of anger, begins to destroy the shop, her passivity in Lucian's hands transformed into a contemporary version of Medusa's revenge, which, as Kathleen Coyne Kelly points out, expresses the "positive and affirming" laughing Medusa of Hélène Cixous as well as the "terrible ... beauty" of the traditional figure (56–57). When Susannah sees Lucian's image multiplied in a mirror, "a cohort of slender, trousered swords-men, waving the bright scissors like weapons" (24–25), the apparently innocent implements of the salon become, in her hands, "bombs or grenades" (25) as the mirror cracks and basins shatter. Here, as often in Byatt's work, glass represents both illusion and truth. Susannah first sees the *Rosy Nude* through the glass of Lucian's shop window, and he himself describes the shop as "a great glass cage" that he is now leaving for the "real world" (28); but it is her own image in the mirror that has shown Susannah the failure of her hopes of arresting physical decay. The full impact of her mock-heroic assault is lost, however, as Lucian calmly reassures her: he had thought, he says of closing the shop, and now he can use the insurance money to pursue his most recent enthusiasm, sell-ing antique jewellery. When Susannah goes home, with her hair still in its "fatal coils," her husband further deflates the glory of her protest, pronouncing her new look youthful. But he, it is hinted, is about to repeat Lucian's pattern of deserting his wife: his movements are "unpredictable and unexplained" (28). Neither of the males has understood Susannah's triumphant moment, when she stepped out of her role as a translator of others' work to make her own unique, original gesture. Nevertheless, she has made her statement. Meanwhile, the *Rosy Nude*, although now re-moved from view, emphasizes the contrast between the ravages of time and the endurance of art.

In "Art Work," too, characters who have been trapped in repetitious lives are freed, in an unexpected way, by art. The story opens with the narrator's meditation on another Matisse painting, *Le silence habité des maisons*. It moves to the "inhabited silence" (32) of 49 Alma Road, where there are no voices, only the hum of machinery: the washer, the dryer, an unwatched television, a young boy's electric train, a girl's vibrating records, a woman's typewriter, a vacuum cleaner. Anticipating the plot's erasure of the line between high art and popular culture and design, the narrator comments that the pattern on the bedspread in the girl's room is one its designer "would never have seen, without Matisse" (34) and that the girl herself, Natasha, resembles one of the painter's "supine women" (34). The owners of the house, Debbie and Robin Dennison, are now introduced; both are artists, and both are at a creative impasse, for opposite, gender-related reasons. To support the family and leave Robin free to pursue his work, which is not commercially successful, Debbie has reluctantly given up her first love, wood engraving, for a job as design editor of a women's magazine. Robin, meanwhile, remains stubbornly faithful to his long-ago vision of the power of colours and to the inspiration of Matisse, which revealed to him "the paradoxical way in which the pure sensuousness of *Luxe, calme et volupté* could be a religious experience of the nature of things" (56). Working doggedly at his painstaking experiments with colour, each colour represented by one of the carefully chosen objects he has arranged in his studio, he paints small, inanimate things, "never anything alive" (52). His studio is spacious, while Debbie's woman's space is cramped and confining: when her drawing board is folded against the window, it blocks out the light and the view of flowers growing in the window box. Debbie is at the beck and call of males: a husband, who has "ritualised his life dangerously" (57) and who rages at the disarrangement of his studio by the cleaning woman; an editor, who "slightly despises the pieces about the guilt of the working mother" (38) that he publishes; and a son, a small symbol of that guilt, at home with chicken pox. Torn between her roles as caregiver and career woman, deprived of her chosen creative outlet, Debbie is caught in stagnation and repetition. Her husband increasingly appears to her as a child to be protected and placated; he even looks "like an adolescent… like a worried colt" (49). When the cleaning woman, Mrs. Brown, disturbs the "fetishes" in his studio, he and Debbie repeatedly engage in a "ritual confrontation" (50), which his wife, seeing his need to insist on the importance of his work, knows "is somehow necessary to their survival" (48). Unable to find her own creative sun, Debbie "turns and hearkens" to Robin's complaints "like a heliotrope" (48), repeating and parodying the old pattern of female response. Robin, for his part, repeats his father's domestic patterns. He is at a dead end, and now experiences his original "vision" as something static: it has "never expanded or diminished or taken its teeth out of him" (55). He is oblivious to Debbie's grief for her "unmade" woodcuts, a loss she feels in her body: "Her fingers remembered the slow, careful work in the wood" (54). She loves her husband for his dedication but also hates him for his blindness to her needs.

Into this household comes Mrs. Brown as a free spirit, despite the fact that she is herself the victim of more overt domestic violence, being sometimes prevented from coming to work by what she labels "acts of Hooker," her abusive sometime partner. Undaunted by male authority, she questions Robin's rigid rules about red and green, using the naturalness of geraniums as proof and arguing that "they're all there, the colours, God made 'em all…, what exists goes together somehow or other" (60). At first viewed as the provider of bizarrely coloured handmade gifts for the children, she turns out to be a secret artist, constructing whole worlds out of found objects. The crisis of the story occurs when Debbie, hoping for a one-man show for Robin, arranges for Shona McRury, a gallery owner, to view his work. Shona puts Robin's problem into words, suggesting that his work is static and forcing him to admit that he cannot imagine moving on to a new phase. Their impasse is demonstrated by the clash between her observation, intended to be encouraging, that his paintings are about "the littleness of our life" and his unspoken response that they are about "the infinite terror of the brilliance of colour" (72). When Shona leaves, Mrs. Brown waylays her, and later Debbie is amazed to see at Shona's gallery a show by Sheba Brown. The centrepiece is an Aladdin's cave of bright, soft sculptures, including deconstructed female bodies and a broken doll-like figure entrapped by washing, "twisted brassières and demented petticoats," with only half a face, guarded by a dragon who is also a vacuum cleaner, "inert and suffocating" (80). Completing the story of the chains of the imprisonment of women's bodies by domesticity are two versions of the ineffectual male rescuer, a tiny toy knight and a toy soldier, both of which have "obviously been through the wheel of the washing-machine, more than once" (81). Identifying her own discarded dress as the source of the dragon's scales, Debbie is not resentful of this appropriation or of Mrs. Brown's opportunistic use of Shona; rather, she is delighted by the splendour of Sheba's newly revealed name and of her treasure trove. By contrast, Robin, predictably, views the exhibit as a (double) theft. The now-famous Sheba, in a television interview, insists that her work has no agenda of feminist anger but is simply a response to the plenitude of experience: "there's so much in the world, isn't there, and making things is a natural enough way of showing your excitement…" (85). For her, the question "Why bother?" which, Debbie reflects, every artist, including (especially) Robin, must ask—"why make representations of anything at all?" (52)—never arises. A genuine producer of "art work," she engages in creative substitution, first by recycling and transforming materials from the households where she works, and then by providing Mrs. Stimpson as her replacement in the Dennison house, with the tantalizing promise that her successor "will do exactly what I did ... no one's unique" (87-88). By showing the persistence of the unique and the unexpected, Mrs. Brown has reasserted the fertility of art. Her exhibit has some concrete results for the Dennisons as well: Debbie begins a series of woodcuts, illustrations for fairy tales, using the faces of Mrs. Brown and Mrs. Stimpson as the models for the bad and good fairies. Robin is jolted into acquiring a new interest; he reads about oriental mythology and paints, with "a new kind of loosed, slightly savage energy" (90), a black goddess who is a travesty of Mrs. Brown. Both Dennisons have been released into creative expression of their anger. And Mrs. Stimpson fulfills at least part of Mrs. Brown's promise that she will replicate her predecessor. Surprisingly identifying Robin's black goddess as "Kali the Destroyer" (89), she reveals herself as a connoisseur of art in her turn, pronouncing that Robin's new work has "*got* something" (90).[1]

In the third story, "The Chinese Lobster," Robin's question, "Why bother," takes on a new urgency. It is asked by Peggi Nollett, a depressed, angry, anorexic art student, in a desperate, misspelled rambling letter to her middle-aged dean of women, Gerda Himmelblau. Peggi is complaining about an instance of alleged sexual harassment by her dissertation supervisor, the distinguished, elderly scholar Perry Diss, whom she also accuses of failing to appreciate her project, which deconstructs Matisse's paintings of women in order to expose what she sees as the painter's misogyny. Faced with Diss's rejection of her work of "*revising or reviewing or rearranging* Matisse" (103) and with her own ongoing apathy and despair, her "Why bother?" interrogates both this project and her life: "Why bother I say to myself and realy there isn't any answer. I realy think I might be better off dead ..." (105). During their discussion of Peggi's accusations, over a restaurant meal of delicious Chinese food, Gerda and Perry discover that both of them, like Peggi, are well acquainted with the thought of suicide. Both reach a realization that their attachment to the "bright forms" of paintings that "go on shining in the dark" (133) helps to hold them back from self-destruction.

In this story the imagery of the enclosed female, also present in the salon that disturbs Susannah in "Medusa's Ankles" and in Debbie's crowded workspace in "Art Work," is more oppressive. When Gerda enters the restaurant for her lunch with Perry, she stops to watch a female lobster imprisoned with some crabs in a glass case, struggling for life in an "unbreathable element" (95); "For a moment, in her bones, Dr. Himmel-blau feels their painful life in the thin air" (96). By the end of the story, this image has acquired more resonance, as it is associated with Peggi's room, with the room in which Perry, years earlier, visited the old and ail-ing Matisse, and with the solitary spaces of Gerda's and Perry's worlds of death. Perry describes Peggi's room, where she eats, sleeps, and furi-ously pursues her project of defacing (with blood or excrement, he spec-ulates) copies of Matisse's paintings, and relates it to Peggi's self-enclo-sure, mummy-like, in layers of wrappings: "You *cannot believe* I could have brought myself to touch her...?" (115). Gerda knows instinctively that he is telling the truth; she has had previous knowledge of Peggi's deep disturbance, which has already led to attempts at suicide. She sees the link between Peggi's vehement rejection of what she calls Matisse's "*distortions* of the Female Body" and "his ways of acumulating Flesh on certain Parts of the Body which appeal to Men and tend to immobilise Women" (102) and to Peggi's anorexia, through which she expresses her loathing of her own body. Yet she can also understand—although as a trained observer she does not share—the feminist objection to Matisse that Peggi confusedly enunciates. When Perry asks why Matisse (rather than, say, Picasso) should be Peggi's target, Gerda replies, "Because he paints silent bliss.... How can Peggi Nollett bear luxe, calme et volupté?" (121). Unlike Peggi, however, Gerda can respond to Perry's passionate insistence on the "*life and power*" (121) of Matisse's work and to his description of the old painter, threatened with blindness, living in a darkened apartment in Nice and telling his young visitor that "black is the colour of light" (131). Meanwhile, the two scholars make the discov-ery that they share their own image of enclosure, a white room where, as Perry says, "There is only one thing possible," death (125).

Gerda's white room is related to the suicide of her friend Kay, the only person she has loved, who killed herself after the suicide of her young daughter. Since then, Gerda has felt herself to be "next in line" (129) and has made some attempts to kill herself: "She believes the impulse is wrong, to be resisted. But at the time it is white, and clear, and simple. The colour goes from the world, so that the only stain on it is her own watching mind. Which it would be easy to wipe away" (129). Now, notic-ing for the first time the scars on Perry's wrists, she sees that he "*knows that she knows*" (129) about the white room. Like her, "he carries inside himself some chamber of ice inside which sits his figure of pain" (130). Silently, she assents to his assertion that "Pleasure is *life*" (123) and that painters like Matisse offer us "*the thing itself*" (124). Their conversation has been accompanied by a silent undercurrent, "a kind of dark river of unconnected thought," and their recognition of its presence is "like the quick slip of a waterfall into a pool, like a drop into darkness" (126). This moment of understanding is, Byatt has said, "the depth of the story" (Chevalier, "Entretien" 23). Such moments are, she says, "the reason why I write short stories" (Chevalier, "Entretien" 12). This experience alters Gerda's death wish: "Something has happened to her white space, to her inner ice, which she does not quite understand" (133). When they leave the restaurant and see again the lobster and crabs, now closer to death, Gerda is able to partially detach herself from their plight. She "experiences, in a way, the pain of alien fish-flesh," but her examination of them is now both "accurate" and "distant" (134). When her new friend comments that he finds the display case "*absolutely appalling*" and yet at the same time doesn't "give a damn" (134), she understands. Through his assertion of the power of Matisse's art, she has experienced a rare moment of *volupté*, and she is at least temporarily relieved of the compulsion to repeat Kay's and Kay's daughter's experience. As a reviewer has observed, the story, which appeared "to be about the battle between intellectual integrity and pity for madness…, has become a meditation on the death wish" (Kelman K12). Byatt has observed that "The Chinese Lobster" is "a story which isn't about what it appears to be"; like Alice Munro, Byatt "changes direction suddenly in the middle" (qtd. in Chevalier, "Entretien" 12–13). Yet although it veers away from Peggi and her problems, refusing to be either a feminist attack on the academy or simply a parody of such attacks, the story does try to answer Peggi's question, "Why bother?"

At the same time, of course, "The Chinese Lobster" does comment, wittily and with insight, on academic politics. Caught between Peggi's accusations and neediness and Perry's fierce defence of art, Gerda makes the necessary compromise, deciding to assign Peggi a new supervisor, one who shares Peggi's ideological position and will overlook her lack of achievement. Gerda and Perry agree that this step, which means that Peggi will get her degree, is a defeat that (like the dying lobster) "matters very much and not at all" (133). The plot does not lead, as a formulaic feminist reading might demand, to a moment of understanding between the older woman and the younger. In an interview, Byatt locates the story's "feminist message" elsewhere, in "this woman's inconsolable grief for another woman" (Miller).[2]

The story offers a warning against the narrowness of imagination that accompanies rigidity. Perry accuses Peggi of failure of imagination and unwillingness to work at understanding Matisse's colours. Gerda links this with Kay's inability to imagine the impact of her suicide on her survivors—but Gerda also knows that "when one is at that point, imagining others becomes unimaginable" (125). For her as for Perry (and as for Byatt herself), the qualities in paintings that Matisse described as "an art of balance, of purity, of quietness" (123) make life bearable. The two new friends will continue to live in their own darkness, knowing that black is the colour of light.[3]

All three of these stories think about the way paintings change the spaces of our lives, challenging us by their visual authority. As a secondary theme, all ponder the relationship between art and the female body. Debbie, unable to find time for her dream of making woodcuts, feels her deprivation in her fingers; Gerda feels the pain of the caged and dying lobster within her body, and only the endurance of art saves her from despair. Relaxed and soothed by the *Rosy Nude*, Susannah becomes violent when black-and-white photographs of young girls replace it, taunting her with the losses of her aging body, and her revenge is a physical rampage. Sheba Brown's art portrays the enslavement of women's bodies with comic exuberance, and Byatt clearly prefers this ludic critique, and Susannah's carnivalesque rampage, to the deadly seriousness of Peggi's attacks on Matisse and on her own body—assaults that arise from an inability both to respond to the paintings' liberating qualities and to accept and enjoy her physical life. Unlike Sheba, who frees herself from the dominance of the male tradition, Peggi is defeated by that tradition and sees no solution but to destroy it. In these stories, in postmodern fashion, the barrier between high art and the furnishings of ordinary life breaks down. As Byatt has said, "the question of the relation between great, individual visions and decoration is not trivial" ("Fashion for Squares" 14). Perry Diss, acting as Byatt's spokesperson, underlines the truth of Matisse's "shocking" statement that art, like a good armchair, should "*please and … be comfortable*" (122). But art also has the power, by engaging the imagination, to break cycles of repetition, to jolt us out of apathy into a renewed perception of the uniqueness of the ordinary, and to release us from enclosure.

9 *The Djinn in the Nightingale's Eye:*
Five Fairy Stories

THE DJINN IN THE NIGHTINGALE'S EYE is subtitled *Five Fairy Stories*. The tales it contains, however, cleverly subvert the fairy-tale genre, subjecting the form to feminist revision without slipping into the propagandizing Byatt so dislikes. In this volume, published in 1994 but containing two stories that had already appeared in *Possession*, Byatt continues to explore the "wonderful, versatile hybrid form" of the "literary fairy tale." Her fairy stories, she says, were written "primarily for the pleasure of entering ... a world of imaginary apples and forest paths ..., of powerful beasts and satisfactory endings" ("Fairy Stories"). As postmodern tales, however, they both think about human experience, as all fairy tales do, and "reflect on the nature of narrative, and of their own narrative in particular. Narration is seen as the goal as well as the medium" ("Fairy Stories"). The heroines of the two longest tales in the volume, the Eldest Princess and Gillian in the title story, find freedom by becoming storytellers, and, since Byatt uses weaving and needlework as images of narration, the tailor in "The Glass Coffin" and Eva in "Dragons' Breath" make stories as well. Gode's always-new telling of an old story is also a creative act on behalf of women.

Anne Cranny-Francis states that "Feminist generic fiction ... critically evaluates the ideological significance of textual conventions and of fiction as a discursive practice" (9–10). In *Imagining Characters*, Byatt observes that "the fairy story says life is full of hazards and horrors and terrors and then you will be married and you will live happily ever after"; her fairy stories reject this formula, moving the form closer to the novel, which she describes as saying that "life is full of energy" and as rejecting the happy-ever-after ending (190–91). By combining features from the two genres, *The Djinn in the Nightingale's Eye* explores both the "hazards" of women's lives and their creative energies. Byatt performs the task of feminist writers described by Cranny-Francis, of "placing the individual (generic) text within the history of that particular (generic) form" (18), to reveal the ideological meaning of that history. In doing so, she gives women power in their own lives.

The two stories originally published in *Possession*, "The Glass Coffin" and "Gode's Story," shift their shape by reappearing in combination with three new stories. Richard Todd shows how these two stories are trans-formed by their presence in "the narrative matrix of *Possession*" (A.S. *Byatt* 43), and the converse is also true. By removing them from their orig-inal context and placing them in her new volume, Byatt makes them part of a history of women's stories. "Gode's Story," the one with the earliest historical setting, stresses most heavily the limitations of women by their culture. "The Glass Coffin" is written in *Possession* by Christabel, a more independently creative woman than those in whose oral tradition Gode follows. Yet Christabel's imagination remains tied to the nine-teenth century. Her story gives its female character more freedom, although her liberation is brought about in the traditional way, by a male. The three new stories, "The Story of the Eldest Princess," "Dragons' Breath," and "The Djinn in the Nightingale's Eye," go further in decon-structing the traditional woman's plot.

In "The Story of the Eldest Princess," the heroine, doomed to failure in the traditional plot that favours the third sibling, succeeds in her quest—and she does so by redefining the quest itself. Rather than bring back the desired object in a plot laid down for her, she abandons the plot and moves outside it. The quest is for a silver bird whose capture will restore the blue sky that has, for some reason apparently related to the three princesses' growth, turned to variable shades of green. Disobeying the instructions of the patriarchal wizard by leaving the straight road of the traditional plot for the wild wood, the eldest princess recognizes in the end that the object of her quest is nothing outside herself; rather, it is nar-rative freedom. In doing so, she violates both the quest plot and the plot of romance—which, for women, usually form one plot.

The princess, knowledgeable about the story she is in, sees this quest plot as a trap: "I am in a pattern I know, and I suspect I have no power to break it" (48). She meets three creatures, all wounded or imprisoned and all in need, they say, of the healing powers of an old woman in the forest. Each creature has suffered, like her, from being caught in a story.[1]

After rescuing the first, a scorpion, the princess decides to "walk out of this inconvenient story"; she realizes that "it would make no difference to the Quest" (52-53). She assumes that the scorpion will sting her, because this is what traditional wisdom tells us; to this, the scorpion retorts that "Most scorpions ... have better things to do" (51). The toad is bleeding because of the false belief that it has a jewel in its head; it has, however, freed itself from its persecutor by using what is true about it, its poisonous skin. Far from being the loathsome creatures constructed by false narratives, the scorpion and the toad are both handsome, although the toad warns the princess about another false story: she "must not suppose I shall turn into a handsome Prince, or any such non-sense" (55). The third creature, a cockroach, which has been caught in a fowler's trap, is the most skilled of all at refuting false stories. After the princess has been attracted by the fowler's whistle and the hunter's horn and has been warned by the scorpion and toad to avoid these humans because of their cruelty, she is enticed by a more threatening temptation in the form of the woodcutter's apparently innocent song. This song, a version of "Come live with me and be my love," promises happy pastoral romance, but the cockroach counters it with the *real* story as he knows it from his observation of the fates of the woodcutter's five wives: "And I will beat your back, and drive / My knotty fists against your head" (59). The cockroach, reputedly the most despicable of the three creatures, is a perceptive truth-teller who, by exposing the despicable habits of the woodcutter, becomes a rescuer in his turn.

Now in her own shared story, the princess reaches the house of the old woman and her true goal, an understanding of the therapeutic value of narrative. The old woman, with a house full of creatures, heals the three newcomers by having them "tell the story of their hurts" (64-65). And the princess discovers her vocation: "telling the story, [she] felt pure pleasure in getting it right" (65). The old woman's completion of the stories of the second and third princesses tells how the second princess is also innovative within the traditional plot, claiming for herself the successful quest for the silver bird. In other ways, however, narrative still imprisons her, for she follows the formula to the letter and, obeying the wizard's instructions, burns the bird. Predictably, the ashes produce a phoenix, the sky turns blue, restoring the norms of narrative,[2] and the second princess in due course becomes queen. The third princess, left with no story, meets an old woman—one of those who, says the old woman storyteller, are "always ahead of you on a journey, and ... behind you too" (71)—and (in this one respect following the convention) chooses the third of three gifts offered to her. She rejects the magic mirror, which would show her her true love and effectively end her story. She also rejects the loom that weaves "thickets of singing birds" (70), providing a ready-made narrative, and chooses instead a fine thread—the narrative of her own free life—which she follows into the forest. By refusing to be caught in the marriage plot, she also rejects the plot of woman's enclosure in a world of simulacra. The women in this story all break the pattern and do so more radically than the figures in the two stories from *Possession*.

Boredom and stagnation in an old plot also lead to the possibility of new stories in the next tale, "Dragons' Breath." Three siblings, Harry, Jack, and Eva, long for escape from the repetitious life of their isolated village. The brothers wish for excitement and variety, while Eva, a weaver working with a limited range of colours to produce traditional designs, dreams of "unknown colours" and an escape from her occupation, which she does not perform well but which is prescribed for her gender. She would like to be "a traveller, a sailor, a learned doctor, an opera singer" (78). When the mountains begin to move and the fixed story of the villager's lives is disturbed, the villagers feel "a certain pleasure in novelty" (79). Then the creatures appear, great wormlike dragons that devastate the village, driving the villagers into the forest (where, despite their terror and suffering, they are still bored) and filling the air with the stench of their breath. But after the destruction—and the subsequent loss of Harry, who dashed into the smoke to rescue his beloved pig, Boris—the family's house emerges untouched, and Boris, too, is restored to them. Now everything is transformed; the people have new stories to tell, and, like the eldest princess, they find delight in making beauty out of danger and suffering. Their stories of the dragons, edited to omit the misery of waiting for Harry to return and the "inevitable fate" (92) of the cherished Boris, take their place with the traditional stories, and these tales become "charms against boredom, … riddling hints of the true relations between peace and beauty and terror" (92). The people create a new folk tale. And although Eva continues to be a weaver, she now sees the old colours freshly, "as though she had never seen colour before" (90). In her unfinished rug, surviving in the ashes, she reads not only the record of her own uneven achievement as an artist—"her moments of flowing competence" as well as of "bunching, tension, anxiety, fumbling"—but also, in the traditional design of the tree, fruit, and birds, the communal narrative of the women of her family, "the past of her mother and grandmother" (91).

This story highlights the possibility of creativity in repetition, insists on the need (especially for women) to continually reimagine personal, family, and tribal history, and faces the inescapability of loss, suffering, and limitation. As in "The Glass Coffin," the female figure's closest ties are familial. Although the predictable patterns of community life necessarily involve becoming "lovers,… parents and grandparents" (76), there is no hint that this future exists for Jack or Eva, and no suggestion that they will fulfill their dreams of enlarged horizons. Unlike the three princesses, they cannot change the plot they are in, but they can change their relation to it by becoming storytellers themselves. And whereas the male hero of the traditional tales rescues the passive female from the dragon, here both sexes share in helplessly witnessing the dragons' devastation and in creatively responding to it.[3]

In the novella that is the *The Djinn*'s title story, the romance plot is again present but involves a love relationship between Dr. Gillian Perholt, a middle-aged narratologist whose name recalls that of Perrault, collector of fairy tales, and a genie whom she has unwittingly released from his imprisonment in a bottle made from a rare and beautiful Turkish glass called nightingale's eye. From one perspective, "The Djinn in the Nightingale's Eye" is an essay in feminist narratology. In it, Byatt performs magic of her own, blending realism and fairy tale. With the djinn's appearance in Gillian's hotel bathroom, the plot slips, apparently effortlessly, across the generic boundary. But long before this moment, the author has highlighted the marvellous elements of everyday life, including the possibility of independent life for women in Western culture.

Byatt's opening paragraph, through its use of the "once upon a time" formula, identifies the story as belonging simultaneously to realism and fantasy by evoking the wonders of the familiar: "Once upon a time, when men and women hurtled through the air on metal wings…." The airplane is now the magic carpet, and Gillian, a denizen of this world, is introduced through apparent paradox: she is "largely irrelevant, and therefore happy" (95). She enjoys being redundant, as "a woman in her fifties, past child-bearing" (101), whose children live far away and whose husband has left her. The reader's creativity is appealed to; we are invited to share Gillian's enjoyment of Milton's description of the serpent "floating redundant" (98), to participate in her reflections on the modern meanings of redundancy, and to construct for ourselves the story of her marriage. We can imagine for ourselves, the narrator says, the fax that arrives by modern magic to tell of Mr. Perholt's decision to leave Gillian for Emmeline Porter, whom we can also imagine for ourselves: "she was twenty-six, that is all you need to know, and more or less what you supposed, probably, anyway" (102). Realistic and fairy-tale elements are smoothly blended in the opening of this story.

As in the other stories in the volume, the marriage plot is marginalized. Gillian has outlived that plot, and, instead of the grief she "imagined herself" feeling, she experiences (in language that anticipates the escape of the djinn from his bottle) "lightness … like a bird confined in a box, like a gas confined in a bottle, that found an opening, and rushed out" (103-04). Gillian is an "unprecedented being" (105), thanks both to modern science, which has extended her lifespan far beyond that of her ancestors, and to the Western world's acceptance of women scholars. Far from being caught in a story like the helpless females in fairy tales, she is a powerful interpreter of narrative and, indeed, ready to create a plot that will enhance her freedom.

Two stories told by Gillian at academic conferences frame the main story. The first, narrated at a conference in Ankara on "Stories of Women's Lives" (105), is Chaucer's tale of Patient Griselda and her testing by her husband Walter. Gillian's analysis, a severe critique of patriarchal control of women's stories, shows, once again, Byatt's concern with the ethics of narrative. After completing her presentation, which is interrupted by a terrifying vision of her own aged and dying self, Gillian becomes a listener to other stories about women, including her friend Orhan Rifat's paper on *The Arabian Nights* (whose principle of embedded stories "The Djinn" follows)[4] and the tales that are told by a mysterious, eloquent guide at the Museum of Anatolian Civilizations. These stories prepare for Gillian's sharing of stories with the djinn and for the second conference, where Gillian creates a story that summarizes the understanding of narrative and of mortality that she has now reached.

In Ankara, Gillian retells Chaucer's "Clerk's Tale," about Griselda's meek endurance of her husband Walter's grotesque tests of her obedience, as a story of the stopping off of women's energies; this, she tells her audience, is the common subject of women's lives in fiction. A resisting reader, Gillian rejects the moral offered by the Clerk that, like Job, we must patiently endure suffering. Noting that the Clerk himself has already rejected the obvious, gender-specific moral that all *wives* should follow Griselda's example—thus showing that interpretation of narrative is an ongoing, communal task—she moves to her own assessment of the story: "The story is terrible because Walter has assumed too many positions in the narration; he is hero, villain, destiny, God and narrator—there is no *play* in this tale" (120). Since Griselda's voice is so effectively silenced, she can, in the end, speak authentically only through her body, clasping her restored children so tightly that she becomes unconscious; "Chaucer does not say … that she was strangling them, but there is fear in his words, and in the power of her grip" (119). Griselda's attempt to rewrite Walter's ending by performing the story of her oppression fails, of course, and Chaucer gives the happily-ever-after ending that Gillian finds so outrageous. Her reshaping of the tale aligns it not with Job but with *The Winter's Tale*, a story with a "plotted dénouement" for a life most of which "has been taken by plotting" (114).

The story of Patient Griselda prepares the way for Orhan's paper, "Powers and powerlessness: djinns and women in *The Arabian Nights*" (106), which itself both builds on Gillian's paper and prepares for the rest of the novella. By focusing on Scheherazade as powerful storyteller and as powerless possession of King Shahriyar, Orhan again links the two subjects of narrative and women's lives. He tells how Scheherazade, by her narrative skill, saves her own life and the lives of the other virgins intended to replace her. This is possible, he says, because her power in "plotting" (125) is powerful enough to overcome Shahriyar's obsessive sexual egotism and vengefulness. Orhan then analyzes one of Scheherazade's stories, one that again brings together freedom, control, and sexuality.

From this point on, Gillian encounters a series of narratives of women's lives. Her self-appointed guide to the museum, whom Orhan identifies as a djinn, tells her of the history of the construction of woman and of Gilgamesh, whose friendship with Enkidu was destroyed by another powerful female, Ishtar, who killed Enkidu because Gilgamesh had rejected her. The tale of Gilgamesh's successful quest—for the flower of immortality, his loss of it to a snake who stole it, and his own death— returns to the topic of mortality, which had interrupted Gillian's conference paper. Then, in Ephesus, Gillian reflects on the figures of Artemis and the Virgin Mary, on the power and powerlessness of women, and on factual versus imaginative truth. She decides that "real-unreal [is] not the point" (166); the point is the imaginative energy generated by well-told stories.[5]

After Gillian buys the bottle that, she is told, may or may not be made of nightingale's-eye glass, the lines between real and unreal simply disappear; wonder becomes naturalized, and language moves easily and often comically between the two realms. After the djinn, fascinated by the television in Gillian's hotel room, which to him is true magic, moves into the reality of the tennis game to pluck the figure of Boris Becker and set it on the chest of drawers, the commentator announces that Becker has had a seizure. This "delighted the djinn, who had indeed seized him" (199). Later, when Gillian tells him she is ready to make her third and last wish, he replies, "I am all ears," and expands his ears "to the size of elephants' ears" (269), erasing the line between word and act. The most telling instance of linguistic boundary-crossing is Gillian's name, which the djinn pronounces "Djil-yan Peri-han" (206), giving her a girl's name, Perihan, from his culture—a name which contains within itself *peri*, a Turkish fairy. Thus transformed, and floating redundant in a new dimension, she understands that "she might move suddenly"—or the djinn might—"into some world where they no longer shared a mutual existence" (207). In her dreamlike state, she does not question his presence, his assurance that the bottle is truly nightingale's eye, or the story he tells of his history; real-unreal is not the point when we meet images from the world of our imagination.

Unlike Sleeping Beauty, who dreams as she sleeps in her glass casket, Gillian, in her dream state, is fully active as her narratologist self; her professional life is enriched, not suspended, by her relationship with the djinn. Again she becomes a listener to and learner from stories, as the djinn, telling the history of his previous incarcerations, explores with her the question of women's freedom. He tells of his relative the Queen of Sheba—the only female he has known who has matched Gillian's description of herself as an independent woman—who willingly gave herself to Suleiman, and, at the other end of the spectrum, of women who, prisoners of patriarchy, had no power of their own at all. One of these, Zefir, was a secret artist, embroidering stories in silk, and feeling herself to be "eaten up with unused power" while she was kept by her husband "like a toy dog…in a cage" (223–24). Zefir and the djinn loved each other, but he sacrificed the possibility of her freedom to his enjoyment of her company. Their story ends in imprisonment for both; as a result of her careless wish that she could forget him, he is enclosed in a bottle again.

Taking her turn as historian of her life, Gillian reciprocates with stories that place herself in relation to women's narratives. She tells about herself as a girl, confused and terrified by the power of her newly emerged perfect body, wishing she were not female. She also tells about her early, abortive attempt to write fiction, when, feeling imprisoned at boarding school, she invented a male alter ego called Julian, who disguised himself as a girl, Julien. This story was abandoned because Gillian was unable to separate realism, reality, and truth; "my imagination failed," and because of this failure, she thinks, "I am a narratologist and not a maker of fictions" (233). Her third story is about an old Ethiopian woman, starving along with all her people, and unable to act: "if only I were not a woman I could go out and do something," she told an interviewer from within the cage-like structure of her body (248). Through this story, Gillian relates herself to the issue in a personal way and exposes the gaps—already indicated by the presence of traditionally garbed Moslem women at the conference in Ankara—between the worlds in which twentieth-century women live.

Up to this point, Gillian has made three wishes. Two are in the ordinary, pre-djinn world, where, at the temple of Artemis, she wishes for an invitation to a conference in Toronto; then, forced against her will to wish on a pillar in the Haghia Sophia, she repeats her girlhood wish to not be a woman. With the djinn, she makes a third wish (the first of three that he is obligated to grant her): to have her body once again as it was at thirty-five, "when I last really *liked* it" (201). Now, her fourth wish is that the djinn will love her—a wish, he says, that might not have been necessary, "since we are together, and sharing our life stories, as lovers do" (250). After their strange and beautiful lovemaking, she and the djinn go to England, where a letter awaits, granting her first wish to attend the conference in Toronto, where she will tell her last story and make her last wish.

This story sums up what Gillian has learned about wishing and about narrative, and shows her understanding of their connection. It also shows that she is now not only a narratologist, "a being of secondary order" (96), but also a maker of fictions. She knows the importance of wishing wisely, and she understands that when narrative control is too rigid, it produces unsatisfactory fictions. Her story of the fisherman and the apes, which introduces her paper, exemplifies these principles. The djinn, in disguise, silently collaborates with her to bring about the ending that both participants desire. Instead of wishing extravagantly for great wealth, Gillian's fisherman asks from the ape he has rescued only a shop, a house with a garden, and a loving wife. There is, however, a snag. With each wish, the ape is diminished; he is wasting away. Gillian now understands what her own last wish must be; she tells how the fisherman gives his last wish to the ape to "wish for your heart's desire" (265). The ape vanishes, and the fisherman lives contentedly to the end of his natural life. As co-operative narrators, Gillian and the djinn have crossed another boundary, obliterating the distinction between the one who wishes and the one who grants the wish. With the djinn's help, Gillian has fulfilled her own requirement that there should be play and freedom in narrative, even to the point of risking loss of control of one's own story. She later accuses her friend of making her paper "incoherent" by introducing "the freedom of wishing-apes" into a story she had intended to be "about fate and death and desire" (269). She concludes her paper with reflections—related to the fisherman's eventual death—on Freud's discovery that death, not pleasure, is humans' deepest wish. This story mirrors the structure of the enclosing main story; it blends the fairy tale, where, as Gillian points out, characters are "subject to Fate and enact their fates," and the novel, where characters have "choice and motivation" (258).

There is no need for women characters as actors in Gillian's new story, for, with the illogical logic of dreams, fisherman and ape stand in for Gillian and the djinn, and the fisherman's wife, who in many versions of tales about fishermen is greedy, is simply one of the rewards her husband's kindness brings. The djinn has indeed introduced freedom: he has contrived his own release from Gillian's control—for he must stay with her until he has granted three wishes—and at the same time has helped her to fulfill her own wish to give him something. With the help of the story, Gillian is able to accept the loss of the djinn and the inevitability of her death. Like the fisherman, she acts generously, giving her last wish to her friend, who, before taking his freedom, chooses to remain with her long enough to give her a gift in return. His gift, a glass paperweight, lends an image for their relationship and the form of their stories by suggesting, in its combination of multicoloured, fluid shapes, what he calls "forever possibilities. And impossibilities, of course" (227). The djinn then disappears, and Gillian resumes her life in "normal" reality, where, "two years ago" (270) in the narrator's time, the djinn returns in another disguise to present her with two weights that image the flower and snake in the tale of Gilgamesh. Holding the snake, which waits to steal the flower, Gillian, though still in her thirty-five-year-old body, notices an age mark on her hand and is able to see this portent as "pretty," a "soft dried-leaf colour" (276). Her body, despite its temporary reprieve, is still travelling toward death, but she no longer finds the sign of mortality terrifying. At the beginning of "The Djinn," Gillian had rejected the image of the wise old crone as applicable to herself. Now, she is ready to become the crone when her time comes. Meanwhile, she is "happy," because she has, for a time, recaptured her childhood ability to recognize "things in the earth … that live a life different from ours, … that cross our lives in stories, in dreams, at certain times when we are floating redundant" (277). Earlier, Gillian's story of the imprisoned Griselda was interrupted by a ghoulish apparition of her own aged self, and she heard her own voice echoing "inside a glass box" (117). Now, she is the possessor and namer of glass, which is "a medium for seeing and a thing seen at once. It is what art is" (274-75). With its paradoxical quality of being "fire and ice, … liquid and solid, … there and not there" (271), glass is a "solid metaphor" (274). Gillian can now see other possibilities in glass besides the story of woman's captivity told in "The Glass Coffin" and its antecedents; glass has become a multiple signifier.

The djinn, who has moved from being the prisoner of glass to the buyer and bestower of glass, has also matured as a storyteller. In his previous incarcerations, he has failed to encourage his temporary owners to use their wishes wisely; he was either too slow to act to change the story and help the woman escape death or, in the case of Zefir, too reluctant to break the tie between them, which depended on her remaining in the cage of her marriage. He wanted, Gillian thought, "to be both liberator and imprisoner in one" (227). Now he and Gillian together achieve as much freedom as is possible for each. In the story of their relationship, furthermore, the ending balances the satisfaction of closure and the promise of open-endedness. As they part, the djinn says that he will "probably" come back to visit her again; Gillian adds, "If you remember to return in my life-time," and he responds, "If I do" (277). Gillian has found what Byatt has described as "ordinary happiness ... to be outside a story, full of curiosity, looking before and after" ("Old Tales" 150). She has achieved this state through her own creative energy, activated by the djinn, who Byatt says is "both death as an invigorating force, and also the passion for reading tales" ("Old Tales" 132).

In the five stories in this volume, Byatt re-visions the traditional female story and questions its ideology. Beginning with the old image of the woman unconscious, enclosed in glass, the collection ends with the woman free, active, and an interpreter of glass. Rescue is a reciprocal act in this story. Even in "The Glass Coffin," in which a male is the rescuer, he is able to free the woman without imposing a new slavery, and the woman lives out her own choices. "Gode's Story," the story most tied to convention, both shows a woman imprisoned by her culture and, at the same time, demonstrates the power of women's imagination, for it is the miller's daughter who, by the force of her language, compels the sailor to see and hear the dancing child. "Dragons' Breath" tells of a woman's discovery of her own and her foremothers' creativity. "The Eldest Princess" and "The Djinn in the Nightingale's Eye" feature women who confront the old stories in a conscious, informed critique and construct new stories demonstrating openness and community.

In all five of the stories, too, a space is opened for the reader. In traditional fairy stories, Rosemary Jackson observes, the closed structure and authoritative narration keep both protagonist and reader passive (154); in Byatt's stories, however, readers as well as characters are active. Familiar with the structure and motifs of fairy tales, we are alert to notice deviations: the absence of evil stepmothers, the transformation of the act of leaving the prescribed path from a dangerous punishable offence to a first step to freedom; most striking of all, the deletion of the marriage ending. The "system of rewards" in the classic tale—summarized by Marcia K. Lieberman as "being beautiful, being chosen, and getting rich" (190)—is displaced. Byatt's heroines are not praised for their youth and beauty, and their riches derive from their own resourcefulness and creativity. These stories all critique the inherited stories described by Karen Rowe as glorifying "passivity, dependency, and self-sacrifice as a heroines cardinal virtues" (210). Whereas the ending of the classic tale answers all our questions, Byatt's tales leave us still wondering. If the guide at the museum was Gillian's djinn in one of his disguises, how did he escape from the bottle of nightingale's eye before Gillian bought it and took it to her hotel? If the two are not the same, how did the second djinn know that Gillian should receive the flower and the snake? We are in a realm where ordinary logic is suspended, where loose ends are irrelevant, and where mysterious forces and beings exist "somehow out there on an unexpected wavelength" (118).[6] Or, to put it in other terms, we are in contact with the "romance of language" that Gillian sees as the meaning of the "golden boy," "more real than reality" (236), whom, as a child, she invented to be her companion, and who is given a new embodiment in the djinn, whose name resembles Julian's.

Byatt's book, described by a reviewer as "an elegant reflection on the nature of narrative" (Adil 20), can be seen as a step toward framing a feminist narratology. The stories do not contain a precise answer to Freud's question, "what do women want?" (about which Gillian speculates), but they point to one clear answer: women want to be free in their own story in a multiplicity of flexible, self-directed plots. Furthermore, they want to participate in shared stories, arising from and constructed around community and reciprocity. These stories are full of "forever possibilities."

Like the adult fairy tales examined by Jack Zipes, the five stories in the *Djinn* volume show "liberation and transformation" for women. At the same time, however, they take what Zipes identifies as a "guarded position...with regard to the possibilities for gender rearrangement" (19). Byatt reveals the potential of the female imagination and envisions the possibility of a male-female relationship that is not based on power and dominance, but only one story, "The Djinn in the Nightingale's Eye," depicts a satisfying sexual relationship, and in it, the male figure is not human. In "The Glass Coffin" and "Dragons' Breath," heterosexual love is marginalized and the sister-brother relationship is privileged; in "The

Eldest Princess," storytelling replaces romantic love; and in "Gode's Story," the result of sexual union is death for both partners. Furthermore, except for "The Glass Coffin," where the language of "happy ever after" is still present, the stories assume that their characters will die. In this sense, the stories also praise the acceptance of limits, the "impossibilities" spoken of by the djinn. In her comment accompanying her contribution of "new" poems by Christabel to the editor of *Victorian Poetry*, Byatt describes *The Djinn in the Nightingale's Eye* as "a self-referring fiction about the life and death of the (female) body" (Letter 2). Certainly both the energy and the vulnerability of women's bodies are highlighted in these stories. But it is important to remember that Byatt is writing to *Victorian Poetry* as Maud Michell-Bailey, and her statement reflects Maud's scholarly interests and language. Similarly, although the multiplicity and bisexuality attributed to woman's experience by Hélène Cixous are present through the relationship of Gillian, the Golden Boy, and the djinn, Byatt's emphasis, I think, is elsewhere. Her paramount interest remains the telling itself, the production of narratives about women that interrogate and revise old stories and create new ones.

10 Elementals: Stories of Fire and Ice

The title of *Elementals* points in several directions. Its subtitle, *Stories of Fire and Ice*, indicates that the six stories in the volume have to do with basic powers or forces: not only fire and water or ice (most prominent in "Cold" and "Crocodile Tears") but earth and air and their psychic equivalents. "Crocodile Tears" and "Cold" are extended narratives, set in climates that mirror the characters' inner states. The remaining four capture brief, sharp moments of realization. All except "Jael" take place in real or imagined settings of intense heat or cold, where mental as well as physical experiences are intensified. In all six, the central characters are stripped of extraneous facts and possessions; they exist in conditions of fundamental neediness and confront primal experiences of love, loss, and betrayal. Extending the metaphor of the title, the stories also depict the terrors of being displaced, "out of one's element," and the possibility of finding or being restored to one's proper state. In four of the stories, "Crocodile Tears," "A Lamia in the Cévennes," "Cold," and "Christ in the House of Martha and Mary," this rescue or restoration occurs; in two, "Baglady" and "Jael," it slips out of reach, and the women are stranded in inauthenticity and equivocation ("Jael") or collapse and disintegration ("Baglady"). In all of the stories except "Lamia," which extends Byatt's reflections on painting (when it first appeared in *The Atlantic Monthly*, Robert Heilman called it a "Matisse story" [610]), the principal figures are women.

In her review of Alice Munro's collection of short stories *The Love of a Good Woman*, Byatt comments on Munro's interest "both in the texture of the 'normal' and the shears that slit it" (D16). This description fits many of Byatt's own stories in *Elementals* and is especially relevant to the first story, "Crocodile Tears." Here, death abruptly ends the happy marriage of Patricia and Tony Nimmo, and the narrative traces the process by which Patricia must come to accept the catastrophic disruption of the pattern of her life. Byatt depicts Patricia's work of grieving—first, denial and flight; then, attempts at suicide; finally, acceptance of the fact of death and return to the place of loss to honour the dead—in terms of physical objects and of Patricia's body. Placing herself at random in an unfamiliar element, the hot, ancient city of Nîmes, surrounded by stones and fountains, Patricia encounters the images of death that make internalization of her loss possible. Unconsciously and, it seems, randomly, she has found the elemental objective correlatives of her loss. As she painfully connects the things of her new environment with her old world with Tony, she is helped by her friendship with another displaced person, Nils Isaksen, a Norwegian who is enduring his own torment and his own form of denial. Together they construct a new, authentic story.

For the Nimmos, the slitting of the normal begins earlier, on the day of Tony's death, when the middle-aged couple quarrel about a piece of art Tony wants to buy. In their frequent visits to galleries, they usually are attracted to the same pieces: "they lingered in the same places considering the same things. Some they remembered, some they forgot, some they carried away to keep" (4). But on this occasion, while Patricia admires a dandelion clock, Tony is drawn to a piece called *The Windbreak*, in which ordinary small objects are combined in a beach scene. Patricia dislikes its banality, pointing out the "dreadful predictability" (7) of its colours; Tony argues that predictability is its subject: "It's a perfectly good complete image of something important" (6). Tony's heart attack, itself a banal, predictable event, occurs after a heavy meal and before the couple have had a chance to repair the rift between them, cutting short their life together, and Patricia must continue alone, suffering the banality of grief.

In shock, her first impulse is to escape to the unfamiliar. Catching sight of Tony's body lying beneath a painting of an avalanche, she flees unobserved, "quick, quick" (9), packs hurriedly, and, without even contacting her grown son and daughter, catches a train to France. She cannot leave her past life so easily, however: she decides to stop in Nîmes because she knows nothing about it and will not be looked for there, but the narrator points out the "almost coincidence" (13) of Nîmes and Nimmo. She finds that "everything was linked to every other thing, and that wasn't good" (13). The ubiquitous crocodile, ancient emblem of the city, elicits her memory of Tony playing Lepidus in *Antony and Cleopatra*

when they were young lovers; according to legend, Augustus's legion-
naires had been given the land and its crocodile symbol to mark the
victory over Anthony and Cleopatra. A newspaper report about the death
of a cyclist releases Patricia's unshed tears, and when Nils offers help,
telling her that he is widowed like her, she dimly recognizes a further
resemblance between them: he is "a driven man" (32). She and Nils
explore the city, and everywhere they see memorials to the dead: the
gladiators' tombs, lovingly erected and inscribed by their loved ones;
the stuffed bulls, victims of bullfights, their mutilated bodies stitched
together; the images of the French Revolution in the Carré d'Art. Meanwhile, Patricia's changing appearance represents her attempts to separate herself from the women who saw Tony's dead body. She buys new
clothes, has her hair cut, and loses weight. Apparently aimless, practising the "indifference" that she recommends to Nils—"The flow of things.
Anything. One thing, then another thing" (39)—she is in fact forced to
glimpse pattern and to see coincidences and connectedness, to acknowledge "the paradox of the formed in the formless" that Byatt identifies in
the writings of Willa Cather and of Munro ("Alice Munro: One of the
Great Ones" D14). Her inner journey during this time is symbolized by her
reading of Proust in French: she "pieced together the world of the novel
in slow motion, like a jigsaw seen through thick, uneven glass, the colours
and shapes hopelessly distorted, the cutting lines of the pieces the only
clear image" (21). Proust's text is a double symbol, in fact, since it insists
on the connectedness and continuity that Patricia is trying to deny. She
avoids looking at the "cutting lines" of one of the pieces of her jigsaw; preferring small, enclosed spaces, she habitually avoids the Arènes, the site
of so much slaughter of humans and beasts. In the story's introductory
paragraph, the narrator comments on the recovery of forgotten events:
"Patches of time can be recalled under hypnosis" (3). Formal hypnosis is
not necessary for Patricia; Nîmes is its own hypnotic atmosphere, and
here she painfully recalls the patches of time in which her traumatic loss
occurred. When she finally goes to the Arènes, first in waking life and
then in a dream, she is able to link up the patches and move toward
acceptance and reparations.

Patricia makes three clumsy, panicky attempts at suicide, and each
time Nils rescues her. Each episode is related to a question Patricia
retrieves from her unconscious: "How do you decide when to stop looking at something?" (3). Visiting the Carré d'Art and finding the ancient
house empty of the museum displays that the guidebook promised, she
asks herself, "What do you do in a dark red space, full of stony art?"
"She remembered wondering when it made sense to stop looking—at a

pictured dandelion, a windbreak, a frozen avalanche" (37). Her repressed memories return, she understands what she has been looking at all along, and she plunges in front of a car. The question is asked again when she has been looking at a painting of frightening images of mountains and snow—"beauty and danger, flat on a wall" (52)—and the image of terror and disaster provokes two questions that bring Patricia closer to the action she must take: "She said in her head, 'What shall I do? What can I do?'" (52). She makes two more attempts, in quick succession.

Now, after pulling her back each time, Nils tells her two stories that facilitate her process of healing. First, he tells a traditional tale of a dead man frozen in ice, waiting for someone to pity him enough to pay for his burial. A young man gives his savings for this purpose, and the iceman, transformed into a servant, helps his benefactor gain the hand of the princess he has dreamed of. Feeling "dread" at the "uncanny aptness," and perceiving that Nils thinks of her as the iceman, Patricia confesses, "I am not the dead man. I left him" (57), and that her action now "feels wrong, terribly wrong" (58).

Acting as her confessor, Nils reassures her: "You can return and set it right" (60). Patricia next sees Nils drunk, angry at the bullfighting that he had come to Nîmes to see but that he has found not mysterious, as he had expected, but disgusting. He now makes his own confession, establishing the crucial connection of the story. He admits that he has not lost a wife, has never in fact been married, and has told himself the false story, embellishing it with a piece of labradorite placed by him on his wife's grave, to avoid the truth. The facts are that after caring for two senile women, his mother and her sister, for years, and eventually burying his mother, he took his helpless aunt to Stockholm and abandoned her in a clinic without identification. He has, he says, done something "much worse" (68) than Patricia: his act of betrayal was premeditated, and he has lied to Patricia. His admission of guilt takes place in the Arènes, where Patricia has followed him. She is acting in response both to the new logic of her connection with him and to requirements of her separate need, that she see the place where people had watched the spectacle of death. Here, she sits beside Nils on a stone seat reminiscent of the imprisoning stone chair in his story of the man in the ice. That night, in a dream, she enters a world of symbols that make explicit the drama of death, acceptance, and renewal in which she has been participating. She dreams that in the Arènes she witnesses a bloody battle between two fencers whose blood then flows back into their bodies so that they can begin again, "hacking, thrusting, bleeding," and finds that Tony is beside her watching the fight. He looks "solid and well." She asks "why are they doing that?"—the same question that had troubled her about the bull-fights. Tony's smile, "as though the slaughter was normal and agree-able," and her recognition that "this very real man was not real" complete her internalization and acceptance. "The bloody men had been real and inescapable" (73), and while she watched "she was not permitted to turn her eyes away, or leave her stony seat…" (72). After Tony's smile, she is freed into action.

With Nils as her companion, Patricia returns to England, finds Tony's grave, and plans to communicate with her son and daughter, whom she had left to bury their father. The inscription she writes with eyebrow pen-cil on the gravestone repeats the memorialization of the gladiators by their loved ones and completes the circle of her marriage. The words are Cleopatra's:

> The odds is gone
> And there is nothing left remarkable
> Beneath the visiting moon. (76)

In the early days of their relationship, Tony had called her Patra. But unlike Cleopatra, Patricia does not become "fire and air" by killing her-self; rather, as she tells Nils in the graveyard, she likes the earth. To Nils, Patricia had praised indifference as a way of dealing with loss. This story about herself is proven false; the elemental forces of life, heightened in the hot, stony city of Nîmes with its ever-present fountains, provide the setting in which she must remember, accept help, and begin to mourn.

Nils's journey is separate but parallel. He has been guilty of covering his guilt with the crocodile tears of false mourning. He has sought the unfamiliarity of Nîmes in order to escape by following the advice he gives Patricia, looking with interest and curiosity: "This," he says, "is human" (41). But, as he himself admits, his kind of interest, like her indifference, is "indiscriminate" (40). He studies Nîmes, "learning these stones" (41), and he wants to understand bullfighting. His discovery that this story of curiosity does not serve his needs, together with Patricia's confession of her own bad faith, makes possible his return in memory to the northern scene of his betrayal. Coincidences have connected the two friends: Nils has told a lie about honouring the dead with a memo-rial stone; Patricia has abandoned her own dead with no memorial. But both have been driven to act against their natures. Both now recognize the uniqueness of both the lost and the living; Nils's counterpart to Patricia's declaration of Tony's uniqueness is his true story of the solitary tree that grows so far north that it must be wrapped by the villagers for protection from the winter's cold. At the end of "Crocodile Tears," Patricia agrees to accompany Nils "to find out—what became of the old lady" (77). With Patricia, he says, this journey "becomes possible" (78).

The second story, "A Lamia in the Cévennes," returns to the topic of painting that was the focus of the *Matisse Stories*. Its central figure, Bernard Lycett-Kean, ponders the same question: "Why bother. Why does [painting] *matter* so much" (87). The Matisse sketch that, with its text by Ronsard, serves as epigraph to the story represents the struggle to resist the lure of the siren, a struggle in which Bernard does not need to engage. Unlike Robin Dennison and Peggi Nollett, however, Bernard has a deep certainty about the answer. In his intense struggles with colour and form, he is "happy, in one of the ways human beings have found in which to be happy" (88). In this story Byatt also continues her exploration of the strategies of postmodern narration, which was especially prominent in the *Djinn* volume, and asserts the freedom of characters to act in plots of their own choosing. Here, it is a man, not (as in "The Story of the Eldest Princess") a woman, who resists the romance plot in order to thrive in a plot based on the successive challenges of work. The first half of Bernard's hyphenated surname, Lycett, suggests the role offered to him: like Lucius, the lover in Keats's poem *Lamia*, he meets a serpent-woman, or lamia, who professes to love him. However, the second part of his name, Kean, aligns him with Keats's philosopher Apollonius, whose keen sight reveals the true nature of the lamia. Bernard is neither Lycius nor Apollonius, however: he has his own perception of the mystery of ordinary things, "serpents and water and light" (111), and no need for magic transformations. Furthermore, he likes snakes but does not like women. Meeting a snake in his swimming pool, Bernard eludes his assigned role in her quest for transformation into a beautiful woman, preferring to use the colours of her body to solve his problem of the colour blue. His friend Raymond, arriving for a visit, steps into the vacant role, and Bernard is left to enjoy his chosen version of Matisse's *luxe, calme, et volupté*. Like other characters in *Elementals*, he finds his element and lives in it.

Once again, as in the title story of *The Djinn*, Byatt crosses the line between reality and fantasy with ease and assurance. The boundary line is already blurred before the appearance of the lamia. After his move from London, with its "lung-corroding ozone" (81), Bernard finds the atmosphere and climate of the south of France intense, a poser of exhilarating, terrifying professional problems; its blue is something "he needed to know and fight" (83). Swimming in the pool, "trying to understand the blue," his body is momentarily—and naturally—transformed into a boat:

his shadow has "paddle-shaped hands" and his chin is a "prow" (84). After the purification of the pool of the algae-fighting substance that, Bernard insists, has polluted it and its refilling with mountain river water, the lamia appears swimming beside him. She is a creature from both the natural world and the world of textualized fantasy. Her size, the colours of her scales, and even her possession of what appear to be eyelashes identify her as the poisonous Montpellier snake that inhabits the Cévennes, but the language through which Bernard perceives her is, he knows, that of Keats's poem. Bernard judges her to be "a mess, as far as her head went" (102) but seizes on the colours of her body as a way of overcoming his impasse. When she is swimming in it, "The colour of the water [is] solved, dissolved, it became a medium to contain a darkness spangled with living colours" (96–97). His refusal to yield to the blandishments of her language, when she speaks, is, paradoxically, not a denial but an affirmation of beauty and mystery, for, unlike the djinn, the lamia speaks from a set text and offers formulaic promises: "If you will kiss my mouth, I will become a most beautiful woman, and if you will marry me, I will be eternally faithful and gain an immortal soul. I will also bring you power, and riches, and knowledge you never dreamed of" (98–99). Whereas the djinn, as a creative agent, devises open-ended plots in a world of true magic, the lamia is a figure from degraded myth, offering worn-out magic. In preferring the natural world, Bernard chooses what to him is genuine mystery.

The debasement of myth in the lamia's narrative is underlined in the second part of the story, when Bernard's friend Raymond Potter arrives. Described by Bernard as "a dreadful Englishman of the fee-fi-fo-fum sort" (103), Raymond is large and loud, like the giant in the fairy tale; he brings an appropriately outsized feast, including a leg of wild boar and a crate of red wine. His given name indicates that he is a twentieth-century counterpart of Raimondin from the story of Melusina, but his surname, taken by Byatt from her own partly autobiographical quartet, comically signals his inability to function in a real fairy tale. The lamia appears the next morning at breakfast, now transformed, presumably by Raymond's kiss, into Melanie, a Melusina who has had her day. Her hair is dyed, her gestures "actressy," and the silver moons of her scales, now downgraded to "little round green spots like peas" (105) in her sleazy, skimpy cheesecloth dress, are, no doubt, the source of the sound of "rattling coins" in her luggage (107). The besotted Raymond announces, "as though he himself had not known this until he said it" (108), that they are to be married; now they are leaving for Cannes to see films and film stars and to buy Melanie a new wardrobe. Falling obediently into the role of Lycius in Keats's poem, he is obviously doomed to a rude awakening. Bernard, making a private joke, tells his friend to "Beware of philosophers" (108); he himself, like Apollonius, has penetrated Melanie's disguise.

Although Byatt's main preoccupation in "Lamia" is with the exhilarating struggle of the artist, her story also makes a wry comment on the objectification of women by the male imagination. For Raymond, who is a professional set designer for television, Melanie is a sexy, star-struck girl. (He does not notice her resemblance to both a snake and a cat, and thus to one of the monsters featured in the children's program he works on.) Bernard reflects that Melanie "made a very good blowzy sort of a woman, just right for Raymond," and wonders "what sort of a woman she would have become for him" (110). But he is not interested in this question; it was her otherness as a snake, not as a woman, that had captured his attention. Meanwhile, Melanie's real self—if she has one—remains hidden.

Left alone, Bernard discovers his next challenge, a butterfly that, at first "nondescript orange-brown," becomes "rich, gleaming, intense purple" then "orange-gold and purple-veiled" and, folding its wings, reveals green, tan, white, and charcoal (110-11). The serious point of this lighthearted, playful story is that the ordinary world contains endless instances of changefulness and variety to engage the attentive imagination. Further, the story asserts that in the demythologized world of the late twentieth century, the enmity between the imagination and science is erased. This Romantic myth, too, is obsolete. Bernard rejects the statement of Keats's narrator that

> Philosophy will clip an Angel's wings,
> Conquer all mysteries by rule and line,
> Empty the haunted air and gnomed mine—
> Unweave a rainbow....

"Personally..., he had never gone along with Keats about all that stuff." He "would rather have the optical mysteries of waves and particles in the water and light of the rainbow than any old gnome or fay," he thinks, as he joyfully identifies the butterfly as his next "mystery to be explained by rule and line" (109-10). Unlike Raymond, he chooses his own plot. "Exact study would not clip this creature's wings," he reflects. "Don't go, he begged it.... Purple and orange is a terrible and violent fate. There is months of work in it" (111).

"Cold," an extended fantasy about love and art, is set in an unspecified time in the past, in two imaginary kingdoms. Simply put, its subject is the attraction of opposites and the price that may be paid for this attraction. A princess, Fiammarosa, a creature of cold, falls in love with a prince, Sasan, from a fiery desert land, and marries him. The story is also about the difficulties and compromises a woman faces in finding an environment in which her mind and body can thrive.

Fiammarosa is given her name because at birth she is "fiery and rosy" (115), but she soon becomes milky white, lethargic, and delicate. Her parents believe that she must be protected, especially from the cold. But as her body matures, it asserts its needs and its difference from the temperate climate that surrounds it. Her subconscious speaks to her through dreams of travelling alone "at high speeds above black and white fields and forests" (121) and hearing the shriek of the wind, which is in fact howling around the palace when she wakes—"She heard with her ears what she had dreamed in her skull" (122). But her "dreams entertained no visitors" (141); her sexual hunger is not linked to any other body. Her favourite childhood possession was a mirror, and she is now narcissistically "possessed" (123) by the image of herself lying naked in the snow. Escaping at night from the palace, she dances in the snow and comes to sensuous life. "Her body was full of an electric charge, a thrill, from an intense cold" (125), "that paradoxical burn" that it contains. "This is who I am," she thinks; "this is what I want" (126). Her tutor, Hugh, is led by his love for her to recognize her true story, that her element is not fire but ice. He offers her a version of her genealogy: she is descended from Fror, an icewoman from the north who was given to Fiammarosa's ancestor King Beriman in a political marriage but could not live away from her cold world. Leaving behind her baby son, Leonin, she returned to "her own air" (130). Fiammarosa cautiously accepts the relationship—perhaps she does have ice in her veins—but does she therefore have "a cold nature?" (132). Did the icewoman have a cold soul? This conversation produces a "clarification" (133).

Urged by Hugh, Fiammarosa's parents construct a cold environment for her. She creates gardens of arctic plants, and instead of producing embroidery and drawings because all princesses must do so, she now creates original art. No longer a passive imitator, she becomes a unique artist, weaving "tapestries, with silver threads and ice-blue threads, with night violets and cool primroses … that were unlike anything seen before in that land" (134–35); she is narrating the story of her own element. She becomes a scholar of both weaving and botany, and corresponds with other experts around the world. She has revised the story of the princess-as-artist to fit her own gifts, which spring from her own body.

But the traditional princess's plot does not, of course, end here. Princesses are expected to be wives as well as artists. Fiammarosa must find her own relationship to the narrative that could imprison her. She has seen, in "both histories and wonder tales" (135), that princesses appear to be commodities, but also that they have, in stories and in real life, some power of choice. Her liberal-minded father wishes to revise this inherited story. He will not impose a political marriage on Fiammarosa, but wishes her "to marry for her own good" (138); she should, he thinks, marry Prince Boris, from the ice kingdom of her ancestress Fror. The metaphor with which he privately represents her imagined marriage reveals his uneasiness about the effect of a sexual relationship on Fiammarosa's identity: "He believed it would be good for his daughter to be melted smooth, although he did not … push this metaphor too far. He had a mental image of an icicle running with water, not an absent icicle and a warm, formless pool" (137). For her part, the princess "vaguely" thinks that she should use her limited powers of "prevarication and intimidation" (136) to avoid marrying anyone.

When the suitors invited by her father arrive, preceded by their gifts, Fiammarosa makes a radical alteration in both her father's version of her story and her own provisional narrative. She rejects Prince Boris's gifts, which include a necklace of bears' claws that even her father, with his hopes for a marriage to Boris, does not wish to see around Fiammarosa's neck. She is unmoved by the other suitors' gifts, too, and is powerfully drawn to the three sent by Prince Sasan. All are made of glass—a castle, a beehive, and a tree of life representing the four seasons—and all are exquisitely wrought metaphors through which Sasan expresses his intuitive understanding of Fiammarosa's body and its needs. Byatt's language is delicately sexual. The castle has an invisible centre "where the thickness of the transparent glass itself resisted penetration"; from here, "little tongues of rosy flame" (142) run through passageways. Sasan's envoy interprets the castle as "an image of my master's heart" (143) waiting for Fiammarosa's warmth to fill it; the reader sees that it also images Fiammarosa's body and her passion—it is a multiple signifier. The beehive and the tree of life take the glass narrative to its conclusion. Bees luxuriate in the depth of flowers, and the tree shows "life flowering and fruiting perpetually" (147). Fiammarosa, already seeing the gifts with the eye of love, assumes that Sasan has created them himself, just as she makes her own art, although Hugh urges another interpretation, that the gifts are made by subject craftsmen. In any case, Hugh says—repeating the thoughts of Fiammarosa's father about Boris—a man and his gifts are not the same thing, and he adds a warning: "And glass is not ice" (148).

When the princes arrive, Sasan confirms that he is the creator of the glass objects and proves himself to be an artist in music as well: he plays on his pipe music of his own composition, whereas the other princes have brought their musicians with them. Both Fiammarosa and Sasan are original artists who create from their bodies. But they also create from their own elements, which are opposites. Fiammarosa struggles to bring the two together, hearing in Sasan's music "water frozen in mid-fall" (150) and seeing glass as resembling "frozen water" (151). Despite Hugh's correction, as he tells her that glass is sand melted by fire, and despite his prediction—"He will melt you into a puddle" (153)—Fiammarosa agrees to marry Sasan and "learn about glass-blowing" (152).

Now the two lovers move from interpreting and misinterpreting each other to composing their mutual story. Sasan's lovemaking literally writes on Fiammarosa's body, leaving rosy marks: "she had an icewoman's skin that responded to every touch by blossoming red" (157). She now rediscovers the "agonizing bliss" (156) of burning cold, which she had previously experienced in solitude. But Hugh's prophecy is beginning to be fulfilled: "inside her a little melted pool of water slopped and swayed where she had been solid and shining" (157). Arriving in Sasan's desert country, she finds the sun "merciless" (165) and becomes once more passive and languid as she was as a child before she found her element. Fiammarosa believes, however, that she can impose a happy ending by an act of will: "She put it to herself that she was delighting in extremity.... She thought she was learning to live for love and beauty, through the power of the will. She was to find that in the end these things are subject to the weather..." (164). She writes to Hugh that she misses their conversations and finds herself confined indoors (in a palace whose beehive-like shape shows the sinister aspect of Sasan's courtship gift), awaiting another confinement. She miscarries, "melting" to the extreme degree her father had not dared to imagine, and lies "moaning in a sea of red blood, lit by flames" (169) in Sasan's workroom. She has indeed learned about glass-blowing; her enclosure in this strange land threatens to choke her, just as she had feared that Boris's bears'-claw necklace would have done. Her body, which she had instinctively felt she must not give to the prince of the north, cannot thrive in Sasan's hot world either. Her studies and her weaving are abandoned; her body becomes heavy and slow. She cannot weave in her new home, although Sasan has thoughtfully transported her loom and wool there.

Responding to Fiammarosa's needs, Sasan packs away the nine vases he had made to tell the story of her pregnancy and sets out in secret to create a new habitat for his wife in the mountains of his country. As they journey toward it, he names the things of his element: "These are the things I am made of…, grains of burning sand, and breath of air, and the blaze of light. Like glass" (173). He sees clearly in this space. Meanwhile, Fiammarosa, still trying to make a story that brings their two worlds together, transforms the sand and stone into objects from her own world: "great lagoons of clear water, great rivers of ice with ice floes…. They could have lived together happily, she reflected, by day and night, in these vanishing frozen palaces shining in the hot desert…. But the mirages came and went" (173). This story, like her story of living in Sasan's world by will and like Sasan's narrative of pregnancy told in the nine vases, must be set aside.

In the end, the story becomes one of compromise. In the mountains Sasan builds a large-scale embodiment of the glass castle that had enthralled Fiammarosa before they met. It is wholly his creation; his breath, his artistic power, controls its doors. He has devised a way to keep the temperature cold; here Fiammarosa's "icewoman's blood stirred to life and her eyes shone" (177). Sasan has provided for Fiammarosa's physical needs; he will visit her when he can; and he hopes that here she can "live, and…breathe, and…be herself, for he could neither bear to keep her in the hot sunny city, nor could he bear to lose her" (178). Best of all, the castle opens into a place above the snow line, where Fiammarosa finds "a field of untouched snow, such as she had never thought to see again" (180). Here they create art together—she dances as Sasan plays his flute—and when Sasan is too cold to play, Fiammarosa warms him with her body. Their lovemaking takes place in Fiammarosa's chamber in an atmosphere that fulfills their separate needs: the currents of air, "first warm, then cooling,…brought both of them to life" (181), and her body is restored to its natural icy form. Together, the two have found a way to make beauty and love, but they have done so at a cost to both. Sasan supplies a hopeful conclusion to their story: "We can make air, water, light, into something both of us can live in" (179). However, they must endure long separations when Sasan is working in his hot city.

In rewriting the story of her ancestress Fror as a narrative of passion and fidelity, Fiammarosa has sacrificed her art. She has proven that she is not cold at heart like Fror, who left her husband and son without a farewell. Moreover, Fiammarosa's children, unlike Fror's son, do not resemble only their father. She has a son, who resembles herself, and a daughter, who is dark like her father, with a "glass-blower's, flute-player's mouth" (181). In the next generation of Sasanians, women will practice arts hitherto deemed to be the prerogative of males; it will no longer be true, as Sasan says, that "princes are glassmakers and glassmakers are princes" (163). But for the present all art has been appropriated by the male. Although Fiammarosa continues her study of botany and her scholarly correspondence, her loom is not present among the furnishings of her new palace. She does not weave tapestries again; she has lost part of her creativity. Her bed curtains, which resemble the tapestries she wove before her marriage, have been fashioned by Sasan in his own medium, glass. Sasan has lovingly provided for the needs of Fiammarosa's body, but he has unwittingly deprived her of the art that was an expression of that body. Fiammarosa has also lost the intellectual stimulus of her conversations with Hugh, either in person or through letters; in his farewell letter, he tells her that he too has compromised, making an ordinary happy marriage. He declares his love for her—"I shall never be *quite* contented … because I saw you dance in the snow"—and completes the interpretation of the narrative of her life that he began before Sasan arrived. He tried to prevent her marriage, but he now sees "that extreme desires extreme, and that beings of pure fire and ice may know delights we ordinary mortals must glimpse and forgo" (167).

Instead of the fairy-tale ending, Byatt offers a realistic one. Fiammarosa understands that "no one has everything they can desire"; she is "resourceful and hopeful" (182). She discovers a new plant that is an image of herself and her losses: "a sweet blueberry, that grew in the snow, but in the glass garden became twice the size, and almost as delicate in flavour" (182).

Reviewing *Elementals* in the *Times Literary Supplement*, Katy Emck observed that Sasan's creations "provide solutions which are simultaneously a question of art and a question of love" and that these "can hardly be separated" (25). In fact, it is only the force of the couple's passion and the tenderness and perseverance of Sasan's concern for Fiammarosa that prevent "Cold," from being a stark, frightening narrative of male power enclosing the female and appropriating her art. In her interview with Nicolas Tredell, Byatt describes the conflict, related to her reading of "The Lady of Shalott," between "the sensuous life, childbearing, therefore men, therefore danger, and making things by yourself of exquisite beauty which can be accused of being unreal" (66). In "Cold," she depicts a Lady who does not die but lives a life of bittersweet compromise. From a feminist perspective, it seems significant that whereas Bernard, the male artist in "Lamia," is free to choose art over the possibility of love, here the female loses her art as the price of loving and being loved. The fact that neither she nor her husband appears to be conscious of her loss only makes the story's commentary on women's choices more poignant. But, like the stories of art versus life that Byatt praises in her essay "Ice,

Snow, Glass," the plots of "Cold" and "Lamia" are "riddles" that "all readers change ... a little" and that "accept and resist change simultaneously"
("Ice, Snow, Glass" 164). Byatt has written a more complex version of the
fairy stories in which the prince rescues the princess from her icy world
of art. In this intricately beautiful story, she again ponders a problem that
has preoccupied her from the beginning of her career.[1]

The fourth story, "Baglady," is a short, chilling tale that represents
Byatt's most pessimistic answer to the question of what happens to the
aging woman. Its closest resemblance is to "The Dried Witch" from the
Sugar collection, a story Kathleen Coyne Kelly aptly compares to Shirley
Jackson's "The Lottery" (49); in "The Dried Witch," however, A-Oa is the
victim of a traditional, ritualized persecution. In "Baglady," Daphne
Gulver-Robinson suffers from a vague and even more frightening process
of marginalization: she is simply left behind and forgotten. Her name
suggests successful male travellers, Gulliver and Crusoe, but her journey
is only to stasis and disintegration.

The narrator deftly constructs Daphne as a lonely woman even when
she is still at home in England. She correctly identifies her element there
as the world of "the donkeys and the geese and the fantails" (186) at the
country house in Norfolk that she shares with Rollo, her husband, a
company director. Rollo agrees that she would be happier not to accompany him on his business trip to the Far East, but insists that she go; the
chairman of his company, the oxymoronic Doolittle Wind Quietus, prefers
that wives accompany their husbands, especially to the Far East in the
age of AIDS. Rollo "doesn't want to see and doesn't see" (187) what matters to Daphne; he fails to recognize that he has betrayed her by making
her into a convenience. In their hierarchical, sexist world, both husband
and wife are marginalized, existing on the fringes of their peer groups.
Rollo is not an influential director, and Daphne does not fit in with the
younger, beautifully groomed wives who are her companions on the
journey. When, following the rigid schedule enforced by Lady Scroop,
the chairman's wife, she joins the others in an expedition to the Good Fortune Shopping Mall, she enters a Kafkaesque nightmare that, in terrify-
ingly heightened fashion, reflects her real situation. At the mall, Daphne,
left behind when the other women rush off, experiences the speeding up
of time. One by one, the marks of her identity and place in the world drop
away: she loses her camera, a heel from her shoe, her purse and credit
cards, her pen, her watch, and, finally, her passport. Her appearance dis-
integrates rapidly, as her hairpins fall out, her lipstick bleeds, her stock-
ings split and wrinkle, and her body sweats. She realizes in terror that she
is trapped in the prison-like building whose signs, "Café" and "Exit," lead

nowhere, and that she has missed both her lunch appointment with the other women and her plane. She releases her desperation in a scream that "helps" (192), but only in that it comes from her real, stripped-bare self. A policeman appears, and she sees herself through his eyes, "a baglady, dirty, unkempt, with a bag full of somebody's shopping, a tattered battery-hen" (193). Is this the fate that is in store also for the younger women, whom she had seen as "hens looking for worms" (188) in their frenzied pursuit of objects to buy? In a few hours, she has become nameless and abandoned, part of the "human flotsam and jetsam" (188) she had seen outside the mall, and the policeman orders her to join them: "People like you…, not allowed in here" (193). Although Daphne protests that her husband will come for her, she in fact "cannot imagine anyone coming. She cannot imagine getting out of the Good Fortune Mall" (194). She is no longer related even to the socially constructed story of the dependent, exploited woman; she is beyond the imagination's power to conceive of change, beyond narrative. The blandly cheerful fortune inscribed in the introductory illustration by Darren Haggar jars harshly with her fate. Echoing the artificial brightness of Lady Scroop's instructions, it proclaims, "You will always have good luck in your personal affairs." For Daphne, time has stopped; the Doolittle Wind Quietus has left her behind, used and discarded. "Baglady" is the blackest and most disturbing of Byatt's portraits of aging, marginalized women.

"Jael" is another tale of disconnectedness. Its central figure, Jess, is much less sympathetic to the reader than Daphne, for whereas Daphne is guilty only of allowing herself to drift with the current, Jess bears moral responsibility for her situation; she comes close to but finally misses the opportunity for full self-recognition. As well, "Jael" makes explicit the theme of betrayal that runs through both *Matisse Stories* and *Elementals* and that is especially evident in "Crocodile Tears." For Jess, however, there is no redemptive making of amends; the story suggests that the cycle of betrayal will be endlessly repeated. In this story, for only the second time in her fiction, Byatt uses first-person narration. But unlike the unnamed narrator of "Sugar," Jess, in her engagement with memory and the imagination's constructions, fails to make the crucial connections that could bring fact to life.

A reviewer of *Elementals* observed that "Jael" contains "three stories from different eras…all sordid little tales of betrayal" (Thomas D20). Jess recalls her childhood experience with the Bible story of the Israelite woman who betrays the laws of hospitality by murdering the Canaanite captain Sisera while he was her guest. Jess half-recalls that, as a child, she perpetrated a similar act of gratuitous violence on a schoolmate. Now, in the present, Jess in turn is about to be betrayed by her ambitious assistant, Lara. The relationship among the betrayals is clear to the reader, but the narrator herself misses seeing them. The reader perceives that Jess, illustrating the story of Jael, revelled in capturing the excitement of the bloodshed with her pencil; searching for excitement as a way out of the boredom of her life as a schoolgirl, she imagined an accident to Wendy, the most popular of her classmates. The adult Jess refuses to admit that she made it happen and thus caused serious permanent damage to the innocent Wendy, who had what "you could call … grace" (210). As an agent of delayed retribution, Lara will supplant Jess in the cutthroat world of advertising. There is, in fact, a fourth betrayer in the story: Mrs. Hodges, Jess's teacher, who substituted illustrating Bible stories for understanding their moral relevance: "she gave us no explanation of why we had to study and illustrate that peculiarly disagreeable and morally equivocal story" (198). Mrs. Hodges, a history teacher "doing her stint at Scripture" (198), had no commitment to the stories; instead, she praised Jess's use of her pointed vermilion pencil to create a "great sheet of blood" (197) spilling from Sisera's body. The language with which Mrs. Hodges is described, "red lips, and wickedly pointed" (198) high heels, suggests her unthinking complicity with Jess. Jess finds the scriptures "both dead and nasty," adding that "all we did was illustrate them" (200). She is unaware of how fully her life has illustrated the story of Jael.

Byatt has described Jess as "an unpleasant and mendacious narrator" ("True Stories" 178 n.13). The narrative order in "Jael" represents the evasiveness of Jess's reflections. Beginning with her memories of illustrating the story, she moves to the present, recounting the story of Jed, her cameraman, and her recent work on a grenadine commercial, then returns to her life at school. Only now, past the midpoint of the narrative, does she introduce the embedded story of her imagining of Wendy's accident and serious injury. At the end, Jess says that she remembers Jael "because the story doesn't quite make sense, the emotions are all in a muddle, you are asked to rejoice in wickedness" and "because of the delicious red, because of the edge of excitement in wielding the pencil-point, because I had a half-a-glimpse of making art and colour" (215–16).

The language shows that Jess has had only "a half-a-glimpse," too, of her own mean-spiritedness and culpability. It moves between insistence on the truth of her version and half-acknowledged admissions that this version suppresses the truth. "Really" is used in conjunction with negatives three times in a sequence of three sentences: "I don't really think I asked myself … why we were being asked to illustrate this very odd tale. I really don't think so. Nor do I really think there is any reason why I remember that drawing…" (198). She calls the moments when she recalls the schoolroom experience "pointless" (199), and later she describes herself as "a pointless poet who doesn't make poems" (205) and sees that the story of Jael provided her with "metaphors": that the point of her pencil and the tent peg that Jael drove into Sisera's skull were images of each other. "Pencil, peg. Another *detached* image, like the grenade" that she had thought of using in her grenadine commercial. "Pointed, pointless" (206), she concludes ambiguously. She now tells the story of her own treachery, which shows that the connection with Jael was *not* "pointless" and which establishes the parallel between her craving for violent colour and her need for some excitement to relieve the boredom of the "yellow-khaki-mustard-*thick* colour" (206) of her days at school. There, two rival "gangs" of girls, Wendy's and Rachel's, had formed, each existing only in order to perpetuate itself and the tension between the two gangs. Apart from this, "Nothing ever happened" (211). The child Jess, on the fringe of the gangs but attracted to Rachel's for its non-conformity, imagines that an act of treachery would create interest. Her language now changes: "I think nothing happened. No, change that, *something* happened, but I do not remember how" (211). The narrative then returns briefly to the present and to Lara's betrayal of Jess, by inventing, "I think" (212), a survey that shows that Jess's commercials are boring the viewers. The parallel between Lara and Jess is acknowledged but not confronted: Jess speaks of Lara using "all the inventiveness of her, our… trade" (212) and of the younger woman's deployment of images that are even more violent than Jess's: "She can fill screens with blood I shall drown in" (213). The cycle of treachery will continue. Juxtaposed with this, still hedged around with ambiguous language, is the younger Jess's plan for Wendy: "I did have another idea, I think, about Wendy and Rachel. I thought, if some girl stretched a dark cord across the path" (213), Wendy would fall in her race and Rachel would feel "secret gratitude" (214) to the unnamed girl who tripped Wendy. But, Jess insists, she "abandoned" this "scenario" (214). Nevertheless, Wendy did fall, exactly where Jess had imagined she would. Jess admits to "a very clear memory of the piece of cord…, such as my father had in his shed" (215) but not to placing it in Wendy's path, and then tries to deny everything: "I remember things I really think didn't happen" (215). Once again, "really" is used with the denying negative, but Jess's disclaimers protest too much; in her evasive narrative, memories she is struggling to repress will not stay buried.

Jess's moral failure comes from an avoidance of connection. She refuses to engage in the arduous work of piecing things together that

Patricia finally accomplishes. Patricia relates herself to Nils's story of the iceman who required burial, and frees herself; Jess lacks the courage to make an open acknowledgment of her role as Jael, and remains trapped. Jess's work reflects a fragmented view of objects: grenadine—pomegranate—grenade—blood. "Attached to nothing, it's just the quirky way my mind works" (205), she says. Her love of colour and movement draws her to violent, sensuous images and disconnected "scenarios"; it is her job to imagine "lighting, the figure entering the frame, and ACTION" (215). In contrast to Bernard in "Lamia," Gerda and Perry in "The Chinese Lobster," and even Robin in "Art Work," Jess has no vision to be true to; she relates to no visual masterpieces, and she has plundered literary works, such as *Jane Eyre*, to serve the commercial interests of her clients. Her metaphors are dangerously ungrounded; they have come loose from meaning. Her memory of having felt, as a child, that she resembled the servant in the Bible story who buried his one talent (while Wendy multiplied her many talents) reveals her sense that she has wasted her potential, but this association is kept at a safe distance by being framed as a parenthetical question. Similarly, Jess, remembering that she and her schoolmates called their school ties "nigger-brown," using the word in an "unloaded" way, confesses that she is now fearful of being "judged without being imagined" (206–07) for this usage. For her much greater failure to connect words with significance, however, Jess is both judged and imagined by the reader; she has betrayed herself through her own words.

The collection ends with an ekphrastic story; its title, "Christ in the House of Martha and Mary," is also the title of a painting by Velázquez, and in her story Byatt imagines the creation of the painting by the young painter (Velázquez was nineteen at the time) and its impact on the young woman who was one of his models. This story's use of ekphrasis differs from that in "Precipice-Encurled," which contains a painting by Monet, and from the three Matisse stories, for here the painting is the central occasion for the story. In addition to providing astute commentary on Velázquez's work, Byatt also engages in biblical exegesis, offering an explication of the story as told in Luke. The story thus becomes a modern parable.

The central figure in both the painting and the story is Dolores, a cook in the wealthy seventeenth-century Spanish household where the young painter (who is never named in the story) is a frequent visitor. A friend of Concepción, the older servant who is Dolores's superior, the painter comes to the kitchen to sketch the food and utensils there, and uses Concepción herself as a model. Dolores, perceiving that he has made the lines of her friend's face into shapes that show her as "wise and graceful" (220), finds her own rage at her lowly lot in life and at her strong, heavy body increased. Her distorted reflection in a copper pan fuels her anger at the family for whom she labours and at God, who has made her as she is—"a mare built for hard work," as Concepción says (219). "I want to live, I want time to think. Not to be pushed around" (220), Dolores tells Concepción. She feels like "a heavy space of unregarded darkness" in the room where the painter works, but she is able to appreciate the patches of "light in darkness" he creates, making "shining fish and white solid eggs" that are "more real" (221) than the objects they represent.

The third woman in the story, Doña Conchita, is the daughter of the house; when the family entertains priests on Sundays, she infuriates Dolores with her demure pose while her real attention is devoted to flirting with another male guest. Waiting on tables, Dolores allows her fury to burst out, breaking a dish and spilling the contents. As one reviewer observed, she believes that "her natural element is that of her mistress" (Gardam 49).

What follows is the heart of the story. The painter first praises Dolores as an artist in her medium, and retells the biblical story of Martha, the worker, busy with serving in the household and her sister Mary, who, Jesus said, chose the better path of learning and contemplating religious teaching. Dolores pronounces this a man's story, pointing out that she, Concepción, and women like them are given no choice. Concepción repeats the traditional interpretation, which relegates both herself and Dolores to an inferior place, but the painter decentres the usual reading, replacing Christ as teacher and providing a commentary that enlarges on St. Luke's brief tale and shows the complexity of its issues. There is more than one way to the "better part," he says. "The cook, as much as the painter, looks into the essence of the creation, not, as I do, in light and on surfaces, but with all the other senses, with taste, and smell, and touch, which God also made in us for purposes" (225). He sees that Dolores's art comes from her body. Both the cook and the painter contemplate the mysteries of the world; the line between the contemplative and the active ways of life is erased, the painter implies, through understanding that "the true crime" is indifference to the world of "light and life" (226). His retelling not only liberates women who work but also obliterates class lines between servants and masters, for the real division, he says, is "between those who are *interested* in the world and its multiplicity of forms and forces, and those who merely subsist, worrying or yawning" (226). At the same time, this interpretation elevates the role of the artists. Unlike Mrs. Hodges, the teacher in "Jael," the Velázquez figure as teacher makes connections. Freeing Dolores to think of herself as an artist, the painter also frees the humble objects with which she works. The eggs and fishes he paints need no theological significance as emblems; they are already holy by virtue of their place in the world. In the painting he makes, using both Dolores and Concepción as models, he transfers his teaching into his own element, making the light fall not on the "holy staring woman" at Christ's feet, but on eggs, fish, a head of garlic, and the figure of the cook who stands beside them with her furious frown. On her other side is Concepción, still admonishing her young friend to look at the biblical tableau (where Concepción has been the model for Martha). This grouping, two women and their work, dominates Velázquez's canvas; the three figures from St. Luke's story appear dwarfed as if seen through a window or as a reflected image. Perhaps it was the oddness of this arrangement in relation to the painting's title that first attracted Byatt's attention, just as in the story she imagines the painter's attention being drawn to the power of the girl's frown. The story ends in celebration: Dolores marvels at the representation of herself, which immortalizes her as she is, and her laughter releases her into time, while her anger remains "still and eternal in the painting" (230). The painter's creation, celebrating the riches of the earth and sea and the human emotion of anger, has replaced the religious stories of damnation and martyrdom to which Dolores's imagination has been limited, as well as the "patient and ethereal Madonnas" (229) that have previously been held up to her as the feminine ideal. Recognizing herself in the painting, she accepts her vocation and her work with the fruits of the earth and sea, with a new perception of their significance. In shared laughter, the three friends eat together.

Again, Byatt explores women's experience of the world through their bodies. The three women artists all create from their bodies. Jess uses her drawing tools as weapons. Fiammarosa, responding to the sexual needs of her body for the Other, risks losing the central core of ice that is her separate identity and does not even seem to notice the loss of the art that expressed her separate self. Dolores, listening to the painter's story, learns to expand her definition of art and to recognize that her own creativity comes from her body. Patricia plunges herself into an extreme climate and relearns the world there; Daphne, on the other hand, enters a foreign setting that accentuates and speeds up the decay of her body and her loss of herself. By contrast, in "Lamia" it is the male whose alert eyes and swimming body respond to the shapes and colours of the world, whereas the Lamia/Melanie female becomes in turn what the males in the story require her to be. Against the realities of treachery, loss, and decay, Byatt places in *Elementals* the richness of things in the world. Nils warns Patricia that indifference, if continued, becomes "cement" and advises her to "look with curiosity, and live" (40). The stories in this collection all offer this wisdom.

11 The Biographer's Tale

The Biographer's Tale (2000) both grows naturally out of Byatt's earlier work and contains new developments. Like *Possession* and *Angels and Insects,* this novel asks questions about the accessibility of the past and about our ability to "know" historical characters. These are problems that have also led Byatt as a reader and critic to study contemporary experiments in historical fiction and to discuss her views in the essays collected in *On Histories and Stories,* also published in 2000. The narrative of *Possession* moves between two time frames, the mid-nineteenth and the late twentieth centuries. *The Biographer's Tale* goes further back, containing one eighteenth-century character and three from the nineteenth, an early twentieth-century biographer of these four, and a late twentieth-century would-be biographer of that biographer, who tries to make sense of all this material. The result, as John Updike observed in his *New Yorker* review, is anything but a "smooth story" (222).

The Biographer's Tale represents, as well, Byatt's growing fascination with biological science and her growing concern for ecology. As early as *The Game,* the herpetologist Simon Moffitt speaks for the integrity of the creatures; twenty-five years later, the entomologist William Adamson occupies a much more prominent place in *Angels and Insects.* In her essay "Ancestors," Byatt defines the new fear, which, for the younger generation of novelists, replaces the terror of nuclear war. Such writers as Lawrence Norfolk portray the nightmare vision of "the destruction of biodiversity, of huge parts of the solid and watery earth." Byatt concludes, "We are part of it, and we are destroying it" (69). In *Babel Tower* and *A Whistling Woman,* scientists at the university detect increasing evidence of irreversible environmental damage. Now Byatt's new hero, Phineas Nanson, becomes an advocate for the threatened natural world. Phineas learns "to look at the *exterior*," as Byatt says we must ("True Stories" 122). His longing to find, not to impose—for he, like his creator, admires Wallace Stevens—and his need for "a life full of *things*" (*Biographer's Tale* 4) drive him to abandon poststructuralist literary theory, through which he and his fellow graduate students repetitively deconstructed texts, finding "the same clefts and crevices, transgressions and disintegrations, lures and deceptions" in every text they examined (3). At the suggestion of Professor Ormerod Goode, Phineas embarks on a biography of a biographer, Scholes Destry-Scholes. Phineas needs, and greatly admires, Destry-Scholes's life of the fictitious Victorian polymath and traveller Sir Elmer Bole, and he takes Destry-Scholes's work to be a model of factual solidity, just what is needed as a corrective of the poststructuralist seminar he has left. He finds, however, that in an unfinished project, Destry-Scholes partly fabricated the stories of his three subjects, the taxonomist Carl Linnaeus (1707-1778), the traveller and eugenicist Francis Galton (1822-1911), and the playwright Henrik Ibsen (1826-1906). After much frustrating research in which he tries to make sense of this mass of material, Phineas gives up biography as "pointless" (239) and turns to the natural world.

Like *Possession*, *The Biographer's Tale* is partly academic satire; it mocks the second-hand quality of scholarly research and the mazes into which it can lead. However—and this is a crucial difference—the primary place that poetry occupies in *Possession* is now given to the physical world, which will always be beyond language. Byatt's fascination with the relationship of words and things, always present in her fiction and non-fiction, is for the first time set squarely at the centre of the text. In a perceptive review, Hal Jensen observed that "the relation of language to things, the arrangement of those things in the world, and exposure of the tricks of literary composition are not just occasional intruders in [*The Biographer's Tale*], they are its very subject" (23). This is a daring move on Byatt's part, and one that risks alienating readers. She has made the decision to confront the reader directly with long passages—some from existing texts, some "confected"—that her narrator encounters in his researches. It is as if the contents of Byatt's essay "True Stories and the Facts in Fiction," describing the genesis of *Angels and Insects*, together with the documents used in her research, were present, unmediated and unorganized, in the novellas themselves. In that essay, Byatt observes that the thought and research that went into the novellas "could have turned into academic papers" (92); in *The Biographer's Tale*, there are many such possible papers. Here, however, the researcher is present as a character and we are looking over his shoulder. Predictably, some reviewers protested against this method. One, pointing out that "Byatt has chosen to write a novel that reads like a research notebook," asked, "But how different is a novel that resembles a haphazard notebook from a haphazard notebook itself?" (Scurr 38). Another found that by making us read the research notes instead of telling us about them, Byatt "pushes the limits of what a novel can be, forcing us to endure an experience rather than receive her story" (Charles 17).

For the reader who perseveres, however, there are many rewards. Updike said in his review that although *The Biographer's Tale* "takes the reader to the edge of exasperation and beyond, that reader must still be grateful to have the art of fiction reworked in such knowing hands" (222). Most readers find the long passages of quotations tedious, and most, perhaps, learn more than they wish to know about the findings of Byatt's research, but as the story reveals more of its allegiance to fable, the reader's path becomes more enticing. Alex Clark, in his review, stressed the closeness of this tale to *Possession*: "For all its obsession with facts, this novel is as much fairy tale as satire, and more dream-like than self-consciously erudite" (10). Updike agreed, finding the world of *The Biographer's Tale* "as fancy-tinged, hovering, and bubbly" (220) as that of *Angels and Insects*.[1] Like the fables and fairy tales published after *Possession*, *The Biographer's Tale* presents us with shining colours and the details of intricately made objects, both artificial and natural. It plays with analogies—the epigraph quotes Goethe on the pleasure of "charming and entertaining" similitudes—and invites the reader to share the fun.

Besides being a serious subject, and one that preoccupies all her characters, naming was evidently a particularly delightful project for Byatt in this novel. Phineas's deconstructionist professor is Gareth Butcher. One of the two women in his life, the one with whom he makes love first, is Vera Alphage, Destry-Scholes's niece. Her name suggests initial truth or true beginning—and points also to Linnaeus's illustration for the plant *Andromeda polifolia*, the bog rosemary, which he shows as both mythic woman and flower, writing between the two drawings,

ficta et vera
mystica et genuina
figurata et depicta (112)

—a description that summarizes Byatt's method of combining the fabulous and the everyday. The name of Phineas's other love, Fulla Biefeld, signifies plenitude and the field of the bees she studies; only on the last page are we told that she is also the handmaid of the goddess Frigga, the Norse Queen of Heaven, and keeper of the jewels of heaven. Fulla, a student of bee pollination and its role in environmental preservation, also keeps the jewels, "tending woodland and forests, fruit trees and hives" (260). Scholes Destry-Scholes (whose birth name was Scholes Destry) is named for the beetle *Scolytus scolytus*, carrier of Dutch elm disease. Phineas Nanson's own name extends the play with analogies further, even beyond the text itself. Early in the story, Phineas, who enjoys being a small man, recalls his pleasure at learning as a schoolboy that *nanus* is Latin for "dwarf": "I felt a *frisson* of excited recognition…. I had a name in a system" (3). Later, he is mistaken for the long-dead Norwegian explorer Fridtjof Nansen, who belongs in a different system of northern travels, one Phineas has been studying. In Vera's collection of Destry-Scholes's possessions, Phineas finds a reference to Galton's unpublished utopian fantasy, *Kantsaywhere*, which contained some "Nonnyson anecdotes" (222) that Galton's niece removed from the text before sending the fragments to Galton's biographer Pearson. Only in the acknowledgments that follow the text does Byatt tell us, in passing, that the mite that preys on the beetle *Scolytus scolytus* is called *Phaeogenes nanus*. Thus, although he is not to know it, Phineas is part of a fourth system. Phineas does take on all these roles, as a small man, an explorer of the real world, a (nonsensical?) figure from fantasy, and a well-intentioned predator on his subject, who was himself a kind of predator.[2] Although we may not pick up every hint, we do enter into the novel's atmosphere of surprise, metamorphosis, and comic juxtaposition. In Byatt's world, there is always something more to be added, another example of the "glitter…of the *facts* in the world" (Byatt, "Nothing Is Too Wonderful to Be True" 12).

As a character, Phineas represents a first for Byatt; although from the beginning she had written from within the consciousnesses of male characters, using males as her alter egos, she had never before used a male narrator. As well, *The Biographer's Tale* is only the third piece of her fiction, and the only extended one, to be narrated in the first person. In "Sugar," the confiding first-person narrator is Byatt herself; in "Jael," she is a figure from whom both author and reader are alienated. Phineas speaks from a space somewhere between the two; like most of Byatt's writer characters, he gives voices to her views on and discoveries about topics to do with language and meaning, but his timid, self-effacing nature, his bumbling, and his fussiness are all his own. As he progresses, his voice becomes less pedantic and more engaging, witty, and daring, and the barrier between him and the reader becomes less obtrusive. Near the end of his story, this diminutive, reclusive young man discovers that he likes his body and finds "a kind of pleasure" (216) in himself and in his relationships with the two women in his life. By this time, the reader, who has felt impatience and frustration with Phineas's exhaustive detailing of the earlier stages of his journey, likes him too.

The Biographer's Tale is both Byatt's most postmodern and her most traditional novel to date. It is postmodern in its self-reflexive meditation on the nature of language, in its representation of the fragmentation and unknowability of self and Other, in its multiplicity of discourses and voices, and in its use of pastiche and mixed media (the written text is accompanied by a painting of Galton and Ibsen, botanical illustrations by Linnaeus, and photographs of sisters and a family composite by Galton made in the course of his work on eugenics). It is heavily intertextual, confronting the reader with long excerpts from the actual writings of the three subjects of Destry-Scholes's research, as well as with fragments Phineas later discovers to be Destry-Scholes's own and with index cards found among Destry-Scholes's possessions in the keeping of his niece Vera. Like many of the recent novels Byatt admires, and which she discusses in On Histories and Stories, this novel makes its own blend of documented history and invention. Phineas's text both analyzes and demonstrates contemporary theories of authorship, language, and genre, and it playfully destroys the idea of linear narrative. It is relentlessly self-reflexive. In her acknowledgments, Byatt says that she suspects that the "germ" of the tale is in her "first reading of Foucault's remarks on Linnaeus and taxonomy in Les mots et les choses" (264). Phineas reflects that "Natural history, for Linnaeus, according to Foucault, was fundamentally designed to order and to name the world" (115), and Phineas's tale relates and critiques projects of naming. Foucault writes that natural history must "reduce" the "distance" between things and language (132); this becomes Phineas's project. In these respects, The Biographer's Tale is the most "papery" of Byatt's novels.

Yet it is also, in an odd way, her most traditional. Phineas makes explicit Byatt's own reflections on contemporary issues. Like her, he distrusts the more rigid application of poststructuralist literary theory. Like her, he moves from a reluctance to speak of his own selfhood to an admission that it is impossible to say some things without taking the existence of some kind of selfhood as a given. Like her, he searches for meaning. As his journey progresses, he makes moral as well as aesthetic judgments, and although he gives up his search for accuracy in biography, he hopes to find it in biology, in the study of plants and insects that has become more and more fascinating to Byatt herself. Most important of all, I think, is the old-fashioned unabashed delight in language and objects that Phineas and his creator share.

The narrative structure of *The Biographer's Tale* is best described in Phineas's metaphor of the mosaic. Phineas introduces the image in relation to his initial work on Scholes Destry-Scholes, when he begins to discover that his new-found hero of fact has not been scrupulous about his use of quotation. With postmodernist sophistication, Phineas judges within his own contemporary framework rather than in terms of "the simplistic ideas about plagiarism which were in force in Destry-Scholes's day" (29). He begins to collect the "lifted" sentences, "intending, when my time came, to redeploy them with a difference, catching different light at a different angle. That metaphor is from mosaic-making" (29). In the course of his research into Destry-Scholes's research into Bole's travels in Turkey and Byzantium, Phineas learns that "the great makers [of tiles] constantly raided previous works … for tesserae which they rewrought into new images" (29). He finds that Destry-Scholes is a master tile-maker and tile-raider; his work on Bole and his three unfinished biographies—or were they to have become a mosaic, a composite like Galton's family photographs?—are filled with both lifted and invented passages. A passage in which Destry-Scholes narrates Linnaeus's journey to the famous Maelstrom in northern Norway is "rewrought" from Poe's story "A Descent into the Maelstrom" (Phineas adds this fact much later, so that the reader who does not catch the echoes takes the passage at face value). Furthermore, Linnaeus in fact never reached the Maelstrom, although he said he did. Fulla, on her first meeting with Phineas, calls this claim "Linnaeus's little untruth. Big lie, maybe" (111), and Phineas sees that Destry-Scholes "had romanced further what Linnaeus had already romanced" (112). Destry-Scholes himself is believed to have perished in the Maelstrom. For Galton, Destry-Scholes went further, narrating a journey to Lake Ngami that his subject not only never made but denied ever intending to make. In his reconstruction of Ibsen, Destry-Scholes abandons narrative altogether, breaking into dramatic format to represent an imagined meeting in a café between Ibsen and a "Strange Customer" (88), who turns out to be Ibsen's illegitimate son, Henriksen. In their hostile dialogue, father and estranged son, who appear as doubles of each other, discuss the father's use of the image of the onion to represent the puzzle of identity.[3]

Phineas begins to see a pattern in the mosaic: all three of these invented experiences are occasions for Destry-Scholes to imagine terrifying visions of violence and death; also, all three subjects, "so to speak, hallucinated themselves" (126), each encountering his own double. Like Gareth Butcher's seminars, where students endlessly deconstructed texts, finding dismemberment everywhere, Destry-Scholes's three fragmentary narratives have "a fatal family likeness" (1). The facts that Phineas longed for are there, but they are embedded in a baffling mosaic where fact cannot be separated from fiction. Destry-Scholes's texts enclose writings by his subjects; Byatt's text illustrates the same principle of eclectic mixing and inventing. In her acknowledgments, using a humbler image than the mosaic, she describes her tale as "a patchwork, echoing book" (264) and identifies her sources; but beyond them she has been imaginative and inventive, and she has provided us with a story after all, a thread as well as a mosaic.

In his research on his Destry-Scholes, Phineas discovers the joys as well as the frustrations of collecting and interpreting facts. At first, as he begins to find and correct Destry-Scholes's mistakes, he thinks of these as rare, "shining little jewels hardly observable in moss—the analogy is from beetle-hunting" (29). In his search for facts about Destry-Scholes—about whom few facts seem to exist—he finds Vera in Willesden, and more collections. In addition to photographs of her professional X-rays of the human body, her flat houses relics of Destry-Scholes: shoeboxes of unsorted cards; a collection of photographs, none of which can be identified as Destry-Scholes; and a bag of 366 glass marbles, together with a list Vera believes to be the names her uncle had assigned to the marbles, one for each. Another kind of collection is offered by Puck's Girdle, where Phineas finds part-time work arranging exotic holidays. He is first attracted by the objects in the window, especially an origami Maelstrom, and by the disconnected words, especially "hurtle" and "periplum,"[4] that accompany the objects. His future employers, Erik and Christophe, tell him that they "sell odd holidays"; they tempt their customers (as he himself has been tempted) with "words and images" (106). Meanwhile, Fulla's passionate study of beetles and bees introduces Phineas to other kinds of collections, bringing him partway out of his paper world and closer to the world of growth and change; "I began to notice bumble-bees on pavements and honeybees in hedges" (130), he says. In his endeavour to name and understand the collections of collections, Phineas finds frustration and disillusionment with the Destry-Scholes grouping and the one at Puck's Girdle, but some sense of usefulness in Fulla's world. At Vera's he tries to sort Destry-Scholes's index cards, making groupings with names such as "drowning and autopsy" (153), "hybrids and mixtures" (154), "composite portrait (photography)" (175), even a possible "subset...on taxonomic collections" (191). But the cards do not fall into a coherent narrative; neither in them nor, "beyond the shoebox," in the "three fictive fragments" (236) is Destry-Scholes to be found. Furthermore, the three subjects of Destry-Scholes's fragments, who themselves studied connectedness, are connected to others. Destry-Scholes as biographer leads to Pearson, the first biographer of Galton, and from there to theories of biography: "the threads ran out all the time" (167), and "no string has an end" (168). Vera's project of replicating her uncle's naming of the marbles also leads nowhere; there is "no fixed taxonomy" (191), and several names from the list seem to fit several marbles equally well. (Byatt has fun with this list, inventing "Crimsonwisp," "Bloodrift," and "Goosegob" [138].) Phineas visits a doddery professor and Maelstrom fanatic, Thorold Jespersen, whose person and surroundings reflect the murkiness of scholarship. Jespersen's skylight resembles the filthy one in Butcher's seminar room, except that Jespersen's has slime growing on it. Even his name, like Butcher's, is "over-determined" (247), although Phineas does not remark on it: it recalls Otto Jespersen, the grammarian of Old and Middle English. Here, Phineas hopes to find the facts about Destry-Scholes's death, but all Jespersen can produce is a newspaper photograph of an empty boat. Destry-Scholes is undiscoverable. Vera, whose work involves a more urgent form of semiotics, signalling life or death, breaks down when a young cancer patient reads his "inevitable death" (218) in the X-ray photographs she has made. Faced with their individual crises of naming, she and Phineas admit defeat; wordlessly, they heap the marbles into a glass bowl to reflect the light. They put away the notebook from which Vera was trying to name the marbles, put the lids on the shoeboxes, and make love. Phineas is moving closer to the "things" he longed for.

Left alone to look after Puck's Girdle while Erik and Christophe are on holiday, Phineas faces another semiotic problem. He is visited by Maurice Bossey, a vaguely menacing figure whom Phineas privately names the Strange Customer. Bossey does not name his requirements, and Phineas—never, he says, good at reading signs—misses the "*point*" (170) of Bossey's possessions: his cigar and cigar-clipper, the knife with which he would "dissect" (142) meat and fruit, his "long, fine corkscrew" (143). However, when Phineas explores the Web sites Bossey orders him to search, he finds that they are pornographic, eliciting from him "little, cold, categorising words. Pederasty. Paedophilia. Sado-machoism. Sadism" (170). Bossey wants Phineas to arrange snuff holidays, as his predecessor, Pym (Pimp?), had done before him. When he next visits the agency, Phineas is able, not surprisingly, to read his sign, a snuff box. The return of Erik and Christophe, bearing a present for Phineas—an Easter basket containing toy bunnies with sado-masochistic tastes—brings the situation to a crisis. There is a carnivalesque confrontation, played out both linguistically and physically. Phineas finds himself screaming, "*limits after all*, everything *doesn't go*," "shrieking words I'd never used and didn't exactly know the import of" (203), throwing the chocolate eggs from the basket at his employers, and stabbing them with a paperknife. His release into a furious new use of language is punctuated by Fulla's arrival and her fiercely urgent discourse of ecological responsibility, and Phineas now moves into new language, new collections, and new work as a namer.

Fulla dismisses Erik and Christophe as "fairy hedonists" who send their customers into "fantasy worlds" to "choke in real forest fires in Indonesia" (205) and bombards them with facts about the pollution of the world and the destruction of species. "You can't fly round and round on your pretty invisible girdle without impinging and being impinged on" (205), she furiously tells them. She rescues Phineas from the retaliation of his former employers—they have, of course, fired him—takes him on a picnic in Richmond Park, shows him a colony of rare stag beetles performing their territorial jousting, and, to his great delight, seduces him. He finds that she "bites nicely," covering his body with "little blue florets" (215), which—still not a good semiotician—he does not at first realize may be dangerous signs for Vera to read when they next make love. Fulla puts him to work on her stag-beetle projects and teaches him some insect names, admitting, however, that (as Phineas has already discovered in his other pursuits) "*all* the naming's arbitrary" (213). She tells him that the elm-bark beetle, once called *Scolytus destructor*, has been renamed *Scolytus scolytus*. The reader picks up the clue Phineas misses: Destry-Scholes, like his namesake, burrowed in "wonderfully patterned interconnecting tunnels" (212). However, Phineas has practical work of identification to do. For his task as an observer of the battles of the beetles, Fulla provides him with a set of coloured, numbered discs, but he cannot resist the pleasure of emulating Linnaeus by giving the insects names from myth, naming the males for horned gods, the females for the Fates. He has progressed from inanimate to living collections, and to work that, Fulla assures him, serves a useful purpose.

As a writer of the notebook that is his text, Phineas has undergone a metamorphosis. Beginning in revulsion against the theory of the "dismemberment of the imagined body" (1), he emerges as a lyricist praising the real, whole bodies of his two lovers. Put off by the "meta-language" (214) of theory, he ends (like Roland in *Possession*) by deriving great pleasure in "forbidden words, words critical theorists can't use and writers can" (250). Fulla helps him to find his direction; on their first meeting, when he tells her of his paper on "literary and popular-cultural images of induced panic and mass fear," she vigorously challenges him to use concrete language: "Literary and popular-cultural images … are neither here nor there. As you say in English. Neither here nor there. Whereas both *here* and *there* and *now* this species is destroying, every day, 6,000 species perhaps …" (120). As he ends his tale, Phineas's writing is as close to "things" as he can get. The "forbidden" words to which he is now "addicted" include metaphors—he and Fulla lie among "starry daisies and dandelion clocks and roaring golden dandelions" (213); "Fulla wandered the plains of my flesh…, and inside my nerve-strings sang Vera" (216)— and words for the scents of Fulla's and Vera's skins: "Fulla is goat and aromatic. Vera is fragrant and—not garlicky—but lily and daffodil" (250). Their hair is more difficult: "Vera's hair is ferny and Fulla's hair is—this is hard—honeysuckle is too sweet, hawthorn too almond, I am thinking *hedges*, not the precise smell—there is a touch of ragwort and fennel, mixed with dogrose" (250-51). The exactness that eluded him in his researches in biography is easier to approach—and more pleasurable— in his new-found preoccupation with the two women's bodies. As for his future writing, he thinks of a way to use "all this persistent itch to write down different words and sentences in English" (257); he could produce a kind of mosaic writing for the "non-destructive ecological tourists" whom Erik and Christophe, now reconciled with him and Fulla, are hoping to attract: "I could mix warnings with hints, descriptions with explanations, science with little floating flashes of literature…. I could combine my two splendidly dovetailed lives as tourist manager and parataxonomist, with a kind of ghostwriting, a ghost of writing" (257). The last pages of the novel are an example of this new writing. He has experienced the breakdown of literary genres—biography blurs into autobiography, narrative into dramatic form, scientific description into mythmaking—and he now sets out to devise his own mix of genres.

Phineas abandons poststructuralist theory because he is weary of its imposition of patterns: "You decided what you were looking for, and then duly found it—male hegemony, liberal-humanist *idées reçues*, etc." (144). In his study of biography he is surprised and dismayed to find the same tendency; the biographer had needs of his own that he filled by inventing what he did not find in the lives of his subjects. As his own biographical project becomes more confusing, Phineas at first resists the idea that he is writing autobiography. "I am writing in the first person for the sake of precision," he says, although he concludes that "if I had been born into an earlier generation I might have had to have some idea of my Self.... I do exist on the earth, and would like to be of some use, and find a meaning or two. (*The* meaning is beyond all of us)" (100). After he and Vera make love for the first time, he is still reticent about the personal, but less certain about how to define his writing and his identity: "I am not going to describe what happened, though I am going to record that it *did* happen, because I am not that sort of writer. I think. It's becoming more difficult to know what sort of writer I *am*. Also, afterwards, I was not the same person" (187). A few pages later, he asserts that he is "not the sort of writer ... to make the most of the undoubtedly fantastic elements of my situation at that time. There I lay, in the bed of the niece of the man whose biography—whose *life-writing*—I was vainly trying to piece together, surrounded by anonymous photographs of living skeletons, of heart muscles and lung tissue and the roots of teeth" (190). Soon, however, he is vividly recounting the even more "fantastic" melee at Puck's Girdle and, later, the appearance of a Dionysos, a man costumed as a stag, "horned and two-legged, its head crowned with fantastic curved and pointed peaks of platinum and shrill rose" (240). This apparition, which crashes into Richmond Park, where Phineas and Fulla are making love, is amorously pursued by Christophe; a giant human materialization of the stag beetles, he seems to be introduced merely for the fun of "overlapping symbolification" (Updike 222). Phineas, now an entirely different sort of writer from the one who refused to give details about going to bed with Vera, has just described Fulla's fingers on his erection and called the reader's attention to both his delight and the banality of his language: "I thought (profoundly, banally) that all sex is the same, and every time is different. I turned to her with a little moan. (I am back in lyrical mode. Note at which juncture)" (240). In his more analytical mode, he notes that he is "trying to avoid the problem of the decay of belief in the idea of objectivity by slipstreaming towards the safer, ideologically unloaded idea of precision," but adds, "I don't think the tactic quite works" (250). As he becomes more and more conscious of Destry-Scholes's "*absence*," Phineas reluctantly perceives his own necessary presence in his writing: he is, in fact, engaged in "autobiography, that most evasive and self-indulgent of forms." Still, he tries to maintain the objectivity he initially believed he had found in Destry-Scholes. Although he uses his own life "as a temporal thread to string my story (my writing) on," he has also tried to "avoid unnecessary dwelling on my own feelings, or my own needs, or my own—oh dear—*character*" (214). He is no longer "the ur-I of this document" (162), but a being who has experienced "liberation" (215) into lyricism and has fulfilled his "burning desire" (214) to describe the differences between making love to Fulla and making love to Vera.

Finally, in a moment of "appalling vision," he sees that in spite of his struggle for accuracy, his writing has paralleled that of Destry-Scholes. For Destry-Scholes, "the imaginary narrative had sprung out of the scholarly one" (237); Phineas, writing about Destry-Scholes's writing, has had to insert his own feelings and interpretations: "Was the composite Destry-Scholes? Was it, since I had had to arrange and rearrange, Phineas G. Nanson?... [W]hatever had driven Destry-Scholes to write the three fictive (lying, untruthful) biographical fragments, was whatever was (is) now driving me to form this mass of material into my own story...." He now understands that Destry-Scholes's inventions of "ghosts and spirits, doubles and hauntings, metamorphoses, dismemberment, death" are variations on the universal experience of mystery. There are "very few human truths" that we can know: "Reading and writing extend—not infinitely but violently, but giddily—the variations we can perceive on the truths we thus discover. Children are afraid of the dark; a double walks at our side, or hangs from our flesh like a shadow; and we put a whole life-time (which is brief indeed in the light *even of history* let alone of the time of the world) to discovering what these things *mean* for us—dark, and shadows" (237). His defection from poststructuralist studies came a week after the burial of his mother, which he thought at the time was not related to his decision, although "it might be construed that way" (1). He had already lost his father, to whose "disappearance" (3) he mysteriously refers. Since then, both Vera and Fulla have shown him death, Vera in her X-rays, Fulla in the perishing of species. Bossey's perversion has led him to witness "Pain. Hurt. Damage" (170) on the Web sites. Phineas has had his own meetings with darkness and shadows.

In nightmares, too, he has witnessed versions of the horrors envisioned by Destry-Scholes: of a man who "was and was not myself" (29), trapped in a man-shaped glass bottle; of Destry-Scholes "pouring head-first into the Maelstrøm," which was made up of the origami Maelstrom and of Bossey's dangerous implements, while Phineas, swimming as he struggles to see Destry-Scholes's face, is swept toward the "funnel of blades and water" (190); Galton's vision of a "hanging figure in agony" (201). In his search for his "own story," he has, inevitably, partly "invented" Vera and Fulla (and those other doubles, Erik and Christophe). He has kept before him his somewhat shaky goal of precision, however, and his invention of others has stopped far short of Destry-Scholes's. He "could say" that the women are, respectively, goddesses of the night and of the day, but he stops himself from using these "dangerous metaphors" (238); he must remember that each is unique. Similarly, he refuses to categorize them, in the way of "novels," as the "real one" and that the other is "*only something or other*" (216) in his life. He has discovered—finding, not imposing significance—two women, each with her "independent and unpredictable reality" (238). Phineas realizes that his narrative has taken on not only a universal but a specific familiar shape. It "has funnelled itself into a not unusual shape, run into a channel cut in the earth for it by previous stories (and all our lives are partly the same story, beginning, middle, end)—in terms of writing, this looks like a *writer's story*. PGN was a mere Critick, steps centre-stage, assumes his life, Finds his Voice, is a Writer." Phineas finds this fate nauseating, but admits that he did, like "the '1920s' version" of himself, experience "very precisely" an epiphany, "so I shall write it down, for pleasure, *cliché* and all, and then *stop writing*. Or how shall I see what to do?" (251). His epiphany was a flock of brilliantly coloured green and pink parrots in Richmond Park. True to form, however, he is unable to read this sign, although he is stirred by its beauty: "It could equally have been a sign that I should stay in England—since all, including bright tropical birds, was possible here—or whether, more eccentrically, I should take it as a good omen, that I should travel, and help Fulla with the pollinators, the swamps, the savannahs, the dry hillsides." (Characteristically, and in tune with his involvement in two simultaneous love relationships, he does both.) But he is clear about what his vision of the parrots told him: "that the senses of order and wonder, both, that I had once got from literature, I now found more easily and directly in the creatures" (254).

Phineas's writing becomes fragmented and disjunct. Leaving the manuscript of his tale in London on his computer, he and Vera go on a holiday (a gift from Erik and Christophe) to Norway, where, his journal records, they are about to see the Maelstrom. His writing is interrupted by Vera, inviting him into her arms. His next entry, a year later, tells of his idea for a new kind of writing, and about his working holiday with Fulla to study beetles and tulips; the tulips are both crafted, as in some of the mosaics viewed by Sir Elmer Bole, and real. Phineas has chosen the natural world described by Sir Philip Sidney as "brazen," as opposed to the "golden" world that poets can describe. Phineas quotes Sidney's famous passage and declares boldly, "Not so. As long as we don't destroy and diminish it irrevocably, the too-much-loved earth will always exceed our power to describe, or imagine, or understand it. It is all we have" (259). His proclamation in his own voice of Fulla's more strident warnings is interrupted, like his writing in Norway, by the real woman. Yet, despite

his choice of the world of living things, he still enjoys the beauty of artifice and he is still a poet at heart. He sends Vera, back in England, post-
cards of mosaics and an artificial counterpart of his ambiguously significant parrots, "a glittering glass peacock, shimmering in tesserae of rich
blue and emerald green, streaked with shocking pink and iridescent
with gold" (258).

The story has a postmodern comic ending. Phineas is a successful
lover, but (like Sir Elmer Bole) of two women, both of whom are happy.
He has discovered that he is a writer, but he has also said "farewell to Literature" (255) and now plans to write "a ghost of writing" (257), which will
reflect his two novels. He has gone in search of the Maelstrom, making
the journey that Linnaeus lied about making and that Destry-Scholes lied
about, plagiarized about, and emulated; Destry-Scholes left behind only
an empty boat, and Phineas leaves only a gap in his text, for he does not
tell us whether he and Vera ever saw the Maelstrom. It has itself become
a multiple signifier—of the natural and the artificial, of the real and the
mythic, of the deadly and the beautiful, and of the compelling force of
narrative itself. Following the well-worn channel of comic narrative,
Phineas's story has moved from his solitary life to a kind of community: in the unlikely milieu of Puck's Girdle, he tells us, he first found himself saying "we" (124), and he says it easily both about himself and Vera
and about himself and Fulla, but his two women remain unaware of
each others' existence. Here is a concrete example of "both/and" rather
than "either/or."

Some of the most memorable passages in *The Biographer's Tale* record
moments when words and the order of things come together to produce delight. The writer knows—and Phineas learns—that in the process
of accomplishing this coming together, clichés and banality must sometimes be risked. In a review essay published in 1986, Byatt praises
Flaubert, "the scourge of the cliché," for "having his commonplaces both
ways." His characters' feelings are "banal 'quotations' from the culture,"
yet "they are also true and real and moving, the 'common places' where
our experiences meet. They are both subversive *and* celebratory" ("Subversion and Stubbornness" 50). Byatt has not been afraid to let her characters experience banality. Like Daniel Orton coming to understand why
the beloved is called "sweet" (*Virgin* 165), the much more linguistically
sophisticated Phineas embraces the clichés of love, writing "lyrical (banal,
but shocking-to-me) sentences about foxgloves and freckles, spider-
webs and hairs" (215). His progress repeats, as it were in slow motion, a
textual gesture of Doris Lessing's about which Byatt has written admir-
ingly. Quoting a passage from *The Golden Notebook* in which Anna, con-

sidering the words "good" and "nice," comments, "these are not words you'd use in a novel. I'd be careful not to use them," and goes on to use the words nevertheless, Byatt recalls that when she read the book in the 1960s she felt "the excitement and freedom of the self-reflexive narrative transgression." Lessing's heroine says "I'd be careful not to," "and then does what she 'cannot' do" ("True Stories" 97–98). Phineas's narrative transgressions define (another cliché) his self-discovery. He "commits" lyricism (219), "perpetrates" hackneyed phrases (250), creates a mixed metaphor and declares "Let it lie" (171). He knows that the dirty window is "an ancient, well-worn trope for intellectual dissatisfaction and scholarly blindness" (2), but it was there in Butcher's seminar room, and its double was in Jespersen's college room, and he records the fact.

With *The Biographer's Tale*, Byatt has returned to her starting point, addressing directly the most basic issues for a writer of fiction: words and things, images and real people. Her negotiation of the relationship between language and life is subtle, rich, and complex, yet she is not afraid to arrive at "subversive and celebratory" commonplaces. In this tale, women's experience, though not central, is not ignored. Both Vera and Fulla are engaging figures whose reality does not require the reader's participation in their thought processes. Vera's act of heaping the marbles together to create haphazard beauty shows that she understands the limitations of naming. As for Fulla, Byatt gives to her some of the most compelling rhetoric in the book. It is Phineas, however, who embarks on a quest dear to Byatt's heart, and it is his voice that records the discoveries made along the way.

12 *Babel Tower* and *A Whistling Woman*

IN THE SEVENTEEN YEARS BETWEEN THE APPEARANCE of *Still Life* in 1985 and the completion of the quartet in 2002 with *A Whistling Woman*, Byatt published four volumes of short stories, two novels, and two novellas. As we have seen, these intervening texts mark significant extensions of her range of genres and discourses as well as her increasing skill in narrative. All four volumes of short stories are concerned with women's lives and art. The *Sugar* stories place women in relation to narrative in a variety of ways, the *Matisse* volume explores the impact of painting on women's minds and bodies, and the *Djinn* tales construct alternative narratives for women in the fairy-tale genre that was already present as one of the facets of the multi-generic *Possession*. The tales in *Elementals*, which, like *The Biographer's Tale*, was published between *Babel Tower* and *A Whistling Woman*, place their women characters at points of extremity for which the subtitle, *Stories of Fire and Ice*, is a metaphor. In *Possession*, Byatt's most momentous achievement during these years, she advanced on a number of fronts, blending historical and invented characters and worlds, interweaving many plots, keeping the subject of language in the centre of the action, and thoroughly integrating theoretical issues into her text. The objection made by Julian Gitzen and others, that in *Still Life* Byatt's inquiry into metaphor "temporarily usurped her role as a novelist, causing her to resort to transparent rhetorical devices" (Gitzen 94), is overcome in *Possession*, where the nineteenth-century lovers are poets, where Byatt's ventriloquistic gifts have free rein, and where issues of language and metaphor are a natural and pressing concern in the lives of the pair of twentieth-century lovers as well. The play between fiction and theory is more spontaneous and sophisticated in these later texts. Here, Byatt found a way to create and fully integrate intertexts whose counterparts are only described in *The Virgin in the Garden* and *Still Life*. In her interview with Juliet Dusinberre, Byatt confessed that she "had some trouble with Alexander's play [*Astrea*] and kept asking myself, what is Alexander writing?" ("A.S. Byatt" 191). In *Possession*, the problem of inventing intertexts is brilliantly solved, and from this point on—especially in *Angels and Insects* and *The Biographer's Tale*—passages of actual and invented poetry, fiction, travel accounts, scientific writing, and biography occupy central positions. Byatt's conclusion of her quartet draws on all these achievements of her maturity. In her ongoing formal innovation, her serious play with the conventions of fiction, she has never abandoned realism's concern for real people.

The experimentation with form and the widening of intellectual horizons after *Still Life* come into play when Byatt picks up the story of the Potter family in the third and fourth volumes of the quartet. Set a decade later than *Still Life*—the action of *Babel Tower* begins in 1964, and that of *A Whistling Woman* ends in 1970—these two texts reflect the fragmented, hectic outer world of the sixties. *Babel Tower*, the author told Nicolas Tredell in 1990, would be "about the cracking-up of language and the tearing-loose of language from the world," it would be "about voices as opposed to writing, and it and Volume Four [would] move much more into different areas of visual art as a kind of paradigm" (73-74). This prophecy is fulfilled through the presence of paintings, mixed-media "happenings," and the activities at the Samuel Palmer School of Art in *Babel Tower*, and of television in its successor. Although her characters continue to produce and study written language, as well as debating how children should be taught to read, Byatt now directs her attention to a wider issue; as Richard Todd points out, "the articulate expression of thought" itself is in danger (A.S. Byatt 64).

In place of a prologue, *Babel Tower* presents the reader with four separate beginnings. The story could begin, says the narrator, with a thrush hammering its prey, a snail, on its stone "anvil or altar" (3). This first opening into the book provides no narrative thread; instead, it introduces a cluster of motifs. The snail as sacrificial victim is to reappear in the novel's embedded text, *Babbletower*; in the persecuted child, Felicitas, curling herself into her cot "like a desperate snail in its shell" (270) in her futile attempt to escape the other children; in the snails that are believed to be magical spirits and must, according to custom, be roasted alive in the New Year celebrations of Misrule; and in the suicide of Felicitas's mother, the Lady Mavis, who leaps from the Tower and hits her head on a rock "like a snail dropped by a thrush" (277). Visually, the snail motif introduces each of the sections of *Babbletower*, which are scattered through the text, and in fact the snail itself is a text. Frederica learns that biologists at the new university in Yorkshire are studying snail populations and can read the snails' DNA on their shells. The scientists find fewer thrush anvils now, and environmentalists are worried about death by pesticides. The shadow of extinction—of literature, of Potter values, and of nature itself—hangs over *Babel Tower*. The thrush motif moves through the book also, both as name and as image. The cook in *Flight North*, the story Frederica's new friend and landlady, Agatha Mond, is writing, is called Dol Throstle, and Turdus Cantor, the name of one of the *Babbletower* company—in contradiction of its scatological suggestiveness—is the Latin name of the song thrush. Stones relate to Jude Mason, author of *Babbletower*, who has renamed himself in honour of Thomas Hardy's Jude, a stonemason; to the student Peter Stone, who fell to his death while stoned; and to the game of paper-scissors-stone, in which John Ottokar and his identical twin, Paul, always made uncannily identical moves. The novel's first beginning concludes by questioning the pleasure we get from the thrush's song, performed in the intervals of killing: "Why does his song give us such pleasure?" (3). The motif of pleasure in pain links all the book's narratives as well, and the novel's closing episode, from *Babbletower*, brings the imagery of the thrush and the snail full circle, as Turdus Cantor and the other two survivors of Culvert's debauched experiment, which began as a quest for pleasure and ended in sadism, view the heap of human bones that is all that remains of the community.

The three other possible beginnings are pieces of narrative. The first of these, the second beginning, shows Hugh Pink, Frederica's old friend from Cambridge, coming upon her and her four-year-old son, Leo, by chance while walking in Laidley Woods on the Reiver estate, Bran House. He has heard from their friends that Frederica has married and is kept by her husband "more or less locked up, more or less incommunicado, in a moated grange, would you believe, in the country, in outer darkness" (5). Although she is "dressed for hunting" when he meets her (and was associated with the huntress Diana in her role as the Virgin Queen), she "no longer looks like a huntress" (6). As he walks, Hugh is composing a poem about Persephone, who ate pomegranate seeds though she knew she should not do so and who was doomed to live for part of the year in the underworld with Dis, its ruler. The thread of Frederica's story is thus retrieved from *Still Life* (where Stephanie was the Persephone figure), and we begin to see her marriage as a kind of death and Hugh as a potential rescuer. One of the conclusions of *Babel Tower* is Frederica's divorce hearing.

The third beginning could be in the crypt of St. Simeon's Church, where Daniel now helps to run a telephone helpline. The two calls he answers both impinge on his own story: a woman is distraught because she has abandoned her children, fearing that she might harm them, and the voice whom the workers have nicknamed "Steelwire" calls to repeat his message that God is dead and therefore there is no law but doing what we please. This voice turns out to be that of Jude Mason, whose book Frederica recommends for publication and whose trial for obscenity is another of *Babel Tower*'s endings.

The fourth beginning introduces "the book that was to cause so much trouble" (12), Jude's *Babbletower*; its characters, fleeing from the Reign of Terror; and the plans of their leader, Culvert, to establish a new society that will be an experiment in freedom, a community from which "no one will ever wish to escape," although, he adds, "no one should be prevented" from leaving (15). Themes of child abandonment, of the need to escape from confinement, and of lawless pleasure are interwoven in these three narrative beginnings.

The four possible beginnings—with, as Michael J. Noble astutely observes (71-73), a fifth constructed by the prologues of *The Virgin in the Garden* and *Still Life*—signal fragmentation and multiplicity; they also draw attention to constructedness. As a poet, Hugh is especially conscious of the diligence and joy with which the mind works with language, as words are remembered and made new in the present. Other main characters are shown constructing things with language and reflecting on this work. Byatt's long concern with the process by which the mind takes in the world persists in this novel in a more acute form, for there is more at stake. The tower image is the object interrogated here, and it is a tower of language that is fragile because of its fragmentation. La Tour Bruyarde, the "noisy tower" in Jude's *Babbletower*, is "only one of the names of the place," Jude's narrator informs us (13). Other "names of the place" are the tower in Kafka's *Castle*, which one of Frederica's adult students, John Ottokar, analyzes as "a *mad* tower" where "words don't hang together" (288); the "Skoob" towers of burning books (*books* spelled backward), which John's hippie twin, Paul, claims are "a new art form" (407); and the twin towers of legal language, by which Frederica's divorce petition and Jude's defence of *Babbletower* are inaccurately and clumsily judged. Pitted against these towers are the buildings of learning at the new North Yorkshire University, but even they are not impregnable, as we will see in the sequel to *Babel Tower*.

Repetition is built into the quartet's narrative. When Frederica was a schoolgirl, her father intentionally burned her *Girl's Crystals* magazines and her Georgette Heyer novels, maintaining that they were not really "books" (*Virgin* 35); as an adolescent, Bill himself watched as the Congregational minister (repeating the action of an earlier cleric) burned Hardy's *Jude the Obscure*, whereupon Bill retaliated by burning the minister's religious tracts. Later, when he learns of Stephanie's intention to marry Daniel, Bill accidentally sets fire to books; this time he is in a rage because of his belief that Stephanie will be wasting her life. Now Paul burns books that both Bill and Frederica value, and *Babbletower*, written by a man who considers himself Hardy's heir, is threatened with similar destruction. Frederica's dream at the end of *Babel Tower* recalls Stephanie's dream before her marriage, and both are prophetic. Stephanie dreams of her loss of language. Frederica dreams of saving Leo, for he is surely the small glowing stone lion on whom she falls at the end of a dream in which great cats (for whom the lawyers in her divorce case are named) are juxtaposed with imagery of beheading from *Astrea* and *Alice in Wonderland*. In her dream, Frederica, wearing the paper skirts she had worn as the young Elizabeth, hears herself derided as "made of paper" (523). In the custody hearing, she is given "care and control" of Leo (601), sharing custody with Nigel, but only after feeling reduced to the paper of her court statements and to feeling that she has been misrepresented and has misrepresented herself. Afterward, Pippy Mammott, Nigel's housekeeper, angrily attacks Frederica and makes her face bleed, repeating in a minor form the bloody injuries of Frederica's battles with Nigel. Frederica, who as the young Elizabeth had said "I will not bleed" and who as her own young self had shed copious hymeneal blood, is more seriously marked by blood in *Babel Tower*. Violence suffered by children, which in *Still Life* is present in Daniel's parish when Gerry Burtt's wife murders their child, exists on a larger scale in *Babel Tower* and its intertext, Jude's novel. In court defending his book, Jude recalls the abuses of the Swineburn School, which is Nigel's old school where he wishes to enrol Leo; Sir Augustine Weighall, in his summing-up of the case, recognizes that Jude has experienced "a circle of deprivation" (591). When Jude disappears after the verdict, which finds *Babbletower* to be obscene, Frederica and Daniel search for him, having been told that he is living in a tower of flats where a child fell or was pushed to its death. They have difficulty in finding him because "More children have fallen" from towers "than they expected" (608). Violence proliferates: Nigel assaults both Daniel in London and Bill in Yorkshire; Jude's personal experience of exploitation becomes part of a long history. In this world of the sixties, violence is commonplace and its circle is much wider than in the first two novels of the quartet. All these motifs—Persephone, books, fire, stone, blood—recur in the final volume.

Pulled between the novel's two main narratives and its many intertexts, confronted by examples of twinning and doubling in plots and characters, as well as of multiple naming, the reader can become perplexed and even overwhelmed. What is the point—or is there one?—in the echo of the Swineburn School's name in that of Alex Swinburn, member of the Steerforth Committee on language teaching? Is there significance in Dol Throstle's being named for the predatory thrush, when she, as a member of the travelling company in Agatha's story, is a benign and helpful figure? Nigel's unmarried sisters, Rosaline and Olive, who live at Bran House, act uniformly but are not twins. John and Paul are identical twins, but John is a sober computer programmer, Paul a wildly exuberant, mentally unstable, often destructive member of the counterculture; Byatt says that they are connected with Kafka's two "assistants" and in turn with Nietzsche's Apollo and Dionysos ("Memory" 49). The jangling dissonance of the clashing images at the art school, where Frederica teaches literature, and in the world of pop "happenings," where Paul and his band, Zag and the Szyzgy (Ziggy) Zy-Goats (their name a punning reference to twinning), perform, seems epitomized in the language of one of Frederica's cut-outs. Feeling "wild and oppressed" (379) on receiving a letter from Nigel's lawyer Guy Tiger objecting to Leo's attending the William Blake School in the working-class, racially mixed area of Kennington and proposing instead that he follow his father to Brock's School and Swineburn, Frederica emulates her friend Desmond Bull's experiments with collage. Bull is superimposing visual images, "Robespierre's eyes in Marilyn Monroe's face above Bronzina Freud's scaly tail" (378). In Frederica's textual collage, made of pieces of Tiger's letter, we read, "my client is informed return to the matrimonial home, a deprived and socially unstable environment, suggests that it will be best that you inhabit a basement, the most beneficial arrangement a near-slum; that you arrange immediately to Brock's preparatory intermediate care for the boy, parents will be free to earn money part-time. His request is both kinds" (379). This chaotic, William Burroughs-like text critiques the illogical forces at work in divorce and custody proceedings by revealing their nonsense. None of the documents involved reflects the state of Frederica's relationship with Nigel, which is more truly imaged in her wordless "double movement of flinching and turning to him" during the hearing (521). Despite her repulsion at Nigel's insensitivity, her terror that he will take Leo from her, and her determination never again to live at Bran House, desire still exerts a counter-tug that is mirrored in the pull their genetic makeup exerts on the Ottokars. The text is full of movement, and much of it is centrifugal: Frederica flees Bran House pursued by Leo, who insists on accompanying her; the people of *Babbletower* leave their ravaged homes; Artegall, the prince in Agatha's tale, escapes with his friends from their invaded country. Dispersal, disconnectedness, and makeshift arrangements seem to prevail. In the book's ongoing debates, voices and versions compete. In the work of the Steerforth Committee, in Frederica's classrooms, in the courtrooms, and in the many conversations that are recorded, there appears to be neither clarity nor anything approaching resolution.

Nevertheless, there is a kind of order in this text, although its principle is at least as difficult to discern as the pattern in John's colourful pullover, which, he points out, has every other triangle in the order of the spectrum while everything between these "building-blocks of order" is random (333). The escapes the characters make are from sites of fear or confinement, and although one, the journey to La Tour Bruyarde, ends in disruption and disaster, the other two involve friendship and reach some measure of safety. In their search for Artegall's uncle, Ragna, the companions in *Flight North* reach a far northern village where the inhabitants need a fire to be built in order for spring to arrive, and accomplish this by co-operation and by tolerance of strangeness—the King of Snakes, who helps Artegall to understand the speech of creatures; the salamander-like, stone-like Dracosilex, who lights the great fire; and Fraxinius, a fragile, fading figure who is transformed by the fire into a force of renewal and who causes a crack to open in an hitherto impassable rock face so that the company can proceed. In London, Frederica is helped by old and new friends, finds work and a place to live (her bond with Agatha is a rare and convincing example of women's friendship in Byatt's fiction), and begins an affair with John Ottokar. Her circle is able to encompass the strange and initially repellent figure, the malodorous Jude, and, at times and even less comfortably, the unpredictable Paul-Zag, who is driven to share all his brother's experiences, including those with women. Small centres of the "civilized" behaviour that Byatt values[1] are found or constructed: the church crypt where Daniel and his co-workers answer calls for help; Agatha's flat, where Agatha tells instalments of *Flight North* to her daughter, Saskia, Saskia's new friend Leo, and black children from the neighbourhood, Clement and Thanos Aygepong; Frederica's classrooms, filled with lively adult talk; the lawyers' office where Jude's supporters organize his defence. An important meeting place is the beautiful old house in Yorkshire to which Bill and Winifred have moved after

Bill's retirement. Here, the grandparents are able to nurture Daniel's children with more warmth than they could give their own children; Winifred becomes happier as the house accumulates a new history, a record of the children's life; and Bill, still busy with extramural teaching, is quieter and more communicative with his wife. Frederica and Daniel return here after their separate estrangements from the family and both are surprised to recognize their likeness to Bill, their old adversary. Here, Frederica brings first Leo, then John; Agatha and Saskia visit; Marcus's old friend Jacqueline, a student at the university, comes here with the geneticist with whom she is studying snail populations (and who is in love with her), Luk Lysgaard-Peacock. The Potter family reshapes itself, and its house becomes a community and a refuge, strong enough to eject Nigel, who comes in search of his wife and son, and to provide a festive Christmas. Much of the narrative exists in tension between fracturing and unifying forces. Its centripetal movements are toward a plurality of centres.

There is also a pattern of fruitful, progressive repetition. Alexander, who provided brief sanctuary to several individuals in *The Virgin in the Garden* and who welcomed the fugitive Daniel at the end of *Still Life*, now finds the fugitive Frederica a place to live in London, with Thomas Poole and the children whom his deserting wife Elinor has left him to care for. One of these children, Simon, who is almost certainly Alexander's son, repeats his father's kindliness by befriending Leo. When Frederica's hopes for a divorce are threatened by the way these living arrangements are perceived, it is Alexander who again arranges a move, this time to the basement of Agatha's flat. Frederica becomes a teacher, following her father and sister, and a publisher's reader. Now in the position of choosing books for her adult students, she implicitly rejects her old idol Raphael's view that realism is dead, and teaches the classics so dear to her father. Her work and her hard experience of life make it possible for her to achieve rapport with Bill: "She imagines his life…, a class in Scarborough reading *Bleak House*, a class in Calverley coming to grips with *Paradise Lost*. She imagines him imagining dinosaurs striding through the foggy London streets and angels shining in the distance through the trees of the Garden" (245). She knows that she and her father share the delight of the imagination's response to language. Meanwhile, growing up in her grandparents' house, Mary Orton loves words; her dead mother's passion lives on in her.

As one reviewer, Philip Hensher, observed, Byatt's subject is "intelligence"; her characters in this novel of ideas are driven by "imaginative energy" (36). Unlike the authors whom Byatt criticizes for having designs on the reader (a phrase the real-life character Anthony Burgess echoes when he appears at the *Babbletower* trial), Byatt practises, as Hensher pointed out, her own value of "authorial civility," permitting the reader "to think about the questions, and not to be bullied into premature conclusions" (34). What Hensher said specifically about the obscenity trial applies to the author-reader relationship in general, in *Babel Tower* and throughout Byatt's fiction. In a sense, this respect for and trust in the reader is the moral centre of what several reviewers recognized as an intensely moral book; beneath its "serious conversation" about many subjects and its mapping of the split between political viewpoints, *Babel Tower*, said John Bemrose, is "about the courage required to cope with change" (59). Lorna Sage concluded that Frederica is, "despite her cut-up and promiscuous life, a most moral character" (24). As usual with Byatt, the moral value is to be found as much in the process of carefully attending to and sifting through the evidence as in any conclusions that may be reached. *Babbletower* is acquitted on appeal, on the grounds that the judge misdirected the jury. Nevertheless, some of the most compelling language in the trial comes from the other side, when Efraim Ziz, who has survived the Treblinka death camp where his family were killed, gently accuses *Babbletower* of having the potential to cause more pain than goodness in the world. Frederica's triumph in her divorce hearing is mixed, and she knows that her evidence, although factual, has failed to tell the truth about her marriage. Within the *Babbletower* story itself, the way in which Culvert and his company perish is left mysterious, for there is a hiatus between the description of Culvert's viciously sadistic plan to torture his wife and the discovery of the bones outside the Tower. It seems, however, that they die at the hands of the savage Krebs, not through any battle of good versus evil. Our sympathetic relationship with Frederica—for most readers, less ambivalent than it was in the preceding texts—is based on our perception of her as beleaguered, jostled by contradictory systems of language, and living in terror of losing both her independence and Leo, who greatly hampers her freedom and whom she fiercely loves with a passion beyond language.

It is language that draws the threads of *Babel Tower* into a complicated whole. In the account of the work of the Steerforth Committee (a fictionalized version of the Kingman Committee, on which Byatt served), the narrator's sympathies are more obvious than in Jude's trial. They are on the side of tradition, of finding ways to continue to teach grammar, and even of showing children the delight of acquiring lines of poetry "by heart." Those—teachers, pupils, and committee members—who support the view that the teaching of grammar was and presumably remains "a series of gates in a maze for rats…, a series of nasty interruptions to … creative flow" (186) get a fair hearing, but (although the committee's report is necessarily cautious and conciliatory and, inevitably, distorted by the media) the most convincing expert is Gerard Wijnnobel. He urges that his hearers distinguish between "the rules devised for political or social control of group behaviour and the forms of the structure of language"; and argues that "if we have no words to describe the structure of our thoughts, we are unable to analyse their nature and their limitations" (187). The debate, Alexander sees, will divide itself around Eros and the Will to Power, "the buddy and the boss" (189). Byatt makes a telling point when Roger Magog, who related grammar to a rats' maze, testifies later against *Babbletower*. The author of articles advocating unlimited free speech (and prematurely defending Jude's novel), he has now, he says, read *Babbletower* and learned that books can do harm. In an abrupt reversal, he now declares that he has "had enough of the Permissive Society" (586). Byatt does not endorse his view wholeheartedly—Magog is depicted as a foolish, excitable, but well-meaning person—instead, she takes the risk of inserting the text of *Babbletower* for her readers to experience for themselves.[2]

Byatt's views on the teaching of language are not gender-specific, but in other respects *Babel Tower* continues and expands her concern with women and language. In the sixties, her women are more aware of their situation and more vocal about it, although their complaints have not changed very much from those of Jennifer Parry. Frederica listens in on and a chorus of wives discussing their husbands, "one indistinguishable He," and creating "the narrative of women talking," which Frederica herself has never participated in but which she now "can recognize [as] an archetypal anonymous female narrative" (282). Connecting this talk with the much more serious narrative she is preparing for the divorce hearing, she thinks about how language changes relationships: "Does the speaking of mocking criticism … strengthen opposition to Him or dissolve Him in laughter?" She knows that in her narrative, Nigel has been changed into "the Husband, herself into the Plaintiff, Thomas Poole into something he is and is not" (283). At Crowe's Christmas party, the guests and their conversations split into groups according to gender, just as they would have done in earlier decades. By default, Frederica becomes part of the group of wives, who are talking, Crowe says dismissively, about "whatever women talk about" (249). Frederica joins them after perceiving that two of the men do not want to talk to her, although they are discussing her subject, novels. She discovers that the wives' topic is depression; "They blamed their mothers for being depressed and that they are now depressed" (253). This women's chorus is being secretly taped by a sociologist, Brenda Pincher, who is doing research on the lives and conversations of university wives and who collects "their speech habits, their sentences, their regrets, their hopes, their circular discussions, their pregnant silences." Lady Wijnnobel makes a violent, drunken attack on Frederica, for admitting that she finds it difficult to work and look after Leo; to Lady Wijnnobel's traditional description of a mother's duty to do nothing but care for her child, Frederica responds, "I can't care for him if I'm *not myself*." Brenda, who judges Frederica to be arrogant, knows that she should erase Lady Wijnnobel's tirade but does not do so. She feels "aesthetic attachment to the disproportionate rage, the moral fury from nowhere" (255). In the fragmented world of *Babel Tower*, where the women's movement of the seventies has yet to make its impact, women's voices are diverse and contradictory, solidarity is not much in evidence, and the language of women's liberation is yet to be articulated.

Nevertheless, there are signs of hope. Frederica, who never has been and still is not comfortable in groups of women, bonds with Agatha over their mutual love for the "doubleness" of the texts and illustrations of Blake's *Songs of Innocence* and *Songs of Experience* and over shared memories of their childhood impatience for adulthood. Delightedly, they recognize that they have "never had this conversation" before, with anyone (300–01). Although Agatha's private life remains mysterious (she will not reveal anything about Saskia's father), she shows Frederica that it is possible to be a single working woman caring for a child. Their co-operative arrangements for their children allow Frederica to plead successfully to be awarded Leo's day-to-day care: "we are two women, two responsible women, Your Honour, two efficient women" (599).

Married to Nigel, Frederica experiences direct oppression as a woman and realizes that the worst oppression is not being allowed to work; for her, work inevitably involves books. Nigel, a practical businessman, has little use for language except as a means of getting what he wants; he attempts to control Frederica by using love-language as well as the appeal—and the brute force—of his body. In his script, Frederica is wife and mother; he chose her for those roles and "wishes to keep her" (41). To his male business associates, she is his "lady wife" (113); they do not include her in their conversations. To Nigel, words are "for keeping things safe in their places" (41). To Frederica, words are fluid, exciting ends in themselves. Despite her education and sophistication, she is sickened by the discovery of Nigel's hoard of pornography, which graphically shows his pleasure in the subjection of women's bodies. There are obvious parallels between her story and that of *Babbletower*, in which a man holds sway over a community largely by the force of his manipulative language and in which, again, women are the chief sufferers. But Mavis can escape only by choosing a violent death—her child, Felicitas, clings to her at the end just as Leo clings to Frederica—whereas Frederica does get away from Bran House. In another parallel, Jacqueline, who in *Still Life* had seemed as much under the spell of the charismatic, hypocritical, lecherous Gideon Farrar as her friend Ruth, now understands what Gideon is doing to young women and tries, unsuccessfully, to stop Ruth from joining Gideon's commune, the Joyful Companions. Nigel, Culvert, and Gideon all use language as a lure, and women escape partly by being discriminating listeners.

The heterogeneous community in which Frederica finds herself is put together, bit by bit, from old friends and newly made ones, students and teachers, people associated with Bowers and Eden, the publishing house for which she is a reader, and her family in Yorkshire. Its centre is books and language. She recommends Jude's *Babbletower* for publication and lends support when Jude and Rupert Parrott, its publisher, are on trial. Of the other books she reviews, one, *A Thing Apart*, is a woman's novel of the kind she dislikes, an undergraduate story filled with sensitivity and, Frederica says, "empty *longing*" (155); it is, in fact, the only kind of novel Frederica herself is capable of writing at this stage of her life. Another, *Daily Bread* by Phyllis K. Pratt, draws praise from Frederica because of the strength of its language and imagery; "it made me feel that the English language can *say* things, deep, funny, difficult things," Frederica writes (156). Celia Wallhead aptly categorizes *Daily Bread* as a "Byatt book" (145). The other two manuscripts of which we are given excerpts are a poor imitation of Tolkien and a repetitive picaresque tale of a hippie's sexual adventures. The former, Frederica discovers afterward, is by the head of liberal studies at the art college, Richmond Bly, who is a Blake enthusiast and who later stages a bardic performance based on Blake and Tolkien, which is demolished by Paul and the Zy-Goats. The four texts represent a small cross-section of possibilities for fiction in the sixties. What is important for Frederica, however, is that this work restores her sense of self. Energy that was unused at bookless Bran House is now released as she feels the "bliss of talking about books" (151) and the "complicated glee" (156) of writing about them.

In its exploration of women and language, *Babel Tower* focuses on women as readers of texts; reviewing it, Ann Hulbert described it as "a portrait of the reader as a young woman" (7). In *Babel Tower*, Frederica has come a long way from her Oxford interview, when, she boastfully recounts, "I've never talked so much *in my life* and they were interested, they were, I got all sort of things in, *Britannicus* and *Henry VIII* and *The Broken Heart* and *The Winter's Tale* and feminine endings ..." (*Still Life* 20). Now she chooses her texts thoughtfully and cares more about sharing than about showing off. To her art students, she teaches *Women in Love*, and she tries to make them see its "brightness and meaning": "The people are made of language, but that is not all they are. A novel is also made of *ideas*," she tells them (214), and goes on to argue that Lawrence's moon "takes her power from *all our imaginings*" of it (215). Like the Somerville dons, the students listen, and Frederica discovers the joy of teaching. She and her father, who once clashed over *Women in Love* when she was a schoolgirl, now agree that Lawrence provokes ambivalent responses in both of them. Bill says, speaking for both Frederica and Byatt, that Lawrence can be "a *silly* man, even at times a *bad* man," but that when you go back to his book, "there's the language, and the vision, *shining* at you, with authority, whatever that is" (245). In our first meeting with Frederica, she raged at her father for holding up *Women in Love* as a text she should admire: "I don't want the immemorial magnificence of mystic palpable otherness, you can keep it" (*Virgin* 34). Now a mature woman who has made a bad marriage partly because she wanted to believe in Lawrence's vision of sexuality, she must try to deal analytically with the mixed emotions that *Women in Love* produces in her. She has a similar problem with E.M. Forster's *Howards End*; Frederica sees that Forster's dictum "Only connect" led her to the false hope that her marriage could relate "the prose and the passion"—Nigel's world and hers— in a satisfying whole. Now she thinks that "Margaret Schlegel was a fool in ways Forster had no idea of, because he wasn't a woman," and she views Margaret's husband, the businessman Henry Wilcox, as a "stuffed man" (36). In an interview in 2001, Byatt told Philip Hensher that she "writes against E.M. Forster" and has "spent most of [her] life writing against *The Winter's Tale*" (74). Both texts can appear to celebrate the waste of women's energies. In *Babel Tower*, Byatt continues her exploration, begun in her first novel, of the ways in which books shape women's imagining of themselves. In *Still Life*, at Cambridge, Frederica "fell in love ... with a face and a concept" (*Still Life* 199); Raphael Faber's face as Frederica saw it "was put together out of floating cultural clichés. It was dark and lean because these qualities went with a delightful wickedness, they had Satanic and Byronic overtones. It was also 'sensitive'" (*Still Life* 208). From her reading and her imagining of what she read, Frederica constructed an ideal face. A parallel but much more damaging association has resulted in her marriage to Nigel, which at the divorce hearing she relates to her reading of Lawrence, "who says we should listen to—to our passions—to our bodies" (*Babel Tower* 492) and to the need to seek the Other. The physical delight she experienced with Nigel was beyond words, but Frederica still needs words and people to discuss them with, and her marriage ended because of this need. Characteristically, Frederica, having learned these lessons about the dangers of Forster and Lawrence, does not reject their novels but chooses to explore them with her students. In notes for a lecture on love and marriage in *Howards End* and *Women in Love*, she works at the problem these texts pose: "Both writers ... assert an antagonism between 'the machine age' and human passion. Both, in this sense, are pastoral ..." (308). She recognizes that she is living in a decade that has its own issues (for her, the pastoral world of Bran House was the opposite of natural), but she also knows that the novels of Forster and Lawrence are still important. She plans to teach *Middlemarch* and *Mansfield Park*, she draws on Iris Murdoch and Doris Lessing in her arguments about fiction, but she continues to assume the value of male-authored texts as well. As she and Wilkie agree, she prefers "both—and" to "binary dichotomies" (342).

Although writing by women—most notably Frederica's own, appears in *Babel Tower*, this is not the story of Frederica as a developing novelist. Byatt's concern goes deeper than this, to the root question of how minds learn and respond to language. The Steerforth Committee provides a forum for an examination of the broad subject of the teaching of language and of its acquisition by young children, a topic already intimately described in *Still Life*. Byatt's passionate belief that "we owe our children experience of our language that is delightful, varied, shocking, profound, powerful" ("Hauntings" 46) is fictionally vindicated, not only in the dialogues within the committee but in the joy with which Leo and Saskia listen to stories. Indeed, one function of Agatha's *Flight North* is to provide experiential proof that children can respond with excitement to intricate narrative that contains words new to them. Agatha the report writer, working with Alexander to co-ordinate the group work of summarizing the committee's findings, has already provided relevant evidence in her role as storyteller.

Frederica's "Laminations" are a strategy for survival; she cuts up and juxtaposes texts as diverse as Blake's "Infant Sorrow," the report of the Steerforth Committee, Norman O. Brown on the polymorphous perversity of infantile sexuality, Hansel and Gretel, T.S. Eliot's *Four Quartets*, one of her own dreams, Wordsworth's "Immortality Ode," R.D. Laing on the restraint of children masquerading as love, the death of eighty-three people in a colliery avalanche, and a passage by W.H. Auden. The process allows her both to make patterns and to call patterning into question. It also helps her to deal with the polyphony of the sixties. In relation to her own life, it helps to demonstrate the requirement to keep things separate, not to insist on or hope for organic wholeness. Her collage of fragments of legal documents represents her defence against and commentary on official language, which—whether it appears in an obscenity trial or a divorce or custody hearing or the reports of a government-sponsored committee—falsifies and distorts its subjects and their human relevance. Frederica knows that the truth about her marriage cannot be conveyed by either the opposing documents or her (or Nigel's) testimony. In this confused world, it is not surprising that Frederica's new acquaintance Avram Snitkin, taping the proceedings of the *Babbletower* trial, makes a career out of studying "what people actually think they are doing when they are in the process of doing whatever they do" (471). Their spoken and written accounts of what they think they are doing are far from what they actually do; as Alexander tells Frederica, the words of schoolteachers who speak of such things as "whole personalities" and "friendly atmospheres" are "like sand slipping through your fingers" (477) when these teachers are at work with real pupils. Fractured language pervades the world of *Babel Tower*.

Still, Frederica clings to books and language. At her custody hearing, she feels that she is on trial for reading, as Olive and Rosalind and especially Pippy Mammott accuse her of neglecting Leo in order to read. In her statement to Judge Plumb, Frederica pleads for Leo to be brought up in a house with Potter traditions—"My family is a bookish family, a *thinking* family"—and counters Nigel's emphasis on the value of "a pony and woods" with that of "a house *full of books*" (599). Although Frederica's experiences with the law offer many instances of discrimination against women, in the end she is heard. Ironically, however, she discovers to her dismay that Leo, who loves words, is not yet able to read.

Byatt's own discomfort with the sixties is clear throughout *Babel Tower*, as Frederica notes the uniform dress of the art students who think they are asserting independence and the ill-thought-out cult of the child (based in part on selective, hasty reading of Blake), which led women to dress as little girls. In an interview, Byatt cuttingly comments on the emptiness of such gestures of rebellion, including the drug culture: "Actually rushing up and down in very short skirts and freaking out is not the way to [prevent] Auschwitz at all. You need a bit of intelligence" (Miller). In the sixties, she said in another interview, she found "a dangerous lack of thought" (Rogers).

Against this threat Byatt pits intelligence, openness, reflection (which Frederica manages despite her harried life), and community. Books and free expression are part of this. Byatt's position on censorship, stated eight years before the publication of *Babel Tower*, is a balanced, thoughtful one: "Free speech is not a value that overrides all others in all situations. If, nevertheless, we have to think that it is important enough to risk the damage and hurt it can and does bring with it, we should do so humbly and with caution" ("Obscenity" 159). The rival claims of the individual and the group, the responsibility to the self and to others, constitute a continuing preoccupation for her. Although one of the threads running through *Babel Tower* is the pressure of groups and mass emotion on the individual, threatening the human need for private places, this thread is crossed by another, the requirement to pay attention to and participate in public debate. Frederica, whose "first experience of passionate public feeling" (*Still Life* 281) was the debate over Suez at Cambridge but whose life was not much affected by this public crisis or by the revolution in Hungary, now is part of three public debates, all directly or indirectly about language, and all directly or indirectly involving her. In each case, the evidence—about education, about divorce, and about obscenity—falsifies the subject. Frederica's experience with the committee for the defence of *Babbletower*, like her ordeal of her divorce petition, leads her to conclude that "life is full of lawyers and committees defining the indefinable, like childhood, tendencies to deprave and corrupt, language, pre-nuptial incontinence, adultery, guilt" (*Babel Tower* 478). The original title for Byatt's text was, in fact, *Evidence* (Dusinberre, "A.S. Byatt" 183), but the title she finally chose encompasses more fully her view that in the sixties the splitting and collapse of language was accelerated to a crisis point.

In her private life, Frederica has come to understand that books can determine behaviour. While not guilty of most of the things Nigel's lawyer accuses her of, she is, she believes, guilty of betraying Nigel simply by marrying him. No wonder she now longs for a way of achieving disconnection—"Keeping things separate. Not linked by metaphor or sex or desire, but separate objects of knowledge, systems of work, or discovery"—and conceives of "an art form of fragments, juxtaposed, not interwoven" (360). Proof of the power of separation is offered by the life of Elizabeth I; in the present, Frederica watches John Ottokar's struggle to live a separate life while remaining responsible, in some sense, for his twin. Byatt continues to explore the problem in the quartet's concluding volume.

In *A Whistling Woman*, Byatt casts her narrative net even wider. The novel's focal point, a conference on Body and Mind at the University of North Yorkshire, enables her to explore the knowledge explosion of the sixties while extending *Babel Tower*'s earlier subjects, the interrogation of literature, painting, and television. She shows that although the conference makes very little room for women except as audience (among the speakers listed, only two are women), its topic is an urgent and practical one for her women characters in the promiscuous late sixties.

Frederica still occupies a central place in the text, Daniel remains a figure of stability, and Alexander produces a play. Characters from earlier volumes — Marcus, Jacqueline, Ruth, Luk Lysgaard-Peacock, Edmund Wilkie, Vincent Hodgkiss, Elvet Gander, Brenda Pincher, the Wijnnobels, and others — now take on larger roles. (Nigel does not appear; he has remarried and there is another family at Bran House.) Two characters from *The Game*, Julia Corbett Eskelund and Simon Moffitt, reappear here. One is a participant, the other an offstage presence; this is, after all, their decade. Their retrieval from the earlier, very different book contributes to the shape-shifting effect. As well, Byatt introduces many new characters, the most striking being Josh Lamb, christened Joshua Ramsden, whose consciousness occupies much of the earlier part of *A Whistling Woman*. His spiritual torment and visionary terrors — attributable in medical terms to epilepsy — provide a concrete example of the body-mind relationship while representing Byatt's ventriloquistic art at its most empathetic. Through him she continues the representation of the paranormal begun in the *Sugar* volume and continued in the seances of *Possession* and "The Conjugial Angel." Less sympathetically portrayed are another group of new characters, the representatives of the student Left and the counterculture forces, headed by student leader Nick Tewfell and professional revolutionary Jonty Surtees. The diversity of the cast of characters, together with the number of minds to which we have access, makes *A Whistling Woman* the most polyvocal of all Byatt's work.

To introduce *A Whistling Woman*, Byatt uses neither a prologue nor, as in *Babel Tower*, a plurality of beginnings. This concluding volume of her quartet opens with a beginning that is also an ending, as Agatha completes the telling of *Flight North*. Her assembled listeners — Saskia, Frederica, Leo, the Aygepong boys, the Ottokar twins, and Daniel — are dissatisfied, even appalled, by the conclusion Agatha offers them. Guided by the creatures called Whistlers, the travellers find a refuge with a kinsman, but they do not meet Artegall's mysterious uncle or find his father. Frederica tries to counter Leo's protest that this ending is not "a *real* end" by asking, "What's a real end?" and adding, "The end is always the most unreal bit," but Leo rejects this: "There are good ends and this isn't one, *this isn't an end*" (10). Saskia can only sob. By beginning her book in this way, Byatt prepares us for the ending of her own story and for the reflections on endings, in art and life, that the book contains; she also gives us the first of the many groupings of performance and audience, action and commentary, with which the book is filled. As well, the travellers' journey introduces one of the subjects that unifies the plot strands of *A Whistling Woman*: the search for a safe place, a physical, emotional, or intellectual home. Furthermore, Agatha's Whistlers, who are bird-women, are an image of bizarre hybridity that recurs throughout the text and that is already present in the title, which Byatt's first epigraph explains: "A Whistling Woman and a Crowing Hen / Is neither good for God nor Men." In the second epigraph, the pigeon accuses Alice, whose neck has grown long in Wonderland, of being a serpent. The idea of the anomalous is thus linked with the questions that run through the quartet concerning women's identity, what they want, how they are represented, and how they represent themselves. The final epigraph, from Marvell's "Garden," uses the bird in its time-honoured way as a metaphor for the soul that casts "the Bodies Vest aside" in order to engage in spiritual flight—an image that introduces both the conference and the problems of women.

The novel is preoccupied with changing definitions of the human; it demonstrates that binaries such as sane/insane, natural/unnatural, innate/learned, and altruistic/selfish became even more inadequate in the second half of the twentieth century. The three groups that constitute the novel's plot—the commune-cult, the university, and the counterculture/anti-university movement—attempt to offer responses to these questions.

Those who find their way to Dun Vale Hall commune are a mixed group that includes the Quaker-led Spirit's Tigers, to which Paul Ottokar belongs; patients, including Paul, from the psychiatric hospital at Cedar Mount; Gideon Farrar's Joyful Companions; Canon Holly, who has worked with Daniel at the helpline at St. Simeon's; and Richmond Bly, suffering from the shock of the student revolution at the art school. Lucy Nighby, a woman who has certainly been hit by her husband and who may have attacked her children with a rake, takes refuge here and eventually turns her farmhouse, Dun Vale, over to the group. Ruth is here, still under Gideon's spell, and Gideon is as sexually exploitive as ever. Others drift through this part of the story: Ellie, a young mental patient of Gander's in search of safety (who, having starved herself, dies there); Lucas Simmonds, also from Cedar Mount; Eva Wijnnobel, the vice-chancellor's wife, now trumpeting the virtues of astrology as the source of essential knowledge and moving between the cult and the anti-university. Commenting on the group's dynamic are observers on the inside: the psychoanalyst Elvet Gander, who writes to his colleague and friend Kieran

Quarrell, and the sociologist Brenda Pincher, now pursuing a new research project, who sends reports and tapes to her colleague and lover Avram Snitkin. These letters form an important part of the text. They trace Gander's increasing attraction to the group (and to drugs)—he assures Quarrell, just before the catastrophe that destroys the community, that "all is under control, or if not under control, expanding splenderiferously" (389)—and Brenda's contrasting revulsion and terror, as she writes frantically to Snitkin, who never responds; her last letter describes Ruth's agonizing childbirth and Ellie's dead body, which Brenda herself discovers. Taking over the leadership position from Gideon, both these commentators attest, is Joshua Ramsden, another of Gander's patients. At the age of eleven, Joshua found the bodies of his mother and siblings, killed by his father as the result of a mad religious rampage from which he himself escaped by chance. He knows that he will always be alone. He sees himself as one of Kierkegaard's knights of faith, an Abraham figure who (as Joshua writes in an essay) knows the beauty and comfort of being an ordinary person, born "with the universal as his home," but is compelled to walk on the "lonely path" of those who live "outside the universal." Joshua, a mystic who does not want sexual contact, who knows that like the knight of faith he is "Humanly speaking ... insane" (121), exerts powerful, unwilled charismatic force by virtue of his fervid visionary conviction, which leads him and the community closer and closer, through blood and fire, to the apocalyptic last battle he has foreseen. In the fire built by the group on his instructions, to "purify" the house that, also on his instructions, is being enclosed by a stone wall, Joshua dies, together with Ruth and Eva Wijnnobel. The other leader, Gideon, leaves, with his wife, Clemency, and no one knows their whereabouts. John has dashed into the flames to rescue his brother; both have been badly burned and, in hospital, they have "uncannily symmetrical" (405) bandages covering their skin grafts—a testimony to their inability to separate. The group's attempt to reach mystic oneness, already split by Gideon's pseudo-Christianity and Joshua's Manichaeism, has collapsed, imploding, as Brenda Pincher knew it would. The stone walls (which would have cut Luk off from the snail population he is researching) are disintegrating along with the aspirations they had contained. The safe place has not endured.

At the University of North Yorkshire, Gerard Wijnnobel has another vision, of a secular place where forms of learning will be represented and connected. His image of rationality and coherence is at odds with his marriage, in which his wife, going her separate way, pursues her obsession with astrology. The two keynote speakers at the conference on Body and Mind, Hodder Pinsky and Theobald Eichenbaum, agree with Wijn-nobel that some human structures and patterns are innate, but both their politics and their disciplines, cognitive psycholinguistics and ethology, lead them in different directions. Other speakers, Luk Lysgaard-Peacock the biologist and Vincent Hodgkiss the philosopher, offer other perspectives. For Pinsky, studies of the chemistry of the brain prove that the "brain, nervous system, and mind were the *same thing*," and there is no soul or spirit apart from this "convoluted layered slab of white and grey matter and its branches and pulses" (353). We are "fated—*not* designed," he says, to use words, metaphors, to describe brain activity, but he warns that "thought is not words, life is not words" (355). Eichenbaum's paper was to be on group behaviour, the natural tendency of humans to act aggressively in herds or packs; because of what were taken to be Nazi affiliations in his youth, he is still suspect. He is prevented from speaking by a concrete example of his topic, the anti-university force acting as a mob. Hodgkiss gives a paper on Wittgenstein's theory of colour; Luk, representing another discourse, delights Frederica with his lecture on meiosis, in which he argues that in ultimate biological terms the losers are the redundant males, despite the fact that in human society women have been oppressed by males. The papers on literature, on topics such as "Lawrence and blood and semen" (363), interest Frederica less than she had expected; she perceives that her education, which had divided learning into science and literature, is now outmoded. F.R. Leavis's insistence on the centrality of English studies, in opposition to the claims of science, now appears to her as a Darwinian struggle for survival, "a territorial snarl and dash" (364). Frederica concludes there is a new battle: "to defend reason against unreason" (364).

The university rebels and the counterculture community, who blur into each other, are the forces of unreason. The leader, the hippie Jonty Surtees, is happy to enlist any who come, especially Nick Tewfell, the legitimately elected student leader, whose aims are more moderate to begin with but who, with the other young men and women from inside and outside the university, is swept up in the mindless language of the revolution; "Prescribe mushrooms not Shakespeare texts," says one of the graffiti at the art school (39), and at the North Yorkshire University the messages are similar. Students who began by asking for the abolition of the compulsory preparatory year of maths and languages so dear to Wijnnobel's heart are inflamed by Surtees's insistence that all authority is evil. The gathering of momentum and unexamined fervour within this group parallels that at the commune; in this case, the public climax comes when Surtees, crying, "Freedom begins, *here*, and *now*," cuts off

Eichenbaum's freedom by hitting him on the head with a microphone, interrupting Eichenbaum's accusation that Surtees is "Pied Piper with a crowd of denatured children draggling behind" (369). After this, a petrol bomb is thrown, fires are started, and Frederica recognizes examples of "Skoob. An art form" (371), Paul's sign. Lab animals and birds are let loose to wander, maimed and bewildered. Damage is done to Long Royston and its art treasures. A private climax, unwitnessed except by the two participants, epitomizes what is most menacing about such mass actions, as Byatt sees them. Nick Tewfell, a "naturally lawful" person, is trying to stop some rowdy and drunk students from smashing museum cases; cornered by Wijnnobel, he, against his nature, smashes a case containing Renaissance glass beakers from Matthew Crowe's collection: "He wished to hurt someone. He was not used to the feeling" (372). Afterward, Wijnnobel picks up some fragments and cuts his hand. This small instance of the pointless breaking of history remains in Nick's memory: "Many years later, when Tewfell was a minister in Tony Blair's government, he would still wake at night and remember that moment, the unbroken box, the bright unbroken beakers, the broken box, the splinters of glass, the dark-faced tall man with his bleeding fingers, the strange dancing light in the room, which was the torches outside, and the flaring behind his own eyes" (372). Wijnnobel never tells anyone who broke the glass; Nick comes to realize that at first "he had hated him for that"; then, as time passed, he "had almost loved him. He had come, in a way, to resemble him" (373). In this brief scene, Byatt captures the shattering of fragile beauty that wisdom acquired after the fact cannot restore. In the present of the narrative, the protesters leave and the university sets about its recovery.

Throughout this text, we are constantly invited to be discriminating in making distinctions. We are both helped and challenged by the multitude of voices that comment on the action. Gander and Brenda both begin as observers of the cult, but one becomes enraptured by apocalyptic possibilities, his language losing any vestige of scientific detachment, and the other grows more aware that the group will follow a predictable course. Gander sees uniqueness, Brenda classifies instances of sameness. Daniel, who also foresees how things will end, speaks wisely to Jacqueline about Joshua: "He's a religious man. He loves the Light. He wants to love God. He is sick.... I was going to say, he's dangerous. But I've no right. I'm just going on the pattern of how it always is, the vision, the intensity, the excess, the—the violence. Maybe it'll be contained, this time" (256). Daniel knows the predictable pattern—he can classify—but hopes for an exception to it. Other interpreters and commentators have their say. To Gander, the counterculture "kids" are dangerously "playing with the things of the spirit as though they were clouds of coloured smoke" (328). To Frederica, it is Gander's world that is menacing; when John moves closer to that world, she is vehement: "It's all nonsense. It's all increasingly frightening *nonsense*" (333). John, in turn, feels pulled into the cult not only by Paul's presence there but by the threats of Luk's biology-based "explanation of everything. From the point of view of cells and organisms. Makes all sorts of ideas meaningless. Kindness, love. God" (322). Luk's ideas, says John, are right, but they take away the meaning and "they don't change the fact" that John's personal fate is Paul, "because he's my genes" (323). Luk, without John's panic at the thought, is able to accept that there are words that have lost their meaning; he names "Reality.... Authenticity. Creation. Love" (408) in a conversation with Frederica, with whom he is beginning a sexual relationship. Frederica, much more drawn to Luk's world than to Gander's, nevertheless challenges Luk's contemptuous dismissal of astrology, which, she says, "lets people think in metaphors." To Luk, it "prevents people from thinking"; he compares it to cobwebs covering a window. To Frederica, all mental constructs, including astrological signs, are interesting because "our brains made them" (350). This conversation with Luk reaches back to the program on creativity that Frederica hosted and that pitted Gander's definition of creativity, as what produces unique works drawn up from the unconscious, against Pinsky's scientific view that creativity is "the generation of new ideas, new explanations" (151); computers may eventually understand the uniqueness of *Hamlet*.

Amid all these attempts to explain the world, each possessing its own attractiveness, the text warns against reductiveness. An extreme example of the all-embracing system is Mondrian's theory of colour and line: "Mondrian believed that everything—the sum of things—could be represented by these three colours [red, yellow, and blue], with black, white, and grey, within the intersections of verticals and horizontals." For Wijnnobel, who loves the paintings, "this system was mad in its man-made purity" yet "endlessly beautiful in its own implacable terms. There were many triads of 'primary' colours, of which, for historical reasons, Mondrian had picked one. It was one vision of necessity, of the building-blocks of the universe. A theory of everything" (28). The cult, the conference, and the counterculture all hope for "a theory of everything"; all fail. Wijnnobel's own dream persists because he is wise enough to know that it is impossible to achieve it in concrete form. He knows that the towers of his university are only metaphors, symbols of the forms of knowledge, "philosophy, bio-chemistry, grammar," which themselves are only "lookouts, from which other forms could be seen, to which other forms could be linked. The world was infinitely multifarious and its elements were simple and could be seen from infinite viewpoints, in infinite rearrangements" (326). The peacock's tail feathers, in Frederica's words, "completely improbable, completely beautiful things" (378) that no theory is able to account for, continue to tantalize and delight. In the moral and religious world, Daniel confronts Joshua's obsessive quest for the Light and rejects both it and humanism. His description of his own life is illogical and confused, based on instinct, not system: "My son says, I'm not a religious. He may be right. I do the things somebody has to do since religion died in the world. Not for 'humanity's' sake, but because we are religious beings, and caring for each other is what is left of what we used to know or believe about how everything worked. I am a religious, and God isn't a man, and I don't know what It is" (400–401). At the end of her story, Frederica's decision to tell Luk that she is carrying his child is impulsive and instinctual; like Daniel's understanding of his vocation, it is an individual, untheorized act. Luk's and Pinsky's ways of seeing the world, which appear to the desperate John to destroy both individuality and God, are only viewpoints, although they are in the ascendancy. Giving them ample space and credibility, Byatt nevertheless suggests that they are only two of Wijnnobel's lookouts from which the multifarious reality of the world can be glimpsed. In fact, although Wijnnobel's ideal of an underlying coherence is presented as admirable, Frederica's experience continues to show her that, in Byatt's words in her 1996 interview with Eleanor Wachtel about *Babel Tower*, "everything doesn't connect"; there are only "local truths."

Nowhere is the danger of reductiveness more threatening than in the lives of women in the Swinging Sixties, when the availability of the pill and the expectation of sexual liberation for women could mean the restriction rather than the enlargement of their freedom to make choices. Power is still in the hands of men; they dominate both the social institutions and the challenges to these structures. Even in the hippie protest group, women follow their male leaders. Wilkie is in control of Frederica's television series although the program on "Free Women" is her idea. Here, the new medium becomes the setting for a self-reflexive consideration of the portrayal of women by the older medium of fiction, while the set itself, with its allusive doll's house and its conglomeration of objects denoting women's domestic roles, asserts that only the externals of women's lives have changed.

Frederica's guests on this program are Julia Corbett and Penny Komuves, both writers about women. Julia, reappearing from *The Game*, does not seem to have changed; a generation older than Frederica, she is "somewhere between a lady novelist and a woman novelist" (140) and writes about women's entrapment. Once again, as in *The Game*, Byatt uses Julia's imaginary novels to represent the kind of "woman's novel" she herself has worked to avoid. Now, in retrospection, with the achievement of all her subsequent fiction to bear witness, she—and we—can measure Byatt's progress. Her reference to Julia as in part a "lady novelist" evokes George Eliot's satirical dismissal of some of her contemporaries, women who portrayed impossibly learned and beautiful heroines and thus betrayed both actual women and the seriousness of the novel as a form. By including Julia's "trapped titles" (141) from nursery rhymes (*Life in a Shoe, The Toy Box*) together with titles we recognize as belonging to real-life author Penelope Mortimer (*The Bright Prison, The Pumpkin-Eater, Daddy's Gone A-Hunting*), Byatt comments dismissively on women's novels of the fifties, at the same time suggesting that, although plots have changed, popular fiction for women has not progressed very far since Eliot published her satire in 1856. Penny's articles about educated young women who are frustrated by current theories of child-rearing (especially John Bowlby's insistence on the need for the mother's constant presence) show the split between the "heads" and "hands" of these women. "Their heads were full of Lawrentian ideology, or particle physics, or the sociology of leisure, or the labour theory of value"—subjects that reflect ironically on their situation—while "their hands were full of suds, and soufflés, and strained purées and stained nappies" (140). Penny herself, unencumbered by children (although there is a hint that she has had an abortion), is free to pursue and write about her other interest, elaborate gourmet cooking. The conversation, which appears as a "knowing parody" of a kaffeeklatsch because of the presence of the male film crew and the unseen viewers, shows the confusion of women's experience in the sixties as well as the control of media by men. The images of food and kitchen gadgets within the doll's house on the set—including tools for "poking and prying," objects that, filmed, recall a "gynaecological theatre" (141)—attest to both the seductiveness of domestic objects and the power of the new medium. Julia observes that wedding gifts are discovered by the bride to be "like the cheese in the mousetrap," assuring that she will remain in her kitchen "thinking how to get out, how to be free" (145) and that in George Eliot's novels, too, "pretty women ... are made to want *things*" (144).

The three women's conversation—introduced by Frederica with Freud's question, "What do women want?"—considers the attractiveness of the male body, the freedom of modern women "to pick and choose," and the persistence nevertheless of the old problem: "Women wanted children, women had to care for children" (143). They move on to the question of abortion. Asked if she would ever choose it, Frederica, seeing a vision of Leo's face, says, "I might…I might like to feel I had the right. I might not" (143). Julia voices the feminist criticism that Eliot punished female beauty and withheld freedom from those who "wanted something else out of life besides sex and marriage"; Frederica responds with Byatt's own feminist view, that Eliot punished only women who exploited their beauty, and that she told the story of "how it was. How clever women's lives *were*" (144). Frederica reflects that girls in Victorian fiction—she names Jane Eyre and Maggie Tulliver—are "wise and attractive and human" but mature women are "monsters, demons, or victims" like Lewis Carroll's Queen of Hearts, Duchess, and Cook. "Perhaps we shouldn't grow up," she concludes (146), and the program ends, its opening question unanswered.

This sketched, selective mini-history of women's writing—Eliot's "lady novelists," Eliot herself, Doris Lessing, whose section "Free Women" in *The Golden Notebook* provided Frederica's title, and Julia's book—acts self-reflexively to call attention to Byatt's own project. In Frederica, Jacqueline, and Agatha, Byatt depicts women (not girls, despite the then-current "little girl" fashions) who resist simple classification and who confront the never-solved problem of women's freedom. Through these women, too, Byatt proposes a more complicated story for women than Julia's latest book. *Just a Little Bit Higher* tells of a woman, at first happily married, who is encouraged by her husband to become a teacher and then, pregnant and "free," is deserted by him for a younger woman. *A Whistling Woman* looks deeply at "how clever women's lives *were*" and avoids both the clichéd outcome of Julia's novel and its "edge of aimlessness," which is more frightening to Frederica than the "ferocity and violence" (141) of Lessing's *Golden Notebook*. In encompassing more of the inner lives of women and of the outer world, Byatt's story stands with Lessing's.

In *A Whistling Woman*, Jacqueline Winwar's story becomes almost as important as Frederica's; their plots play against each other not as opposite paths but as complementary ones. Both women are caught in the struggle between sexuality, marriage, and motherhood on the one hand and the life of the mind on the other; both experience, in different ways, Stephanie's dilemma. Byatt places them in a context of other women and their choices. Agatha, her private life hidden until the novel's conclusion, stands alone in the security of her career as a public servant, the unexpected success of *Flight North*, and her life as mother of an apparently fatherless daughter. Brenda Pincher's sojourn at Dun Vale Hall displays professional ambition, determination, and courage—she is energetic in her rescue work during the fire—but she relies on a weak, foolish male, Avram Snitkin, to keep her tapes and letters safe, although she knows from experience that he is irresponsible and may "wind them round [his] head" during a drug trip (192). When she finds him asleep at the anti-university, which everyone else has abandoned, her fears are justified, for he has left all her letters unopened, believing them to be bills. In the commune, Lucy and Clemency, both victims of male abuse, are drawn by Joshua's power to make a mysterious, identical vow to him, declaring, "All my life. All my life" (207). Do they mean, asks Gander as he reports this, that they have waited all their lives for him or that they are offering him their lives? In any case, they—and Ellie, who joins them—have given up what independence they had. Clemency has emotionally deserted Gideon, who is almost certainly the father of Ruth's sickly baby girl, but she does not leave him. As for Ruth, she rejects her child, not even acknowledging her sex or naming her. "Take it away," she says to Luk and Daniel. "Give it to Jacqueline" (401). The more forceful woman associated with the commune, the crazed astrologer Eva, does not fare any better, despite the fact that her husband has risked his reputation and authority by leaving her at liberty to pursue her version of independence. Clearly, this is a world where female identity and autonomy are precarious.

In the lives of the two principal women characters, we hear, once again, the cry for independence that Christabel and Maud utter in *Possession*: in Maud's words, "I must go on *doing my work*" (*Possession* 506). At the beginning of *A Whistling Woman*, Jacqueline is hopeful that she can continue her affectionate relationship with Marcus, more maternal than sexual, and that Luk's passionate interest in her can be transferred to someone else. She recognizes the force of her scientific curiosity, "her desire to know the next thing, and then the next, and then the next," which "lived in her like a bright dragon in a cave, it had to be fed, it must not be denied, it would destroy her if she did not feed it…" (24). In her research on the physiology of memory, she makes discoveries that she tries—with only partial success—to protect from appropriation by her supervisor, Lyon Bowman, who also adds her to his harem of young women students. At the conference, Bowman gives a paper that "smoothly" incorporates "months of trial and error, failure and triumph" (361) from Jacqueline's research; the only acknowledgment he gives her is an introduction to Pinsky's new discussion group.

Poignantly, Byatt explores the dilemma of an ambitious woman in the sixties who is aware that the best way to get her work done is to try not to be noticed as a woman. Still amorously pursued by Luk, Jacqueline agrees to a weekend with him. Their lovemaking is an ordeal for her, and she is uncomfortably aware of the similarity between Luk's language, as he waits on her attentively at the dinner table, and that of Lyon Bowman at the climax of their much more casual sexual encounter. Bowman says "Good *girl*," and she thinks, "Like a rider encouraging a horse" (167); Luk's "My lady is served" moves the language from the discourse of the stable to that of courtly love, but Jacqueline's mind puts them together: "'Good *girl*' said Jacqueline's mind. And 'my lady is served'" (174). Both phrases are condescending; both imply inequality. The simplicity and power of Jacqueline's own language, both internally and as she struggles to explain herself to Luk and then to Daniel, is striking. Painfully aware of how much their continuing relationship would mean to Luk, she utters the "cool sentence" "I need time to think." Unlike the women at Dun Vale Hall, she sees clearly what is at stake: "She was trying to make sensible decisions about her own life—it was *the whole of her own life* she was disposing of..." (179). In a few weeks, believing herself to be pregnant, she tries to force herself to want marriage; to Luk's ecstatic response to the news, she can only say, weeping, "I think this decides everything. I will. I do want to marry you" (181). When her body makes its own decision and she miscarries, she looks at the "kind of jelly bundle" in the toilet bowl, and her body responds with a flood of blood and tears. She is distanced from both her body and her feelings, "appalled by her body, which shook, and trembled, by the sense that emotion was a bodily, unnameable, unmanageable thing" that she cannot call "grief. Or mourning, or anger, or fear" (184). Her disconnection from both the fetus and Luk is clear in her fragmented speech when she tells Luk what has happened—"There isn't. I wasn't. I'm *not*, anyway, pregnant"—and her torment comes through in the starkness of the verbs she uses: "I came to say, I can't. I don't want to get married. I can't. I want to want to get married, but I don't" (185). The simple progression of her intellectual life, knowing things one after another, in logical sequence, clashes violently with the fits and starts of her words to Luk and with her physical and emotional turmoil.

The sadness of Jacqueline's narrative is that she feels compelled to label her choice of work and separateness as unnatural, inhuman. Confiding in Daniel as they go by bus to visit Ruth—who has made very different choices—at the commune, she says that she refused Luk "because I want to concentrate on what I'm doing. Because I don't want to be split.... I always assumed everything would fall into place, work and life and sex and so on. It won't." She continues, "I wanted to be human, and I'm—not" (255). She and Daniel can talk easily, and Daniel shows her that they have chosen similar paths, both involving a kind of scientific detachment, "not like ordinary love" (255). In his presence, the tension in Jacqueline's body relaxes, as he helps her to feel at ease with her choice. After Ruth's death in the fire, Daniel helps Jacqueline again. Knowing that Jacqueline cannot take responsibility for Ruth's baby (whom Eva has named Sophy) and still do her work, he argues against altruism, pointing out that it is "hard to think that what's right, might be what you want *for yourself*, because the world we grew up in said, always put others before yourself" (414). Reversing the usual gender roles, Daniel declares Sophy to be his own problem; he will try to find a home for her. Then, unexpectedly, he does something that Jacqueline, taken by surprise, thinks Daniel "doesn't *do*": he kisses her. Jacqueline's part of the narrative concludes on this surprising note, with Daniel the celibate religious man advocating selfishness, kissing a woman, and finding that "nothing seemed to hold him back" (415).

For Frederica, the problem of separateness versus connectedness is even more complicated than it is for Jacqueline. The two women share a hunger for knowledge, and Frederica is becoming more aware of how important it is to her. Hosting the first of her television programs, on which her guests are "two very clever men," Richard Gregory and Jonathan Miller (both real-life characters whom Byatt thanks in her acknowledgments), she feels like Carroll's Alice, a clever child; they have "their own knowledge, vastly greater than hers." She reflects, "she had thought she had wanted womanhood and sex. Knowledge had been there, and she had swallowed it wholesale, because she had a good digestion, but hadn't seemed to be what mattered. Now, perhaps after all, it did" (137).

Surrounded by the proliferating scientific language of the late sixties, Frederica continues to think about the discourse of literature. Reading and teaching novels still gives her deep pleasure: teaching *The Great Gatsby* to her extramural class, she excitedly shares with them her experience of "*really reading* every word of something she had believed she knew." Frederica knows that she is "both by accident and by inheritance constructed to understand … the setting of words in order, to make worlds, to make ideas" (270). Earlier, confronted by Wilkie's enthusiasm for television, she protests, "Novels won't go away.…We *need* images made of language" (48). Despite the unexpected success of her *Laminations*, she declares that she is not a writer; she reflects that Agatha's mind "naturally inhabited the world of living metaphor which was myth or fable, whereas she, Frederica, was confined to stitching and patching the solid, and you could still see the joins" (240). Nostalgically recalling her abandoned thesis topic, she thinks, sadly, that instead of following her plan of studying the nature of literary metaphor, she herself has become a metaphor in her role as television personality: "She sat about dressed as a clever metaphor, in an easy-to-grasp metaphorical glass box, like a mermaid in a raree show, and posed trivial superficial questions with trivial superficial brightness" (326). Nevertheless, she is intrigued by what the new medium can do. Her new colour television brings her images of a world "outside the classroom, outside the book-covers." "The Golgi-stained slide, the flashing movements of the snooker balls, the new-born child sliding out in its bloody caul, the killing of the countryside (her next *Looking-Glass* project)"—and concludes that "these existed.... These were real. These were also real" (270). At the conference, Frederica hears Pinsky talk about metaphors for the mind and realizes, as his language becomes more technical, that "though she had *understood what he had said*, which was lucid, and interesting, she was profoundly ignorant, blackly, thickly ignorant, of *what he was talking about*" (355). Rather than dismiss his world and the referents of his language, she wants to know more. Near the book's conclusion, she tells Luk that she does not want to return to English studies, as John had urged her to do when he had hoped they would marry; she has been convinced that "the *new* metaphors" are in "that box," television, and that, as "air hostess" in that box, she can have in her cabin all kinds of languages — "Simon Moffitt explaining the Amazon flora and fauna — and Pinsky, and you.... Explaining genes, and chromosomes, and the language of the DNA" (411). What she wants most of all, however, is "to *think*" (410).

In the passage from *Flight North* that begins *A Whistling Woman*, the Whistlers tell Artegall their history. They were once women, they say, living in a far northern region called Veralden, where the men are shapeshifters who can move freely while women are confined to the valley, "spinning and teaching, tending fruit-trees and flowers"; "We wanted to go out, we wanted the speed and the danger of the wind and the snow and the dark" (6). Using their female charm, they learned from a student how to make feather-coats and became shape-shifters themselves, free at night and returning to their prescribed, enclosed roles at dawn. Their deception discovered, they were driven from the city and now suffer because no one understands their speech. In the terms of this tale, Frederica and Jacqueline are both Whistlers—intelligent, curious women who want freedom to explore the world and who need someone to comprehend their language.

For Frederica, much more sexually alive than Jacqueline and a passionately loving mother as well, the problem is even more acute. She puts one aspect of the issue bluntly on the "Free Women" program: "The body … wants to be pregnant. The woman often doesn't" (143). At this point in her life, she is attracted by celibacy, and when John is away at the university in Calverley, she enjoys living without sex in London, her "most intense physical pleasure" the smell of Leo's hair and skin (148). When John arrives for the weekend, her flat is "full of heat, and tension, and pleasure, and tension," yet in the midst of their lovemaking, Frederica experiences a sharper version of her old wish for separateness. She "had the usual feeling—this is the *real thing*—and the new, niggling feeling; 'this is the *usual* feeling.' Now I feel this is the real thing. And outside all this, I am something else, someone else, I walk alone" (149). Our glimpse of Frederica and John in the prologue to *The Virgin in the Garden* is put in context when, immediately after these thoughts of Frederica's, John tries to stop her from meeting Alexander and Daniel at the National Portrait Gallery. In the *Virgin* prologue, we watch with Alexander as Frederica arrives with a stranger who catches her wrist; she kisses him and twists away, and he runs his hand down her spine in "a gesture of complete, and public, intimacy" (11) before leaving her there. Now, in *A Whistling Woman*, we see John's "possessive sweep" of her spine from Frederica's perspective: "She felt briefly weak, and gave herself a little shake, and went in to see Elizabeth" (150). We also understand the double gesture of her kissing John and twisting away from him (which recalls the attraction/revulsion of her relationship with Nigel) and the continuing force of her fascination with Elizabeth I, whose separateness was her power. Later, John frantically pleads with Frederica to marry him, saying that she is the way for him to be "an *individual* in an ordinary world" (340), separate from Paul and also from the threats to the individual he perceives in Luk's discoveries. Frederica, who has always feared Paul's hold on John, again has a dual response: "a terrible sense of a weight of responsibility and an even more violent urge to escape, to get out, to go away" (341). Weeping, she falls asleep and dreams of herself as the young Elizabeth naked beneath her cut-paper dress but being raped by Luk. Her affair with John is over.

True to her dream, Frederica and Luk do begin an affair. Despite the violent sex in the dream, the narrator's rather ominous description of Luk as "a man who appeared gentler and kinder than he was" (188), and Luk's earlier intense dislike of Frederica, this relationship seems promising. With Frederica, Luk performs none of the courtship ritual with which he had self-consciously wooed Jacqueline. Their sexual encounters are satisfying to both, and they are able, as well, to discuss their work with mutual respect. Luk is not in the least possessive, and Frederica appears to have found a way of life that suits her: "She had space to breathe and be—and so had he—and they met eagerly and happily. That would do" (413). Both of them, "for different reasons," feel that the discourse of love is "dead words" (413). Nevertheless, when he agrees with her that "what matters" is that she, who as a woman must "whistle harder," will come to "*know more*," Frederica finds herself "perturbed in body and mind"; he has not said "you are lovely" or "I want you exclusively to be *mine*." She feels that the "laminations" of her life are "slipping," being put into "new patterns." She is both "full of life, and afraid" (411). Soon after returning to London, she discovers that she is pregnant; the "new, fluent, elegantly provisional shape" (412) that her life appeared to have acquired is an illusion; her life is now biologically determined by the inexorable process of the multiplication of cells that will give her body a predictable shape. She does nothing to interfere with this process, letting nature follow its course; she recalls the terror of being "trapped by her own body" (415) during her first pregnancy but also knows that the love that binds her to Leo will tie her to the new baby. It is Leo who insists that she tell Luk and who forces her to go north to Yorkshire to find him. Leo's argument is based on Saskia's unhappiness at not knowing who her father was; parents and children, he believes, should know each other. Frederica, who understands that in the sixties the nuclear family is seen as oppressive ("Who is the father was an outdated Victorian question" [416]) has recently seen, in Holland, an example of this apparently obsolete grouping—a man, woman, and child who turn out to be Wijnnobel, Agatha, and Saskia—and takes this, as does the reader, to be the answer to the "outdated" question of who is Saskia's father. Frederica gives Luk the news in a conversation we do not hear but only see through Leo's perspective as he watches from a distance—he hears them shouting, sees Luk put his arm around Frederica, and is reassured that it is "all right." The ending is left open.

Frederica Potter is the most fully developed and many-sided of all Byatt's women. Simply by virtue of her presence in four long narratives that trace her progress from the age of seventeen to thirty-four, she becomes a dominant figure. Beyond this, however, she possesses a convincingly fluid, complex, at times self-contradictory reality. Most readers find that she is more likeable in the later two volumes, when, as reviewer Michèle Roberts observed, she is "mellowed by suffering" (40). She retains some of her gingery sharpness, however, and the curiosity and greed for life that marked her teenaged self only enlarge and deepen with maturity. Displaying ruthless rationality at some times and intuitive impulsiveness at others, she is an imperfect woman who becomes an endearing one. Although often arrogant, she is able to feel humiliated, inadequate, or unworthy; her outburst on hearing that Mary confided in Agatha that she was having her first period both echoes Jacqueline's language and reflects Byatt's awareness of the prescriptive images of femininity. "I'm a dreadful failure, Agatha," Frederica says. "If I was a real human being—she should have told *me*" (235). Despite her passionate love for Leo, Frederica, like Jacqueline, feels herself to be lacking in maternal responses, and therefore failing in humanity. The quartet preserves Frederica's capacity to surprise us.

Byatt's retrospective look at the situation of women in the fifties and sixties succeeds in showing, as George Eliot did in her time, how "clever women's lives *were*" (144) at the same time as it leaves its characters' futures open. Readers in 2004 may smile at the prediction of the usually astute Tony Watson concerning "the First Woman Prime Minister, an imaginary figure who would rise to power in about 2020" (140). At the same time, these readers can identify what has *not* changed for women in the past thirty-odd years. Never preaching, seldom theorizing, Byatt leaves these observations up to us. "What's a real end?" (10), Frederica asks when Agatha's ending fails to satisfy her listeners. In the quartet, Byatt has found her most intriguing and engaging solution so far to the problem of ending. As she had done in *Possession*, she accomplishes a strategic balance of openness and closure.

In *Still Life*, a hint is given about what for Frederica will become "a later obsessive subject, *her* subject," as she already, at Cambridge, ponders "the strange relations between the niceties of human perceptions and creations of style and the discriminations of the moral, and political life" (*Still Life* 125). As for Frederica's career, several reviewers of *Babel Tower* believed that she would eventually become a novelist. For J.M. Coetzee this was an "implicit promise" (18), and Sage went so far as to say that as the quartet moves on it "more and more resembles a game of hide-and-seek" that Byatt is playing with herself: "Her creature, Frederica, keeps *not quite* turning into a novelist, and Byatt continues to avoid catching up with herself" (24). The prologue to *Still Life* shows Frederica at the Royal Academy of Arts, signing the Visitors' Book, "Frederica Potter, Radio 3 Critics' Forum" (3). Since the conclusion of *A Whistling Woman*, she has, it seems, acquired more professional security, and now at least part of her work on "*her* subject" is for the older medium, radio, not for television. But we do not know whether she has married Luk; we learn nothing about the baby she was carrying ten years earlier or about Leo.

Frederica remains elusive, "protean," as John House says women are "these days" (3).

After the publication of *Babel Tower*, Byatt told Eleanor Wachtel that she had found a way to end the story without killing off all the characters. She envisioned a "last battle" like that in *Ragnarök* (Wachtel, interview), which would feature an invasion of the North Yorkshire campus by "anarchic riffraff" (Rogers). Elsewhere, Byatt writes of her admiration for the ending of *Ragnarök*, in which, after years of "emptiness," life returns to the earth. This image, Byatt says, provides her with hope within her "gloomier moments"; she can think that "we are destroying biodiversity and the earth we inhabit, [only] temporarily." This narrative from *Asgard and the Gods*, she says, "gives the writer a perfect paradigm of all sorts of narrative—the linear, ending in defeat, the cyclical, ending in rebirth, the riddling, box-in-box full of alternative versions, characters who may be the same, or different, or change their names and natures" ("Hunger" 10). The ending of the quartet draws on this paradigm.

The final paragraph of the quartet reads, "They stood together and looked over the moving moor, under the moving clouds, at the distant dark line of the sea beyond the edge of the earth. In the distance, the man-made Early Warning System, three perfect, pale, immense spheres, like visitors from another world, angelic or daemonic, stood against the golds and greens and blues. Frederica said to Leo: 'We haven't the slightest idea what to do.' Everyone laughed. The world was all before them, it seemed. They could go anywhere. 'We shall think of something,' said Luk Lysgaard-Peacock." This passage, combining echoes of Arnold's sad vision in "Dover Beach" of the receding of the tide from the edges of the world with the conclusion of *Paradise Lost*, blends the linear and the cyclical, defeat and rebirth, at the same time placing the three figures against the huge forms of the Early Warning System, themselves both ominous and beautiful. Frederica and Luk speak hopeful words, and the dominant sense is of optimism and the exuberance of possibility and choice. Nevertheless, both adults, especially Frederica, have forfeited some of their autonomy, and the larger threat of the destruction of the world remains. On the personal level of women's experience, Byatt seems to be undercutting Frederica's vision, only a few weeks earlier, of herself and Jacqueline as "free women, women who had incomes, work they had chosen, a life of the mind, sex as they pleased" (415). This spectrum of possibilities has dimmed for Frederica, but the exhilaration of the struggle remains. The events that lead to this conclusion also combine the linear and the cyclical. The deaths of three people by fire, the destruction of the cult-commune, the dispersal of the protestors, the disruption of the conference, and the damage to the university buildings all in their different ways represent defeat. Nevertheless, the story has moved toward recovery and rebirth. Through Mary, Byatt finds a way to "resurrect" her mother, Stephanie, who, Byatt said to Nicholas Tredell, "also goes with Hermione in *The Winter's Tale*" (71). It is this play, a story of rebirth and recovery, that is Alexander's fitting choice as his contribution to the renovation of the damaged university. In the production, Mary plays Hermione's daughter, Perdita, speaking the powerful lines about Proserpina's flowers, and bringing her grandfather and her father to tears as they see the mother in the daughter. Leo is being taught to read by his grandfather Bill who, now more patient and gentle and less angry, declares himself "a reformed character" (249). Daniel rescues Will from the commune and thus, possibly, from sharing the fate of the other three killed in the fire, and tries to explain his vocation to his son, who has accused him of not believing in God: "If you can't see what Mary saw, then you must make do with Martha, who lived with what's solid" (401). Although Will makes no response—he is recovering from a drug trip— there seems to be hope after all for this troubled father-son relationship. Vincent Hodgkiss, with great delicacy, tact, and gentleness, has helped Marcus, to acknowledge that he, like Vincent, is homosexual, and the two men are to share a house in Cambridge. Although Vincent is "not in any sense part of the family," the Potters accept this new beginning, smiling their "encouragement" when Marcus, "with almost complete ease," speaks about Vincent (413). The Potter family is continuing to reconstitute itself, and, meanwhile, another family emerges, as Wijnnobel, freed from the misery of his marriage, joins Agatha and Saskia.

As for the "riddling, box-in-box" ending, it does not consist of the presentation of fixed, clearly defined alternative endings; we recall Byatt's dislike of Fowles's two endings in *The French Lieutenant's Woman*, which, she says, "do not suggest a plurality of possible stories"; they are "neither future nor conditional" ("People in Paper Houses" 174). Rather, throughout the quartet the reader is invited by passages like *A Whistling Woman*'s concluding paragraph to find not endings so much as varied possibilities for ongoing life. In the quartet, as in Byatt's other work, things are always reconfiguring themselves. Like Frederica and Alexander coming upon Agatha in her new family grouping and recalling past "stories they could never substantiate or deny, stories of committee-journeys, meetings" (417) that now have new meaning as possible lovers' trysts, we must re-see and reassess. We have insight into Agatha's failure to provide a parent-child reunion at the end of her characters' long journey: "Even a discovered uncle, Frederica thought, appeared to be too much for Agatha"

(11). Now will Agatha feel freed to write a sequel that will reshape her tale? But Agatha remains a mystery; she is one of the few important characters in all Byatt's work whose minds we never enter (Christabel is another; these two represent both the hiddenness of women's identity and their power to speak through their texts). The brief scene in which Wijnnobel, alone while Eva is in London appearing on Frederica's program, continues his reading of *Flight North*, finds it "a good story," and feels "things looming, in the world outside" (345) also takes on new possibilities in retrospect. The passage Wijnnobel reads is about the relation of words and things and the usefulness of books—topics dear to the hearts of Agatha and himself, as we know. Has he contributed to the writing of *Flight North*? Although the question of whether Wijnnobel is Saskia's father, like that concerning Gideon and the baby Sophy, is left without a final answer, the discovery of Wijnnobel and Agatha's love for each other and his probable fatherhood reconfigures the past.

Throughout the four volumes, the two prologues, together with scattered references in the main narrative to Frederica's later life, give glimpses of a future whose details remain unknown. Although the linear narrative ends when Frederica is thirty-four, we have already seen her at forty-four in the *Still Life* prologue and, as well, have been provided with glimpses of her at other points in her life through narrative asides in the main texts. In the 1968 prologue to *Virgin*, Frederica comes to the National Portrait Gallery with an unnamed man; in *Babel Tower*, we realize that the man is John; in *A Whistling Woman*, we witness the troubled situation that precedes this scene, and read it differently in retrospect. At the end of *A Whistling Woman*, Frederica is with Luk; in the 1980 prologue there is no mention of him. Our hopes for Daniel and Will are diminished when we remember the 1980 prologue. Similarly, the tentative and fragile relationship between Daniel and Jacqueline at the end of *A Whistling Woman* is called into question not only by Daniel's appearance alone at the Royal Academy of Arts but by the air of solitude and vocational commitment that continues to surround him; at forty-eight, he thinks of himself as "a battered and grizzled survivor" (*Still Life* 4). No real questions concerning Alexander's sex life arise, however; past liaisons have shown his predictability in finding the imagining of sex more satisfying than the performance. The changes within him are shifts in perspective, as both prologues reveal his dissatisfaction with both of his plays, *Astrea* and *The Yellow Chair*, and from *A Whistling Woman* we learn why he did not write a new play for the university fundraising: his inspiration is "burned out," he tells Frederica (385). In the terms of Byatt's comment on the *Ragnarök* paradigm, the three friends are both the same and different, but their friendship endures. At several points, *The Virgin*'s narrative looks ahead to 1973, as when we learn about Frederica's thoughts about the coronation twenty years after the event (and three years after the conclusion of *A Whistling Woman*). Another passage shows two future Fredericas who contrast with the seventeen-year-old Frederica: "She did not know then, that as an ageing woman walking along a London street she could almost with certainty tell herself: I have come to the end of desire. I should like to live alone. Or that, shaken by desire at forty, she could know with a very comfortable despair that desire will always fail, and still shake. At seventeen it was virginity that was, like the grasshopper, a burden" (*Virgin* 325). In the first book of her chronicle, Byatt prepared carefully for what was to follow. *Babel Tower* contains a reference to a trip Frederica will make at an unspecified date in the future to the Rio Negro, where a South American sloth with its infant wrapped around its neck will remind her of "the worst moment" of her life (*Babel Tower* 129), when Leo clung to her as she left Bran House. In *A Whistling Woman*, we read that "Frederica who had felt old at thirty was surprised at how she did not feel old at sixty" (49). We share in her more mature reflections on the youth-obsessed sixties: "it takes a few decades to learn that younger generations than 'the young' sprout like mushrooms, that if the young of the 60s could not remember the War they were followed rapidly by generations who could not remember Vietnam, who were followed by generations who could not remember the Falklands" (49). (Interestingly, since Byatt gives Frederica the same birthday as her own, both would be sixty in 1996, the year *Babel Tower* was published.) The time span of the quartet's story overflows the chronological boundaries of its narrative.

Early in *A Whistling Woman*, reflecting on Agatha's unsatisfactory ending, Frederica asks herself what endings she has found most moving, and answers that they are "reunions of parents and children, separated by danger" (11). In her own ending, Byatt both offers these endings—for Wijnnobel and Saskia, Daniel and Will, Luk and the unborn baby—and refuses to solidify them. The other plot lines also remain open. The quartet's ending is real in the way in which life's endings are real; this highly artful story does not provide the finality of traditional narrative. It captures, instead, the fluidity of real experience. In doing so, it shows that our relationship with art itself is altered and enriched by changes. Like Gillian in "The Djinn," Bill Potter has "always hated" *The Winter's Tale* "for making comedy out of tragedy by ignoring real feelings" (385), Frederica tells Alexander before his production at Long Royston. As Bill watches and listens to Mary perform Perdita, the lost daughter who is restored to her parents, he weeps and reaches a "revelation," which he tries to share with Frederica: "I've just *understood*. Never too old. Never too old to understand something. The thing about the late comedies—the thing is—that what they do, the effect they have, isn't anything to do with fobbing you off with a happy ending when you know you witnessed a tragedy. It's about art, it's about the necessity of art. The human need to be *mocked with art*—you can have a happy ending, precisely because you know in life they don't happen, when you are old, you have a right to the *irony* of a happy ending—because you don't believe it" (395). The re-visioning of art and life is both commented on and exemplified by Byatt's text. In Holland, Frederica, exhausted by the lethargy of early pregnancy and her confused emotions, falls into "a drowse of defeat" in front of Vermeer's *View of Delft* and wakes to perceive how time is "very quietly arrested" in the painting: "She saw it as though she was in it, and saw, simultaneously, the perfect art ..." (418). The experience parallels her father's revelation, which, at the time, she was too preoccupied to share. Vermeer's canvas has itself undergone changes during the process of restoration; Wijnnobel pronounces it a "mystery of survival and renewal.... But it is still there" (418). Like Shakespeare's play, which has lived through so many interpretations, it retains its integrity.

Among the losses during the protest at the university are Alexander's costume designs for *Astrea*. Viewing them in Wijnnobel's museum cases, Frederica sees herself there, running through Crowe's garden, "her red hair streaming, her thin legs visible through the streamers of her scissored skirts" (329). These paper skirts have recurred in her dreams since that time in 1953 when she was a young virgin acting a young virgin's role. Later, a sexually experienced woman fearing the loss of her son, the skirts are rearranged by her dreaming memory to signify the flimsiness of her case for Leo's custody. The paper skirts reappear shortly after this, in her dream, after refusing to marry John, of being raped by Luk. Looking at the *Astrea* museum, Frederica thinks, "Time had not stopped there, oh no" (329). The mind's reassembling of images is endless, and endlessly interesting.

Through the open structures of her texts, Byatt gives her characters—especially her women—the only form of freedom that can be imagined in the real world. Frederica, Christabel, Maud, Matilda, the Eldest Princess, Gillian, and the rest live in the fluidity of process, where death is the only predictable. Like the paperweight the djinn describes to Gillian, the world of Byatt's fiction is filled with "forever possibilities. And impossibilities, of course."

Epilogue

In 1993, Byatt published a poem about clichés, taking her epigraph from Toni Morrison, who cites the longevity of clichés as proof of their value. Byatt's "Working with Clichés" is about Proteus, who is himself a cliché of the paradox of constancy in flux and the impossibility of grasping the meaning of change. In the poem, Proteus displays himself as multiplicity: he is many-coloured, his texture both smooth and rough, his body both cold and warm, seeming "both dead / And alive" (21-22). He both "burns" and "trickles silky" (43). He seduces us with both male and female qualities, yet is "always one fish" (1). The encounter with him is unavoidable, and it must take place in his own element. The speaker does not try to approach Proteus on dry land, where, according to Virgil, he will tell of the future if he is unable to escape into one of his many shapes. For Byatt's speaker, the prophecy is the encounter with metamorphosis; there is no separate truth: "You must take hold. / You must grasp tight" (10-11), "You must grip" (27), "You must go down" (37), "You must hold on." As the intensely sensual struggle reaches its climax, Proteus is both gentle, "His soft lips kissing your hurt knees," (49) and threatening, "The rows of needle-teeth bristling / Inside his ravenous grin" (50-51). He leaves you "gasping and retching" while he "disports himself still / Wreathed in sunlight" (53-55). The poem concludes: "You do not know him. / But you have something to say" (57-58). In her long, loving, and courageous encounter with the living, changing world, Byatt does not achieve a fixity of either knowledge or form. She knows that, in Michael Levenson's words, "There is no one true metaphor. There are only new attempts to describe the world, resurrecting dead cliché into living speech, and straining to point at a world beyond the words" ("*Angels and Insects*" 173). Proteus is unknowable, but Byatt's engagement with process and multiplicity in language, in the experienced world and especially in the lives of women has given her a seemingly inexhaustible number of things to say.

Appendix 1: The Placing of *Possession*

IN AN ESSAY FIRST PUBLISHED IN 1996, Jackie Buxton prophesied that critical consensus would eventually place *Possession* outside "the canon of postmodernist texts" (103): it gives "ideological priority" to the Victorian world (98), advocates "traditional conceptions of readerly and writerly practice" (100), and represents the love relationship of Roland and Maud as "a productive, liberating affair" (102). In fact, Buxton suggests that despite its "postmodern gestures" (98), *Possession* resists and critiques postmodernism's epistemology. Other critics also note the traditional values in the book. Kelly A. Marsh finds that the plot privileges "honesty of motivation and emotion" (113) in both scholarship and sexual relationships. Along with other "Neo-Sensation" novelists such as Graham Swift and Margaret Drabble, Marsh argues, Byatt questions "the poststructuralist tenet that morality is socially constructed by asserting that there can and must be truth, at least of feeling" (115). In her exploration of Byatt's "repossession" of the romance, Thelma J. Shinn stresses the permanence of our need for romance, showing that in Byatt's text "form is content and the past is the present; when the Romance is realized in our lives, we realize that reality is in itself a Romance and that life is a construct that needs to be retold in the present moment and can be transformed with each retelling" (113). Deborah Morse explores the centrality of the transcending power of the romantic imagination, and also draws attention to the text's richness of allusion.

Two critics who stress the postmodern aspects are Chris Walsh and André Brink; both view language as the novel's primary subject. Walsh praises the freedom of reading that *Possession* fosters: the text "shows up restrictive, monologic, authoritarian, closed, coercive readings for what they are, and promotes an ideal that is the product of thoughtfulness—liberal, dialogic, democratic, open, pluralistic" (194). Brink, who provides the fullest and most subtle and cogent account of the book's postmodern qualities, focuses on language as "the primary form" of possession (292) and sees the text as "a *performance* to be enacted and entered into" (302). In the course of this process, the difference between Self and Other becomes central, fixed gender roles are called into question along with fixed views of history, and, in fact, the concepts of male and female "are subsumed in one another" (305). For Brink, *Possession* is postmodern in the primacy it gives to "the *fact* of narrative, of fiction, of lies, and of language" (308). He notes, however, Byatt's "reservations about the extreme Postmodernist view of language as the *only* reality" (305).

The consensus that appears to be forming supports Elisabeth Bronfen's description of *Possession* as "a hybrid cross between the postmodern text, whose ethical gesture consists in a self-conscious reference to its own significatory process, and the text of moral realism, aimed at the discovery of an ethical truth" (131). A helpful summary of the book's dual aspects is offered by Kate Flint. Byatt, she says "refuses the assumptions of post-modernism" in her belief in "character" and in her preoccupation with creating "the illusion of the immediacy of experience" (300). Nevertheless, like David Lodge's *Nice Work* and John Fowles's *The French Lieutenant's Woman*, *Possession* deliberately poses "some of the problematics of identity, of writing history, and of narrative discontinuity" (303) that are typical of postmodernist writing. Much of the critical response to *Possession* has consisted of attempts to place the novel in terms of its use of history and of its generic affiliations. *Possession* has been variously categorized as a "Neo-Sensation Novel" (Marsh), a "Neo-Victorian Novel" (Shiller), a "Retro-Victorian Novel" (Shuttleworth, "Natural History"), and an example of "Postmodern Moral Fiction" (Bronfen). In a negative assessment of its treatment of history, Louise Yelin argues that *Possession* "mystifies past and present alike.... [Byatt] locates Victorianists—those in her novel and those of us 'outside' its pages—in a critical wilderness from which we cannot escape. But at the same time, she makes at least an implicit claim to possess Victorian secrets known or knowable by no one else" (40). On the other hand, Frederick M. Holmes, Dana Shiller, Del Ivan Janik, and Sabine Hotho-Jackson see the representation of history as liberating rather than imprisoning. Holmes wisely observes that *Possession*'s "recognition that the imagination is an intertextual construct is not in itself grounds for dismissing its efficacy in providing us with provisional structures with which to make sense of the past" ("Historical Imagination" 331). For Shiller, *Possession* recuperates the past, by foregrounding the "frustrating, imprecise and finally rewarding *process* of 'reaching back'"; the novel "constructs a notion of history predicated on interpretation, not on the discovery of historical 'truths'" (552). Janik shows how the reader learns with the characters that "in what we call history there are infinitely many histories—known, unknown, discovered, invented, overlooked, or avoided" (166). Hotho-Jackson argues that in rewriting history "from the female perspective," Byatt aims "to give a fuller picture of history"; the concept of history in *Possession*, then, is both modernist and postmodernist: the text "combines a deconstructivist perspective with a conventional attempt at reaffirmation" (118). Byatt's text supports Linda Hutcheon's definition of historiographic metafiction as "both/and."

Appendix II: The Fourth Ending of *Possession*

In 1994, as Maud Michell-Bailey, Byatt sent a letter to the editor of *Victorian Poetry*. Maud enclosed two newly discovered fragments of poetry by Christabel, with a scholarly note linking them to Christabel's oeuvre. The first piece begins, "When I come to my last home," and imagines "two angry spirits," one white and one grey, struggling to claim the speaker's "remnants" in the grave. Maud identifies the spirits as Blanche and Ash. On the second, Maud makes a personal comment relating the central image, a thread binding mother and child, to Maud's experience of maternity since the birth of her own daughter, Rowan: "Feminist criticism admits the validity of the personal response, so I can say that before the birth of my daughter I had quite failed to imagine the nature of the pain LaMotte must daily have experienced, seeing her child and being unable to acknowledge the tie—so literally, the tie" (Letter 2). This contribution adds to the histories of both sets of main characters in *Possession*. It takes the plot further into the future while at the same time returning to fill a gap in the nineteenth-century narrative. Maud, we learn, did marry Roland, and entered a life that combined motherhood and work, something her great-great-great-grandmother was not able to do. Maud's coded naming of her daughter for the mountain ash tree belatedly acknowledges Ash's paternity. The fact that Christabel's poems were found "on the reverse side of a drawing of the Winter Garden at Seal Court, done by May, or Maia LaMotte, and ... signed LaMotte" (Letter 1) presents Maia and her mother as artistic collaborators. The poems, Maud says, were "preserved in a folder of [Maia's] schoolwork" (1). Presumably, then, Christabel kept this folder, wrote her fragments on the reverse of one sheet, and bequeathed it, together with all her other papers, to Maia (whom Maud, in what I take to be a slip on Byatt's part, calls her great-grandmother). In *Possession*, Maud recalls that Sophia Bailey, carrying out her sister's last wishes, sent the package to Maia upon Christabel's death, telling Maia that "she [Christabel] believed strongly in the importance of handing things on through the female line" (434–35). What was handed on included half of the truth of Maia's lineage, and the signature on the drawing may indicate that the adult Maia—she was thirty when Christabel died—read the poem and understood that she was the child, ignorant of the truth, to whose "gold head" and "small bed" the witch's thread in the second poem is forever painfully attached, and that the "witch" who is the "bobbin" was Christabel, who now could safely reveal her maternity. Appropriately, Maia signed her newly revealed name to her drawing of the Winter Garden, which had been "much loved" by her mother (*Possession* 141). For the reader, this is the most satisfying explanation of the signature; on the other hand, Christabel may herself have written the name under the drawing as another coded message to her daughter, which may or may not have been "delivered" (511) to Maia's full comprehension.

Maud's extratextual contribution fits its context, an issue of *Victorian Poetry* devoted to the recuperation of Victorian women poets. It is notable too that this issue includes a review of a book by Byatt's friend Isobel Armstrong, to whom *Possession* is dedicated. This mini-sequel thus points back to a page of *Possession* that precedes the text itself, suggesting ever-widening circles in which the worlds of text and reader, and of nineteenth-century poets (real and imagined) and twentieth-century scholars (real and imagined), endlessly connect.

The letter, which Linda K. Hughes, editor of *Victorian Poetry*, aptly calls "meta-meta-metadiscourse" (Introduction 6), thus constitutes a second, extratextual postscript to the novel. What status, now, has this additional document whose immediate audience is not the readers of *Possession*, but readers of a journal existing in the "real" world? André Brink's conclusion about the postscript is that although by "the rules of the conventional contract between narrator and reader we 'could not have known' this ending, yet we *do* know—because it has been *told*, because it has found its way, by hook or by crook, into language" (308). Perhaps our best course is simply to enjoy the letter, which also finds its way to us "by hook or by crook" to offer further satisfaction for our narrative curiosity—and further proof that Byatt has succeeded in her "passionate plea for readers to be allowed to identify with characters" (qtd. in Tredell 62).

Notes

1 Introduction

1 Christien Franken gives a detailed discussion of the complex influence of Leavis on Byatt's thinking; see chapter 1 of her *A.S. Byatt: Art, Authorship, Creativity*.

2 In 1994, when she included Levenson's review of *Angels and Insects*, "The Religion of Fiction," in the new edition of *Degrees of Freedom*, Byatt said somewhat enigmatically that Levenson "took some of the ideas [in *Degrees of Freedom*] further than I might have done myself and in a direction which surprised and excited me" (viii). Levenson's later essay expands on and develops the argument in his original review.

2 *The Shadow of the Sun*

1 Kuno Schuhmann states that Anna's story is "an example of a rather simple realism" but that Henry's requires that the novel move to "what has traditionally been regarded the domain of the poet" ("In Search" 80).

2 Richard Todd interprets these experiences of Anna's in a more positive way, as contributing to her "sense of autonomy": "Anna sees things in this way not because she is a woman but because she is not a visionary." Byatt's problem at this point, he adds, is to find a language for female vision (*A.S. Byatt* 9-10). In a fascinating feminist analysis, Christien Franken argues that Henry is an example of "the instability of the Burkean [male] sublime"; Anna can be seen as "the failed sublime" but is more properly viewed as a woman who, like one of Clarice Lispector's heroines as interpreted by Luce Irigaray, can experience "a sublime of nearness" that is based not on conquest but on love (*A.S. Byatt* 45, 53, 58).

3 *The Game*

1 Kuno Schuhmann argues that it is Simon whose "view of reality ... sets a standard for this novel" and points to Simon's statement that "Our picture of real-

ity is never fixed but can always be elaborated and made more accurate. And this changes us" (Schuhmann, "In Search" 82; see also, *The Game* 25). In her more detailed account of Simon, Christien Franken stresses his ambivalence and observes that in the course of the novel, "Simon himself becomes increasingly uncertain about his own conceptualizations of cognitive vision" (*A.S. Byatt* 67). My reworking of my earlier essay on *The Game* has been greatly enriched by my reading of Franken's thoughtful and discriminating discussion.

2 The fullest biographical reading is Joanne Creighton's "Sisterly Symbiosis." Giuliana Giobbi explores the subject of sisterhood more generally.

3 Some examples cited by Gayle Greene are Penelope Mortimer's *The Pumpkin Eater* (1962), Sue Kaufman's *The Diary of a Mad Housewife* (1970), and Fay Weldon's *The Fat Woman's Joke* (1967). For a study of these and other novels, see Greene, *Changing the Story: Feminist Fiction and the Tradition*, especially chapter 3, "Mad Housewives and Closed Circles." Byatt's work receives only a passing reference in Greene's book, however.

4 *The Virgin in the Garden* and *Still Life*

1 Kathleen Coyne Kelly cites Byatt's use of "Powerhouse" to denote a "good and liberal family" like the Potter family and her own (63 and 121 n.2).

2 In *After the War*, D.J. Taylor points out Byatt's role as an early commentator on the "burgeoning media culture," beginning with *The Game* (205–206).

3 In a recent short story, "Heavenly Bodies," Byatt whimsically depicts the process by which the signs of the zodiac overthrow a degraded, commercialized pop version of the figure of the Virgin and restore the eternal figure with all its rich associations, to its place in the heavens.

4 Richard Todd comments on *The Virgin's* engagement with "the erotic power exercised both by the work of art and by the mythic power of art" and makes suggestive parallels with Murdoch's *The Black Prince* (*A.S. Byatt* 15–16).

5 In "A Modern 'Seer Blest,'" Judith Plotz sees Marcus as an embodiment of "the terrors and loneliness of childhood that are inseparable from the condition of not knowing oneself" (43).

6 Todd suggests that in this encounter, Stephanie and Daniel are "'taken over' by Eros the trickster under his guise as Venus Anadyomene," and points to Byatt's revisioning of the Anadyomene myth, again with reference to Filey, "within the context of the gender politics of *Possession*" (*A.S. Byatt* 17). The myth appears again in "Crocodile Tears" in the name of Patricia Nimmo's chain of bath specialty shops. Here, it is a sad ironic emblem of the life from which Patricia flees after Tony's death.

7 Michael Westlake comments on the appearance of an "authorial simulacrum" in each of the two prologues, and quotes Byatt's statement that she is present in "the person scanning" rather than in the "story" told in her texts (33).

8 See Tess Coslett for a full account of Byatt's depiction, from the "participant point of view," of this "previously undocumented experience" (263).

9 In her interview with Philip Hensher, Byatt speaks of her intention to represent Stephanie's death in such a way that "the reader [would] be upset as you are by a real death, and not as you are by a fictional death" (52). This abrupt cutting of the knot of an individual life is praised by Todd as an example of Byatt's

"moral honesty…, coupled with her conviction that her characters must be depicted as having thoughts, that these thoughts are frequently important, exciting, and painful, and that neither the act nor the depicting of thinking must be confused with specious attempts to make sense of the world" (A.S. Byatt 54). In two very personal poems, "A Dog, a Horse, a Rat" and "Dead Boys," Byatt conveys the cutting of the knot from the opposite perspective, that of the mourner confronting what Sue Sorensen calls "death's vitality" (131). In a reading that contrasts with Todd's, Sorensen asserts that Stephanie's death is "unquestionably constructed as a religious sacrifice of some sort" (132). In my view, the immediacy and directness of the event represents sheer, senseless accident.

5 Sugar and Other Stories

1 Laurent Lepaludier offers a fine analysis of the forms of discourse in the story and of the role of the reader as narratee. Drawing on Bakhtin's theory, he shows that the narrator "aims at saving the character of Emily" from Miss Crichton-Walker's "totalitarian" discourse "with the threads of his/her polyphonic discourse" (38). In her essay "Arachne," Byatt speaks of her changing relationship to the "woman's art" of needlework. She "hated it as a child," rebelled as a schoolgirl against her headmistress's praise of tablecloth-making as "useful," and later came to see embroidery as "the image I had in my own mind of the things I wrote" (138).

2 In his essay "The Ghost Written and the Ghost Writer in A.S. Byatt's Story 'The July Ghost,' Claude Maisonnat argues that the ghost-story genre is used "to foreground the problematic element of the work of mourning which it in fact describes, the latter functioning as a metaphor of the act of writing" (49). In a subtle Lacanian analysis, Maisonnat draws attention to the narrator's self-censoring and hesitation, to the layers of narrative, and to the narrative confusion that produces "a sort of overall denial of narratorial responsibility, exactly as if the narrative agency had a ghost-like status, in that it is at the same time visible and out of reach" (61). I am not certain, however, that his conclusion, that the lodger "enables her [Imogen] to complete the work of mourning which had proved impossible before" (62), is justified by the story's open ending. The last words of Imogen in the text, spoken after their attempt at sex, imply that she is still frozen in the "grip" of her grief: "Sex and death don't go. I can't afford to let go of my grip on myself. I hoped. What you hoped. It was a bad idea. I apologize" (54). Strangely, Maisonnat, in his argument that the lodger as ghost-writer "has laid the ghost of the ghost written in the text" (62), omits any mention of the failed sexual encounter and its hoped-for result, or of the story's inconclusive ending.

3 Byatt relates "The Dried Witch" to a perception she shared with other women at University College, London (where she taught from 1972 to 1981): "we had all observed that women, once they got over the age of 45, began to be persecuted by groups of people…." The story was also inspired by her reading of Chinese stories by Shen Tsunh Wen, which, she told Jean-Louis Chevalier, "moved me in a way I didn't quite understand" ("Entretien" 14).

4 In On Histories, Byatt describes the genesis of "Precipice-Encurled," beginning with Meredith's footnote: "Absence of information sets the imagination work-

ing—I wondered about the young person whose life and death were contained in a footnote" ("True Stories" 102–03).

5 Daniel Sargent Curtis, "Robert Browning 1879 to 1885," in Meredith, Appendix C, 167, records that on being shown the first proposition for a Browning Society, Browning responded, "Il me semble que cela frise le ridicule." Byatt substitutes "ce genre de chose" for "cela."

6 Before Meredith, Betty Miller had interpreted "Inapprehensiveness" as expressing Browning's feelings for Mrs. Bronson (see Meredith lxxvi n. 71). Meredith's argument is more extended, however. Mrs. Bronson, "Browning in Asolo," in Meredith, Appendix A, 132, quotes Browning as saying that "The Lady and the Painter" was composed during a drive from Bassano to Asolo and was suggested by "the birds twittering in the trees."

6 Possession: A Romance

1 Compare Emily Dickinson's appeal to her mentor Thomas Higginson: "Are you too deeply occupied to say if my Verse is alive?" (888). Byatt comments on Dickinson's and Christabel's "spider" poems in her essay "Arachne" (151–55). See also Nancy Chinn's exploration of the similarities between the two poets.

2 On Melusine, see especially Christien Franken and André Brink. Franken emphasizes Byatt's revision of the Melusine myth in order "to write a woman artist's story" (A.S. Byatt 99). Brink sees Melusine as the "figure of intertextuality" (300) in Possession. In the novel's project of "restitution and rewriting," he says, "Melusine is restored to her position of benign power through an act of historical correction" (304–305). In her discussion of Possession as a "fairy tale romance," Victoria Sanchez argues that Christabel's fairy tales serve "the expressly feminist purpose of giving the female voice control and subjectivity" (33).

3 For a very helpful discussion of Ellen as journal writer, see Adrienne Shiffman's argument that Ellen "collapses the generic boundaries of the female diary" (103). Shiffman concludes, "Ultimately, Ellen Ash is both private and public, subject and object, Poet and Poem and as such, she baffles" (103).

4 Elisabeth Bronfen sees the relationship with the earlier pair of lovers as one that enables Maud and Roland to overcome "postmodern scepticism." They "can now consciously accept the discourse of love, even though it is a disempowering discourse, given that it performs a plagiarism of their predecessors and the illusion of a coherent self and a coherent story. Crucial, however, is the fact that this discourse of love is acknowledged as precisely a marvelous illusion" (133).

5 Two critics, Louise Yelin and Monica Flegel, have objected to Byatt's use of the romance plot and of fairy tale on the grounds that these forms encourage uncritical reading. "We are asked," says Flegel, "to overlook the unrealistic qualities of Byatt's novel and embrace a fairy-tale world" (427). Both single out Euan's rescue of Val as particularly problematic. Such views, I believe, pay insufficient attention to the novel's ethical commitments and to the self-conscious playfulness with which the happy ending is produced. And although, as both critics point out, Byatt does not highlight issues of poverty and of class, neither does she simply pass over them.

6 For a discussion of Byatt's use of the epistolary form, see Lucille Desblache.

7 Angels and Insects

1 I am grateful to Judith Fletcher for information about Dame Cottitoe's name, and for allowing me to read a draft of her illuminating essay "The Odyssey Rewoven: A.S. Byatt's *Angels and Insects*" prior to its publication.

2 In "True Stories," Byatt seems to confirm this conclusion of mine: "I realized unexpectedly that from the beginning I had set up *Morpho Eugenia*, the aphrodisiac butterfly of sexual selection against Matty, the Sphinx, the night-flyer, who 'hath both kinds in one'" ("True Stories" 121). For a parallel between this game of anagrams and the one in Nabokov's *Ada or Ardor: A Family Chronicle*, see Sally Shuttleworth, "Writing Natural History," n. 17. In Nabokov's game, the story ends with "incest," however.

3 In her feminist study of "Morpho Eugenia," Margaret Pearce argues that Matty acts to overcome the "reductive narrative perspective" with which William begins, thus decentralizing him; she "undermines the chief namer in the story" (399, 406). Rather pessimistically, however, Pearce stresses that in the book's last scene, William is still imparting information, "still locked in his system of naming" (410). My reading of the novella differs from Pearce's in seeing Matty and William as co-operative narrators who enrich each other's perspectives, who are not polarized by gender, and who are at least to some extent able to free themselves from systems. Michael Levenson sees Matty as "the chief protagonist" of the novella: "Partly, her importance lies in rousing Adamson to recover the realist vocation; more substantially, it lies in finding a vocation of her own" (*"Angels and Insects"* 165). My view is closer to Levenson's; we both see Matty as a creative force of change.

4 Fryn Jesse was a writer herself; *The Feminist Companion to Literature in English* describes her as "novelist, journalist, playwright and crime writer" (Blain, Clements, and Grundy 575).

5 In "The Gender of Mourning," Christien Franken makes a convincing argument for reading Tennyson's continued grieving as an example of melancholy, whereas Emily, for reasons tied to her gender, experiences and completes the stages of mourning.

6 In "The Double Voice of Metaphor," Heidi Hansson comments on this statement of William's: "Ultimately the development and choices of the individual matter, and as a consequence a reading that tries to explain the analogies in universal terms collapses" (460). Hansson's insight applies with equal validity to "The Conjugial Angel."

8 The Matisse Stories

1 In her essay "Mr Cropper and Mrs Brown," Helen Wilkinson examines "good and bad collectors" in works by Byatt and other contemporary writers. Taking "Art Work" as a "case study," she sees Sheba Brown as "perhaps the epitome of the good collector" because for her, "collecting is part of an ongoing process of transformation and transfiguration" (97). Her collections and Robin's, Wilkinson argues, respectively represent female and male collecting. (It should be noted, however, that although Robin's collecting habits are gently mocked, his passion for colour and his enunciations of the challenge of representation are very much Byatt's own.) Wilkinson extends her discussion to include, among

others, Cropper and Ash in *Possession*, Josephine in "The Changeling," and Julia, Cassandra, and Simon in *The Game*; her division of collectors along gender lines is not continued beyond "Art Work," however.

2 In this interview with Laura Miller, Byatt acknowledges that she received many letters complaining about her treatment of sexual harassment in this story. Even Michèle Roberts, "an extremely subtle writer and a terribly good critic," failed to see "the feminist message that was there" because she was looking for a different feminist message; the story "seemed not to fit her pattern.... It was feminism that caused her to misread this story in my view."

3 Byatt's short story "Repeating Patterns," published in 1989, is a more light-hearted depiction of a bond established between two people through their common love of Matisse. This time the two are a young woman and her fiancé's mother; on the occasion of their first meeting, they are wearing identical dresses made of a fabric whose pattern was inspired by Matisse.

9 *The Djinn in the Nightingale's Eye*

1 Byatt has praised Terry Pratchett's fantasies for their ability to portray "the misery of animal minds trapped in human metamorphoses" ("Old Tales" 149).

2 I owe this valuable suggestion to my former graduate student Sally Braun-Jackson.

3 Byatt wrote "Dragons' Breath" to be read aloud as part of a benefit project for Sarajevo. She comments, "I wanted to write about people who believed themselves to be trapped by boredom in peace, and who are truly trapped by destruction—and rediscover, and see differently, the fragments of their world, their culture, in the ruins" ("Fairy Stories"). In a recently published short story, "The Thing in the Forest," a new version of the dragon figure traumatizes two young girls, evacuees in wartime Britain. Here again, the dragon is associated with the terrors of displacement.

4 Robert Irwin draws attention to Todorov's analysis of embedded narrative in the *Arabian Nights* (226). (It seems fitting that Todorov himself should be present to hear Gillian's last story, told at the Toronto conference.) Byatt acknowledges her indebtedness to Irwin's book (*Djinn* 279) and also comments on the effect the device has on the reading experience: it "turns the writer into a reader and it turns the reader into a reader of a reading; and it somehow lines the reader up with the writer as a reader of this text within a text" (qtd. in Chevalier, "Entretien" 20).

5 Annegret Maack helpfully shows how Gillian "learns the law of metaphorical identity" through her experiences with narrative: "Through the act of retelling, Gillian participates in the cultural memory of the community" (125, 132).

6 Todd (*A.S. Byatt* 44) points out the "veiled puzzlement" Byatt creates in "The Glass Coffin" by the unexplained vanishing from the story of the "little grey man" who initiated the tailor's quest. The mystery surrounding the djinn/museum guide is another instance of this effect.

10 *Elementals: Stories of Fire and Ice*

1 The reviewers of *Elementals* devoted surprisingly little attention to "Cold." Those who gave it more than passing mention stressed Sasan's creative act of

love. Although one, Alex Clark, acknowledged that readers might feel sorrow over Fiammarosa's "exile" (10), neither this reviewer nor any other I have found made reference to the heroine's loss of her art.

11 The Biographer's Tale

1 The reviews of The Biographer's Tale were mixed, with more negative assessments than usual. John Updike, Hal Jensen, Alex Clark, Richard Eder, and Pamela Norris are representative of the more positive reviewers, who stressed the richness of Byatt's language, the seriousness of her intellectual engagement with issues, and the lure of the fairy-tale and fabular aspects. Others, such as Ruth Scurr, John Bayley, Ron Charles, and Stephen Amidon, praised some of these qualities but found the erudition laboured and the theoretical preoccupations intrusive.

2 Noting that Byatt provides her sources for these names in her acknowledgments, Norris further points us to a justification of predation, Destry-Scholes's note on the ecological function of parasites (50).

3 Ibsen's biographer Michael Meyer records that such a meeting was in fact planned as a prank by Ibsen's acquaintances but never took place. It was to involve, as Destry-Scholes's playlet does, dressing Henriksen to resemble Ibsen and shocking the father with the encounter with his double (see Meyer 206). Byatt records that she chose Ibsen because in his centreless onion (peeled by Peer in Peer Gynt) he "gives one of the earliest modern images of the absence of a central self" ("Nothing is Too Wonderful to Be True" 13).

4 Byatt seems to have found this coinage in Ezra Pound. See her review of Helen DeWitt's novel The Last Samurai, where Byatt comments on the depiction of a boy "going round and round the Circle Line—the periplum, as Pound kept saying of the circle of the Mediterranean around which Odysseus journeyed" ("The Kurosawa Kid" 100-102).

12 Babel Tower and A Whistling Woman

1 In her conversation with Jean-Louis Chevalier, Byatt describes her image of civilized behaviour: "the human community holding itself together by decorum, by good manners, by handing each other carefully cooked food, by talking to each other with consideration, by keeping certain rules, and beyond that is violence and terror…" (19).

2 Several of the reviewers of Babel Tower were critical of the inclusion of so much of the Babbletower text. J.M. Coetzee, for example, called it a "sorry miscalculation" (19); Michèle Roberts objected to "the fake mediaeval pastiche of the language" and found Jude's narrative "insufficiently authentic and convincing," whereas Byatt's main narrative is "resonant with emotion and sympathy" for Frederica. For Roberts, the critique of the sixties in the Babbletower story is done in "rather too post hoc a manner" (40).

Works Cited

Novels and Collected Short Stories by A.S. Byatt

The Shadow of the Sun. London: Chatto and Windus, 1964 (as *Shadow of a Sun*). London: Vintage, 1991.

The Game. London: Chatto and Windus, 1967.

The Virgin in the Garden. London: Chatto and Windus, 1978. London: Penguin, 1981.

Still Life. London: Chatto and Windus, 1985. London: Penguin, 1986.

Sugar and Other Stories. London: Penguin, 1987.

    Contains:

    "Racine and the Tablecloth."

    "Rose-Coloured Teacups."

    "The July Ghost." First published in *Firebird I.* Ed. T.J. Binding. Harmondsworth, UK: Penguin, 1982. 21-37.

    "The Next Room."

    "The Dried Witch."

    "Loss of Face."

    "On the Day that E.M. Forster Died." First published in *Encounter* December 1983: 3-9.

    "The Changeling." First published in *Encounter* May 1985: 3-7.

    "In the Air."

    "Precipice-Encurled." First published in *Encounter* April 1987: 21-31.

    "Sugar." First published in *The New Yorker* 12 January 1987: 28-50.

Possession: A Romance. London: Chatto and Windus, 1990.

Angels and Insects. London: Chatto and Windus, 1992.

    Contains:

    "Morpho Eugenia."

    "The Conjugial Angel."

The Matisse Stories. London: Chatto and Windus, 1993.
  Contains:
  "Medusa's Ankles." First published in *Woman's Journal* September 1990:
    182+.
  "Art Work." First published in *The New Yorker* 20 May 1991: 36–51.
  "The Chinese Lobster." First published in *The New Yorker* 26 October 1992:
    90–100.
The Djinn in the Nightingale's Eye: Five Fairy Stories. London: Chatto and Win-
  dus, 1994.
  Contains:
  "The Glass Coffin." First published as part of *Possession: A Romance*.
  "Gode's Story." First published as part of *Possession: A Romance*.
  "The Story of the Eldest Princess." First published in *Caught in a Story:
    Contemporary Fairytales and Fables*. Ed. Caroline Heaton and Christine
    Park. London: Vintage, 1992. 12–28.
  "Dragons' Breath." First published in *Index on Censorship* September–Octo-
    ber 1994: 89–95.
  "The Djinn in the Nightingale's Eye." First published in *Paris Review* 133
    (Winter 1994): 14–112.
Babel Tower. London: Chatto and Windus, 1996.
Elementals: Stories of Fire and Ice. London: Chatto and Windus, 1998.
  Contains:
  "Crocodile Tears." First published in *Paris Review* 146 (Spring 1998): 1–41.
  "A Lamia in the Cévennes." First published in *Atlantic Monthly* July 1995:
    56–59.
  "Cold."
  "Baglady." First published in *Daily Telegraph* 15 January 1994: 11.
  "Jael." First published in *Guardian* 27 Dec. 1997, The Week: 1–2.
  "Christ in the House of Martha and Mary." First published in *Mail on Sun-
    day* 31 May 1998, *You Magazine*: 71–74.
The Biographer's Tale. London: Chatto and Windus, 2000.
A Whistling Woman. London: Chatto and Windus, 2002.

Uncollected Short Stories by A.S. Byatt

"Repeating Patterns." *Storia* 2 (1989): 137–46.
"Heavenly Bodies." *Sunday Times* 20 Dec. 1998: Culture 12+.
"The Thing in the Forest." *The New Yorker* 3 June 2002: 80–89.

Poetry by A.S. Byatt

"A Dog, a Horse, a Rat." TLS 24 May 1991: 22.
"Working with Clichés." *The Timeless and the Temporal: Writings in Honour of
  John Chalker by Friends and Colleagues*. Ed. Elizabeth Maslen. London: Dept.
  of English, Queen Mary & Westfield College, 1993. 1–3.
"Dead Boys." TLS 2 December 1994: 27.
[Writing as Maud Michell-Bailey]. Letter [with poems]. *Victorian Poetry* 33.1
  (1995): 1–3.

Collected Non-fiction by A.S. Byatt

Degrees of Freedom: The Early Novels of Iris Murdoch. London: Chatto and Windus, 1995 (as *Degrees of Freedom: The Novels of Iris Murdoch*). London: Vintage, 1994.

Wordsworth and Coleridge in Their Time. London: Nelson, 1970. New York: Crane, 1973. Rpt. as *Unruly Times: Wordsworth and Coleridge in Their Time.* London: Hogarth, 1989.

Iris Murdoch. Writers and Their Work 251. Harlow, UK: Longman, 1976.

Passions of the Mind: Selected Writings. London: Chatto and Windus, 1991.
Contains:
Introduction.

"Still Life/Nature morte." First published in *Cross References: Modern French Theory and the Practice of Criticism.* Ed. David Kelley and Isabelle Llasera. London: Society for French Studies, 1986. 95-102.

"Sugar/Le sucre." 21-25. First published as an introduction to A.S. Byatt. *Le sucre.* Trans. Jean-Louis Chevalier. Paris: Editions des Cendres, 1989. 11-19.

"Robert Browning: Fact, Fiction, Lies, Incarnation and Art." An expanded version of the introduction to *Robert Browning: Dramatic Monologues.* London: Folio Society, 1991. vii-xxxi.

"George Eliot: A Celebration." First published as a pamphlet for inclusion with a boxed set of George Eliot's novels. Harmondsworth, UK: Penguin, 1980.

"George Eliot's Essays." An edited version of the introduction to *George Eliot: Selected Essays, Poems and Other Writings.* Ed. A.S. Byatt and Nicholas Warren. Harmondsworth, UK: Penguin, 1990. ix-xxxiv.

"Accurate Letters: Ford Madox Ford." Based on "Impressions and Their Rendering." TLS 13 Feb. 1981: 171-72; and the preface to *The Fifth Queen*, by Ford Madox Ford. Oxford: Oxford UP, 1984. v-xiv.

"The Omnipotence of Thought: Frazer, Freud, and Post-modernist Fiction." First published in *Sir James Frazer and the Literary Imagination: Essays in Affinity and Influence.* Ed. Robert Fraser. London: Macmillan, 1990. 270-308.

"People in Paper Houses: Attitudes to 'Realism' and 'Experiment' in English Post-War Fiction." First published in *The Contemporary English Novel.* Ed. Malcolm Bradbury and David Palmer. London: Arnold, 1979. 19-41.

"William Golding: *Darkness Visible.*" Rpt. of "A.S. Byatt on *Darkness Visible.*" Rev. of *Darkness Visible,* by William Golding. *Literary Review* 5 October 1979: 10.

"The TLS Poetry Competition." Rpt. of "Writing and Feeling." TLS 18 November 1988: 1278.

"A Sense of Religion: Enright's God." First published in *Life by Other Means: Essays on D.J. Enright.* Ed. Jacqueline Simms. Oxford: Oxford UP, 1990. 158-74.

"Willa Cather." Based on the afterword and introductions to Willa Cather. *O Pioneers!* London: Virago, 1983; *The Professor's House.* London: Virago, 1981; and *Death Comes for the Archbishop.* London: Virago, 1981.

"Elizabeth Bowen: *The House in Paris*." Rpt. of the introduction to *The House in Paris*, by Elizabeth Bowen. Harmondsworth, UK: Penguin, 1976. 7-16.

"Sylvia Plath: *Letters Home*." Rpt. of "Mirror, Mirror on the Wall." Rev. of *Sylvia Plath: Letters Home*, ed. Aurelia Schober Plath. *New Statesman* 23 April 1976: 541-42.

"Toni Morrison: *Beloved*."

"An Honourable Escape: Georgette Heyer." Rpt. of "Georgette Heyer Is a Better Writer Than You Think." *Nova* August 1969: 14+.

"Barbara Pym." Rpt. of "Marginal Lives." Rev. of *An Academic Question*, by Barbara Pym, and *Barbara Pym*, by Robert E. Long. *TLS* 8 August 1986: 862.

"Monique Wittig: The Lesbian Body." Rpt. of "Give Me the Moonlight, Give Me the Girl." Rev. of *The Lesbian Body*, by Monique Wittig. *New Review* July 1974: 65-67.

"Coleridge: An Archangel a Little Damaged." Rpt. of "Coleridge: 'An Archangel a Little Damaged': An Analysis of the Power and Failure of the Poet's Mind in Solitude and in Companionship." *Times* 2 December 1972: 8.

"Charles Rycroft: *The Innocence of Dreams*." Rpt. of "Downstream." Rev. of *The Innocence of Dreams*, by Charles Rycroft. *New Statesman* 4 May 1979: 646.

"Van Gogh, Death and Summer." An expanded version of "After the Myth, the Real." Rev. of *The Van Gogh File: A Journey of Discovery*, by Ken Wilkie; *Young Vincent: The Story of Van Gogh's Years in England*, by Martin Bailey; *The Love of Many Things: A Life of Vincent Van Gogh*, by David Sweetman; and *Vincent Van Gogh: Christianity Versus Nature*, by Tsukasa Kodera. *TLS* 29 June 1990: 683-85.

(With Ignês Sodré). *Imagining Characters: Six Conversations about Women Writers*. London: Chatto, 1995.

On Histories and Stories: Selected Essays. Cambridge: Harvard UP, 2001.
  Contains:
  "Fathers."
  "Ancestors."
  "True Stories and the Facts in Fiction."
  "Old Tales, New Forms."
  "Ice, Snow, Glass." First published in *Mirror, Mirror on the Wall: Women Writers Explore Their Favourite Fairy Tale*. Ed. Kate Bernheimer. New York: Doubleday, 1998. 64-84.
  "The Greatest Story Ever Told." Rpt. of "Narrate or Die: Why Scheherazade Keeps on Talking." *New York Times Magazine* 18 April 1999. 105-07.

Uncollected Essays and Reviews by A.S. Byatt

[Untitled contribution.] *The God I Want*. Ed. James Mitchell. London: Constable, 1967. 71-87.

"The Battle between Real People and Images." Rev. of *The Solid Mandala*, by Patrick White. *Encounter* February 1967: 71-78.

"The Lyric Structure of Tennyson's *Maud*." *The Major Victorian Poets: Reconsiderations*. Ed. Isobel Armstrong. London: Routledge, 1969. 69-92.

Introduction. *The Mill on the Floss*. By George Eliot. Harmondsworth, UK: Penguin, 1979. 7-40.

"The Art of Stanley Middleton." *The Best of the Fiction Magazine*. Ed. Judy Cooke and Elizabeth Bunster. London and Melbourne: Dent. In association with *Fiction Magazine*, 1986. 201–07.

"Subversion and Stubbornness." *Encounter* November 1986: 46–51.

"Identity and the Writer." *The Real Me: Post-modernism and the Question of Identity*. Ed. Lisa Appignanesi. ICA Documents 6. London: Institute for Contemporary Arts Document, 1987. 23–26.

"Obscenity and the Arts: A Symposium." *TLS* 12–18 February 1988: 159–61.

"Chosen Vessels of a Fraud." Rev. of *The Darkened Room*, by Alex Owen. *TLS* 2–8 June 1989: 605.

"First Impressions, Lasting Memories." *Guardian* 16 August 1990: 21.

"A Hundred Years After: Twelve Writers Reflect on Tennyson's Achievement and Influence." *TLS* 2 October 1992: 8.

"Reading, Writing, Studying: Some Questions about Changing Conditions for Writers and Readers." *Critical Quarterly* 35.4 (1993): 3–7.

"A New Body of Writing: Darwin and Recent British Fiction." *New Writing 4*. Ed. A.S. Byatt and Alan Hollinghurst. London: Vintage, 1995. 439–48.

"Alice Munro: One of the Great Ones." Rev. of *Selected Stories*, by Alice Munro. *Globe and Mail* 2 November 1996: D18+.

"Fashion for Squares." *Observer* 3 August 1997: 14–17.

"Hauntings." *Literacy Is Not Enough: Essays on the Importance of Reading*. Ed. Brian Cox. Cambridge: Cambridge UP, 1998. 41–46.

"Memory and the Making of Fiction." *Memory*. Ed. Patricia Fara and Karalyn Patterson. Cambridge: Cambridge UP, 1998. 47–72.

"Munro: The Stuff of Life." Rev. of *The Love of a Good Woman*, by Alice Munro. *Globe and Mail* 26 September 1998: D16.

"A Hunger for the Marvellous." *Guardian* 5 Dec. 1998, Saturday Review: 10.

"Fairy Stories: The Djinn in the Nightingale's Eye." 1999. *A.S. Byatt Page*. 30 November 2001. <http://www.asbyatt.com/fairy.htm>.

"Arachne." *Ovid Metamorphosed*. Ed. Philip Terry. London: Chatto and Windus, 2000. 131–57.

"Nothing Is Too Wonderful to Be True." *Times* 7 June 2000, sec. 2: 12–13.

"The Kurosawa Kid." Rev. of *The Last Samurai*, by Helen DeWitt. *The New Yorker* 30 October 2000: 100–02.

"Justice for Willa Cather." Rev. of *Willa Cather and the Politics of Criticism*, by Joan Acocella. *NY Review of Books* 30 November 2000: 51–53.

Translations

D'Aulnoy, Marie-Catherine. "The Great Green Worm." Trans. A.S. Byatt. *Wonder Tales*. Ed. Marina Warner. London: Chatto and Windus, 1994. 189–229.

Films

Angels and Insects. Dir. Philip Haas. Screenplay by Belinda Haas and Philip Haas. Perf. Mark Rylance, Patsy Kensit, Kristin Scott Thomas, Douglas Henshall, Jeremy Kemp, and Annette Badland. Samuel Goldwyn, 1995.

Possession. Dir. Neil LaBute. Screenplay by David Henry Hwang, Laura Jones, and Neil LaBute. Perf. Gwyneth Paltrow, Aaron Eckhart, Jeremy Northam,

Jennifer Ehle, Trevor Eve, Toby Stephens, Anna Massey. Odean Films and USA Films, 2002.

Interviews with A.S. Byatt

Chevalier, Jean-Louis. "Entretien avec A.S. Byatt." *Journal of the Short Story in English* 22 (Summer 1994): 12-27.

Dusinberre, Juliet. "A.S. Byatt." *Women Writers Talking*. Ed. Janet Todd. New York: Columbia UP, 1980. 181-95.

Hensher, Philip. "A.S. Byatt: The Art of Fiction CLXVIII." *Paris Review* 159 (Fall 2001): 39-77.

Kenyon, Olga. *The Writer's Imagination*. Bradford: University of Bradford, 1992.

Miller, Laura. "Limeade Seas and Bloody Cobblestones: The Salon Interview— A.S. Byatt." *Salon* 17 June 1996. 30 November 2001. < www.salon.com/weekly /interview960617.html >.

Rogers, Shelagh. Interview with A.S. Byatt. *Morningside*. CBC Radio. 3 June 1996.

Ross, Val. "Art, Myth and A.S. Byatt." *Globe and Mail* 28 May 1996: D1.

———. "Booker Fuss Keeps Byatt Busy." *Globe and Mail* 7 November 1991: C5.

Rothstein, Mervyn. "Best Seller Breaks Rule on Crossing the Atlantic." *New York Times* 31 January 1991: C17+.

Stout, Mira. "What Possessed A.S. Byatt?" *New York Times Magazine* 26 May 1991: 13-15, 24-25.

Tredell, Nicolas. "A.S. Byatt." *Conversations with Critics*. Manchester: Carcanet, 1994. 58-74.

Wachtel, Eleanor. "A.S. Byatt." *Writers & Company*. Toronto: Knopf, 1993. 77-89.

———. Interview with A.S. Byatt. *Writers & Company*. CBC Radio. 15 September 1996.

Cited Criticism of A.S. Byatt's Fiction

Alexander, Flora. "A.S. Byatt." *Post-war Literatures in English: A Lexicon of Contemporary Authors*. Ed. Theo D'haen et al. Groningen: Nijhoff, 1992. 1-10, A1-2, B1.

———. "Versions of the Real: A.S. Byatt, *Still Life*." *Contemporary Women Novelists*. London: Arnold, 1989. 34-41.

Alfer, Alexa. "Realism and Its Discontents: *The Virgin in the Garden and Still Life*." *Essays on the Fiction of A.S. Byatt: Imagining the Real*. Ed. Alexa Alfer and Michael J. Noble. Westport, CT: Greenwood, 2001. 47-59.

Alfer, Alexa, and Michael J. Noble, eds. *Essays on the Fiction of A.S. Byatt: Imagining the Real*. Westport, CT: Greenwood, 2001.

Brink, André. "Possessed by Language: A.S. Byatt: *Possession*." *The Novel: Language and Narrative from Cervantes to Calvino*. Basingstoke, UK: Macmillan, 1998. 288-308.

Bronfen, Elisabeth. "Romancing Difference, Courting Coherence: A.S. Byatt's *Possession* as Postmodern Moral Fiction." *Why Literature Matters: Theories and Functions of Literature*. Ed. Rüdiger Ahrens and Laurenz Volkmann. Heidelberg: Winter, 1996. 117-34.

Buxton, Jackie. "'What's Love Got to Do with It?': Postmodernism and *Posses-sion.*" *English Studies in Canada* 22.2 (1996): 199-219. Rpt. in *Essays on the Fiction of A.S. Byatt: Imagining the Real.* Ed. Alexa Alfer and Michael J. Noble. Westport, CT: Greenwood, 2001. 89-104.

Chevalier, Jean-Louis. "Conclusion in *Possession* by Antonia Byatt." *Fins de romans: Aspects de la conclusion dans la litterature Anglaise.* Ed. Lucien LeBouille. Caën: PU de Caën, 1993. 109-31. Rpt. in *Essays on the Fiction of A.S. Byatt: Imagining the Real.* Ed. Alexa Alfer and Michael J. Noble. Westport, CT: Greenwood, 2001. 105-122.

Chinn, Nancy. "'I Am My Own Riddle'—A.S. Byatt's Christabel LaMotte: Emily Dickinson and Melusina." *PLL* 37 (2001): 179-204.

Cosslett, Tess. "Childbirth from the Woman's Point of View in British Women's Fiction: Enid Bagnold's *The Squire* and A.S. Byatt's *Still Life.*" *Tulsa Studies in Women's Literature* 8 (1989): 263-86.

Creighton, Joanne V. "Sisterly Symbiosis: Margaret Drabble's *The Waterfall* and A.S. Byatt's *The Game.*" *Mosaic* 20 (Winter 1987): 15-29.

Desblache, Lucille. "Penning Secrets: Presence and Essence of the Epistolary Genre in A.S. Byatt's *Possession.*" *L'esprit createur* 40.4 (2000): 89-95.

Dusinberre, Juliet. "Forms of Reality in A.S. Byatt's *The Virgin in the Garden.*" *Critique: Studies in Modern Fiction* 24 (Fall 1982): 55-62.

Flegel, Monica. "Enchanted Readings and Fairy Tale Endings in A.S. Byatt's *Possession.*" *English Studies in Canada* 24 (1999): 413-30.

Fletcher, Judith. "The Odyssey Rewoven: A.S. Byatt's *Angels and Insects.*" *Classical and Modern Literature* 19 (1999): 217-31.

Flint, Kate. "Plotting the Victorians: Narrative, Post-modernism, and Contemporary Fiction." *Writing and Victorianism.* Ed. J.B. Bullen. Harlow, UK: Addison, 1997. 286-305.

Franken, Christien. *A.S. Byatt: Art, Authorship, Creativity.* London: Palgrave, 2001.

———. "The Gender of Mourning: A.S. Byatt's 'The Conjugial Angel' and Alfred Lord Tennyson's *In Memoriam.*" *The Author as Character: Representing Historical Writers in Western Literature.* Ed. Paul Franssen and Ton Hoenselaars. London: Associated UP, 1999. 244-47.

Giobbi, Giuliana. "Sisters Beware of Sisters: Sisterhood as a Literary Motif in Jane Austen, A.S. Byatt, and I. Bossi Fedrigotti." *Journal of European Studies* 22 (1992): 241-58.

Gitzen, Julian. "A.S. Byatt's Self-Mirroring Art." *Critique: Studies in Modern Fiction* 36 (Winter 1995): 83-95.

Hansson, Heidi. "The Double Voice of Metaphor: A.S. Byatt's 'Morpho Eugenia.'" *20th Century Literature: A Scholarly and Critical Journal* 45 (1999): 452-66.

Holmes, Frederick M. "The Historical Imagination and the Victorian Past: A.S. Byatt's *Possession.*" *English Studies in Canada* 20 (1994): 319-34.

———. *The Historical Imagination: Postmodernism and the Treatment of the Past in Contemporary British Fiction.* Victoria, BC: English Literary Studies, University of Victoria, 1997.

Hope, Christopher. *Contemporary Writers: A.S. Byatt.* London: Book Trust/British Council, 1990.

Hotho-Jackson, Sabine. "Literary History in Literature: An Aspect of the Contemporary Novel." *Moderna Sprak* 86.2 (1992): 113-19.

Hughes, Linda K. Introduction. *Victorian Poetry* 33.1 (1995): 5-11.

Janik, Del Ivan. "No End of History: Evidence from the Contemporary English Novel." *Twentieth Century Literature* 41 (1995): 160-90.

Kelly, Kathleen Coyne. *A.S. Byatt*. Twayne's English Authors Series 529. New York: Twayne, 1996.

Kenyon, Olga. "A.S. Byatt: Fusing Tradition with Twentieth-Century Experimentation." *Women Novelists Today: A Survey of English Writing in the Seventies and Eighties*. Brighton: Harvester, 1988. 51-84.

Lepaludier, Laurent. "The Saving Threads of Discourse and the Necessity of the Reader in A.S. Byatt's 'Racine and the Tablecloth.'" *Journal of the Short Story in English* 22 (Summer 1994): 37-48.

Levenson, Michael. "*Angels and Insects*: Theory, Analogy, Metamorphosis." *Essays on the Fiction of A.S. Byatt: Imagining the Real*. Ed. Alexa Alfer and Michael J. Noble. Westport, CT: Greenwood, 2001. 161-74.

Maack, Annegret. "Wonder-Tales Hiding a Truth: Retelling Tales in *The Djinn in the Nightingale's Eye*." *Essays on the Fiction of A.S. Byatt: Imagining the Real*. Ed. Alexa Alfer and Michael J. Noble. Westport, CT: Greenwood, 2001. 123-34.

Maisonnat, Claude. "The Ghost Written and the Ghost Writer in A.S. Byatt's Story 'The July Ghost.'" *Journal of the Short Story in English* 22 (Summer 1994): 49-62.

Marsh, Kelly A. "The Neo-Sensation Novel: A Contemporary Genre in the Victorian Tradition." *Philological Quarterly* 74 (1995): 99-123.

Morse, Deborah Denenholz. "Crossing the Boundaries: The Female Artist and the Sacred Word in A.S. Byatt's *Possession*." *British Women Writing Fiction*. Ed. H.P. Werlock-Abby. Tuscaloosa, AL: U of Alabama P, 2000. 148-74.

Musil, Caryn McTighe. "A.S. Byatt." *Dictionary of Literary Biography*. Ed. Jay L. Halio. Vol. 14. Detroit: Gale, 1983. 194-205.

Neumeier, Beate. "Female Visions: The Fiction of A.S. Byatt." *(Sub)Versions of Realism: Recent Women's Fiction in Britain*. Ed. Irmgard Maassen and Anna Maria Stuby. Spec. issue of *Anglistik und Englischunterricht* 60 (1997): 11-25.

Noble, Michael J. "A Tower of Tongues: *Babel Tower* and the Art of Memory." *Essays on the Fiction of A.S. Byatt: Imagining the Real*. Ed. Alexa Alfer and Michael J. Noble. Westport, CT: Greenwood , 2001. 61-74.

Page, Malcolm. "Byatt, A(ntonia) S(usan)." *Contemporary Novelists*. Ed. James Vinson. London: St James, 1972. 214-15.

Pearce, Margaret. "'Morpho Eugenia': Problems with the Male Gaze." *Critique: Studies in Contemporary Fiction* 40 (1999): 399-411.

Plotz, Judith. "A Modern 'Seer Blest': The Visionary Child in *The Virgin in the Garden*." *Essays on the Fiction of A.S. Byatt: Imagining the Real*. Ed. Alexa Alfer and Michael J. Noble. Westport, CT: Greenwood, 2001. 31-45.

Sanchez, Victoria. "A.S. Byatt's *Possession*: A Fairytale Romance." *Southern Folklore* 52.1 (1995): 33-52.

Schuhmann, Kuno. "The Concept of Culture in Some Recent English Novels." *Anglistentag 1981: Vorträge*. Ed. Jörg Hasler. Trierer Studien zur Literatur 7. Frankfurt: Lang, 1983. 111-27.

———. "In Search of Self and Self-Fulfilment: Themes and Strategies in A.S. Byatt's Early Novels." *Essays on the Fiction of A.S. Byatt: Imagining the Real.* Ed. Alexa Alfer and Michael J. Noble. Westport, CT: Greenwood, 2001. 75-87.

Shiffman, Adrienne. "'Burn What They Should Not See': The Private Journal as Public Text in A.S. Byatt's *Possession.*" *Tulsa Studies in Women's Literature* 20 (2001): 93-106.

Shiller, Dana. "The Redemptive Past in the Neo-Victorian Novel." *Studies in the Novel* 29 (1997): 538-60.

Shinn, Thelma J. *Women Shapeshifters: Transforming the Contemporary Novel.* Westport, CT: Greenwood, 1996.

Shuttleworth, Sally. "Natural History: The Retro-Victorian Novel." *The Third Culture: Literature and Science.* Ed. Elinor Shaffer. Berlin: De Gruyter, 1998. 253-68.

———. "Writing Natural History: 'Morpho Eugenia.'" *Essays on the Fiction of A.S. Byatt: Imagining the Real.* Ed Alexa Alfer and Michael J. Noble. Westport, CT: Greenwood, 2001. 147-60.

Sorensen, Sue. "Death in the Fiction of A.S. Byatt." *Critique: Studies in Modern Fiction* 43.2 (2002): 115-35.

Taylor, D.J. *After the War: The Novel and English Society since 1945.* London: Chatto and Windus, 1993.

Todd, Richard. *A.S. Byatt.* Plymouth, UK: Northcote/British Council, 1997.

———. "The Retrieval of Unheard Voices in British Postmodernist Fiction: A.S. Byatt and Marina Warner." *Liminal Postmodernism: The Postmodern, the (Post-) Colonial, and the (Post-) Feminist.* Ed. Theo D'haen and Hans Bertens. Amsterdam: Rodopi, 1994. 99-114.

Wallhead, Celia M. *The Old, the New and the Metaphor: A Critical Study of the Novels of A.S. Byatt.* London: Minerva, 1999.

Walsh, Chris. "Postmodernist Reflections: A.S. Byatt's *Possession.*" *Theme Parks, Rain Forests and Sprouting Wastelands: European Essays on Theory and Performance in Contemporary British Fiction.* Ed. Richard Todd and Luisa Flora. Amsterdam: Rodopi, 2000. 185-94.

Westlake, Michael. "The Hard Idea of Truth." *PN Review* 15.4 (1989): 33.

Wilkinson, Helen. "Mr Cropper and Mrs Brown: Good and Bad Collectors in the Work of A.S. Byatt and Other Recent Fiction." *Experiencing Material Culture in the Western World.* Ed. Susan M. Pearce. London: Leicester UP, 1997. 95-113.

Worton, Michael. "Of Prisms and Prose: Reading Paintings in A.S. Byatt's Work." *Essays on the Fiction of A.S. Byatt: Imagining the Real.* Ed. Alexa Alfer and Michael J. Noble. Westport, CT: Greenwood, 2001. 15-29.

Yelin, Louise. "Cultural Cartography: A.S. Byatt's *Possession* and the Politics of Victorian Studies." *Victorian Newsletter* 81 (Spring 1992): 38.

Cited Reviews of A.S. Byatt's Fiction

Shadow of a Sun
    "Living with a Genius." *TLS* 9 January 1964: 21.
The Game
    Bradbury, Malcolm. "On from Murdoch." *Encounter* July 1968: 72-74.

Still Life

    Conant, Oliver. "A Portrait of Two Sisters." *New Leader* 10 February 1986: 17-18.

    Lewis, Peter. "The Truth and Nothing Like the Truth: History and Fiction." *Stand Magazine* 27.2 (1986): 42.

    Lewis, Roger. "Larger Than Life." *New Statesman* 28 June 1985: 29.

    Mars-Jones, Adam. "Doubts about the Monument." *TLS* 28 June 1985: 720.

    Naughton, John. "Potters' Tale." *Listener* 8 August 1985: 31.

    Parrinder, Patrick. "Thirty Years Ago." *London Review of Books* 18 July 1985: 17.

    Sage, Lorna. "How We Live Now." *Observer* 23 June 1985: 22.

Sugar and Other Stories

    Spufford, Francis. "The Mantle of Jehovah." *London Review of Books* 25 June 1987: 22-23.

Possession: A Romance

    Jenkyns, Richard. "Disinterring Buried Lives." *TLS* 2 March 1990: 213-14.

    Karlin, Danny. "Prolonging Her Absence." *London Review of Books* 8 March 1990: 17-18.

Angels and Insects

    Butler, Marilyn. "The Moth and the Medium." *TLS* 16 October 1992: 22.

    Levenson, Michael. "The Religion of Fiction." *New Republic* 2 August 1993: 41-44. Rpt. in A.S. Byatt. *Degrees of Freedom*. London: Vintage, 1994. 337-44.

The Matisse Stories

    Kelman, Suanne. "The Painted Words of A.S. Byatt." *Toronto Star* 19 March 1994: K12.

The Djinn in the Nightingale's Eye: Five Fairy Stories

    Adil, Alev. "Obeying the Genie." *TLS* 6 January 1995: 20.

Babel Tower

    Bemrose, John. "The Dark Side of Utopia." *Maclean's* 1 July 1996: 59.

    Coetzee, J.M. "En Route to the Catastrophe." *New York Review of Books* 6 June 1996: 17.

    Hensher, Philip. "Her Shaping Spirit of Imagination." *Spectator* 11 May 1996: 34-36.

    Hulbert, Ann. "Hungry for Books." *New York Times Book Review* 9 June 1996: 7.

    Roberts, Michèle. "The Sixties on Trial." *New Statesman* 3 May 1996: 40.

    Sage, Lorna. "Frederica's Story." *TLS* 10 May 1996: 24.

Elementals: Stories of Fire and Ice

    Clark, Alex. "*Elementals: Stories of Fire and Ice*." *Guardian* 5 December 1998, Saturday Review: 10.

    Emck, Katy. "The Consolations of a Kindly Genie." *TLS* 13 November 1998: 25.

    Gardam, Jane. "Women Breaking Out." *Literary Review* November 1998: 49.

    Thomas, Joan. "Windows on the Oddity of Life." *Globe and Mail* 18 December 1998: D20.

The Biographer's Tale

    Charles, Ron. "Note Cards That Can't Be Put in Any Reasonable Order." *Christian Science Monitor* 1 February 2001: 17.

    Clark, Alex. "Mischief Maker." *Guardian* 3 June 2000, Saturday Review: 10.

Jensen, Hal. "Unexaggerated Lions." *TLS* 2 June 2000: 23.

Norris, Pamela. "Better Write Novels." *Literary Review* June 2000: 50.

Scurr, Ruth. "Underlinings." *London Review of Books* 10 August 2000: 38–39.

Updike, John. "Fairy Tales and Paradigms." *New Yorker* 19 February 2001: 216–22.

Additional References

Anderson, Linda. Preface. *Plotting Change: Contemporary Women's Fiction*. London: Arnold, 1990. vi–xi.

Atwood, Margaret. *The Edible Woman*. Toronto: McClelland and Stewart, 1967.

Blain, Patricia, Patricia Clements, and Isobel Grundy, eds. *The Feminist Companion to Literature in English*. New Haven and London: Yale UP, 1990. 575–76.

Browning, Robert. "De Gustibus —." *Poetry and Prose*. Selected by Simon Nowell-Smith. London: Hart-Davis, 1950. 352–53.

———. "Parleyings with Certain People of Importance in Their Day: With Christopher Smart." *The Complete Works of Robert Browning*. Ed. Susan Crowl and Roma A. King, Jr. Vol. xvi. Athens, OH: Ohio UP, 1998. 48–57.

———. *Sordello. The Complete Works of Robert Browning*. Ed. Roma A. King, Jr. Vol. 2. Athens, OH: Ohio UP, 1998. 125–335.

———. *The Ring and the Book*. Ed. Richard D. Altick. New Haven: Yale UP, 1981.

Buck, Claire, ed. *The Bloomsbury Guide to Women's Literature*. London: Bloomsbury, 1992. 38–39.

Cranny-Francis, Anne. *Feminist Fiction: Feminist Uses of Generic Fiction*. New York: St. Martin's, 1990.

Dickinson, Emily. "Letters." *Norton Anthology of Literature by Women: The Traditions in English*. 2nd ed. Ed. Sandra Gilbert and Susan Gubar. New York: Norton, 1996. 888–92.

DuPlessis, Rachel Blau. *Writing beyond the Ending*. Bloomington: Indiana UP, 1985.

Fetterley, Judith. *The Resisting Reader: A Feminist Approach to American Fiction*. Bloomington: Indiana UP, 1978.

Foucault, Michel. *The Order of Things: An Archaeology of the Human Sciences*. A translation of *Les mots et les choices*. London: Tavistock, 1970.

Gilbert, Sandra, and Susan Gubar. *The Madwoman in the Attic: The Woman Writer and the Nineteenth-Century Imagination*. New Haven: Yale UP, 1979.

———. *No Man's Land: The Place of the Woman Writer in the Twentieth Century*. Vol. 3. New Haven: Yale UP, 1988.

Greene, Gayle. *Changing the Story: Feminist Fiction and the Tradition*. Bloomington: Indiana UP, 1991.

Hutcheon, Linda. *A Poetics of Postmodernism: History, Theory, Fiction*. New York: Routledge, 1988.

Irwin, Robert. *The Arabian Nights: A Companion*. London: Allen Lane, 1994.

Jackson, Rosemary. *Fantasy: The Literature of Subversion*. London: Methuen, 1981.

James, Henry. "The Private Life." *Stories of the Supernatural*. Ed. Leon Edel. New York: Taplinger, 1970. 212–49.

Kelley, Philip, and Ronald Hudson, eds. *The Brownings' Correspondence*. Vol. 7. Winfield, KS: Wedgestone, 1989.

Kolb, Jack, ed. *The Letters of Arthur Henry Hallam*. Columbus, OH: Ohio State UP, 1981.

Kristeva, Julia. "Woman Can Never Be Defined." Trans. Marilyn A. August. *New French Feminisms: An Anthology*. Ed. Elaine Marks and Isabelle de Courtivron. Amherst: Massachusetts UP, 1980. 137-41.

Lieberman, Marcia K. "'Some Day My Prince Will Come': Female Acculturation through the Fairy Tale." *Don't Bet on the Prince*. Ed. Jack Zipes. New York: Methuen, 1986. 185-200.

Lodge, David. "The Novelist Today: Still at the Crossroads?" *New Writing*. Ed. Malcolm Bradbury and Judy Cooke. London: Minerva, 1992. 203-15.

MacDowall, M.W. *Asgard and the Gods: The Tales and Traditions of Our Northern Ancestors: Forming a Complete Manual of Norse Mythology Adapted from the Work of Dr. W. Wagner*. Ed. W.S.W. Anson. London: Swan Sonnenschein, 1902.

McHale, Brian. *Postmodernist Fiction*. New York: Methuen, 1987.

Meredith, Michael, ed. *More Than Friend: The Letters of Robert Browning to Katharine de Kay Bronson*. Waco, TX: Armstrong Browning Library of Baylor University, Wedgestone, 1985.

Meyer, Michael. *Henrik Ibsen: The Top of a Cold Mountain*. London: Hart-Davis, 1971. Vol. 3 of *Henrick Ibsen*. 3 vols. 1967-71.

Miller, Nancy K. "Arachnologies: The Woman, the Text, and the Critic." *The Poetics of Gender*. Ed. Nancy K. Miller. New York: Columbia UP, 1986.

Milton, John. *Paradise Lost*. Ed. Northrop Frye. New York: Holt Rinehart & Winston, 1951.

Moi, Toril. *Sexual/Textual Politics: Feminist Literary Theory*. London: Routledge, 1988.

Murdoch, Iris. "Against Dryness." *Encounter* January 1961: 16-20.

Rowe, Karen E. "Feminism and Fairy Stories." *Don't Bet on the Prince*. Ed. Jack Zipes. New York: Methuen, 1986. 209-26.

Shakespeare, William. *As You Like It*. Ed. Alan Brissenden. Oxford: Clarendon, 1993.

Showalter, Elaine. *A Literature of Their Own: British Women Novelists from Brontë to Lessing*. Princeton: Princeton UP, 1977.

Smart, Christopher. *Song to David*. Ed. J.B. Broadbent. Cambridge, UK: Rampant Lions, 1960.

Tennyson, Charles, and Hope Dyson. *The Tennysons: Background to Genius*. London: Macmillan, 1974.

Waugh, Patricia. *Feminine Fictions: Revisiting the Postmodern*. London: Routledge, 1989.

———. *Metafiction: The Theory and Practice of Self-Conscious Fiction*. London: Methuen, 1984.

Zagarell, Sandra A. "Narrative of Community: The Identification of a Genre." *Signs: Journal of Women in Culture and Society* 13 (1988): 498-527.

Zipes, Jack. Introduction. *Don't Bet on the Prince*. Ed. Jack Zipes. New York: Methuen, 1986. 1-36.

Source Acknowledgments

An earlier version of chapter 3, "*The Game*," was published under the title "The Hunger of the Imagination in A.S. Byatt's *The Game*" in *Critique: Studies in Modern Fiction* 29.3 (Spring 1988). Used by permission of *Critique* and Heldref Publications.

Earlier versions of parts of chapter 5, "*Sugar and Other Stories*," were published under the titles "'The Somehow May Be Thishow': Fact, Fiction, and Intertextuality in Antonia Byatt's 'Precipice-Encurled'" in *Studies in Short Fiction* 28.2 (6) and "Confecting *Sugar*: Narrative Theory and Practice in A.S. Byatt's Short Stories," in *Critique: Studies in Contemporary Fiction* 38.2 (Winter 1997). Used by permission of *Studies in Short Fiction* and *Critique* and Heldref Publications.

An earlier version of chapter 9, "*The Djinn in the Nightingale's Eye: Five Fairy Stories*," was published under the title "'Forever possibilities. And impossibilities, of course'" in *Essays on the Fiction of A.S. Byatt: Imagining the Real*. Edited by Alexa Alfer and Michael J. Noble. Copyright © 2001 by Alexa Alfer and Michael J. Noble. Reproduced with permission of Greenwood Publishing Group, Inc., Westport, CT.

Extract from THE SHADOW OF THE SUN by A.S. Byatt published by Chatto & Windus. Used by permission of The Random House Group Limited. Excerpts from *The Shadow of the Sun: A Novel*, copyright © 1964 and renewed 1992 by A.S. Byatt, reprinted by permission of Harcourt, Inc.

Extract from THE GAME by A.S. Byatt published by Chatto & Windus. Used by permission of The Random House Group Limited. Reprinted by permission of Sll / sterling Lord Literistic, Inc. Copyright by Antonia Byatt.

From *The Virgin in the Garden* by A.S. Byatt, copyright © 1979 by A.S. Byatt. Used by permission of Random House, Inc. Reprinted by permission of Sll / sterling Lord Literistic, Inc. Copyright by Antonia Byatt.

Extract from STILL LIFE by A.S. Byatt published by Chatto & Windus. Used by permission of The Random House Group Limited. North American rights held by Simon and Schuster.

Extract from SUGAR by A.S. Byatt published by Chatto & Windus. Used by permission of The Random House Group Limited. Reprinted by permission of Sll / sterling Lord Literistic, Inc. Copyright by Antonia Byatt.

From *Possession* by A.S. Byatt, copyright © 1991 by A.S. Byatt. Used by permission of Random House, Inc. Reprinted by permission of Sll / sterling Lord Literistic, Inc. Copyright by Antonia Byatt.

From *Passions of the Mind* by A.S. Byatt, copyright © 1991 by A.S. Byatt. Used by permission of Random House, Inc. Reprinted by permission of Sll / sterling Lord Literistic, Inc. Copyright by Antonia Byatt.

From *Angels and Insects* by A.S. Byatt, copyright © 1992 by A.S. Byatt. Used by permission of Random House, Inc. Reprinted by permission of Sll / sterling Lord Literistic, Inc. Copyright by Antonia Byatt.

From *The Matisse Stories* by A.S. Byatt, copyright © 1993 by A.S. Byatt. Used by permission of Random House, Inc. Reprinted by permission of Sll / sterling Lord Literistic, Inc. Copyright by Antonia Byatt.

From *The Djinn in the Nightingale's Eye* by A.S. Byatt, copyright © 1994 by A.S. Byatt. Used by permission of Random House, Inc. Reprinted by permission of Sll / sterling Lord Literistic, Inc. Copyright by Antonia Byatt.

From *Babel Tower* by A.S. Byatt, copyright © 1996 by A.S. Byatt. Used by permission of Random House, Inc. Reprinted by permission of Sll / sterling Lord Literistic, Inc. Copyright by Antonia Byatt.

From *Elementals: Stories of Fire and Ice* by A.S. Byatt, copyright © 1998 by A.S. Byatt. Used by permission of Random House, Inc. Reprinted by permission of Sll / sterling Lord Literistic, Inc. Copyright by Antonia Byatt.

Extract from THE BIOGRAPHER'S TALE by A.S. Byatt, published by Chatto & Windus. Used by permission of The Random House Group Limited. From *The Biographer's Tale* by A.S. Byatt, copyright © 2000 by A. S. Byatt. Used by permission of Alfred A. Knopf, a division of Random House, Inc.

Extract from ON HISTORIES AND STORIES by A.S. Byatt published by Chatto & Windus. Used by permission of The Random House Group Limited. Reprinted by permission of the publisher from *On Histories and Stories* by A.S. Byatt, Cambridge, Mass.: Harvard University Press. Copyright © 2000 by the President and Fellows of Harvard University. Reprinted by permission of Sll / sterling Lord Literistic, Inc. Copyright by Antonia Byatt.

Extract from A WHISTLING WOMAN by A.S. Byatt published by Chatto & Windus. Used by permission of The Random House Group Limited. From *A Whistling Woman* by A.S. Byatt copyright © 2002 by A.S. Byatt. Used by permission of Alfred A. Knopf, a division of Random House, Inc.

Acknowledgement is made to PFD < www.pfd.co.uk > on behalf of A.S. Byatt for permission to reproduce excerpts from STILL LIFE (Copyright © A.S. Byatt 1986) SUGAR (Copyright © A.S. Byatt 1987) THE GAME (Copyright © A.S. Byatt 1967) and ON HISTORIES AND STORIES (Copyright © A.S. Byatt 2000).

Index

282n6; postmodern, 5, 71, 136, 137, 219, 228; and reality, 106, 205; social, 149–52, 153–54, 246, 250; and traditional endings, 115–16, 203, 205, 247–48, 266, 280n5(6)

Sugar and Other Stories (Byatt), 1, 5, 169, 170, 231; "The Changeling," 11, 14, 82, 91–92, 93–95, 282n1(8); "The Dried Witch," 82, 86, 88–89, 206, 279n3; haunting in, 86–88, 95, 166, 247, 279n2; "In the Air," 82, 95–96; "The July Ghost," 81, 82, 86–87, 95, 166, 279n2; language in, 87, 102–103; "Loss of Face," 82, 88, 89–91; narration in, 22, 81, 82, 85, 86, 92, 95, 96, 98, 100, 101–105, 207, 279nn1–2; "The Next Room," 82, 86, 87–88, 166, 279n2; "On the Day that E.M. Forster Died," 82, 91–93; "Precipice-Encurled," 8, 82, 96–103, 107, 109, 210, 279n4; "Racine and the Tablecloth," 11, 20, 82, 83–85, 279n1; reader in, 82, 83–84, 85, 94; "Rose-Coloured Teacups," 82, 85–86; scholarship on, 4, 84; structure in, 82, 84–85, 86, 87, 96, 98, 99–101, 102, 105–106, 279n2; women's entrapment in, 81, 83–85, 88; "Sugar," 11, 82, 103–105, 145, 207

Sugden, Mrs. (character), 95–96. See also *Sugar*

Swammerdam, Jan, 110

Swedenborg, Emanuel, 13, 148, 159, 162, 165

Swift, Graham, 18, 271

Swinburne, Algernon Charles, 109–10

symbolism, 6, 54–58, 63

Taylor, D.J., 77, 278n2(4)

Tennyson, Alfred, 13, 23, 110, 111, 153; as character, 149, 163–65; *In Memoriam*, 24, 150, 157, 159–60, 162, 163–64, 165, 167; *Maud*, 12, 127, 144; "The Palace of Art," 165; *Recollections of the Arabian Nights*, 163. See also "Lady of Shalott"

Thomas, Joan, 207

Todd, Richard, 2; *A.S. Byatt*, 3, 4, 24, 138, 151, 152, 154, 180, 232, 277n2(2), 278nn4,6,9, 282n6

Tolkien, J.R.R., 242

Tredell, Nicolas, 1, 19, 25, 136, 205, 232, 264, 276

truth, 104, 185, 253, 271; in fiction, 58, 102–103, 107, 108–110, 125, 145, 186, 272; and language, 147, 208–209, 245, 246; and myth, 13, 105, 131, 142

truth-telling, 4, 11, 181

Updike, John, 215, 217, 225, 283n1(11)

van Gogh, Vincent, 33, 41, 76; accurate representation by, 7, 67–70, 104; *Poet's Garden*, 67

Velázquez, Diego, 8, 210–12

Vermeer, Johannes: *View of Delft*, 267

Victorian period, 6, 23–24, 147–48, 275–76; gender in, 156, 159, 163, 165; social structures in, 150–52. See also under *Possession*

Virgin in the Garden, The (Byatt), 1, 3, 5, 228, 232, 238, 278n5; identity in, 64, 266; myth and metaphor in, 61, 63, 278nn4,6; prologue to, 63–64, 68, 77, 234, 260, 265, 278n7; relationship between representation and reality in, 63, 64–66, 73, 75–76, 97, 243; time in, 63–64, 68. See also "Powerhouse" quartet

Wachtel, Eleanor, 18, 113, 136, 137, 253, 263

Wallhead, Celia: *The Old, the New and the Metaphor*, 3

Walsh, Chris, 271–72

Waugh, Patricia, 82–83; *Feminine Fictions*, 129

webs, 54–55, 57

Wedderburn, Alexander (character), 7, 23. See also *Babel Tower*; *Still Life*; *Virgin in the Garden, The*; *Whistling Woman, A*

Weil, Simone, 14, 139

Westlake, Michael, 72, 278n7

Whistling Woman, A (Byatt), 1, 2, 8, 24, 68, 215–16; art in, 61, 232, 252, 267; cultural context in, 5, 232, 246–47, 248, 253–55, 257–58, 262; hybridity in, 248, 250; language in, 251–53, 257–59, 260–61; reason in, 248–51, 253; scholarship on, 4, 5; structure of, 247–48, 261–67; women's freedom in, 254–57, 260. See also "Powerhouse" quartet

White, Patrick: *The Solid Mandala*, 5